IN CHICKEN DRIPPINGS SAUCE

ON RAW SCALLOPS

SPICED LAMB MEATBALLS WITH CHICKPEAS, PICKLED PARSLEY & YOGURT

COUSCOUS, SAUSAGE & PICKLED SAGE

ON SEARED STEAK

TUNA SALAD SANDWICH WITH PICKLED PARSLEY & RED ONION

ON AVOCADO

MANY-HERB SALAD, SCALLION-HERB SALAD

PICKLED HERBS

D057Z827

HERB TANK

use all

pickle

PICKLED PARSLEY RELISH

ANY-HERB LEMONADE

store

herbs

RAW YELLOWFIN TUNA WITH PARSLEY VINAIGRETTE

THE LITTLE NOTO COCKTAIL

infuse

make

ANY-HERB SIMPLE SYRUP

HERB-INFUSED BUTTER

The Nimble Cook will teach you how to

→ get the most from your ingredients and your efforts in the kitchen

→ use parts of ingredients you might normally throw away

→ prep foods so they're easier to cook

→ put ingredients, not recipes, first

→ learn new techniques for releasing flavor so you can eventually cook without recipes

SPRING VEGETABLE & HERB SAUTÉ

QUICK SPRING-STOCK RISOTTO WITH HERB BUTTER

WITH ROASTED POT...

RUSTIC POLENTA

STEAMED CHERRYSTONE CLAMS

the Nimble Cook

the Nimble Cook

NEW STRATEGIES FOR GREAT MEALS THAT MAKE THE MOST OF YOUR INGREDIENTS

Ronna Welsh

Illustrations by DIANA VASSAR

A RUX MARTIN BOOK
HOUGHTON MIFFLIN HARCOURT
Boston | New York | 2019

For information about permission to reproduce selections from
this book, write to trade.permissions@hmhco.com or to Permissions,
Houghton Mifflin Harcourt Publishing Company,
3 Park Avenue, 19th Floor, New York, New York 10016.

hmhbooks.com

Library of Congress Cataloging-in-Publication Data
Names: Welsh, Ronna, author.
Title: The nimble cook : new strategies for great meals that make
the most of your ingredients / Ronna Welsh ; illustrations by Diana Vassar.
Description: Boston : Houghton Mifflin Harcourt, 2019. |
"A Rux Martin Book."| Includes index.
Identifiers: LCCN 2018043608 (print) | LCCN 2018044780 (ebook) |
ISBN 9780544936843 (ebook) | ISBN 9780544935501 (paper over board)
Subjects: LCSH: Cooking. | LCGFT: Cookbooks.
Classification: LCC TX714 (ebook) | LCC TX714 .W346 2019 (print) |
DDC641.5—dc23
LC record available at https://lccn.loc.gov/2018043608

Book design by Toni Tajima

Printed in China
C&C 10 9 8 7 6 5 4 3 2 1

To my dad, who framed all of our accomplishments, no matter how small. This particular one is for you.

Acknowledgments

My work began at a sweet café in Austin, Texas, where a group of women forged long-lasting friendships cooking terrific food. Jane Lilly, thank you for giving this forlorn graduate student and wayward soul a chance at the stove. Thanks too for your friendship and advice. Thanks to John Trimble, who taught me how to edit boldly and so, how to write. To the late Virginia Wood, who gave me a first chance at publication.

Thanks to Peter Hoffman, who saw, underneath some serious angst, an earnest cook. To Barbara Rich, a kitchen co-conspirator, who gave me my first independent platform as a chef. Thanks to Corrado Assenza of Noto, Sicily, for unforgettable hospitality and encouragement, not to mention unspeakably good sweets. Thanks to the late Fernando Abadia of Huesca, Spain, for showing me the highest standards of professionalism, and, along with Enrique Torrijos, making me feel like family.

There are many great cooks and smart thinkers who have come through Purple Kale Kitchenworks' doors. To them collectively, I give bottomless thanks. Your hard work and generous input let me grow my business beyond a small city apartment. Together, we hauled equipment and ingredients from rented kitchen to kitchen. We labored through dishes, collated papers, scrubbed oven doors, fixed water filters, and more. We made great food and changed people's minds.

Foremost among them is Diana Vassar, who signed on to this project before even

I knew what it would become, and who turned her life upside down to work on the phenomenal illustrations for this book. I am your biggest fan.

Thanks to other friends, near and far, including those who lent me their roomier kitchens for those early classes, and those who gave a sharp eye to proposal and manuscript drafts.

Also, thanks to Rachel Holtzman, who rescued the big ideas of this book from a draft that had been drowning in revisions. Your belief in it—and me—got us to the end.

To Roy Finamore, who transformed a behemoth of a manuscript into an accessible, aspirational book. I am grateful for your instruction, support, diligence, and commitment to keeping the bar high.

To Rux Martin, who was quick to see the possible "long tail" in an ambitious proposal from this small-platform cook. Your pencil is this writer's best weapon. I am honored to be part of the terrific band of authors under your wing.

To copyeditor Suzanne Fass, for her speedy, thorough, and thoughtful work. Your sharp eye gave the book a final polish I didn't know it needed. And to Sarah Kwak, Jamie Selzer, and Crystal Paquette for all your help pulling everything together.

To the talented and very patient art team, including designer Toni Tajima and art director Melissa Lotfy, who added order and elegance to the book's interlinking content. No small task.

To my agent, Janis Donnaud, who saw in a jumbled book proposal an idea worth championing. I cannot overstate how lucky I feel to have you at my back.

To Dorothy Yang, Sara Kay, and Jess Ziman, for bringing to the test kitchen a rare combination of talent, drive, integrity, and humor, and for committing to this cookbook as if it were your own. I am a better cook, and person, for our time together.

To my mom, who taught me how to trust myself, persevere, take risks, and make things. You are my strength.

To my sister, a person of boundless generosity and goodwill. You always drop everything to help others, as you did for me in many times of my life and especially for this book.

To Matthew, whose commitment to my work, ideas, and passions sometimes held out longer than mine. Thank you for putting up with my indignations, for lending me patience when I needed it most, and for having the confidence for both of us to see me through the long play.

To my daughters, Eleanor and Sophie. You are the ultimate improvisers, always true, spirited, optimistic, and original, and my reasons for everything.

Contents

HOW TO USE THIS BOOK

This book is organized to guide you through the three-step process of making a meal. I divide it first by the kind of ingredient, arranged by season. Then I give you favorite preparations for each ingredient (Starting Points), followed by ways to build these prepared ingredients into other dishes (Explorations).

If you're curious about what to do with an ingredient you have, whether because it is new to you, you have too little of it left, or you are tired of your standard way to cook it, you can refer to the Starting Points. If you want ideas for different dishes you can make, consult the Explorations that follow the Starting Points.

Because the Starting Points are set up to see you through more than one dish—sometimes many more—they are written to minimize your time and maximize your efforts so you usually get the dish you set out to make, plus ingredients ready for another use. Your kitchen starts to sustain itself.

A Note About Serving Sizes

Going against convention, most of the Explorations in this book are written for a single serving, while the Starting Points serve more than one.

Why?

I want to show you how to do amazing things with the food you have on hand—no matter how much or how little. This sometimes means dropping typical expectations of what constitutes a meal. These preconceptions can stop us from

recognizing the makings of one when we have it. Consider this: A great meal doesn't have to be any more than an assembly of fresh, delicious things to eat. For the nimble cook, a meal is sometimes several different, simple-to-assemble plates of food for all to share, the separate dishes tied together with little more than good conversation. We can ignore the standard that each dish must "serve four."

Plus, when you scale up Explorations, rather than make more of the finished dish than you need, you make the exact number of servings you want and still have its components ready for making other dishes. These components usually reheat and store better than typical leftovers.

Besides, not everyone eats as a family of four. Even families of four aren't always at the table at the same time, or always eating the same thing. A recipe "for four" alienates the single woman cooking only for herself, the couple forced to divide every recipe by two. What about families of five, or three? In this book, I decided not to play to a stereotype of how we *think* people eat, because it ignores what many of us actually *do*. When you do want to cook for any number more or less, it's easy to scale the recipes up or down, and I've provided information, where necessary, to help you do that.

However, where I thought quality would suffer at a smaller scale or where the effort put into one dish justifies having more of it, I've written dishes for multiple servings. It's easier to make gazpacho as a big batch than try to pull together small pieces of raw vegetables for a single serving.

A New Way to Cook

You know this moment.

You come home late from work, hungry, maybe with kids to feed, with nothing prepared or planned for dinner. You plunk your bag on the kitchen counter, on top of last month's unread magazines, accumulating bills, a pair of earbuds. You glance at the clock. Inside the refrigerator perishables hide—once filled with promise, now triggering regret. Even a package of chicken thighs, purchased with a specific recipe in mind, offers no inspiration, since the zucchini for that dish is now withered in the produce drawer. "Damn!" you think to yourself. "There's nothing to eat."

When the cupboards are almost bare, tired ingredients fill the produce bin, and you're hungry, you need valuable strategies for getting meals started. In this book, I'll teach you how to get the most from your ingredients and your efforts in the kitchen, how to prep foods so they are easier to cook when you're pressed for time or short on ideas. This includes new ways to store ingredients (wrapping lettuce, saving watermelon as juice), so they remain delicious, keep fresh longer, and are poised for service. It also involves seeing how far an ingredient—and its cooking water, peel, stem, and bones—can take you. I'll show you how to use recipes strategically, which will allow you to take the first steps toward being able to cook without any recipe at all. With this book, you'll soon be able to move confidently, unhesitatingly, from raw ingredients to

finished plates, saving time, effort, and money while putting out consistently delicious food. You'll have the know-how to walk into a kitchen—any kitchen—no matter your skills or experience, or what ingredients you have (or don't), and comfortably, confidently start making great food. To do this, I'll help you rethink what a "meal" means and open up a new world of options for how and what to eat.

In short order, you'll set aside traditional meal plans and gain an empowering sense of freedom and control. What's more, your new practice will encourage everyone's participation. You'll watch as your spouse delves into the refrigerator to pull together a late dinner, and the kids step up to make their own lunches. This approach will change the way you cook, immediately and for years to come. Under your guidance, your kitchen will make everyone who enters it a better cook.

The Nimble Cook

To start, imagine shopping not for one specific recipe, but for ingredients you want to eat. Think about prepping these ingredients not just for a specific dish, but by how they taste best and how much of them you have. Excellently prepared, versatile ingredients open up the possibility of many dishes, even some unplanned. You wash some herbs for a pasta, but instead of sentencing the rest to the produce drawer, you put them in a "tank" with other fresh herbs, infuse them in butter, or dunk them in pickle brine. You now have extra herbs washed and ready, a seasoned butter, and a unique condiment at your call.

Next, picture having more than the herbs on hand—maybe roasted chicken legs or boiled potatoes. The possibilities for what you can put together begin to grow: chicken soup with potatoes and herb butter, potato-herb salad with crisp chicken skin, chicken salad with pickled herbs. You get a few steps closer to quickly assembling not just one, but several great, original meals.

Nimble, in 3 Steps

I'll bet you are more likely to make something—anything—with one of your favorite ingredients if it is already prepped than if it's whole and raw. If you come home hungry to a bowl of raw, unpeeled shallots, for instance, making dinner requires more commitment and thought than if you have some already sliced and ready to cook.

THE NIMBLE COOK . . .

→ Shops for ingredients, not recipes

→ Cooks by circumstance, not by rote

→ Eats something delicious, not just expected

Better yet, think of the quick, imaginative dishes a jar of jammy roasted shallots inspires that whole bulbs do not: an omelet with shallots, goat cheese, and tomato; a sandwich with shallots, arugula, mustard, and leftover roast pork; pasta with shallots, Parmesan, and herbs. These improvised ideas—I call them Explorations—do not derive from what you planned but are inspired by the found treasures in your fridge.

Step 1: Take Stock

Condiments crowding your refrigerator door, spices competing for space on a rack, specialty oils hidden in cabinet corners, open bags of pasta spilling on a back shelf, months-frozen chicken legs blocking access to the container of bacon fat you forget why you were saving: This is the food we overlook every day.

We're blind to other ingredients too: a few loose carrots, jars of pickles, leftover sour cream. So, in our practice of making a meal, we reach for the same ingredients to make the same tried-and-true (and tired) dishes, or we conclude, again, "There's nothing to eat."

Thinking about what dish we'll make before taking stock of what we actually have and whether we'll have the time or inclination to do it is a common error in starting a meal. If we start with the repertoire of meals we're familiar with—those seven or eight or ten meals we make again and again—then the fate of those tomatoes and onions is already sealed. But what if we let our ingredients take the lead and show us what they can do? It's rarely the ingredients that stand in our way of cooking great food, but the unimaginative expectations we have of them.

Find your pantry blind spots. Use everything on your refrigerator door. Rather than shop for a specific recipe or meal plan, shop for ingredients you want and can afford. Buy great ingredients at their peak, because the best cooking depends on it.

Step 2: Create Starting Points

Starting Points are ingredients at their most "ready." An onion, sliced, is a great Starting Point for a sandwich or fresh salad. Caramelized, it's there to sauce braised meat or get turned into soup. The best Starting Points are personal and of the moment, and fit how you cook and eat.

For example, if you enjoy salad with dinner, you might set up your ingredients for several salads all at once. You could wash, dry, and store your greens; peel and slice your cucumbers; toast your nuts; make some dressing. Then, on a busy weeknight, rather than staring down at a gritty head of romaine, you have a salad in prepped parts ready to be thrown together.

But while you might prep these ingredients with salad in mind, you can use them to make other dishes too: Put the greens in a soup; pair the cucumber with cold noodles; stir the nuts into oatmeal; spoon the dressing on grilled fish. You've not only made parts of the salad; you've made Starting Points for other meals.

Starting Points give ideas for what you can do with what you have, and they act as prompts to get you cooking. They give you an important leg up to a number of meals, without committing in advance to just one. You might boil all your potatoes, roast a head of garlic, make your herbs into vinaigrette, and cube and freeze day-old bread, all without any specific dish in mind but just for the sake of stocking up. The care you give to these Starting Points will transfer to any dish you make with them.

Step 3: Turn Starting Points into Meals

You'll see that many of the Starting Points in this book stand on their own as ready-to-eat dishes. For a meal, you can serve several Starting Points on a table, side by side— Seared and Roasted Duck Breast (page 270) with Crisp Sautéed Shiitakes (page 199). But every Starting Point can also be partnered with other prepared ingredients in original, sophisticated ways, such as for a duck, shiitake, and scallion soup (page 272). I call these pairings Explorations.

THE STARTING POINTS IN THIS BOOK INCLUDE

→ Familiar ingredients prepared in common ways, where it's especially helpful to have ingredients ready to go (sliced raw fennel, diced celery)

→ Familiar ingredients prepared in original ways (braised celery, pickled garlic, seared kale)

→ Parts of ingredients you'd otherwise throw away (celery leaves and ends, stems from herbs and greens, peels from potatoes and beets, apple cores, cooking water from pasta, grains, and potatoes)

→ Ways of storing ingredients for longer life or convenient use (forming ground meat into patties, cutting lettuce into wedges, mixing herbs into butters)

The Starting Points help you put together dishes not only quickly and effortlessly, but more ambitiously than if you didn't have any ingredients prepped at all. For instance, with pickled beets and some braised pork in your refrigerator as Starting Points, it takes just minutes—and not much skill—to put together a quick borscht (page 163). In fact, having different ingredients prepared in different ways builds a refinement absent from the typical soup. As a bonus, preparing these ingredients separately means the extra braised pork can be used for a sandwich (page 290), the beets for a salad.

From drinks to pasta to flatbreads to fish stews, the Explorations in this book can be assembled in minutes and, I hope, will both teach and inspire you. In total, you'll explore more than 250 ideas for making the most of your ingredients, skill, and time.

The Wastefulness of Meal Planning

Having a dish in mind ahead of time does provide direction, guidance, assurance, a place to start. But recipes don't always take into account the food we have on hand, not to mention our appetite, available time, and mood.

Meal plans are worse. Meal planning often lands on the list of things we feel we should do more of and do better. We like meal plans because they do all the thinking for us. But they require too much effort to sustain. They offer tight scripts for putting meals on the table without room for changing moods or situations. Even when we stick rigidly to the plan, they entail a good deal of waste and extra work. When one dish calls for a bit of parsley, what do you do with the rest of the wilted bunch? If you buy a special spice for a new dish, how long will it sit in your spice rack before you use it up?

When we flip the traditional model of making a meal on its head and put ingredients, not recipes, first, we still get dinner—but in a manner tailored to the particular quantities and quality of our ingredients, and to our personal circumstances. The power of this approach is its compounding, even exponential effect. After we're through with this recipe, we'll have stocked our system with all kinds of preparations that we can call on for many other meals. We no longer feel an obligation to leftovers, but see promise in prepared ingredients.

An Ingredient-First Approach

"The Celery Sort" is a staple routine in my classes and a great way to illustrate how to identify and make good use of an ingredient's unique properties and distinct parts. Celery gives crunch to salads, carries dips to our mouths, and lightens soups and stews. Yet few of us crave this vegetable for its own sake. It's the one ingredient that traditional recipes always call for in tiny quantities, yet is only sold in large.

Go ahead: Grab a bunch. Hold it in one hand; it has a heft rarely attributed to something made mostly of water. It is sizeable, perhaps even the largest item in your produce bin. It is perishable, though we're rarely moved by the threat of its demise.

Now pull the celery apart, stalk by stalk, leaf by leaf. Sort the separate components by color, texture, form. Celery's tender yellow inner stalks don't belong with the dark outer ones. The rough green leaves are unlike the feathery yellow ones. Celery's fibrous outer stalks soften with gentle, moist heat. Braised (page 90), they become cunningly decadent. The stubby stalk ends can anchor a stock made entirely of scraps (page 88); the often-discarded tops yield enough syrup for a Celery Sour (page 92). The flexible inner stalks are delicious on their own, the truly snackable part of the celery, but they also explode when tossed with Mustard Vinaigrette (page 364). The darker stalks hold up in a nice dice, which you could use to cook lentils (page 344) or as a sturdy partner to chicken livers and pickled apples. The yellow leaves are at once surprisingly astringent yet delicate. Tossed with peaches, herbs, buttermilk dressing, and the rest of the stalk, they become a celery salad full of itself (page 86).

Processed ingredients like shrink-wrapped, factory-trimmed, warehouse-stored celery hearts don't come to us full of possibilities. But a whole, minimally processed bunch, with more and tastier parts, offers at least seven different directions to dinner. You may not know how to make a single dish off the cuff, but you'll be able to see the celery's potential. Your perspective has expanded, and in the long run, so have the possibilities for many meals.

Otherwise Trash

Seeing ingredients for their fullest potential—beyond how you might normally prepare them—is an important shift in perspective that puts ingredients, not recipes, first. It also leads to using not just more of these ingredients, but also the parts of them you might otherwise throw away. This is simply good cooking. After all, a "scrap" is just food you haven't figured out how to use. When you save a scrap, you bank a possibility. The more you save, the more possibilities you accumulate. This is true even when you don't recognize a scrap's value specifically. Because many scraps (including cooking water, pan drippings, skin, and peels) can be easily stored, you are under little immediate pressure to come up with ideas for using them. Sometimes it's only when you step away from the kitchen that you see kimchi in a pile of cucumber peels (page 130) or gazpacho in watermelon rind (page 155).

Let's turn an ingredient-first eye toward a familiar apple to shake up our ideas for how to eat it. You can use its peel for a slaw (page 206) and its core for a sweet-and-sour syrup (page 210). The syrup is perfect for game and pairs well with bourbon for a winter cocktail (page 211).

Sustaining Your New Way of Cooking

Once you see the value of Starting Points to put together a meal, you can use the vantage point they provide to help manage your kitchen better.

Build a personalized pantry.

Will you use herbs more if they are folded into butter (page 377)? Spices, if they are in a spice salt (page 372)? If you make a vinaigrette, how many things can you think of to use it for? Salad, sure. But what about poached chicken or fish? What about slathering it on some bread with grilled vegetables? If that vinaigrette alone gives you many directions to dinner, you should consider always having some around. A pantry should be filled not just with the right ingredients, but with ingredients that are prepared the right way for you.

Organize your spices for how you cook.

Keep your spices accessible, but don't put them in an unnatural alphabetical arrangement. Team up spices that work especially well together. Fennel seed and thyme make great partners for bread and meat, cumin and cinnamon for fruit desserts.

Prep for indulgences.

You may not care to freeze wine and stock for braising kits, but you could make a variety of herb syrups for cocktails or a large batch of Balsamic-Poached Figs (page 366), ready to spoon onto pancakes or even ice cream.

Take notes as you go.

Write directly in your cookbook—yes, in *this* book. Read through a recipe completely before you start. Highlight instructions most relevant to you.

Bring along your favorite recipes.

Good recipes are good instruction and, happily, contain many starting points for stocking up. Enlist the dishes you like to provide a familiar framework for getting started. If a recipe for pasta calls for cooking one onion, what if you cooked two and stored the extra for later use? You can make a sauce just for tonight's pasta, but what if you made extra for tomorrow's fish too?

Use takeout as a tool.

Takeout can be part of your strategy to put more home-cooked meals on the table. Can you use the time you save by ordering pizza to roast a chicken for tomorrow? If you call for a plain pizza, can you quickly cook the nubs of vegetables in your refrigerator to put on as toppings when it arrives? It gives you a clever way to use up the food you have on hand and buys you more time to cook.

Make excess useful.

If you anticipate feeling stuck with leftover ingredients—say, half a container of ricotta cheese—get even more of it and make the extra into something else, such as the Savory Ricotta Custard on page 386, which is versatile enough to slice for a sandwich, with a shelf life twice as long as plain ricotta. If you buy basil and fear tossing away most of the bunch, buy two bunches so you'll have enough to make a batch of pesto.

Keep your tools and ingredients in sight.

Most kitchen organizers suggest that you store appliances you don't use frequently. But this usually means you'll use them even less. If you now hide your food processor in a cabinet, try putting it next to your toaster instead. Maybe with it so close, you'll call on it when you think, on a whim, to make bread crumbs from that day-old loaf.

Putting away things like olive oil, salt, and your favorite spices just forces you to take more steps the next time you cook.

Use crib notes.

I write shorthand recipes for a quick pickled brine or a poaching broth on sticky notes or index cards—even the inside of kitchen cabinets—so I can refer to them without delay. They are handy for when I am deterred not by the prospect of cooking itself but by the interruption of having to look something up. For many cooking tasks, I don't need to read the full recipe each time, but could use a reminder about the ingredients and quantities it requires.

Hone the three-step habit.

Take stock ("What do I have?"), then create your Starting Points ("What can I do with what I have?"), before exploring options for what to eat ("How can I serve what I've prepared?"). With these three steps as your guide, you'll have the tools to cook terrific food, even when you have no ingredients readied and nothing specific in mind. Let this book help you develop a practice that extends far beyond its pages.

Remember one thing: How we "do" dinner is not a valid metric of how much we care about ourselves, those we feed, the environment, or anything else. Home cooking is about bringing humor and love to the table and giving ourselves permission to be less than any ideal. It's about taking stock, keeping up, being there to provide in whatever ways work to surround ourselves with friends, family, and delicious food.

THE INGREDIENTS I USE MOST

Excellent olive oil

The best olive oil is cold pressed and from a specific, identifiable source. It is extra-virgin, but not all extra-virgin olive oil is excellent. It should smell fruity and taste full and "green," not thin or acrid; occasionally it will have a spicy finish, but it should not be overly bitter. While professional tasters sip olive oil to grade it, I suggest you taste yours with good, plain bread.

Coarse kosher salt and flaky sea salt

The call to "salt to taste" doesn't provide enough guidance to the cook who typically underseasons food—and this is most people. So in each recipe, I have tried to be as specific as possible about when and how much salt to use. But I also want to encourage you to taste as you go, as flavors develop, so you'll recognize "perfectly seasoned" when you arrive at it. I use Diamond Crystal kosher salt (without preservatives) to season food as I prepare it, and sometimes a crunchier flaky sea salt, such as Maldon, to finish.

Aromatics

Garlic

Poached Garlic, Garlic Broth, Poached Garlic Puree, and Poached Garlic Skins 20

Garlic Stock 21

Poached Garlic Soup with Bread Salad 22

Bread Salad for Garlic Soup 23

Garlic-Skin Vinegar 23

Wine-Pickled Garlic Cloves 24

Oysters with Wine-Pickled Garlic and Dill 25

Wine-Pickled Garlic Relish 26

Roasted Garlic 27

Leeks

Wine-Braised Leeks 28

Skewered Wine-Braised Leeks with Sunchokes 30

Squid with Wine-Braised Leeks and Bacon 30

Wine-Braised Leek and Potato Broth Soup 30

Blanched Leek Greens 31

Dill-and-Leek-Greens Pesto 32

Creamed Leek Greens 32

Leek Greens Cream Cheese 33

Onions

Onion Jam 34

✔ Fast French Onion Soup 35

Cheese Stock and Onion Jam Soup 35

Pickled Red Onions 36

✔ **Spicy Lemon-Onion Slaw 36**

Celery Leaf, Fennel, and Spicy Lemon-Onion Slaw 37

Lemon-Onion Tzatziki 37

Scallions and Ramps

Ramp Leaves for Salad 39

Ramp Leaf, Cucumber, and Avocado Salad 39

Scallion-Sesame Magic Mix 40

Scallop Crudo with Scallion-Sesame Magic Mix 40

Shallots

Shallots Roasted with Sugar and Vinegar 41

Roasted Shallot Dressing 42

Roasted Shallots, Prunes, and Walnuts 42

Roasted Shallot and Bread Salad 42

Classic Shallot Vinaigrette 43

Poached Garlic, Garlic Broth, Poached Garlic Puree, and Poached Garlic Skins

Cooked slowly in water, garlic cloves turn mellow, deeply fragrant, and, curiously, a bit sweet. I make poached garlic more often than the pungent roasted garlic, which for me has more limited range. Poached garlic is silky and smooth. With it, you can enrich plain broth or flat beans and give light body to countless other things. It makes a delicious spread for sandwiches too. Put out a plate of poached garlic cloves, their skins slit with a knife, next to little bowls of good olive oil and salt. Dip a clove into the oil, then the salt, then squeeze the soft garlic straight into your mouth.

Poached garlic requires no prep work beyond breaking off the cloves from their stem. You don't even need to peel them. Although you don't need to cook six heads at once, the more you cook, the more flavorful the resulting broth.

This recipe yields a golden broth. You can turn it into stock with the help of the garlic skins, messy with the clinging pulp of slipped-out cloves. Or save the sticky skins to rinse off for a future batch of tomato sauce.

makes **ABOUT 2 CUPS POACHED GARLIC CLOVES, 1⅔ CUPS POACHED GARLIC PUREE,**
1⅓ CUPS GARLIC BROTH, AND PACKED ½ CUP GARLIC SKINS

6 garlic heads, broken up into cloves, unpeeled

2 to 2½ cups water

½ cup excellent olive oil (optional)

¾ or more teaspoon coarse kosher salt (optional)

Place the garlic cloves into a small saucepan. Add the water to just cover the cloves. Cover and cook on medium heat, at a meaningful simmer, until the garlic is very tender, about 15 minutes. Remove the cloves from the liquid to cool, reserving the garlic broth for soup or Garlic Stock.

Once the cloves are cool, you can either slip them from their skins and submerge them in the cooking broth or the oil, or make the cloves into puree.

To make the puree: Press the garlic cloves through a fine-mesh strainer. Discard any rough ends. Reserve the sticky and fragrant skins, either storing them in the garlic broth or setting them aside for Garlic-Skin Vinegar (page 23). Whisk in the oil, a little at a time; the puree will emulsify. Add the salt. You can puree the garlic in a food processor, instead of pushing through a strainer, but you'll have to peel and trim the ends of the garlic first.

The cloves and puree will keep in the refrigerator for up to 2 weeks, the broth for 5 days, or freeze for up to 3 months.

Use Poached Garlic in

—▸ Poached-Garlic Scrambled Eggs (page 353)

—▸ Tagliatelle with Poached Garlic and Egg Yolk (page 313)

Use Garlic Broth in

—▸ Garlic Stock (below)

—▸ Poached Garlic Soup (page 22)

Use Poached Garlic Skins in

—▸ Garlic-Skin Vinegar (page 23)

exploration

Garlic Stock

Use this stock as you would any vegetable stock, even re-pairing it with the Poached Garlic and some potatoes for Poached Garlic Soup (page 22).

Feel free to adjust the proportions of onion, fennel or celery, and carrots, as long as you use a total of 2 cups vegetables. Carrots add color and make the broth sweet; fennel and onion embolden the garlic. You can save batches of Garlic Broth in the freezer to make a big batch of stock at once. Keep in mind that in a larger batch of stock, the vegetables need more time to sauté and the liquid takes longer to reduce.

—▸ **MAKES 3 TO 3½ CUPS**

1 cup thinly sliced onion

½ cup thinly sliced fennel or celery

½ cup thinly sliced carrot

1 tablespoon excellent olive oil

¼ cup crisp white wine

1 cup **Garlic Broth** (opposite)

Packed ½ cup **Poached Garlic Skins** (opposite)

4 cups water

Up to 1 teaspoon coarse kosher salt

Put the onion, fennel, carrot, and oil in a medium saucepan over medium-high heat and cook, stirring frequently, until very soft and beginning to color, about 5 minutes.

Add the wine and cook for 1 full minute, until reduced.

Add the garlic broth, garlic skins, and water. Bring to a boil, then reduce to a meaningful simmer and cook for 30 minutes, until the flavor deepens. To judge, spoon a bit of stock into a small bowl and taste with a pinch of salt. Once done, cool the stock in the saucepan for 5 minutes, then season. (If you plan to use Garlic Stock in other dishes, do not fully season it now.)

Strain before using or storing. Store in the refrigerator for up to 5 days or in the freezer for up to 3 months.

Poached Garlic Soup with Bread Salad

Some people like pureed soups, but I quickly tire of their uniform texture. A bread salad moistened with good olive oil, placed in the bottom of the soup dish, lends the texture I crave and stretches the soup too.

If you don't want to add the bread salad, be sure to give the soup a drizzle of great olive oil at the end. Its fruitiness and slight bitterness give structure and weight to the soup.

If you don't have Garlic Stock, use whatever Garlic Broth you have from poaching the cloves, supplemented by another light stock, such as Light Chicken Broth (page 264).

⟶ **FOR 6 TO 8 SERVINGS, OR 4 WITHOUT BREAD SALAD**

¾ pound Yukon Gold potatoes (2 small), peeled and cut into ½-inch dice (about 1⅓ cups)

⅓ to ½ cup **Poached Garlic** (page 20) or ¼ cup **Poached Garlic Puree** (from 1 large garlic head, page 20)

3 cups cold **Garlic Stock** (page 21), or see headnote

2 teaspoons coarse kosher salt

Freshly ground white pepper

Bread Salad for Garlic Soup (opposite; optional)

Excellent olive oil (for serving; optional)

Place the potatoes and garlic in a small saucepan with the cold stock over high heat. Bring to a boil, cover, then lower the heat and simmer until the potatoes are just tender.

Pour the stock, potatoes, and garlic into a blender and puree just until smooth. Because the soup will be very hot, you may need to do this in smaller batches. Season with salt and a big pinch of pepper. Serve hot, either over bread salad or with a drizzle of olive oil. Store leftovers in a covered container for up to 3 days.

BREAD SALAD FOR GARLIC SOUP

FOR 4 SERVINGS

Cut peasant or sourdough bread into 1-inch cubes to equal 2 cups. Heat a cast-iron pan on medium-high heat. Add enough excellent olive oil to just coat the bottom of the pan. Once it runs loosely over the surface, but before it begins to smoke, add the bread cubes. Cook until the bottoms are golden, about 2 minutes, then turn the pieces to brown the other sides, adding drops of oil at a time if the pan becomes too dry.

Once the croutons are toasted, transfer them to a bowl. Drizzle with additional oil to moisten, then toss with flaky sea salt and a generous pinch of fennel fronds or fresh tarragon.

Garlic-Skin Vinegar

On my way to the trash with a handful of messy poached garlic skins, I knocked over a bottle of cheap red wine vinegar. I tossed the peels onto the counter, freeing my hands to grab paper towels—the flavored vinegar practically made itself.

With mustard and oil, this vinegar makes a quick dressing for asparagus, young beets, or dandelion greens. Sometimes I put it on the table instead of olive oil for dipping good bread.

→ **MAKES 1 CUP**

Pinch of fennel seeds

1 bay leaf

1 cardamom pod, smashed

10 black peppercorns

Packed ½ cup **Poached Garlic Skins** (page 20)

1 cup red wine vinegar

Place all the ingredients into a glass bottle or canning jar and cover. Shake well. Leave at room temperature to marinate for 48 hours. Refrigerate to store; do not strain. The vinegar is best after at least 1 week and only improves with time. It will keep, refrigerated, for 2 months.

Use in

→ Roasted Eggplant with Tomatoes and Garlic-Skin Vinegar (page 132)

→ Triple-Braised Wild Mushrooms and Garlic-Skin Vinegar (page 196)

Wine-Pickled Garlic Cloves

Pickled garlic cloves are mellow enough in their brine to snack on whole. I dilute the vinegar brine with white wine, which is less acidic. This is also a good way to use the end of a leftover bottle of wine.

When you brine garlic cloves raw, they turn greenish blue. It doesn't change their taste, but they are off-putting to eat. You only need to cook them for a minute to preserve their color; they stay crisp once cooled.

makes **ABOUT 3 CUPS PICKLES AND 3 CUPS BRINE**

6 garlic heads, cloves separated and peeled

2 cups distilled white vinegar

1 cup dry white wine

1 tablespoon coarse kosher salt

1 tablespoon sugar

Use in

—> Collard Ribbons with Pickled Garlic (page 49)

—> Oysters with Wine-Pickled Garlic and Dill (opposite)

—> Wine-Pickled Garlic Relish (page 26) for hot dogs or sausages

If your garlic cloves are particularly large, cut them in half lengthwise.

Mix the vinegar, wine, salt, and sugar in a saucepan over high heat and bring to a boil. Add the garlic and boil for 1 minute. Remove from the heat and let cool in the brine. Refrigerate in the brine to store. The garlic cloves will keep for 1 to 2 months.

Oysters with Wine-Pickled Garlic and Dill

Traditional garnishes for raw shellfish use vinegar along with black pepper and shallots. Here pickled garlic brings the expected acidity and bite instead. Serve the dressing on the side of a plate of iced shucked oysters, or drizzle on top as described below.

⟶ **FOR 12 OYSTERS**

12 oysters

24 to 36 very thin slices **Wine-Pickled Garlic Cloves** (page 24)

1 tablespoon or more **brine from Wine-Pickled Garlic Cloves**

12 fresh dill sprigs

Coarsely ground black pepper

Shuck the oysters. Top each with 2 or 3 slices of garlic, then ¼ to ½ teaspoon of the brine, a dill sprig, and a pinch of pepper. Serve immediately.

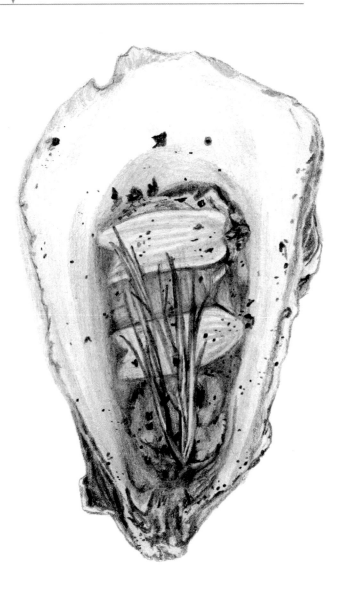

Wine-Pickled Garlic Relish

Good on hot dogs and other sausages, this relish beats store-bought sauerkraut every time. Serve it with stone-ground or whole-grain mustard; you can even mix the two together.

—> **MAKES ABOUT ½ CUP**

¼ cup minced onion

¼ cup slivered **Wine-Pickled Garlic Cloves** (page 24)

½ teaspoon caraway seeds

4 teaspoons **brine from Wine-Pickled Garlic Cloves**

Mix the onion, garlic, caraway seeds, and brine together. Let the relish sit for at least 5 minutes before using. Refrigerate in a covered container for up to 5 days.

Roasted Garlic

Pungent roasted garlic is a force of flavor. I like it best in small quantities to shore up other ingredients. Try substituting it for poached garlic in scrambled eggs (page 353) or Tagliatelle with Poached Garlic and Egg Yolk (page 313). Use in Mushroom Risotto with Nut Stock and Roasted Garlic (page 325).

for **EACH GARLIC HEAD**

1 garlic head

2 teaspoons excellent olive oil

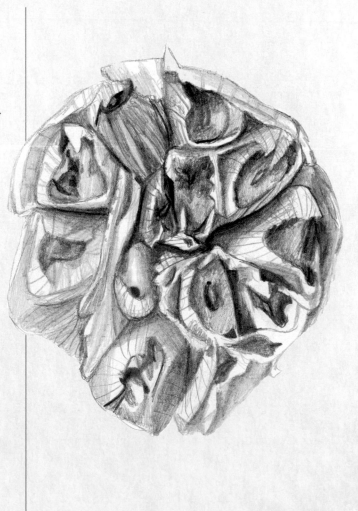

Preheat the oven to 400°F. Cut off the papery end of the garlic head, exposing the tips of most of the cloves. Place the garlic, cut side up, in the middle of a piece of foil large enough to enclose the head completely.

Drizzle the oil all over the head and wrap tightly. Place in the oven and roast until the tip of each clove is straw-colored and as soft as butter, about 40 minutes. Do not let the cloves get too dark; they will turn bitter.

Remove from the oven and cool in the foil package. Once cool, refrigerate as is or gently slip the cloves out of their skins with your fingers, refrigerating them in a jar in their roasting oil.

Wine-Braised Leeks

Leeks release a good deal of their own water when they cook. They reduce considerably in volume and swim in their own fragrant broth by the end. Keep a stash of these on hand to layer on sandwiches, serve alongside chicken legs, or stuff into a quiche. You can easy double the recipe (increasing the cooking time by half) and freeze extra cooked leeks for later use. Save the leek greens for Blanched Leek Greens (page 31).

I like the crunch of whole spices, so I scatter the peppercorns and coriander seeds among the leeks. If you'd rather contain them, first tie them in a cheesecloth sachet.

makes 2½ **TO 3 CUPS**

4 large leeks, white and light green parts only

2½ tablespoons excellent olive oil

3 tablespoons water

4 tablespoons (½ stick) unsalted butter, cut into bits

⅓ cup crisp white wine

6 fresh thyme sprigs

10 coriander seeds

5 white peppercorns

2 teaspoons coarse kosher salt

Preheat the oven to 325°F. Trim the leeks of any roots without cutting into the bulbs. Slice each leek lengthwise through the bulb into long halves, then slice once more into quarters. Fill a large bowl with ice water and submerge the leeks in it. Swish them around and carefully bend back the pieces, using your fingers to release any dirt trapped between layers of the bulbs.

Once clean, lift out the leeks, drain, and place in a snugly fitting roasting pan or Dutch oven, no more than two layers deep. If your leeks are extra long, cut them to fit.

Add the remaining ingredients. Cover and place in the oven. Braise, stirring once or twice, until the leeks have dulled in color, are quite tender to a knife, and bend and flex effortlessly, about 45 minutes. Taste for salt, though you shouldn't need any. Cool to room temperature before storing. Store in the refrigerator for up to 1 week or in the freezer for 3 months.

Use in

→ Linguine with Braised Leeks and Ricotta Custard (page 312)

→ Shaved Cabbage and Braised-Leek Salad (page 113)

→ Pork and Leek Meatballs (page 291)

→ Wine-Braised Leek and Potato Broth Soup (page 30)

→ Squid with Wine-Braised Leeks and Bacon (page 30)

→ Skewered Wine-Braised Leeks with Sunchokes (page 30)

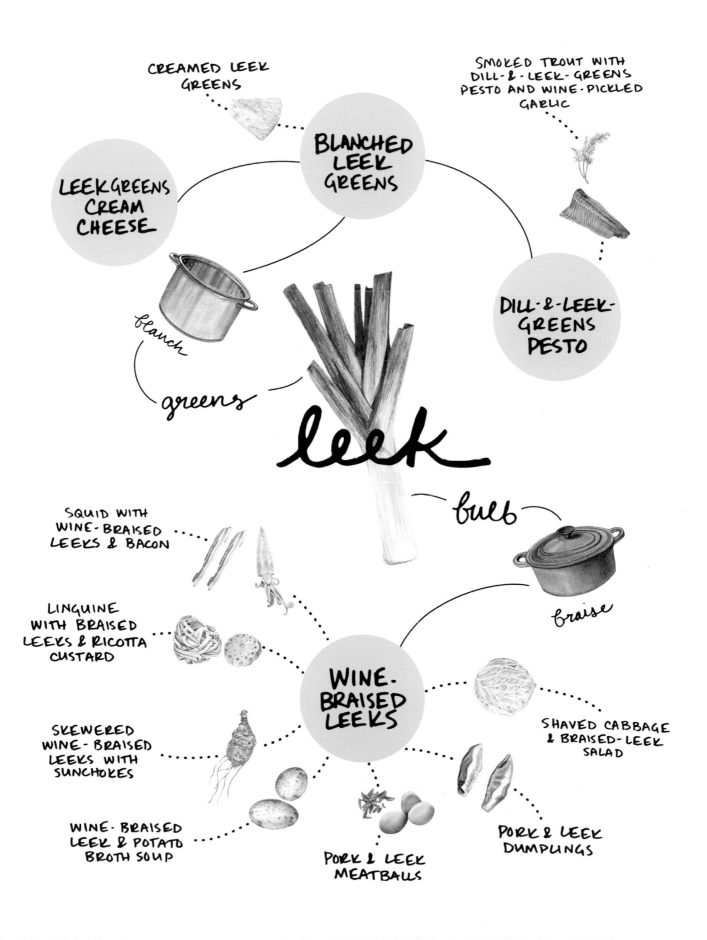

CREAMED LEEK GREENS

SMOKED TROUT WITH DILL-&-LEEK-GREENS PESTO AND WINE-PICKLED GARLIC

BLANCHED LEEK GREENS

LEEK GREENS CREAM CHEESE

DILL-&-LEEK-GREENS PESTO

blanch

greens

leek

bulb

SQUID WITH WINE-BRAISED LEEKS & BACON

LINGUINE WITH BRAISED LEEKS & RICOTTA CUSTARD

braise

WINE-BRAISED LEEKS

SHAVED CABBAGE & BRAISED-LEEK SALAD

SKEWERED WINE-BRAISED LEEKS WITH SUNCHOKES

WINE-BRAISED LEEK & POTATO BROTH SOUP

PORK & LEEK MEATBALLS

PORK & LEEK DUMPLINGS

SKEWERED WINE-BRAISED LEEKS WITH SUNCHOKES

The combination of creamy, acidic, and earthy ingredients works nicely as an hors d'oeuvre, salad, or side dish.

Cut **Wine-Braised Leeks** (page 28) into thin strips, enough for one small bite. Wind each leek around the tip of a small skewer, then stab into a **Roasted Sunchoke** (page 183). Spoon some crème fraîche on top of the leek, thinning it with a few drops of water if it is too thick. Serve at room temperature.

Squid with Wine-Braised Leeks and Bacon

Seafood and cured meats are especially great together, here tangled with soft, buttery leeks. I marinate the just-cooked bacon in sharp red wine vinegar to balance the richness. You can easily scale down the dish.

—> **FOR 4 SERVINGS**

¼ pound sliced bacon

1 tablespoon red wine vinegar

1 pound squid, cleaned and blotted dry, body sliced into 1-inch rings

1 cup roughly chopped **Wine-Braised Leeks** (page 28)

2 handfuls fresh spinach, stemmed and torn in large pieces

Cook the bacon in a heavy skillet over medium-low heat until the fat is rendered and the bacon is crisp. Transfer the bacon to a paper towel, leaving the fat in the pan. Break the bacon into

approximately 1-inch pieces, place in a serving bowl, and pour over the vinegar.

Turn the heat under the skillet to high and sauté the squid in the bacon fat until it's almost opaque, 2 to 3 minutes. Do not overcrowd the pan, which would steam the squid. Cook in batches, if necessary, then return all the squid to the pan.

Add the leeks and any leek juices and sauté until the leeks are just warmed through. Toss in the spinach and sauté for 1 minute more to barely wilt.

Add the squid, leeks, and spinach to the bacon. Toss well and serve immediately.

Wine-Braised Leek and Potato Broth Soup

If you have potato broth in the freezer, this soup is quick to put together, still tasting as fresh as if made entirely from scratch. It is very "leek forward," which I like. If you cooked your peeled potatoes well and with plenty of salt, the resulting potato broth will be potent but light and silky.

—> **1 RECIPE OF WINE-BRAISED LEEKS YIELDS ABOUT 6 SERVINGS SOUP.**

—> **FOR EACH SERVING**

¾ cup **Wine-Braised Leeks** (page 28), with any extra braising liquid

1½ cups **Potato Broth** (page 175)

Heat the leeks and potato broth in a saucepan. Transfer to a blender and puree until very smooth. Serve warm, or refrigerate and serve chilled.

Blanched Leek Greens

When blanched, leek greens taste like chives, although they chew like rubber hose; you need to chop or puree them to be able to eat them. Once you do, you can transform the greens into Dill-and-Leek-Greens Pesto to serve with smoked fish, make Creamed Leek Greens to stand in for spinach at your next Thanksgiving meal, or fold the pulp into softened cream cheese for your bagel.

makes **ABOUT 2 CUPS**

6 cups water

1 tablespoon coarse kosher salt

½ pound dark green leek leaves (from about 2 large leeks), cut into 1-inch pieces and well washed (about 4 cups)

Use in

—> Dill-and-Leek-Greens Pesto (page 32)

—> Creamed Leek Greens (page 32)

—> Leek Greens Cream Cheese (page 33)

Mix 3 cups of the water, a large handful of ice, and 1½ teaspoons of the salt in a large bowl.

Bring the remaining 3 cups water to a boil. Add the remaining 1½ teaspoons salt. Add the greens all at once, submerging them with a spoon or tongs. Cook until they turn bright green and become soft and very pliable, about 1 minute. Drain the leaves and immediately plunge them into the ice bath to stop cooking.

Once completely cool, drain well. The leaves will range in color from rich green to bright yellow. Discard any that are yellow-brown. To store, place a paper towel in the bottom of a container. Place the drained leaves on top. Cover and refrigerate for up to 3 days.

Dill-and-Leek-Greens Pesto

The leek greens give this herbal paste a little bit of heat. Use as you would any pesto. It's especially good whisked together with the brine from Wine-Pickled Garlic (page 24) for a vinaigrette to go on smoked fish (page 242).

⟶ **MAKES 1½ CUPS**

   1 recipe **Blanched Leek Greens** (page 31)

   Packed ½ cup fresh dill

   1 garlic clove, roughly chopped

   Heaping ½ cup freshly grated Parmesan cheese

   ½ to ¾ cup excellent olive oil

   1 teaspoon coarse kosher salt, or more to taste

Pulse the leek greens, dill, garlic, cheese, and ½ cup of the oil in a food processor. If the pesto is too thick, add the remaining oil and pulse to emulsify. Season with salt. To store, place in a container covered with a thin layer of olive oil. Store in the refrigerator for up to 3 weeks or in the freezer for up to 3 months. Bring to room temperature before using.

Creamed Leek Greens

Like creamed spinach, Creamed Leek Greens are endlessly versatile: delicious as a side dish or stretched with a little pasta water and paired with peas over orecchiette; swirled into a frittata with ricotta cheese; or chilled and spread on crackers. I use ground coriander instead of the nutmeg typically found in creamed spinach.

⟶ **MAKES ABOUT 3½ CUPS, ENOUGH FOR 4 SIDE SERVINGS**

   1½ cups heavy cream

   ½ cup sour cream

   2 recipes (4 cups) **Blanched Leek Greens** (page 31), well drained

   ¾ cup freshly grated Parmesan cheese

   1 to 1½ teaspoons freshly ground white pepper

   1 teaspoon ground coriander

   1¾ teaspoons coarse kosher salt

Whisk the cream and sour cream together in a small, heavy-bottomed saucepan. Bring just to a boil over high heat, then turn the heat down to medium and maintain a brisk simmer, stirring frequently to make sure the cream doesn't scorch. Reduce to 1⅓ cups. This could take up to 30 minutes, depending on the width of your saucepan.

Meanwhile, place the greens in a food processor. Pulse until they resemble torn herb leaves; do not puree. You'll have about 3 cups. Scrape the greens into a large bowl.

When the cream has reduced, add the cheese, pepper to taste, the coriander, and salt. Pour on top of the chopped greens and mix well. Taste for salt. Serve warm or at room temperature; the creamed greens will thicken as they cool.

Store any leftovers in the refrigerator for up to 3 days. The mixture will stiffen when chilled. Use straight out of the refrigerator as a spread on a bagel or toast, or let sit at room temperature for at least 30 minutes to soften.

LEEK GREENS CREAM CHEESE

This spread is excellent on bagels, on baked potatoes with sour cream, and folded into scrambled eggs.

Finely chop a heaping ⅔ cup **Blanched Leek Greens** (page 31). Fold into 1 pound softened cream cheese. Season with salt. Store in the refrigerator for up to 10 days or freeze for up to 2 months.

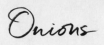

Onion Jam

This jam is the royal cousin of griddled diner onions. Balsamic or sherry vinegar, a heavy hand with butter, and good chicken stock turn a ubiquitous burger topping into a rich, versatile condiment. This is my cooking studio's most requested recipe.

Don't rush this. Give yourself at least 2 hours to make the jam properly. The batch will keep for a few weeks in the refrigerator and longer in the freezer.

makes 1¼ CUPS

2 pounds onions (4 or 5 large), peeled and very thinly sliced (about 10 cups)

8 tablespoons (1 stick) unsalted butter

1 cup excellent chicken stock (such as Worth-It Chicken Stock, page 267)

1 tablespoon balsamic vinegar or sherry vinegar

1 tablespoon coarse kosher salt

1 teaspoon sugar

In large, heavy-bottomed pot (such as a Dutch oven), combine the onions and butter over medium heat. Stir continuously until the butter melts and the onions are well coated. Turn the heat down to low, cover, and cook until the onions are completely translucent, at least 15 minutes, stirring frequently. If the onions begin to brown, turn the heat down even lower. Do not rush this step.

Remove the lid and add the stock, vinegar, salt, and sugar. Turn the heat up to medium and stir well.

Cook, uncovered and stirring occasionally, until the onions are a deep nut-brown, creamy, and highly aromatic, 1½ to 2 hours. As the onions begin to absorb the liquid, stir more frequently. If they begin to stick to the bottom of the pot, scrape them loose and turn down the heat. (For a more hands-off approach, put the onions into a 300°F oven after you add the stock, vinegar, salt, and sugar. Increase the cooking time by about 30 minutes. You'll still need to stir occasionally.)

Cool completely, then scrape every last bit of jam from the pot—do not leave any of the rich liquid behind. Store, covered, in the refrigerator for up to 3 weeks, or in the freezer for up to 6 months. Consider freezing the jam in smaller portions, such as 4 to 6 tablespoons, for individual servings of soup. Bring to room temperature or warm the jam to use.

Use in

—> Freekeh with Onion Jam (page 338)

—> Fast French Onion Soup (opposite)

—> Cheese Stock and Onion Jam Soup (opposite)

—> Glazed Seared Brussels Sprouts with Balsamic-Onion Jam Glaze (page 119)

Fast French Onion Soup

This one best exemplifies how you can use a Starting Point to make a sophisticated dish in little time. In fact, because the base, Onion Jam, is richer than typical caramelized onions, this soup is not only quicker, but better than the classic. Also, unlike classic French onion soup, it is easy to make this at the last minute and for as few or as many portions as you want.

—→ **FOR EACH SERVING**

> **1 cup excellent chicken stock (such as Worth-It Chicken Stock, page 267)**
>
> **1 fresh thyme sprig**
>
> **¼ cup Onion Jam (opposite)**
>
> **1½ teaspoons dry sherry, plus more for serving**
>
> **Coarse kosher salt**
>
> **1 thick slice good bread**
>
> **Loosely packed ¼ cup finely grated raw-milk Gruyère cheese**

Preheat the broiler or preheat the oven to 450°F. Place the stock and thyme in a saucepan. Cover and bring to a quick boil. As soon as it boils, add the onion jam and cook just long enough to heat it through. Remove from the heat; add the sherry and, if necessary, a little salt.

Transfer to a heatproof bowl, add the bread, then scatter the Gruyère on top. Broil or bake until the soup is bubbly and the cheese has browned, 3 to 5 minutes. Drizzle with a little bit more sherry to serve.

Cheese Stock and Onion Jam Soup

By using cheese stock instead of chicken stock, you can make another, richer version of French onion soup. It's the most delicious soup you can ever assemble in under a minute.

—→ **FOR EACH SERVING**

> **6 tablespoons Onion Jam (opposite)**
>
> **1 cup Cheese Stock (page 385)**
>
> **Freshly ground black pepper**

Bring the onion jam and cheese stock to a quick boil. Season with pepper and serve immediately.

ONION JAM + CHEESE-STOCK

↓

CHEESE-STOCK & ONION JAM SOUP

Pickled Red Onions

Pair these onions with fried fish, a hamburger, or a spinach salad with hard-boiled egg.

makes ABOUT 2½ CUPS

2 cups apple cider vinegar

2 teaspoons coarse kosher salt

2 teaspoons black peppercorns

2 tablespoons plus 2 teaspoons light brown sugar

2 cups water

5 cups thinly sliced red onions (about 4 medium)

Fill a saucepan large enough to hold all the onions with water and bring to a boil.

Meanwhile, in another saucepan, combine the vinegar, salt, peppercorns, sugar, and 2 cups water. Bring to a boil to dissolve the sugar. Turn off the heat.

Add the onions to the boiling water and cook for a few seconds. Drain and transfer to a heatproof container or canning jar. Pour the brine over the onions to completely submerge them. Cool to room temperature. Store, covered, in the refrigerator for up to 1 month.

Use in

→ Roasted Beets and Pickled Onions with Pistachios and Bay Salt (page 162)

Spicy Lemon-Onion Slaw

Lemon juice is sufficiently acidic to slow-pickle thinly cut onions, making for a bright slaw. Toss it with fresh watermelon and feta (page 154) or mix with yogurt for a variation on Greek tzatziki (opposite). The slaw is a fine complement to smoked fish (page 242), but it is just as good on thin slices of avocado. This recipe is adapted from the editors of *The Guardian*.

makes ⅔ CUP

1¼ cups very thinly sliced onion (1 medium)

1 teaspoon coarse kosher salt

½ teaspoon hot red pepper flakes

3 tablespoons fresh lemon juice

Place the onions in a small bowl and toss with the salt. Add the red pepper and lemon juice and mix well.

Pack down into the bowl, cover with plastic wrap directly on the surface of the onions, then place a small weight (such as another bowl) directly on top, pressing the onions into the lemon juice. Refrigerate for at least 8 hours, but preferably overnight. Store the onions in their pickle brine.

This will keep for a couple of days, but it's best if used just after the onions finish pickling.

exploration

SPICY LEMON-ONION SLAW + celery leaves fennel salt olive oil →

CELERY LEAF, FENNEL & SPICY LEMON-ONION SLAW

Celery Leaf, Fennel, and Spicy Lemon-Onion Slaw

The addition of herbal celery and fennel turn this tart slaw into a crunchy salad, great on its own at the beginning of a meal or between courses. It's also outstanding with grilled or poached shrimp (page 228).

→ **FOR EACH SERVING**

½ cup thinly sliced fennel

Coarse kosher salt

¼ cup celery leaves (from light green stalks and the yellow heart)

2 tablespoons **Spicy Lemon-Onion Slaw** (opposite), and a bit of the brine

Excellent olive oil

Fennel fronds

Toss the sliced fennel with a pinch of salt; let sit for 5 minutes.

Add the celery leaves, onion slaw, a bit of the brine, and a drizzle of oil. Mix well. Taste to see if it needs additional onion brine. Top with fennel fronds and serve immediately.

LEMON-ONION TZATZIKI

Spoon this tangy, spicy sauce on a bagel with smoked salmon, or scoop it up with toasted pita bread. You can scale this up and use as a dip.

For each serving, mix ¼ cup whole-milk Greek yogurt or sour cream with 1½ tablespoons finely chopped **Spicy Lemon-Onion Slaw** (opposite), ¾ teaspoon excellent olive oil, and a pinch of coarse kosher salt.

Scallions and Ramps

You know the scallion. Meet the ramp, its short-season, svelte sister. You can grill scallions and ramps whole—never mind that the tender green leaves wilt before the crisper white bulb is cooked. But if you break them into parts, you have more possibilities: the leaves for a salad, the bulb cooked with sesame seeds into a delicious condiment.

The white bulbs of each can be used interchangeably, though scallions are crunchier and spicier. Short-seasoned ramps are a fleeting find.

Sliced scallions and sliced ramp bulbs keep for 1 week in the refrigerator, covered directly with a slightly damp paper towel, in an airtight container. Cut your scallions and ramps by the bunch and you'll have them ready for quick use.

Ramp Leaves for Salad

The most perishable part of the ramp is its leaf, pretty as a petal, soft as a ribbon, delicate like baby greens. It tastes like lettuce and onion, and at the same time like young olive oil. It is a singular find for a spring salad, with or without its white bulb. The idea of a ramp leaf standing in for lettuce is so simple that it's funny how novel it seems.

I like to buy ramps in big bundles, clean them all at once, and cut the leaves from the stems, just at the point where the stems turn pink and tough. I store the leaves separate from the bulbs, layering them alternately with paper towels (which I reuse) to absorb any water.

Use any dressing you like with the leaves, as long as it's not too weighty. Sometimes just excellent olive oil and lemon juice is best.

Ramp Leaf, Cucumber, and Avocado Salad

Ramp leaves are so pretty; I like to leave them whole. However, I slice the cucumbers in this salad thin so they'll tangle with the ribbony leaves, and I salt them lightly in advance so they don't get lost among the other assertive flavors.

→ **FOR 4 SERVINGS**

2 small cucumbers (such as Kirby or Persian), peeled and cut into thin half-moons

Coarse kosher salt

Leaves from ¾ pound ramps, washed and dried well

Up to ¼ cup **Coriander Vinaigrette** (page 362)

1 avocado, sliced

2 ounces soft goat cheese, crumbled (optional)

Toss the cucumber slices in a bowl with a few pinches of salt and let them sit for 10 minutes.

In another bowl, toss the ramp leaves with the vinaigrette. Add the cucumbers and fold gently to coat. Divide the salad among four plates and top with the avocado and goat cheese, if using.

Scallion-Sesame Magic Mix

Here's a great, quick way to use up and store scallions, pairing them with standby favorites ginger and sesame. Spoon the "magic mix" over rice, drizzle it over Scallop Crudo, or stir it into Braised Parsnip Velouté (page 173). Raw and without the oil, the mix is exceptional smeared on Charred Corn (page 125) or stirred into Worth-It Chicken Stock (page 267).

makes 1 CUP

1 cup excellent olive oil

2 cups finely sliced scallions, greens and whites

¼ cup toasted sesame seeds

1 teaspoon flaky sea salt

½ teaspoon hot red pepper flakes

2 teaspoons grated fresh ginger

Heat the oil in a small saucepan over medium heat. When you see it glimmer, add the remaining ingredients and lower the heat. Cook until the scallions begin to brown lightly, about 10 minutes; do not let the mixture burn. Store in the refrigerator for up to 2 weeks.

Scallop Crudo with Scallion-Sesame Magic Mix

If you have Scallion-Sesame Magic Mix around, you are a fresh catch away from a wonderful hot-weather appetizer. Of all raw fish for crudo, I like scallops in particular. But be sure to buy them dry packed, which means they haven't been treated with phosphates for storage. Dry-packed scallops are expensive, but you'll need only a couple.

→ **FOR EACH SERVING**

2 (1-ounce) scallops (see headnote)

¼ teaspoon coarse kosher salt

1 teaspoon fresh lime juice

2 teaspoons Scallion-Sesame Magic Mix (at left)

Very thinly slice the scallops (no more than ¼ inch thick). Fan them out onto a small plate and sprinkle with salt. Dress with the lime juice and then the Magic Mix. Serve immediately.

Shallots

Shallots Roasted with Sugar and Vinegar

These shallots are infinitely better than your typical roasted onions. They are sweet and rich; saucy, not dry. Because they stay largely intact, they keep their concentrated flavor locked in. In this recipe, I use parchment paper to prevent the shallots from sticking and burning (they are lightly coated with sugar) and—this is key—to create a pouch for marinating them in vinegar at the end. Put them in a salad with radicchio, drizzled with lemon, or blend them into a salad dressing (page 42).

makes **4 CUPS**

2½ pounds shallots

Excellent olive oil

1½ teaspoons coarse kosher salt

1 tablespoon sugar

2 teaspoons white wine vinegar

Preheat the oven to 350°F. Line a baking sheet with parchment paper. Peel the shallots, separating any double bulbs. Very lightly trim the root tendrils but keep the root ends themselves intact. If the shallots are very large, halve them lengthwise, through the root ends. You should have a few dozen almost-even-sized pieces.

Toss the shallots in a bowl with just enough oil to coat evenly. Sprinkle with the salt and sugar and neatly align them on the parchment, close together, cut (flatter) side down. Roast until they brown all over and are very soft. If they begin to burn before you can easily slide a sharp knife through them, pull up the sides of the parchment, forcing the shallots to tumble to the center, and fold the paper onto itself, enclosing the shallots in a loose pouch. The indirect heat will continue to cook the shallots, but the pouch will prevent further browning.

Once the shallots are very soft, remove them from the oven. If you made a parchment pouch, undo it now. Sprinkle the hot shallots with the vinegar. Carefully fold (or refold) the parchment over the shallots, tucking the pouch ends under. Allow to cool, then toss the shallots around gently in their pouch. Taste. If the vinegar is too sharp, consider adding a bit more salt, but remember that the shallots will sweeten as they cool. Scrape the cooled shallots and the glazed juices into a container to store. They'll keep in the refrigerator for up to 1 week.

Use in

→ Roasted Shallot and Bread Salad (page 42) and serve with braised chicken (page 257)

→ Roasted Shallots, Prunes, and Walnuts (page 42)

Roasted Shallot Dressing

Tart-sweet and jammy, this dressing is ideal for large, thick leaves of fresh spinach.

→ **MAKES 1½ CUPS**

1½ cups **Shallots Roasted with Sugar and Vinegar** (page 41)

2 teaspoons whole-grain mustard

1 teaspoon soy sauce

4 teaspoons sherry vinegar

½ teaspoon or more coarse kosher salt, to taste

1 teaspoon or more honey, to taste

2 tablespoons water

½ cup excellent olive oil

Place all the ingredients in a food processor. Pulse until creamy. Refrigerate for up to 5 days.

Roasted Shallots, Prunes, and Walnuts

Slather this chutney on buttered toast or serve with game meat.

→ **MAKES ABOUT 1¾ CUPS**

½ cup walnuts, roughly chopped and lightly toasted (page 368)

½ cup pitted prunes, cut in half

1 cup **Shallots Roasted with Sugar and Vinegar** (page 41)

1 tablespoon sherry vinegar

Heat all the ingredients in a saucepan over medium heat, covered, for 5 minutes. Serve warm or cool. Refrigerate, covered, for up to 2 weeks. Bring to room temperature or warm before serving.

Roasted Shallot and Bread Salad

Like all bread salads, this one tastes better the longer it sits. The toasted bread cubes turn deliciously chewy—not soft and soppy—as they marinate. This dish also makes a great alternative to a traditional stuffing.

→ **FOR EACH SERVING**

1 thick slice good peasant bread, cut into 1-inch cubes (about ¾ cup)

½ teaspoon sugar

Coarse kosher salt

4 teaspoons sherry vinegar, or more to taste

¼ cup excellent olive oil

¼ cup roughly chopped fresh flat-leaf parsley

½ cup **Shallots Roasted with Sugar and Vinegar** (page 41), at room temperature

¼ cup chopped pitted kalamata olives

Preheat the oven to 400°F. Place the bread cubes on a baking sheet and brown, about 5 minutes.

Meanwhile, place the sugar, 1 teaspoon salt, and the vinegar in a bowl. Whisk together well. Drizzle in the oil, whisking continuously to emulsify. Add the parsley.

While the bread is still warm, add to the vinaigrette. Toss well. Season with salt. Add the shallots to the bowl, pulling the pieces apart lengthwise so they mix with the bread cubes. Stir in the olives. Let marinate for at least 45 minutes and up to 3 hours, at room temperature, stirring occasionally. Taste for salt.

You can wrap the salad and refrigerate it overnight to serve the next day. Bring to room temperature and mix well before serving.

Classic Shallot Vinaigrette

This is a great way to preserve shallots. You can make the vinaigrette in bulk, doubling or tripling the recipe, or keep extra minced raw shallots on hand to pull together a batch at the last minute.

You can use this dressing on any salad, but I particularly like the way it tames thicker, heartier greens like Raw and Ribboned Collard Greens (page 48). If you're not using the whole batch of vinaigrette at once, strain it and discard the shallots after you've infused the vinegar. Otherwise, the shallots will overtake the vinegar flavor.

makes ABOUT 1 CUP

¼ cup sherry vinegar

¼ cup finely minced shallots (about 2 shallots)

½ teaspoon coarse kosher salt, plus more to taste

2 teaspoons Dijon mustard

¾ to 1 cup excellent olive oil

Mix the vinegar, shallots, and salt in a small bowl. Let stand for 10 minutes. If not using immediately, strain the vinegar and reserve the shallots as you would pickled onions.

Whisk in the mustard, then the oil, until emulsified and the vinegar is somewhat tamed. Taste; you may want an additional pinch of salt. Store in the refrigerator for up to 5 days, in a container with a tight lid.

Leaves

Hearty Greens: Kale, Collards, Spinach, and Chard

Save the stems for Swiss Chard Stems Jam (page 54) or for Braised and Pickled Kale Stems (page 52).

starting point

Washed and Ready: Cleaning and Storing Hearty Greens and Their Stems

I try to wash all greens as soon as I bring them home.

Fill a large bowl or a clean sink with plenty of ice water (yes, add ice) to thoroughly clean and invigorate the leaves. If you plan to use the leaves apart from the stems, fold the leaves in half, top sides together, to expose the stem. Then either cut or carefully tear the stem off. Wash and dry the leaves and stems separately. Submerge each in the ice water, in batches. Swish around to revive the leaves and release any dirt. Let sit for a few minutes for the dirt to settle.

Lift out of the water and place in a strainer or colander to drain. Many people use a salad spinner for the leaves, but I don't think spinners do much good; they rarely get the greens completely dry. Instead, do this: Lay the well-drained leaves in a tight, single layer on a long continuous sheet of paper towels. The paper towels will wick water away from the leaves while preventing them from drying out in the refrigerator. Place another layer of paper towels on top of that. Continue layering

greens and towels, ending with a final layer of towels on top. Finally, roll up the towels all together from one of the shorter ends into a fat bundle. Secure this bundle with a band of plastic wrap and store in the refrigerator. To access the leaves you need, just unwrap. This will keep your greens both dry and fresh for up to a week. And you can reuse the paper towels for general kitchen cleanup.

After you drain the stems well, store them loosely in a plastic bag or container lined with dry paper towels. See pages 52 to 54 for some ways to use them.

Whole Leaf "Frittata"

Rather than adding chopped greens to a batch of eggs, I dip whole leaves into beaten eggs, layering them like crepes in a skillet. The egg layers set and the leaves retain some crunch.

 Like most frittatas, this is best at room temperature, even cold. You can also put a wedge in a sandwich on crusty peasant bread with spicy mustard and melt on a slice of provolone cheese.

—→ **FOR 8 SERVINGS**

1 pound whole collard greens washed and ready (opposite)

4 large eggs

Packed 1¼ cups finely grated pecorino cheese

¼ teaspoon coarse kosher salt

1 tablespoon excellent olive oil

1 tablespoon unsalted butter

½ cup crème fraîche or sour cream, for serving

Preheat the oven to 350°F. Trim the collard greens at the base of each leaf to remove the thicker part of the stem. Trim a bit more of the stem if the leaves are extra large and the stems are more than ¼ inch thick, but don't bother cutting the stem out from the center of the leaves entirely.

Beat the eggs in a large bowl. Place the cheese in a small bowl. Add the salt and toss.

Heat a heavy-bottomed 10-inch ovenproof skillet (such as cast iron) over medium-high heat. Add the oil and butter to the pan. When the butter begins to foam, begin dunking your largest collard leaves into the eggs, letting excess egg drip back into the bowl. Place a coated leaf in the pan and top with 1 tablespoon of the cheese, evenly sprinkling it over the leaf. Top with another coated leaf, pressing down firmly with a spatula all over; add another tablespoon of cheese. Continue in this fashion, pressing down firmly on each leaf as you go either with a spatula or—even better—your egg-smeared palm, and layering each leaf with cheese, until all of the leaves are used up. Unfold the leaves if they curl into themselves. If a leaf is extra large, let the extra length run up the sides of the pan; it will find its way into the frittata by the end. If the leaves are small, use multiple leaves to make one layer, overlapping the smaller leaves as necessary to make a layer that covers the entire surface. Do not put cheese on the very top layer.

When all the leaves are in place, lay a sheet of foil on top of the pan and, with your hand or a heavy pot, press down firmly on the frittata for 1 minute.

Remove from the heat. Use a spatula to peek underneath the frittata to see that the bottom is nicely, evenly browned. When it is, invert a heatproof plate facedown directly over the pan, pressing down firmly so it doesn't slip when turned over. Quickly, carefully, and with commitment—and oven mitts—flip the pan upside down so that the frittata lands on the plate. Then slide the now-inverted frittata back into the pan, browned side up, and place in the oven for 5 minutes.

Leave the frittata to cool slightly in the skillet before unmolding. Serve with crème fraîche or sour cream. Cut with a sharp knife. Refrigerate leftovers for up to 5 days.

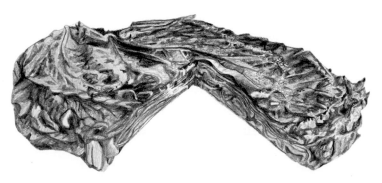

Raw and Ribboned Hearty Greens

Ribboned big, sturdy raw greens—collards, Swiss chard, and kale—are malleable enough to eat with a fork, can carry the creamiest dressings, and are ready to toss into soup and pasta.

To ribbon the leaves, first stem them, then wash and dry them well. Stack about 5 leaves. Starting from one of the longer sides, roll up the leaves like a cigar. Holding the roll tight, slice it ¼ inch thick. Unravel the slices to release ribbons. One and a half pounds greens will give you about 12 packed cups ribboned leaves, depending on the type of green and weight of the stems; this makes 4 servings.

If properly dried, raw, ribboned greens keep for up to 5 days, stored in a plastic bag or container lined with a dry paper towel. Use for a raw salad one night and sauté the rest of the cut greens with Wine-Pickled Garlic Cloves (page 24).

To soften and season for a salad, toss the ribbons gently with salt (½ teaspoon for every 3 cups leaves) and, for collards, a bit of sugar. I do not "massage" my greens to soften them. Instead, I let them relax on their own, resting with salt for at least 10 minutes. They will shrink to about half their volume, but stay airy and crisp. Then I toss them with a dressing thick enough to cling to the now-moistened leaves, about 1 tablespoon per serving.

Collard Ribbons with Sharp Vinaigrette

Raw collard greens are underappreciated. Here, appeased with a little salt and sugar, they benefit from a light dressing. The formidable leaves tenderize, yet don't wilt. They make a great salad for lunch, tossed with Perfect Hard-Boiled Eggs (page 349) and chopped toasted walnuts. I like this dish alongside rich meat. Or instead of shallot vinaigrette, dress them with Spiced-Apple-Cider-Honey Vinaigrette (page 365), crumbling in blue cheese or soft goat cheese.

⟶ **FOR EACH SERVING**

3 cups **Raw and Ribboned Collard Greens** (at left; from a scant ½ pound whole collards)

½ teaspoon coarse kosher salt

Scant ¼ teaspoon sugar

4 teaspoons **Classic Shallot Vinaigrette** (page 43)

Place the greens in a bowl and rub gently and evenly with the salt and sugar. Set aside for 10 minutes.

Place the vinaigrette in a small bowl. Pile the seasoned greens on top and stir gently with your fingers to coat. Taste once more for salt. Serve.

Collard Ribbons with Pickled Garlic

It's traditional to finish sturdy sautéed greens with garlic and a splash of vinegar. Here, I use pickled garlic and a bit of its brine instead. These collard ribbons are quick to make and hard to stop eating; it's worth cooking a large batch at a time.

⟶ **FOR 4 SERVINGS**

8 to 10 **Wine-Pickled Garlic Cloves** (page 24), very thinly sliced

4 tablespoons excellent olive oil

5 cups **Raw and Ribboned Collard Greens**, very thinly sliced (opposite; from about ¾ pound whole collards)

2 tablespoons or more **brine from Wine-Pickled Garlic Cloves**

1 teaspoon coarse kosher salt

Place half of the garlic and 2 tablespoons of the oil in a skillet large enough to hold half of the greens. Warm over medium heat until the garlic begins to sizzle, about 1 minute. Continue to cook until very fragrant, about 2 minutes more, without letting the garlic brown. Add half of the greens all at once, and cook, tossing continuously with tongs, until just limp and well coated with the garlic and oil, about 3 minutes. Take off the heat and immediately add at least 1 tablespoon of the brine (enough so that you can smell it rising from the greens) and ½ teaspoon salt. Toss and taste. Transfer to a serving bowl.

Repeat with the remaining ingredients and serve.

Hearty Greens with Bacon and Fig, Olive, and Walnut Relish

Using bacon grease in addition to oil for body and flavor, this relish stretches to become a dressing for the greens.

⟶ **FOR EACH SERVING**

1 slice bacon, cut into 1-inch pieces

½ small garlic clove, minced

Packed 1¼ cups **Raw and Ribboned Lacinato Kale** or **Collard Greens** (opposite; from a scant ¼ pound greens)

Coarse kosher salt

1 tablespoon or more **Fig, Olive, and Walnut Relish** (page 367)

1 tablespoon crumbled blue cheese

Choose a skillet large enough for the greens. Fry the bacon over medium heat until crisp. Remove from the pan. Pour off all but a couple tablespoons of the remaining fat.

Return the pan to low heat and add the garlic. Cook until lightly golden, about 1 minute. Turn the heat to high and immediately add the greens, turning them with tongs to coat thoroughly with the fat and mopping up the garlic from the pan. Cook until the greens wilt and turn tender, about 2 minutes. Taste for salt. Transfer to a serving bowl.

Mix the bacon and relish together. Add to the greens and toss. Taste and add more relish if desired. Add the blue cheese and gently toss once more. Serve warm or at room temperature.

Seared Kale with Garlic and Lemon

Steaming or wilting greens often leaves them waterlogged, and they turn flat and tinny after a day. Instead, you can sear your greens—brown them in a hot pan—so they extrude all their water and take on deeper flavor. I sear the leaves by weighting them down in a hot, oiled pan. Searing is more work than quickly wilting the kale, but it's worth the extra effort. If you have the cookware, sear in two pans at once.

makes 4 CUPS, ENOUGH FOR 4 SIDE SERVINGS

3 pounds kale, preferably lacinato, stemmed, leaves washed and dried completely (page 46)

½ cup or more excellent olive oil

8 garlic cloves, slivered

Coarse kosher salt

2 tablespoons fresh lemon juice

Tear the kale leaves into 3-inch pieces.

Heat 2 tablespoons of the oil in a large skillet over medium-low heat. Add the garlic and cover. Cook until it is just translucent, up to 30 seconds. Don't let it burn. Pour the garlic and oil into a bowl large enough to hold all the seared kale. Don't wipe the skillet dry.

Turn the heat to high and immediately add just enough kale to cover the bottom of the pan; toss to coat it with the residual oil in the pan. Season lightly with salt and weight down the leaves with the clean bottom of a heavy pot, pressing firmly to flatten them and force out all the water in them. Once they are yellow-brown on the bottom, about 2 minutes—be careful not to let them blacken—turn the pieces and sear on the other side; you will likely not need to weight down the now-flattened leaves.

Once both sides are seared, taste the kale for salt. Transfer to the bowl with the garlic and oil and repeat with the remaining kale in batches, adding a slick of fresh olive oil to the pan each time, as needed. The pan will retain heat to cook the subsequent batches of leaves more quickly; be careful that they don't burn.

Once all the kale is seared, mix it well with the garlic and oil. Add the lemon juice and mix again. Cover with plastic wrap and let rest for 5 minutes, then taste again. Serve warm or at room temperature. Store in the refrigerator for up to 5 days.

Use the leaves in

⟶ Seared Kale with Dates and Cream (opposite)

⟶ Pork Loin and Seared Kale in Broth (page 287)

⟶ Seared Kale with Roasted Lemon and Parmesan (opposite)

Save the stems for

⟶ Braised and Pickled Kale Stems (page 52)

SEARED
KALE

+

ROASTED
WHOLE LEMON

+

almonds

Parmesan

→

SEARED KALE WITH
ROASTED LEMON
& PARMESAN

Seared Kale with Dates and Cream

One of the first dishes I was asked to make as a young line cook was cooked greens paired with cream and dried fruit. The combination was revelatory. I have riffed on this trio many times since. Using the cooked and well-seasoned kale means you need to do little but warm the three ingredients together.

⟶ FOR EACH SERVING

1 cup **Seared Kale with Garlic and Lemon** (opposite)

⅓ cup chopped pitted dates

2 tablespoons water

¼ cup heavy cream

1 teaspoon fresh lemon juice

Coarse kosher salt and freshly ground black pepper

Place the kale, dates, and water in a pan over medium heat and cook until just warmed through, about 2 minutes. Add the cream. Stir the kale as the cream reduces, to coat. Turn off the heat and stir in the lemon juice, salt (if necessary), and pepper to taste. Serve warm.

Seared Kale with Roasted Lemon and Parmesan

Whole roasted lemons have a concentrated flavor similar to that of dried fruit. Used sparingly, they are further kept in check by the cheese and garlicky greens. It's a quick dish to pull together and makes a really good packed lunch. You can also serve it warm, with just-cooked kale.

⟶ FOR EACH SERVING

1 cup **Seared Kale with Garlic and Lemon** (opposite), warm or at room temperature

1 tablespoon chopped **Roasted Whole Lemons** (page 220)

2 tablespoons chopped almonds or pistachios

¼ cup freshly grated Parmesan cheese

Toss the kale with the roasted lemons and nuts. Top with the Parmesan and serve.

Braised and Pickled Kale Stems

These pickles are the best surprise on the table. The stems combine bitter and sharp in a bite that remains vegetal even after long cooking. I like them on their own, perhaps swiped through deli mustard or alongside sharp cheddar and a cold beer. They are terrific next to cured meats or grilled fish.

Lacinato kale has thinner, more tender stems than the larger curly kale, and I prefer them for this recipe. To yield about ½ pound stems, start with about 1 pound lacinato kale.

To stem kale, see page 46.

⟶ **MAKES 2 CUPS**

½ **pound kale stems**

¼ **cup white wine vinegar**

½ **cup water**

1 **teaspoon coarse kosher salt**

2 **pinches of sugar**

Cut the stems into 3-inch pieces; you'll have about 3 cups. Place the stems in a heavy medium saucepan with a tight-fitting lid. Add the remaining ingredients, cover, and place over very low heat. Cook, stirring now and again, until the stems become very tender when pierced with a sharp knife, about an hour. There may be just a little liquid remaining in the saucepan, but it should not all evaporate.

Alternatively, put the covered pan in a preheated 300°F oven and cook, stirring occasionally, for up to 1½ hours. (While the oven takes longer, it is more hands-off and eliminates any risk of burning.)

The vinegar bites sharply when the stems are hot, so cool the pickle to room temperature before serving. It will mellow nicely, as the vinegar and bitterness come to a balance. Store the pickle in a tightly covered container with any remaining liquid in the refrigerator for up to 3 weeks.

WASHING SPINACH

⟶ Fill a clean sink with enough cold water to submerge the spinach. Add a handful of ice. For whole-bunch spinach, carefully strip the leaves from their crunchy stems. Swish the leaves and stems in the ice-cold water to release dirt and revive the leaves. Lift out of the water and drain well in a colander.

⟶ Dry and store large leaves in a roll of paper towels (page 46). Drain the stems well to store; no need to dry completely if you're going to sauté them right away. If your leaves are smaller, store them—tender, edible stems still attached—in dry paper towels in a plastic bag.

Sautéed Spinach Stems with Warm Garlic and Lemon

Sautéed spinach stems taste like Chinese broccoli. The stems are best at room temperature, as their flavors settle in. Serve them on their own as a small plate or pile them on sticky rice.

This recipe depends on whole-bunch spinach, with sturdy, crunchy stems. They should be crisp, full of water, and chew down to sweetness. Don't use them if they taste bitter or like wet grass. The fresher the spinach, the more delicious the stems.

Instead of the garlic, lemon, and red pepper, you can use garlic, ¼ teaspoon fresh ginger, and a splash of soy sauce.

→ **MAKES ABOUT 2 CUPS, ENOUGH FOR 4 SMALL PLATES**

1 large garlic clove, finely minced

2 tablespoons excellent olive oil

Stems from 2 large bunches very fresh spinach, washed and dried

Coarse kosher salt

½ lemon

Pinch of hot red pepper flakes

Cook the garlic with 1 tablespoon of the oil over very low heat in a wok or large skillet until it begins to sizzle and color slightly at the edges, about 45 seconds. Turn the heat to high and add the spinach stems all at once. Toss continuously until they begin to soften in a steamy mass, about 1 minute; if necessary, turn the heat down to make sure the garlic doesn't burn.

Season with salt, a good squeeze of lemon juice, and the red pepper, tossing well. Turn off the heat and drizzle with the remaining 1 tablespoon oil. Let rest for a few minutes, tasting the stems once they have cooled a bit, and adjust the salt and lemon as needed. These are best the day you make them.

Save the leaves for

→ Squid with Wine-Braised Leeks and Bacon (page 30)

Swiss Chard Stems Jam

Swiss chard leaves are tough when raw but take well to a slow simmer. But too often the stems get discarded because they break down even more slowly than the leaves. I cook the stems on their own into a rich and tart jam that will become your new favorite poultry condiment or sandwich spread. It's especially good with game or cured meats. Multiply the recipe to feed a crowd, allowing additional time for the stems to brown and reduce.

The following recipe is for a single bunch of stems (about 12 pieces). I prefer multicolor or rainbow chard. The lighter stems are slightly sour, and the red taste more vegetal. The combination of the two works well.

→ **MAKES 1½ CUPS**

3 tablespoons unsalted butter

Stems from 12 ounces rainbow Swiss chard, cut into ¼-inch dice (2 cups)

¾ cup diced shallots

3 tablespoons light brown sugar

2 tablespoons sherry vinegar

1½ cups excellent chicken stock (such as Worth-It Chicken Stock, page 267)

Combine the butter, stems, and shallots in a small, heavy saucepan. Cover and cook over low heat, stirring frequently, until the stems are well coated and turn translucent, about 10 minutes.

Add the sugar and vinegar and stir well. Cover again and cook, stirring often, until nut brown, 20 to 25 minutes.

Add the chicken stock and bring to a bare simmer. Stir well, then continue to simmer, uncovered, until the jam is reduced to 1½ cups, about 40 minutes.

Remove from the heat and stir the jam occasionally as it cools to prevent the butter from separating out. Store in the refrigerator for up to 2 weeks or in the freezer for up to 1 month. Warm to serve.

Save the leaves for

→ Raw and Ribboned Hearty Greens (page 48)

→ Shaved Brussels Sprout and Swiss Chard Slaw (page 116)

Fried Rice with Sautéed Mushrooms and Swiss Chard Stems Jam

Even without mushrooms, fried rice and this jam make a meal that can be put together in minutes by the most novice cook.

If you don't have day-old rice, spread just-cooked rice on a baking sheet and place it in a preheated 350°F oven for no more than 5 minutes, until it is just slightly dried out and has lost some of its gumminess.

Melt the butter in a skillet or wok over medium-high heat. Add the mushrooms and cook until golden and crisp at the edges, about 2 minutes. Turn the heat up to high and add the grapeseed oil, then the rice, tossing continuously to coat it with the oil. Add the soy sauce and toss well to combine. Add the egg and toss together quickly and thoroughly. Remove from the heat and stir in the sesame oil. Taste for salt.

Transfer to a plate. Quickly heat the jam in the same pan until just warm. Spoon on top of the rice. Top with the scallions and serve.

—> **FOR EACH SERVING**

1 tablespoon unsalted butter

1 cup shiitake mushrooms, stemmed and thinly sliced

2 teaspoons grapeseed or canola oil

1 cup day-old cooked white rice (see headnote)

2 teaspoons soy sauce

1 large egg, beaten

½ teaspoon sesame oil

Coarse kosher salt

2 tablespoons **Swiss Chard Stems Jam** (opposite)

2 tablespoons sliced scallions, greens and whites

Lettuces

I understand the temptation to buy prewashed greens in plastic tubs, but they are much shorter-lived than lettuce and have little taste.

Make sure to dress your lettuce according to its kind. Watery greens like romaine require thicker, creamier dressings unless they are cooked, in which case they deserve a loose, sharp vinaigrette. Tender leaves like arugula do well with a light vinaigrette, although they can hold up to the light, creamy Buttermilk Dressing on page 380.

starting point

Lettuce Washed and Ready: The Wedge

Sometimes, the work of washing and drying lettuce seems disproportionate to the attractive ease of the salad itself. That's why I found a quicker way to put up my greens. Enter The Wedge.

You can cut any head of lettuce, including romaine and butter lettuce, into wedges before washing, a cleaning shortcut that also opens options for serving. Drizzle a lettuce wedge with vinaigrette (no dirtying a bowl) or cook quickly in a pan. Stack multiple wedges on a platter for a crowd, or snip them into a bowl in bite-sized pieces. The core acts like a handle, turning a wedge of lettuce into finger food.

No matter the size or shape of the lettuce, you make wedges the same way: Cut the unwashed head lengthwise in half through its core, then cut each half into long, even wedges—the number and thickness are up to you.

To wash lettuce wedges: Trim to remove any brown edges or leaves, then submerge the wedge in ice water, swishing lightly. Drain well for at least 10 minutes in a colander, with the cut sides facing down and the core ends slanted up.

To dry, roll out a length of paper towels six times the width of the wedge. Place a wedge facing the lower left corner of the line of towels, core end down, and roll up as you would a bouquet of flowers, tucking in the towels at the bottom and leaving the tops of the leaves loosely exposed. Roll sturdy lettuces like romaine tightly; roll tender ones like red leaf or butter lettuce gently.

Store the bundles in the refrigerator, laying them flat. Do not place in a plastic bag. The paper towels will wick the water away from the lettuce, while preventing the lettuce from drying out. Wedges will keep for well over a week.

When you unwrap the wedges, you may notice that "rust" has formed at the cut sides of the wedges' cores, sometimes after only two days. Not to worry; just trim it away when you're ready to serve.

Caper Caesar Salad

This Caesar gets a hit of strong flavors beyond anchovy, unmediated by egg yolk. The salad stands up well to grilled meat and spicy mustards and can be dressed up to an hour in advance.

→ **FOR EACH SERVING**

2 tablespoons Refrigerator-Door Vinaigrette (page 383)

1 wedge romaine lettuce (about ¼ large head), washed, thoroughly dried, and cut crosswise into 2-inch pieces (opposite)

2 tablespoons freshly grated Parmesan cheese

Squeeze of lemon juice

Using your hand, loosely spread the vinaigrette over the bottom and sides of a salad bowl. Add the lettuce and toss until lightly coated. Add the Parmesan and toss again. Add a squeeze of lemon juice and serve.

Wedge Caesar Salad

In a typical Caesar salad, the mild flavor of the romaine disappears under the thick pool of pungent dressing. But served as a wedge, the crunchy, cool, juicy, sweet lettuce is a confident match for it. The Wedge Caesar is the easiest of any salad to put together, especially when you have aioli ready-made. You can also dress this Caesar with Anchovy Dressing (page 379). If you'd rather skip the anchovy, fortify the aioli with spicy mustard instead, or extra lemon juice.

→ **FOR EACH SERVING**

½ teaspoon minced anchovy (2 fillets)

¼ cup Whole-Grain Mustard Aioli (page 381)

2 teaspoons water

1 wedge romaine lettuce (opposite)

Mix the anchovy, aioli, and water together. Drizzle liberally over the romaine wedge. You may have some leftover dressing, which you could save to smother on sandwiches or serve alongside roast chicken.

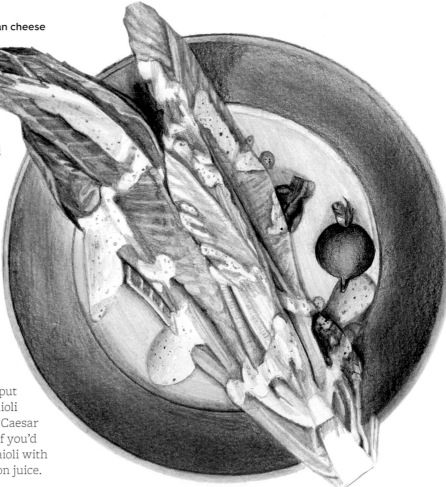

Sautéed Wedge Salad with Warm Vinaigrette

You can sauté a variety of summer lettuces, but I think romaine is best.

This dish takes minutes to bring together, especially when you have washed wedges on hand. The lettuce yields to the heat, releasing its juices, which mingle with and mellow the sharp Parsley Vinaigrette. A single wedge makes a pretty plate by itself, but many wedges piled high on a platter are striking. It's excellent warm or at room temperature, with grilled or seared steak (page 280). I also enjoy leftovers cold, tossed with plump canned sardines.

⟶ **FOR 4 SERVINGS**

12 **wedges romaine lettuce** (from about 2 large heads, page 56)

1 tablespoon excellent olive oil

½ teaspoon coarse kosher salt

6 tablespoons **Parsley Vinaigrette** (made with red wine vinegar, page 69)

Freshly ground black pepper

Cut the romaine wedges in half crosswise. Keep the pieces with the core separate from the loose leaves. Heat the oil in a large skillet over medium heat. Add the core pieces to the pan, cut side down. Season with ¼ teaspoon of the salt. Place the remaining leaves on top. Season with the remaining ¼ teaspoon salt. Toss with tongs as the leaves begin to wilt. Brown the lettuce lightly all over, using the tongs to turn the cores and leaves. Once the cores become tender and the greens wilt and darken, about 1 minute, remove from the heat.

Place in a large bowl, add the vinaigrette, and toss. Add lots of pepper. Cover the bowl with plastic wrap and let sit for 5 minutes. Toss once more. Serve warm or at room temperature.

Peaches and Radicchio with Refrigerator-Door Vinaigrette

This is a striking salad for any meal. You can interchange the herbs, using tarragon or dill, but use a variety, if you can. Because thinly sliced, really ripe peaches drip with juices, this salad becomes limp not long after it's made. To prevent this, dress all the other ingredients first, then fold in the peaches right before eating.

⟶ **FOR EACH SERVING**

½ perfectly ripe peach, very thinly sliced

½ head thin **wedges radicchio** (page 56)

2 tablespoons roughly chopped fresh flat-leaf parsley

2 tablespoons roughly chopped fresh mint

2 tablespoons roughly chopped scallion greens or chives

1 tablespoon or more **Refrigerator-Door Vinaigrette** (page 383) or **Green-Peppercorn Vinaigrette** (page 362)

Toss all the ingredients together lightly (see headnote), being careful not to bruise the peach slices or the herbs. Serve immediately.

Roasted Radicchio

To successfully roast radicchio, you need to harness its concentrated bitterness with ample vinegar and salt. Wedges of marinated roasted radicchio are bold tasting, addictive, and filling. Serve them alongside grilled meat or tucked into a sandwich with a thick slice of cheese.

makes 12 WEDGES

1 large radicchio head (10 ounces)

2 tablespoons excellent olive oil, plus more if needed

1 teaspoon coarse kosher salt, plus more if needed

1½ teaspoons red wine vinegar, plus more if needed

Preheat the oven to 450°F. Trim any tired outer leaves from the radicchio. Cut through the core into 12 even wedges, keeping each wedge intact. Lightly toss the wedges with the oil. Some leaves will detach from the core. You'll roast those too. Sprinkle everything evenly with 1 teaspoon salt.

Place the wedges and any loose leaves in a single layer in a roasting pan or baking sheet. Roast until the leaves are grey-brown at the edges, possibly a little crisp, and the white cores are soft and withered, 12 to 15 minutes. Transfer to a bowl and toss immediately with the vinegar.

Let sit for 10 minutes before serving, tossing occasionally while it rests. Taste for salt. Roasted radicchio is best served the same day, but can last for 1 more day, covered, in the refrigerator. Bring it to room temperature to serve and, if necessary, refresh with more oil, vinegar, and salt.

Use in

→ Roasted Radicchio, Fontina, and Eggplant Sandwich (opposite)

→ eggplant and radicchio antipasto (see headnote, opposite)

Dress with

→ Refrigerator-Door Vinaigrette (page 383)

Roasted Radicchio, Fontina, and Eggplant Sandwich

Distinctively roasted summer vegetables, along with a pungent vinaigrette, give options for a terrific, almost instant picnic lunch. While this sandwich is open-faced, you can close it, then wrap the warm sandwich in foil. Or you can turn the sandwich components into an antipasto, piling together the radicchio (tossed with the mustard) and eggplant, and serving them alongside the bread and cheese.

You can make each individual component of this sandwich at least 1 day in advance of when you want to serve. Check if you need to refresh the flavor of the cold, refrigerated eggplant with a squeeze of lemon and a bit of salt.

⟶ **FOR EACH SERVING**

1 small baguette (about 6 inches), sliced in half lengthwise

2 ounces Italian Fontina cheese, grated (packed ¼ cup)

6 wedges **Roasted Radicchio** (opposite)

1½ teaspoons **Refrigerator-Door Mustard** (page 383)

3 pieces **Cumin-Roasted Eggplant** (page 131), cold or at room temperature, cut into 1½-inch chunks

Red wine vinegar

Preheat the oven to 450°F. Place the bread in the oven and toast until light brown and crisp, 3 to 4 minutes. Divide the cheese on top of each piece of bread and return to the oven until the cheese is bubbly and the edges are beginning to brown, 2 minutes more.

Toss the radicchio with the mustard in a bowl.

Remove the cheese toast from the oven. Add a layer of eggplant and then of radicchio. Drizzle the top with red wine vinegar and serve.

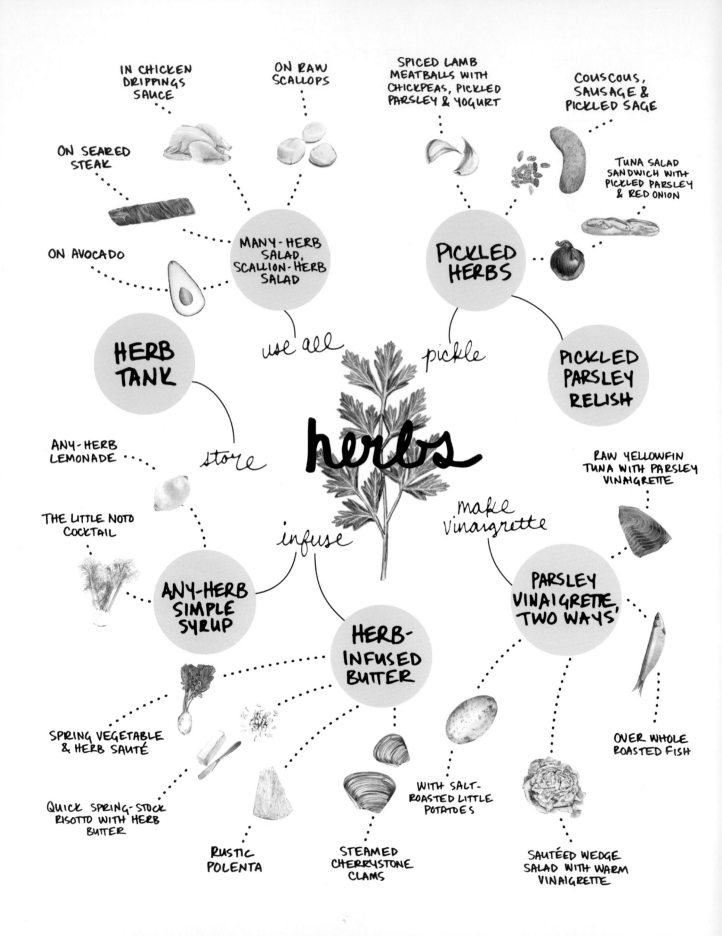

IN CHICKEN DRIPPINGS SAUCE

ON RAW SCALLOPS

SPICED LAMB MEATBALLS WITH CHICKPEAS, PICKLED PARSLEY & YOGURT

COUSCOUS, SAUSAGE & PICKLED SAGE

ON SEARED STEAK

TUNA SALAD SANDWICH WITH PICKLED PARSLEY & RED ONION

ON AVOCADO

MANY-HERB SALAD, SCALLION-HERB SALAD

PICKLED HERBS

HERB TANK

use all

pickle

PICKLED PARSLEY RELISH

ANY-HERB LEMONADE

store

herbs

RAW YELLOWFIN TUNA WITH PARSLEY VINAIGRETTE

THE LITTLE NOTO COCKTAIL

infuse

make vinaigrette

PARSLEY VINAIGRETTE, TWO WAYS

ANY-HERB SIMPLE SYRUP

HERB-INFUSED BUTTER

SPRING VEGETABLE & HERB SAUTÉ

OVER WHOLE ROASTED FISH

QUICK SPRING-STOCK RISOTTO WITH HERB BUTTER

WITH SALT-ROASTED LITTLE POTATOES

RUSTIC POLENTA

STEAMED CHERRYSTONE CLAMS

SAUTÉED WEDGE SALAD WITH WARM VINAIGRETTE

The Herb Tank

I've stumbled upon a way to preserve fresh herbs, keeping them flavorful and crisp for at least a week at a time: an "Herb Tank." I submerge sturdy fresh herbs in a clear container of ice water, so they are always in sight, clean, and ready to use. The herbs' flavor does not leach into the water. Choose herbs at their freshest. A tank will only hasten the decline of tired herbs.

This method is far superior to storing herbs in 1 inch of water in a jar, which turns them dark. That setup is at risk of tipping over and blocks a clear view of other refrigerated things. With the herb tank, herbs like rosemary, sage, thyme, parsley, mint, and oregano retain their fresh texture and taste. However, delicate herbs, like tarragon, chervil, cilantro, dill, and basil, suffer if left in an herb tank too long. It's best to store these herbs washed, well drained, and loosely wrapped in paper towels (see page 46).

You'll need a clear plastic or glass container large enough to lay the herbs down comfortably. If your herbs are bundled by a band, release them. Wash them well in ice water and pick off any yellowed leaves. Leave the stems on but trim the ends if necessary for them to fit into the container.

Place a few ice cubes in the container. You can store different herbs together, as long as you keep herbs with woody stems separate from those with soft stems. Add the herbs. Top with a few more ice cubes and fill with cold water to submerge. If your herbs float and the stems stick out of the water, cover them with a wet paper towel. Place the lid on tightly.

Store in a cold part of your refrigerator—not in the door. When the water begins to cloud (this may happen after a couple of days), change it and add fresh ice.

When you're ready to use the herbs, use clean hands to pull out the amount you need, shaking off excess water. To dry, spread in a single layer on paper towels. Cover with another paper towel and gently roll into a log. Gently press this log to encourage the towels to absorb the water.

Many-Herb Salad

If you need convincing that fresh herbs are worth buying, try this salad. I use it as a light topping (similar to a slaw), scattered on top of sliced raw scallops, mixed with toasted bread crumbs and chopped hard-boiled eggs, or sprinkled over shredded poached chicken.

I also like it piled on top of white beans, and over avocado, mixed with little dice of sweet summer squash. I serve it alongside Seared Skirt Steak (page 281) and with Whole Roasted Fish (page 246). It is the key to never letting another herb go to waste.

Tarragon, basil, parsley, mint, dill, cilantro, and chervil are all good, as are fennel fronds and young celery leaves. Thyme and oregano, picked from their stems and used sparingly, will also work. Avoid rosemary and sage, which are too strong.

Keep the leaves whole. Use any thin, crisp, flavorful stems, like parsley, and use a sharp knife when you chop them to prevent bruising.

1 medium shallot, thinly sliced

1 small fennel bulb, cored and thinly sliced, or 2 small, tender celery stalks, thinly sliced

½ cup finely chopped soft herb stems (see headnote)

Grated zest and juice of 1 lemon

3 tablespoons excellent olive oil

1 teaspoon coarse kosher salt

Packed 2 cups mixed fresh herb leaves and fronds, cleaned and dried

Combine the shallot, fennel, herb stems, and lemon zest and juice in a large bowl. Whisk in the oil and salt. Gently fold in the herbs with your hands, keeping them airy and unbruised. Serve immediately.

Scallion-Herb Salad

The pairing of scallions and a good deal of fresh thyme makes this a more assertive variation on Many-Herb Salad. Toss with sliced grilled flank steak or Poached Chicken Breasts (page 264) and Whole-Grain Mustard Aioli (page 381), or spoon on top of garlic-rubbed toasted bread.

—> FOR ABOUT 4 SIDE SERVINGS

2 cups thinly sliced scallions, greens and whites (10 to 12 scallions)

Grated zest and juice of 1 lemon

3 tablespoons excellent olive oil

1 teaspoon coarse kosher salt

2 tablespoons minced parsley stems

2 tablespoons minced tender yellow celery stalk

Packed 1 cup assorted fresh soft herb leaves (such as yellow and green celery leaves, flat-leaf parsley, and/or cilantro)

⅓ cup fresh thyme leaves, picked carefully from the stems

Combine the scallions, lemon zest and juice, oil, and salt in a bowl. Let sit for 5 minutes. Gently fold in the parsley stems, celery, and herbs with your hands, keeping them airy and unbruised. Serve or store in a covered container in the refrigerator for up to 2 days.

Pickled Parsley or Sage

This sweet brine mimics the taste of store-bought relish and helps the herbs retain their brightness. I like to keep parsley leaves on the stem to pickle. This makes it easier to pull them from the brine, and saves time all around. You just pick off the leaves as you use them and toss the stems back in the jar for later. I don't use sage stems, so I discard them from the start.

The terrific brine, which I think was originally published in a Denver newspaper, is from John Broening, when he was the chef of Spuntino there. Here, I've applied it to herbs.

makes ABOUT 2 CUPS HERBS AND 2½ CUPS BRINE

2 cups white wine vinegar

½ cup sugar

½ cup water

2 teaspoons coarse kosher salt

4 garlic cloves, sliced

1 tablespoon mustard seeds

1 teaspoon hot red pepper flakes

1½ teaspoons coriander seeds

2 small bunches fresh flat-leaf parsley, stems left on (about 2 packed cups), *or* 2 packed cups fresh sage leaves

Combine the vinegar, sugar, water, salt, garlic, mustard seeds, red pepper, and coriander in a small saucepan. Cover and bring just to a boil over high heat. Immediately turn off the heat; steep until cool. Transfer to a 1-quart container. Do not strain. (*You can make the brine up to 1 week ahead; store it in the refrigerator.*)

When you are ready to pickle, wash the herbs well in plenty of cold water. Plunge them into the cool brine, submerging the leaves and stems completely. Store in the refrigerator. They will be ready to use within 1 hour.

Though the herbs may darken, they retain great flavor and texture for up to 2 weeks.

Use in

→ Tuna Salad Sandwich with Pickled Parsley and Red Onion (page 68)

→ Couscous, Sausage, and Pickled Sage (page 67)

→ Spiced Lamb Meatballs with Chickpeas, Pickled Parsley, and Yogurt (page 300)

Couscous, Sausage, and Pickled Sage

In this dish, deeply browned sausage and onions fortify a sauce finished with the sweet-and-sour brine of pickled herbs. Plain couscous soaks up this sauce, cushioning the rich flavors.

⟶ **FOR 4 SERVINGS**

> 1 tablespoon grapeseed or canola oil
>
> 1 pound spicy Italian sausage, cut into 1-inch pieces (keep the casings on)
>
> 1¼ pounds onions (about 4 small), sliced ¼ inch thick
>
> 1 teaspoon coarse kosher salt
>
> 1 cup couscous
>
> Freshly ground black pepper
>
> 1½ cups water
>
> Scant ½ cup golden raisins
>
> ⅓ cup **brine from Pickled Sage** (opposite)
>
> 1½ tablespoons roughly torn **leaves from Pickled Sage**

Heat the oil in a large skillet over medium-high heat. Just as the oil begins to ripple, add the sausage. Sear until well browned on all sides, 4 to 5 minutes per side. Do not let the pieces burn.

Toss the onions on top of the sausage and turn the heat down to medium. Cook, stirring occasionally, until the onions are very tender, about 20 minutes. Watch that they don't burn. Season with ½ teaspoon of the salt.

Meanwhile, place the couscous in a large bowl. Add the remaining ½ teaspoon salt and a good deal of pepper. Bring the water to a boil and pour into the couscous. Cover the bowl tightly with plastic wrap and let the couscous steam until the water is absorbed, about 5 minutes. Remove the plastic wrap and fluff the couscous with a fork, breaking up any large chunks.

Set the sausage aside and add the onions to the couscous. Return the pan to medium heat and add the raisins and pickle brine. Use a heatproof spatula to scrape the browned bits off the bottom of the pan and incorporate them into the sauce. Simmer until reduced to 1 tablespoon.

Pour the sauce into the couscous and mix well. Taste one last time for salt. Transfer to a serving platter or bowl, top with the sausage and sage leaves, and serve.

Tuna Salad Sandwich with Pickled Parsley and Red Onion

The best processed tuna I've had comes from Spain or Italy, packed in glass jars. The pieces of fish are large, not to mention rich in color and flavor. But good processed tuna can be hard to find, and it is expensive. If you can't find any worth eating straight from the jar, consider substituting good-quality canned sardines— equally terrific with the sweet-and-sour dressing here.

—> **FOR EACH SERVING**

1 (4- to 5-ounce) jar excellent tuna (see headnote)

1 tablespoon minced red onion

1 tablespoon **leaves from Pickled Parsley** (page 66)

Pinch of coarse kosher salt

1 tablespoon **brine from Pickled Parsley**

2 to 3 teaspoons excellent olive oil

Squeeze of fresh lemon juice

2 slices toasted bread

Mix all the ingredients *except the bread* together with a fork, lightly flaking the tuna. Pile onto 1 slice of bread. Top with the other piece of bread, slice in half, and serve.

Pickled Parsley Relish

Like a pesto but with more punch, this sweet, sharp relish goes well on a sandwich with ham or sharp cheese. I frequently use it as a condiment for fish or steak.

—> **MAKES ABOUT ½ CUP**

Loosely packed ½ cup **Pickled Parsley** (page 66), leaves and stems

2 tablespoons finely chopped lightly toasted walnuts (page 368)

1 large garlic clove, finely chopped

2 tablespoons excellent olive oil

Remove the parsley from the brine, shaking off excess. Any spices clinging to the leaves are okay. Chop the parsley leaves and stems finely. Stir together with the nuts, garlic, and oil. Serve at room temperature. The relish lasts in a tightly covered container in the refrigerator for up to 2 weeks.

Parsley Vinaigrette, Two Ways

I keep one of these two dressings on hand at all times. They are versatile and keep quick salads within reach. You can substitute other soft herbs for the parsley, such as cilantro or dill.

EACH VERSION *makes* **ABOUT ¾ CUP**

WITH LEMON

Grated zest of 1 small lemon

3 tablespoons fresh lemon juice

2 teaspoons white wine vinegar

1 garlic clove, smashed

1 teaspoon coarse kosher salt

Packed ¼ cup chopped fresh flat-leaf parsley

½ cup excellent olive oil

WITH RED WINE VINEGAR

½ cup red wine vinegar

4 garlic cloves, smashed and roughly chopped

1 teaspoon sugar

1 teaspoon coarse kosher salt

Packed 2 tablespoons roughly chopped fresh flat-leaf parsley leaves

¼ cup excellent olive oil

To make with lemon: Combine the lemon zest and juice, vinegar, and garlic in a small bowl. Let stand for up to 10 minutes, then remove the garlic.

To make with red wine vinegar: Combine the vinegar, garlic, and sugar in a small bowl. Whisk to dissolve the sugar. Let stand for up to 10 minutes, then remove the garlic.

To each dressing base, add the salt. Gently stir in the parsley. Add the oil in a thin stream, whisking until all incorporated. Chill for 15 minutes for better body. Whisk again right before using. The herbs will darken after 1 day, though the vinaigrettes will taste fresh for up to 1 week in the refrigerator. Bring to room temperature and whisk well before using.

Use the lemon version

→ with Salt-Roasted Little Potatoes (page 178)

→ over roasted or seared fish

Use the vinegar version in

→ a simple salad of leaf lettuce with slivered raw onions

→ Sautéed Wedge Salad with Warm Vinaigrette (page 58)

Use leftover macerated garlic in

→ Lamb Shanks Braised in Two Vinegars (page 302)

Use leftover herb stems in

→ Quick Spring Stock (page 88)

Raw Yellowfin Tuna with Parsley Vinaigrette

This is a special dish, not just because the fish is costly, but because it is effortless to make. I prefer to cut the tuna into small dice and serve it as an appetizer or part of a light lunch.

Use the best tuna you can find and afford. If you prefer your fish cooked, sear the tuna (page 239), then chill it before dicing and tossing with the vinaigrette.

→ **FOR EACH SERVING**

4 ounces raw sushi-grade tuna, cut into ¼-inch dice

1½ tablespoons **Parsley Vinaigrette** (made with lemon, page 69)

Coarse kosher salt

Toss the tuna in a bowl with the vinaigrette. Taste for salt. Serve immediately.

Any-Herb Simple Syrup

Any-Herb Lemonade

Use this syrup to make Any-Herb Lemonade (at right), a soda with seltzer water, or a phenomenal Little Noto Cocktail (page 112). Steeping overnight gives the most flavor, but you can increase the strength of a just-made syrup by pureeing the herbs and sugar water together, then passing the mixture through a fine strainer or piece of cheesecloth. In that case, both the flavor and color will intensify, but the color will dull after 1 day. I prefer syrup with a subtle tinge of color, so I like to allow for overnight infusion.

Ready-made simple syrup and fresh lemon juice give you instant lemonade—no waiting for heated sugar water to cool. Try a combination of herb syrups, if you have more than one on hand. I especially like mint and parsley together.

→ **FOR 6 TO 8 SERVINGS**

1 cup fresh lemon juice

1 cup **Any-Herb Simple Syrup** (at left)

6 cups water

Combine all the ingredients in a big pitcher and stir well. Store in the refrigerator, covered, for up to 3 days. Pour over ice to serve.

makes **ABOUT 1½ CUPS**

1 cup sugar

1 cup water

Pinch of coarse kosher salt

1 cup well-washed soft fresh herbs (such as cilantro, mint, dill, or parsley), *or* ½ cup leaves from woody fresh herbs (such as rosemary, oregano, lavender, or thyme)

Bring the sugar, water, and salt to a quick boil in a small saucepan. As soon as the sugar dissolves, submerge the herbs in the hot syrup. Turn off the heat, cover, and let cool. Store in a container or jar in the refrigerator overnight. If you strain out the herbs, the syrup will keep for up to 2 weeks.

Beans, Stalks, and Shoots

Spring Vegetables

PREPPING SPRING VEGETABLES

Asparagus

Look for asparagus with firm tops and smooth stalks. Most preparations instruct you to break the asparagus at the "natural" bending point. But because an asparagus spear has many such points, most cooks shorten their asparagus more than necessary. Instead do this: Holding the asparagus in one hand, grasp the spear at the woody end with your thumb and forefinger of the other. Try to bend the stalk as close to this end as possible; you'll see it won't break. Creep up the stalk a bit and try again. Do this incrementally until the stalk snaps.

For thin spears, I generally leave the skin intact. For wider spears, whose base is thicker than the tip, I gently peel the spear about 1½ to 2 inches from the bottom. The peeler should practically glide down the spear, taking just the very outer, bright green layer. If you've exposed the white interior, you've dug too deep.

Fresh Peas

Generally, 1 pound of peas is a little less than a cup shelled, but always buy more than you think you will need. To shell, hold the pod in one hand over a bowl. With the other hand, snap back the stem end of the pod and pull down to unzip its two halves. With your thumb, push out the peas.

Garlic Scapes

Garlic scapes are the curly stalks of young garlic plants, harvested to encourage the growth of full, flavorful garlic bulbs. When cooked, the sturdy scapes taste somewhat like green beans, with a hint of garlic but without the astringency.

It's usually necessary to trim the tough end of garlic scapes, but do so lightly, taking off no more than 2 inches. Leave the ribbony tops intact, as well as the flower, unless yellowed or wilted. Cut the scapes in manageable pieces by piling them up on your cutting board and chopping through the pile a few times crosswise for pieces 1½ to 2 inches long. One pound of scapes yields about 5 cups cut.

Green Beans

Green beans should be crisp, firm, and full of water. They should not be bruised, nor bend. Trim only the stem end of the beans, leaving the wispy tails intact. The freshest green beans are delicious raw. Slice large beans thinly on the bias. One pound yields about 4 cups sliced.

Fava Beans

Shelling fava beans requires two steps. Begin by removing the beans from the pod: Hold the pod in one hand over a bowl. With the other hand, snap back the stem end and pull down to unzip the two halves. Pull out the beans. Next, you'll need to peel the beans from their skins, best done by blanching. One pound pods gives you about ¾ cup peeled beans.

To blanch: Bring 4 cups water to a boil. Add 4 teaspoons kosher salt. Place 4 cups cold water in a medium bowl; add 2 teaspoons kosher salt and lots of ice. Add the fava beans to the boiling water. Cook until the skins turn from bright to mint green, only about 15 seconds. The skins will begin to pull away from the beans. Drain and plunge them into the ice bath. Drain again. Peel by pinching the loosened skin from each bean. Discard the skins. The beans are now ready to cook, but taste and judge for yourself if they need more cooking.

Spring Vegetable Medley

Cut to approximately equal size, mixes of vegetables are more versatile and flavorful than a single kind alone. You can blanch the vegetables or use them raw.

   If you increase or decrease the amount of vegetables you blanch, make sure you keep the ratio of salt to water the same: 1 teaspoon salt to 1 cup water.

makes **1 CUP**

4 cups water

4 teaspoons coarse kosher salt

1 cup prepped assorted spring vegetables (shelled fava beans, peas, garlic scapes, and/or green beans, separated; see opposite)

½ cup 1½-inch pieces asparagus (peeled if necessary; see opposite), cut on the bias

Bring 2 cups of the water to a boil in a small saucepan. Add 2 teaspoons of the salt. Place the remaining 2 cups water in a medium bowl. Add the remaining 2 teaspoons salt and ice.

Add the fava beans to the boiling water and blanch for 15 seconds. Remove them with a slotted spoon and plunge them into the ice bath. Turn off the heat while you slip the favas out of their skins. Taste one; they may not require additional blanching. If they do, remove them from the ice bath.

Bring the water back to a boil. Blanch the remaining vegetables in batches, removing them with a slotted spoon and adding them to the ice bath, and bringing the water back to a boil after each vegetable.

Blanch the peas until sweet, around 30 seconds, depending on their size.

Blanch the garlic scapes until bright and just tender to a knife, 15 to 20 seconds.

Blanch the asparagus until bright and only just loses its rawness, 20 to 30 seconds.

Blanch the green beans for about 1 minute.

If need be, blanch the peeled favas for a few seconds more, until spring green and tender as butter.

Once all the vegetables are completely cooled, drain them well. Store in a container lined on the bottom with clean paper towels. Use immediately, or refrigerate for up to 2 days.

Use raw vegetables in

→ Chicken Stock with Spring Vegetables and Parmesan (page 77)

→ Ricotta Dumplings with Spring Stock and Seasonal Vegetables (page 78)

Use blanched vegetables in

→ Spring Vegetable and Herb Sauté (page 77)

Spring Vegetable and Herb Sauté

The combination of vegetables and herbs upgrades an otherwise predictable dish. It makes a good warm starter.

⟶ **FOR EACH SERVING**

1 teaspoon excellent olive oil

1 cup **Spring Vegetable Medley** (page 75)

Grated zest of 1 lemon

1 tablespoon **Herb-Infused Butter** (page 377)

¼ cup assorted fresh herbs (such as dill, tarragon, parsley, and/or chives), roughly chopped

Freshly ground black pepper

Flaky sea salt

Place the oil in a skillet just large enough to hold all the vegetables and warm over medium-low heat. Add the vegetables and heat, stirring once, just until gently sizzling. Turn off the heat; add the zest and butter. Swirl the pan to melt the butter and coat the vegetables. Add the herbs and season with a little pepper. Let rest for a few minutes to let the flavors come together. Serve with a couple of pinches of flaky salt and more pepper.

Chicken Stock with Spring Vegetables and Parmesan

Like the vegetables it showcases, this soup is delicate. But the broth, fortified with Parmesan, makes it filling too. It comes together in not much more time than it takes to heat up.

⟶ **FOR EACH SERVING**

1 cup excellent chicken stock (such as Worth-It Chicken Stock, page 267)

½ cup chopped small potatoes (such as Yukon Gold or Red Bliss)

Coarse kosher salt

¾ cup raw **Spring Vegetable Medley,** raw (page 75)

¼ cup freshly grated Parmesan cheese

Freshly ground black pepper

1½ teaspoons excellent olive oil or unsalted butter

Place the stock and potatoes in a saucepan over medium-high heat. Bring to a simmer. Cook until the potatoes are just tender, about 10 minutes. Season well with salt. Add the vegetables and cook until only just tender but still bright, 2 to 3 minutes. Pour the soup into a bowl and top with the cheese, pepper to taste, and the oil or butter.

Ricotta Dumplings with Spring Stock and Seasonal Vegetables

If this seems complicated, look at the recipe closely. The Quick Spring Stock takes only about 15 minutes to make, from start to finish. Use whatever combination of vegetables you have, as long as they are at their peak. If you don't have Savory Ricotta Custard to make these beautiful, bite-sized dumplings, swirl a spoonful of fresh ricotta and a bit of good Parmesan into each bowl of hot broth, at the end.

—→ **FOR EACH SERVING**

2 teaspoons **Savory Ricotta Custard** (page 386; optional)

2 square dumpling wrappers (optional)

1 cup **Quick Spring Stock** (page 88)

½ teaspoon grated fresh ginger

Coarse kosher salt

½ cup **Spring Vegetable Medley**, raw (page 75)

Freshly grated Parmesan cheese, and fresh ricotta cheese if not making dumplings

1 tablespoon roughly chopped fresh herbs (such as dill, flat-leaf parsley, or chives)

Excellent olive oil

Freshly cracked black pepper

To make the dumplings: Place 1 teaspoon of the ricotta custard in the center of each dumpling wrapper. One at a time, use your finger to wet the edges of the wrapper with water. Lift up each of the wrapper's four corners so the edges cleanly align when they meet above the filling without trapping air bubbles, forming a neat purse. Pinch the edges together so that the purse is well sealed. Set aside.

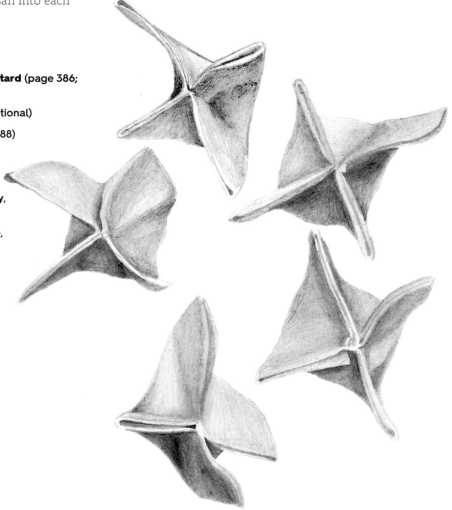

Bring the stock just to a boil in a saucepan over high heat. Add the ginger and enough salt to make the broth flavorful. Remove the stock from the heat and immediately add the vegetables. Cover and let sit for 30 seconds to 1 minute. The vegetables should remain fresh and crunchy, and not taste starchy. Add the dumplings, if using, cover the saucepan, and leave to just cook through, about 30 seconds more. If you cook more portions at once, the cooking will take longer.

Transfer to a bowl. Top with Parmesan and fresh ricotta (if you haven't made the dumplings), the herbs, a swirl of oil, and pepper.

Asparagus

Slivered Raw Asparagus

Young asparagus is terrific raw, especially when cut thin, on the bias. It remains crunchy, its wider cut surfaces season easily, and the slivered shape mixes effortlessly with aromatics like scallions and herbs. Cut thin, one spear goes quite a long way. Just a few spears gives you about ¼ cup asparagus, which you can add to a soup or scrambled eggs, or toss with pickled garlic and spoon on top of toast.

Slivered asparagus can substitute for the vegetables in the Spring Vegetable and Herb Pasta (page 311) or Cheese-Stock Risotto (page 325).

Snap and peel asparagus spears (page 74). Cut on the bias into equal thicknesses, such as ½ inch. Store raw cut asparagus, draped with a slightly damp paper towel, in a covered container in the refrigerator for up to 5 days.

Roasted Asparagus

To roast asparagus well, you must brown it sufficiently without cooking it to mush. High heat is key, as is turning the spears so they cook evenly.

for 4 TO 6 SERVINGS

2 bunches thin asparagus (about 40 spears), snapped (page 74)

4 teaspoons excellent olive oil

2 teaspoons coarse kosher salt

Fresh lemon juice (optional)

Preheat the oven to 450°F. Gently toss the asparagus with the oil and season evenly with the salt. Arrange in a single layer on a baking sheet and place in the oven. Roast until the asparagus browns lightly and softens, about 7 minutes. Gently turn the spears to brown all sides; a wide heatproof spatula is good for this (tongs may cut the spears). Roast until completely tender, about 3 minutes more.

Remove from the oven and cool for a few minutes. Taste for salt. If you like, hit the asparagus with a squeeze of lemon juice, to taste. Serve immediately or store in the refrigerator in a covered container for up to 1 day. Once chilled, do not reheat.

Top with

→ crumbled Perfect Hard-Boiled Eggs
(page 349), lemon zest, and Toasted Bread
Crumbs (page 355)

Toss with

→ Buttermilk Dressing (page 380), then top with
Crispy Fish Skin (page 226)

USING COLD ROASTED ASPARAGUS

→ Dress it with **Parsley Vinaigrette** (made
with lemon, page 69) and toss with
Toasted Bread Crumbs (page 355).

→ Top with crumbled **Perfect Hard-Boiled
Eggs** (page 349) and **Pickled Red
Onions** (page 36)

→ Layer in a sandwich with **Dill-and-Leek-
Greens Pesto** (page 32) and ham.

exploration

Za'atar-Roasted Asparagus

This is as special as it is simple, and its success
depends entirely on the quality of its few
ingredients: height-of-season asparagus and
fragrant za'atar. Za'atar is a spice blend from the
Middle East, made up primarily of dried herbs
such as thyme, sesame seeds, and up to eight
other spices, such as sumac or cumin. I use it
to season asparagus as well as roast chicken
(page 253) and Skillet Flatbread (page 357). In
this dish, I call for a generous amount of za'atar,
which might look like overkill, but is just enough.

→ **FOR 4 SERVINGS**

1½ bunches **Roasted Asparagus** (opposite),
hot out of the oven

Juice of ½ lemon

1¼ teaspoons za'atar (see headnote)

Flaky sea salt

Transfer the hot asparagus to a serving platter.
Squeeze on the lemon juice, then coat generously
with za'atar. Add a healthy pinch of salt and serve.

Pickled Asparagus

Pickling keeps even thin asparagus stalks crisp and pleasantly green-tasting. You can make the brine up to a week in advance, but leave out the tarragon until you add the asparagus. The asparagus must be completely submerged in brine to pickle; if necessary, cut the spears into smaller lengths.

makes **ABOUT 24 PIECES PICKLED ASPARAGUS AND ABOUT 2½ CUPS BRINE**

8 small garlic cloves, slivered

¼ cup coarse kosher salt

1 tablespoon sugar

1½ cups white wine vinegar

¾ cup water

12 ounces asparagus (about 12 thin spears), snapped (page 74)

Loosely packed ¾ cup fresh tarragon leaves

Combine the garlic, salt, sugar, and vinegar in a small saucepan. Heat, stirring just to dissolve the salt and sugar. Remove from the heat and add the water. Let cool to room temperature, then place in the refrigerator to cool completely.

Meanwhile, cut the asparagus in half lengthwise (unless it is pencil thin) and then once widthwise. Once the brine is cold, pour it into a 1-quart jar, add the tarragon, and submerge the asparagus in it, tips up. Cover and refrigerate.

The pickle will be ready to serve in 12 hours and will keep for 2 weeks, refrigerated.

Use in

→ Pickled Asparagus and Egg Toast (opposite)

→ Triple-Braised Wild Mushrooms with Quinoa and Pickled Asparagus (page 195)

Serve whole with

→ butter and soft goat cheese, on toast

→ Confit Duck (page 276) and mustard

Pickled Asparagus and Egg Toast

Though the ingredient pairings here are common—asparagus and egg; mustard and pickles—this little snack is much more than just topping on toast. I toast the bread in a skillet first, so it is crisp on the outside but still soft on the inside. Then I moisten the toasted bread with some of the asparagus pickle brine. In the same pan, I use a bit more of the brine, along with mustard and butter, to coat slightly softened onions.

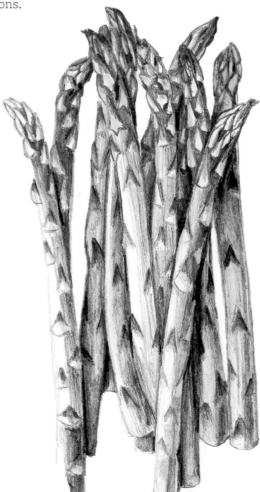

→ **FOR 1 TOAST**

1½ tablespoons unsalted butter, plus more for buttering the bread

1 slice country bread

3½ teaspoons **brine from Pickled Asparagus (opposite)**

½ teaspoon whole-grain mustard

¼ cup thinly sliced red onion

1 **Perfect Hard-Boiled Egg** (page 349), chopped or sliced

2 or 3 pieces **Pickled Asparagus**, roughly chopped

1 teaspoon roughly chopped fresh tarragon

Liberally butter both sides of the bread and toast in a skillet over medium-high heat until both sides are golden. Transfer to a plate and sprinkle with 1½ teaspoons of the pickle brine.

Melt 1½ tablespoons butter in the same skillet over medium heat. Add the mustard, the remaining 2 teaspoons brine, and the red onion. Cook, stirring, just until the onion begins to soften, about 1 minute. Place the onion mix on the toast, then pile on the egg, asparagus, and tarragon.

Celery, Raw and Ready

Celery is a crisper-drawer staple. Yet after using a few stalks, we often let the remaining stalks languish in the fridge, where they become limp. But one bunch of celery, broken into dark and light leaves, tender yellow hearts, and crunchy green stalks, gives us many different tastes and textures. Use the green stalks for fresh salsa or, in small bites, for adding crisp texture to heavier dishes. The green leaves are similar to flat-leaf parsley, but with a slightly more astringent flavor. The hearts—the inner butter-yellow stalks—are sweet and perfect for crudités. Don't discard the tops of the celery, where the dark green leaves begin to branch off the stalk; trim them lightly.

Wash and cut your celery to store: Separate the stalks and run under cold water to remove dirt. Cut into lengths with the leaves still attached and submerge in cold water in a covered container. Refrigerate for up to 10 days, changing the water if it becomes cloudy. The stalks and leaves are now easy to access and quick to use.

When cooking celery stalks in large pieces, such as for Creamy Braised Celery (page 90), you'll find it worth the extra effort to peel them.

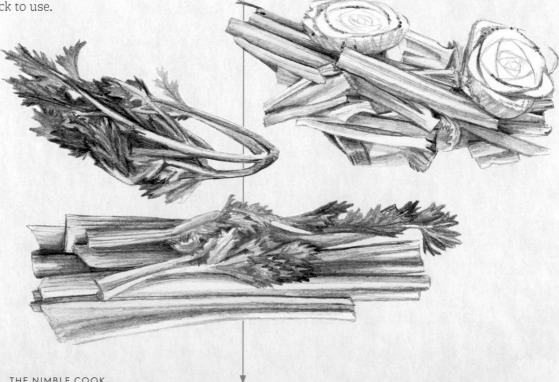

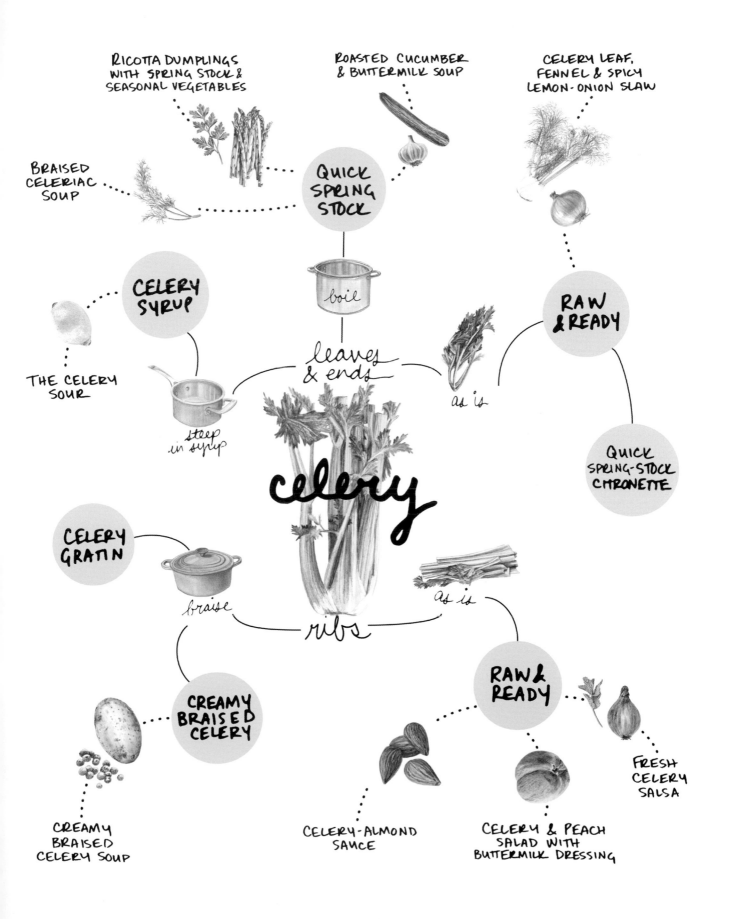

RICOTTA DUMPLINGS
WITH SPRING STOCK &
SEASONAL VEGETABLES

ROASTED CUCUMBER
& BUTTERMILK SOUP

CELERY LEAF,
FENNEL & SPICY
LEMON-ONION SLAW

BRAISED
CELERIAC
SOUP

QUICK
SPRING
STOCK

CELERY
SYRUP

boil

RAW
& READY

THE CELERY
SOUR

*leaves
& ends*

as is

*steep
in syrup*

celery

QUICK
SPRING-STOCK
CHRONETTE

CELERY
GRATIN

braise

as is

ribs

CREAMY
BRAISED
CELERY

RAW &
READY

FRESH
CELERY
SALSA

CREAMY
BRAISED
CELERY SOUP

CELERY-ALMOND
SAUCE

CELERY & PEACH
SALAD WITH
BUTTERMILK DRESSING

Celery and Peach Salad with Buttermilk Dressing

This is one of my favorite summer dishes, and a great showcase for underrated celery, which on its own offers several different textures and tastes. Each of celery's parts is used in this salad: Crunchy stalks are cut into thin slices, hearts into more tender, forkable chunks, and leaves—usually not recognized as the herb we get for free—are tossed whole with other fresh herbs.

Because celery is mostly water, the pieces begin to weep after half an hour and thin the tangy buttermilk dressing. If you prepare the salad in advance, dress it just before serving.

—> **FOR 4 SERVINGS**

½ large bunch celery, washed and divided into leaves, hearts, and stalks

½ teaspoon coarse kosher salt

1 tablespoon fresh tarragon leaves

2 tablespoons chopped fresh dill

2 tablespoons fresh flat-leaf parsley leaves

1 peach (slightly firm is good), pitted and cut into ¼-inch slices

Generous ½ cup **Buttermilk Dressing** (page 380)

Slice the celery stalks very thinly on the bias. Put in a large bowl and toss with the salt. Let sit for 10 minutes while you prepare the rest of the salad.

Cut the hearts into ½-inch chunks. Combine the celery leaves and the remaining herbs on a cutting board and run your knife through the mixture once, barely chopping them.

Drain the salted celery of any liquid and pat dry with paper towels. Return to the bowl and add the celery hearts, peach, and herbs. Just before serving, add the dressing and toss to coat all the ingredients liberally.

Fresh Celery Salsa

This is a refreshing salsa—herbal, bright, and a bit tart. Celery and apple provide the bulk and crunch, and are cut finely enough to release their own juices too. Raw garlic gives a bit of welcome spice, as does a fiery chile.

It's not a salsa I'd eat with chips. I like it as a cold sauce for sliced avocado or seared tuna (page 239). I eat it by the spoonful straight from the container. Even if you have no plan to serve the salsa soon, it's a smart use of celery that might otherwise wither in the fridge.

→ MAKES 2 CUPS

2 cups roughly chopped celery stalks (about 8 stalks)

½ shallot, quartered

1 small garlic clove, chopped

½ serrano chile, seeded and chopped (optional)

1½ cups chopped cored green apple, with peel (1 small)

6 large mint or 10 cilantro leaves, finely chopped

Juice of ½ lime

Coarse kosher salt

¼ teaspoon coarsely ground coriander seeds

¼ cup excellent olive oil

Combine the celery, shallot, garlic, and serrano chile, if using, in a food processor. Pulse about 10 times. Add the apple and pulse again, scraping the sides, until the ingredients are finely chopped but not pureed.

Scrape into a bowl. Fold in the mint, lime juice, a couple of pinches of salt, and the coriander. Stir in the oil. Let sit at room temperature for 30 minutes before serving, to ripen the flavors. This will keep, covered, in the refrigerator, for 5 days.

CELERY-ALMOND SAUCE

This sauce has my vote to pair with a fish like halibut or skate. It's terrific with chilled Poached Chicken Breasts (page 264) too. It tastes rich, but it is light and refreshing.

MAKES ABOUT 2 CUPS, ENOUGH FOR 6 TO 8 SERVINGS

1 recipe **Fresh Celery Salsa**, at room temperature

½ cup toasted slivered almonds, finely ground in a food processor

2 tablespoons heavy cream

Stir all the ingredients together in a small bowl. Serve immediately or store in the refrigerator for up to 3 days, mixing well before serving. If you like, warm slightly in a saucepan over low heat.

Quick Spring Stock

My favorite "otherwise, trash" recipe is for a five-minute stock made from the scraps of green and white vegetables. Alone, it is slightly acidic and tastes a little grassy. But in soups like Roasted Cucumber and Buttermilk Soup (page 128) and Braised Celeriac Soup (page 171), and in Risotto with Herb Butter (page 325), it is elegant. It exposes boxed vegetable stock for the food-coloring sham it is.

This is likely the only "stock" you can make in minutes. In fact, if you cook it much beyond the simmer, you risk dulling its bright flavors.

Be precise about preparing your ingredients. A little white pith from the lemon rind or a few extra dark green celery leaves can turn the stock too bitter. If you have more vegetable tops and stems than you need for the stock, save some for Quick Spring-Stock Citronette (opposite).

makes **ABOUT 6 CUPS**

1 cup roughly chopped fennel stalks and fronds

½ cup roughly chopped parsley stems

1 cup roughly chopped celery tops, ends, and leaves (not including any dark leaves)

Zest of 1 lemon, removed in strips with a vegetable peeler

1 small onion wedge, chopped

6 cups water

2 tablespoons white wine vinegar

4 garlic cloves, unpeeled but roughly chopped

½ teaspoon coarse kosher salt

Put the fennel, parsley stems, celery, lemon zest, and onion in a food processor. Pulse until finely ground. Transfer to a medium saucepan; do not wash the processor bowl. Add the water and vinegar to the pan and turn the heat to high. Finely chop the garlic in the food processor.

Monitor the stock closely as it nears a simmer. As the water heats up, the herbs that touch the side of the pot will begin to dull in color. When this happens, remove the pot from the heat and immediately strain the stock. Add the garlic while the stock is still very hot. Let cool completely, then strain once more. Add the salt. Store in the refrigerator in a covered container for up to 5 days or freeze for up to 3 months.

QUICK SPRING-STOCK CITRONETTE

This remarkably refreshing vinaigrette is made by rerouting the chopped vegetables from Quick Spring Stock on their way to the pot. Of course, you can cut up additional bits and pieces of vegetables to make this vinaigrette and the stock at the same time. Use it on thin slices of raw fish or tossed with just-boiled potatoes.

MAKES 2 CUPS VINAIGRETTE

For every cup of finely chopped vegetables, including the garlic (peel it first) from **Quick Spring Stock**, stir in up to 5 tablespoons excellent olive oil, up to 3 tablespoons fresh lemon juice, and about ¼ teaspoon coarse kosher salt. Store in an airtight container in the refrigerator. The dressing will keep for almost 2 weeks, but it will begin to lose some of its bright color after a few days.

Creamy Braised Celery

Braised celery is the confident expression of an otherwise timid vegetable. In the braising, juices are coaxed from the celery to mix with wine, herbs, and spices in the roasting pan. The flavorful broth then gets reabsorbed by the celery.

Because celery is mostly water, it shrinks considerably when cooked. Peeling the fibrous strings from each stalk is essential, since they remain tough after the stalks have turned tender.

Use any ends and trimmed tips for Quick Spring Stock (page 88); use the leaves for syrup (page 92) or salad—but only if they aren't too dark and bitter.

makes **ABOUT 4 CUPS, ENOUGH FOR 4 SIDE SERVINGS**

4 pounds celery (about 2 large bunches)

1 cup dry, crisp white wine

1 cup water

4 tablespoons (½ stick) unsalted butter, cut into pieces

2 teaspoons coarse kosher salt

4 large garlic cloves, very thinly sliced

2 pinches of freshly ground white pepper

4 (3-inch) strips lemon zest (with no white pith)

½ cup heavy cream

Preheat the oven to 375°F. Lightly trim the root ends of the celery. Pull the stalks apart; reserve the innermost yellow ones for another use. Trim the leaf tips of the remaining stalks. Holding a stalk in one hand and a vegetable peeler in the other and starting at the trimmed end, use the peeler to hook the fibrous outer strings. Pull it down the length of the stalk, peeling only the most sheer ribbons from each stalk's "backside." Don't worry about missing the occasional string. Cut the stalks into 1½-inch pieces. You'll have about 11 cups.

Place the celery in a Dutch oven. Add the wine, water, butter, salt, garlic, pepper, and lemon zest. Bring to a quick boil on the stove, then cover and place in the oven.

After 30 minutes, stir the celery gently. Re-cover and put back in the oven. Stir every 15 minutes until the celery turns a uniform muted green, like the color of split peas, and is pierced effortlessly with a knife, up to 45 minutes more.

Place the pot on the stove over medium-low heat. Add the cream and cook, turning the celery frequently, until the sauce reduces and the salt level is just right to your taste, 5 to 10 minutes. The cream may or may not thicken much; either way, it will continue to thicken and the flavors will settle in as it cools. Serve warm or at room temperature. Refrigerate in a covered container for up to 5 days. Serve cold or rewarm gently in a covered pan over low heat.

CELERY GRATIN

Fortified with wine and aromatics, celery is delicious topped with cheese, bread crumbs, and butter. The pieces are tender but remain intact.

FOR 4 SERVINGS

Follow the recipe for **Creamy Braised Celery,** opposite, through the third step. When the celery is tender, remove it from the oven. Turn the oven up to 425°F.

Spoon ¼ cup of the hot celery broth into a small bowl. Whisk in 1½ tablespoons all-purpose flour. Add this slurry to the pot of celery and stir well. Add 2 pinches of freshly ground white pepper, ½ cup heavy cream, and ¼ cup freshly grated Parmesan cheese. Stir. Top with ⅓ to ½ cup dry bread crumbs and ¼ cup grated Parmesan. Dot with 1 tablespoon unsalted butter.

Return the pot, uncovered, to the oven and bake until the top is golden and crisp and the cream has thickened, 5 to 10 minutes. Serve warm.

Creamy Braised Celery Soup

This soup is delicate, yet rich and silky, with the color of light egg yolk. Freeze any leftover potato cooking water for Wine-Braised Leek and Potato Broth Soup (page 30).

→ **FOR EACH SERVING**

1 small russet potato, peeled and quartered

4 cups water

1 tablespoon coarse kosher salt

½ cup **Creamy Braised Celery** (page 90)

Freshly ground white pepper

Put the potato in a medium saucepan. Add the water and salt. Cover and bring to a quick boil over high heat, then cover, reduce to a simmer, and cook until the potato is soft, 10 to 15 minutes. Drain, reserving the potato broth.

Combine the potato, 1 cup of the potato broth, and the celery in a blender, in batches if necessary for multiple portions. Puree until very smooth. Pass the soup through a fine-mesh strainer to remove any stubborn celery strings. Season with pepper and serve hot, or chill in the refrigerator to serve cold.

Celery Syrup

I turn celery leaves into simple syrup for The Celery Sour. The syrup can be also used in Any-Herb Lemonade (page 71). The syrup keeps well in the refrigerator, and the flavor improves overnight.

makes ABOUT 1½ CUPS, ENOUGH FOR 8 COCKTAILS OR A PITCHER OF LEMONADE

1 cup sugar

1 cup water

Tops and leaves from 1 bunch celery, finely chopped (about 1½ cups)

Combine the sugar and water in a small saucepan. Stir well. Cook on medium-high heat just until the sugar completely dissolves. Add the celery and bring just to a boil. Lower the heat to a simmer and cover tightly. Cook for 5 minutes, then turn off the heat and let the syrup steep until completely cool, about 1 hour.

If you plan on using the syrup immediately and want a vibrant green tint, puree everything in a blender and pass through a very fine strainer. (Keep in mind that a blended syrup will darken after a couple of days.) Alternatively, refrigerate the celery and syrup together overnight. Strain and store the syrup in a tightly covered jar in the refrigerator for up to 3 weeks.

The Celery Sour

Lemon, gin, and sugar make a sour, with celery amplifying the gin's botanical flavors.

⟶ FOR 1 COCKTAIL

2 ounces gin

1½ ounces **Celery Syrup**

½ ounce fresh lemon juice

Either pour all the ingredients into a rocks glass filled with ice and stir, or pour into an ice-filled shaker, shake well, and strain into a cocktail glass.

Garlic Scapes and Green Beans

Garlic scapes, the shoots of young garlic plants, arrive in the market a couple of weeks before the bulbs they've sprouted from. They're sold by the untamed tangle. Scapes are often compared to scallions, but their flavors are more like that of green beans, which is why I group them here and use them interchangeably in the Spring Vegetable Medley (page 75). Like green beans, garlic scapes are wonderful blanched, with a resolute texture; they hold their own with spice salts (page 372), meats, and sour cream. Raw scapes keep for longer than beans, at least a week in the refrigerator.

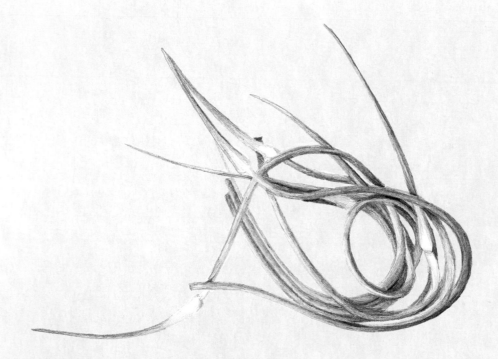

Braised Garlic Scapes

Oh, these are so good! I cook them well beyond the point of tenderness, so they pick up all the flavors from the braising juices. If you make them with a good stock, they'll taste as if they were slow-roasted under a chicken. They turn out best when cooked by the bundle.

I use whole lemons to braise the scapes, rather than lemon juice, because the bitter pith complements the sweetness of the long-cooked onions in the dish. The lemon pulp helps thicken the pot broth.

for **4 SERVINGS**

4 cups sliced onions

2 lemons, well washed, halved

2 tablespoons plus 2 teaspoons excellent olive oil

5 teaspoons coarse kosher salt

4 small garlic cloves, sliced

2 cups excellent chicken stock (such as Worth-It Chicken Stock, page 267)

4 tablespoons (½ stick) unsalted butter

1½ pounds garlic scapes, trimmed (page 74) and cut into 2- to 3-inch pieces (about 8 cups)

1½ teaspoons ground cumin

1 teaspoon hot red pepper flakes

Put the onions, lemon halves, oil, and 4 teaspoons of the salt in a large pot or Dutch oven over medium-high heat. Cook, stirring frequently, until the onions begin to brown, 8 to 10 minutes. Add the garlic, stock, butter, and then the scapes.

Cover and bring to a quick boil, then lower the heat to a simmer. Keep covered and cook, stirring occasionally, until the scapes are very tender and the braising juices are deep brown and rich, 25 to 30 minutes.

Season with the cumin, red pepper, and the remaining teaspoon of salt. Give one of the soft lemon wedges a squeeze with a pair of tongs to release its juice into the broth, and stir. Let the scapes remain in the pot, covered, for 5 minutes to absorb the flavors. The braising juices will begin to thicken as they cool. Serve, or cool in the pan and refrigerate in an airtight container for up to 5 days. Gently reheat in a covered pan over low heat.

Blanched Garlic Scapes or Green Beans

Blanched, green beans and scapes become crunchy, juicy, refreshing, and a bit sweet. I often use them interchangeably, sometimes favoring the scape because it keeps longer.

I like to feature cold blanched scapes or beans on their own plate, dressed with mustard vinaigrette and radishes (page 96), or with crème fraîche and pancetta (at right).

makes 4 CUPS, ENOUGH FOR 4 SERVINGS

6 quarts water

4 tablespoons coarse kosher salt

¾ pound garlic scapes, trimmed (page 74) and cut into 1½-inch pieces, *or* 1 pound green beans, trimmed

Fill a large bowl with 2 quarts of the water. Add a large handful of ice and 2 tablespoons of the salt.

Bring the remaining 4 quarts water to a boil in a large pot over high heat. Add the remaining 2 tablespoons salt. Add the scapes all at once, submerging them with tongs or pressing them down with a large strainer.

When they are tender, 2 to 3 minutes for scapes and 1 to 2 minutes for green beans, drain them and plunge them into the ice bath. Stir them a couple of times in the ice water so they cool faster and evenly. Once completely cold, drain well. Serve, or refrigerate in a covered container for up to 5 days.

Garlic Scapes or Green Beans with Crème Fraîche and Pancetta

You'll make this dish many times over garlic scapes' short season, and it's equally good with green beans. Tossed with tangy crème fraîche or sour cream, fragrant with citrus, cumin, and coriander, speckled with crisp pieces of salty pancetta—it's great for a crowd, or a picnic. Consider making extra Cumin-Coriander Salt for your pantry. Or substitute about ¼ teaspoon ground cumin, ¼ teaspoon kosher salt, and ¾ teaspoon well-crushed coriander seeds.

→ **FOR 4 SERVINGS**

Grated zest and juice of ½ lemon or lime

4 teaspoons excellent olive oil

¼ cup crème fraîche or sour cream

1 small garlic clove, minced (optional; for green beans)

4 cups **Blanched Garlic Scapes or Green Beans** (at left)

2 teaspoons **Cumin-Coriander Salt** (page 372), or see headnote

4 thin slices pancetta or 2 slices bacon, crisped

In a serving bowl large enough to hold all the scapes, mix together the lemon zest and juice, oil, crème fraîche, and (for green beans) the garlic. Add the scapes and toss to coat. Add the salt and toss again. (*The dish can be made to this point up to 1 hour in advance and kept covered in the refrigerator.*) Bring back to room temperature if refrigerated. Crumble in the pancetta, toss once more, and serve at room temperature.

Garlic Scapes with Mustard Vinaigrette and Radishes

Radishes bring crunch and celery seeds add a slight bitterness to a classic vinaigrette salad, which is a terrific first course or side dish for spring.

⟶ **FOR EACH SERVING**

1 cup **Blanched Garlic Scapes** (page 95)

1 tablespoon **Mustard Vinaigrette** (page 364)

Heaping ½ teaspoon celery seeds

Coarse kosher salt, if necessary

2 or 3 radishes, thinly sliced

Toss the scapes with the vinaigrette in a bowl. Add the celery seeds and taste for salt. Fold in the radishes. Serve.

Green Beans and Corn with Ricotta Salata

In this salad, green beans—briefly blanched—are tossed with a compound butter seasoned with oregano, cumin, and lemon. Add raw, crunchy corn, and salty ricotta salata, and you have an outstanding side dish. The salad is especially quick to assemble if you have corn already off the cob and beans already blanched. If you do not have precooked beans, you can blanch them right before mixing them with the seasoned butter, skipping the ice bath altogether.

If you don't plan to serve all the salad at once and your vegetables are especially fresh, you can store the dressed corn and beans in the refrigerator for a couple of days, adding the ricotta salata just before serving.

⟶ **FOR 4 SERVINGS**

1½ tablespoons minced fresh oregano

1 teaspoon ground cumin

1 teaspoon coarse kosher salt

Juice of 1 lemon

2 tablespoons unsalted butter, at room temperature

1 pound **Blanched Green Beans** (page 95), cut into 1- to 2-inch pieces (about 4 cups)

2 cups yellow corn kernels (from 2 to 3 ears; page 123)

2 ounces ricotta salata cheese

Put enough water to cover the beans in a saucepan. Bring to a boil. Meanwhile, put the oregano, cumin, salt, lemon juice, and butter in a large bowl. Whisk or beat with a fork to combine well.

Add the blanched beans to the boiling water and reheat for 5 to 10 seconds. Immediately drain well and add to the seasoned butter. Add the corn. Toss until well coated. Let sit for another minute to cool slightly, then toss again. The butter will become creamier as the beans cool.

Arrange the beans and corn on a serving plate. Use a sharp vegetable peeler to shave thin slivers of ricotta salata on top. Serve immediately.

Rhubarb

starting point

Rhubarb Compote

You can mix this compote with mustard and olive oil for a salad dressing, or stir it into the sauce from Braised Whole Chicken Legs (page 257). It's terrific next to a creamy goat cheese, or as a sandwich spread with cold roast poultry. Sometimes I use whole cardamom pods or half a piece of star anise. Place the spices in a cheesecloth sachet, if you don't want to fish them out later.

Cooked in a covered pot, the vegetable steams itself. Rhubarb that's green on the inside will turn a dull khaki color once it's cooked. You can add a few slices of peeled raw red beet to the rhubarb when it cooks to keep it pink. I usually do this only when I'm serving the compote for dessert.

makes **2 CUPS**

4 cups thinly sliced rhubarb (about 1 pound)

¾ cup plus 1½ teaspoons sugar

¼ teaspoon black peppercorns or other whole spices (see headnote)

1 bay leaf

Place the rhubarb in a medium saucepan. Add the sugar, peppercorns, and bay leaf. Turn the heat to low and cover. Cook, stirring occasionally, until the sugar has dissolved and the rhubarb is completely tender, 12 to 15 minutes. Be careful that it doesn't scorch. Remove from the heat and cool to room temperature. Refrigerate for up to 2 weeks or freeze for several months.

exploration

Rhubarb Lemonade

This lemonade is one of the best reasons to make large batches of Rhubarb Compote. The compote freezes on its own, but it also may be frozen as rhubarb-lemon puree, before adding the simple syrup and water. You can flavor the simple syrup with any number of spices or herbs. I use cardamom with fruit, every chance I get.

You can keep the spice syrup for up to 3 weeks in the refrigerator.

→ **MAKES ABOUT 2½ CUPS SPICE SYRUP, 2½ CUPS RHUBARB-LEMON PUREE, AND ABOUT 2½ QUARTS LEMONADE, ENOUGH FOR 6 TO 8 SERVINGS**

7 cups water

¾ cup sugar

16 cardamom pods, smashed open

1½ cups **Rhubarb Compote** (at left)

1 cup fresh lemon juice

Refrigerate 5 cups of the water. Place the sugar, the remaining 2 cups water, and the cardamom pods in a small saucepan. Bring the sugar water to a quick boil, stirring to dissolve the sugar, then turn off heat, cover, and cool to room temperature.

Place the compote and lemon juice in a blender and puree until smooth. If you don't want your lemonade pulpy, strain this puree.

Pour the puree into a large pitcher. Strain in the cardamom syrup and stir well. Stir in the chilled water. Store in the refrigerator for up to 3 days, mixing well before serving over ice. You can also freeze the lemonade itself—or freeze the rhubarb-lemon puree—for up to 1 month.

Rhubarb Sangria

American standards for sangria are embarrassingly low. I don't know how apples and peaches ever wound up in the sangria glass, but tart fruits like citrus and rhubarb are a good match for red table wine. You can make sangria with a whole fresh bottle of wine or with a collection of leftover wines (to freeze wine, see page 359).

for 4 TO 6 SERVINGS

1 pound rhubarb, diced or thinly sliced (4 cups)

½ cup sugar

¼ teaspoon coarse kosher salt

1 (750-ml) bottle red table wine, or 3¼ cups leftover red wine

Juice of 1 small orange

Juice of 1 small lemon

Juice of 1 small lime

Seltzer water (optional)

Place the rhubarb in a large pitcher or medium bowl and mix with the sugar and salt. Let sit for 20 minutes. The rhubarb will release some liquid and will be sitting in its own syrup. Add the wine and refrigerate for at least 30 minutes and up to 3 hours.

No more than 20 minutes before serving, add the orange, lemon, and lime juices and stir.

To serve, fill a glass halfway with ice. Strain the sangria into each glass, spooning in some rhubarb, and serve. If you like, top with a splash of seltzer just before serving.

Pickled Rhubarb

Sugar and apple cider vinegar tame the sour rhubarb in this quick pickle. I like to pair it with fatty meats like Orange-and-Fennel Pulled Pork (page 288) or Confit Duck (page 276), or with Green Lentils with Cardamom (page 344).

Be sure to cut the rhubarb into small pieces, so it becomes tender in the brine. This lets you sidestep pulling the fibrous strings from each stalk.

makes ABOUT 3 CUPS PICKLED RHUBARB
AND ABOUT 2½ CUPS BRINE

2 cups apple cider vinegar

1 cup plus scant 2 tablespoons sugar

1½ teaspoons powdered mustard

¾ teaspoon ground turmeric

½ teaspoon ground cumin

1 pound rhubarb, sliced no more than ¼ inch thick

Bring the vinegar, sugar, mustard, turmeric, and cumin to a quick boil in a small saucepan over high heat. Reduce the heat and let simmer for a few minutes to meld the flavors.

Put the rhubarb in a bowl. Pour in the hot brine. Place a piece of parchment paper or plastic wrap over the rhubarb and press down to keep it submerged. Let cool to room temperature.

Transfer the pickle to jars and store in the refrigerator for up to 2 weeks.

Heads and Bulbs

Best Roasted Broccoli

You can't do better than to roast broccoli. Cutting it into flat slices, through the stems, when necessary, rather than snipping off single florets, uses a good deal more of the crown and creates wider surfaces that brown and cook evenly. More surface area concentrates the vegetable's flavor and rids it of excess water, so it becomes chewy-tender. Once roasted, bunches of broccoli shrink considerably in size. I finish it while it's still warm, with an assertive dressing like Roasted Lemon Dressing (page 221).

I never cook more than 1 inch of the stem below the crown of broccoli; it usually doesn't stand up well to heat. If it's not too woody, you can pickle the stem with the brine for Pickled Asparagus (page 82), ¾ cup brine for every cup of broccoli stem. Peel off the outer layer to reveal its light green core. Slice the core ½ inch thick, cover it with brine, and refrigerate, covered, for up to 3 days.

for **4 SERVINGS**

3½ pounds broccoli (2 large bunches), stalk trimmed to 1 inch (see headnote)

¼ cup excellent olive oil

1 tablespoon coarse kosher salt, plus more if needed

Preheat the oven to 400°F. Cut each broccoli crown in half lengthwise, starting at the shortened stalk and up through the group of florets. Place each half cut side down, then slice into ½-inch-thick pieces, from the stalk through the florets. You want evenly thick slices that will lie flat on the baking sheet, rather than loose, single florets. If any florets are greater than 1 inch wide, cut those lengthwise in half too. Don't worry about any pieces of broccoli that fall to the side. You'll gather and roast them as well.

Brush the larger slices with most of the oil and arrange them in a single layer on a couple of baking sheets. Toss any smaller pieces and bits of floret with the rest of the oil. Season well with the salt, sampling a thicker piece raw to judge if it is sufficiently seasoned.

Roast until well browned on the bottom, 15 to 20 minutes. Flip the pieces over and roast on the other side another 10 to 15 minutes, until the thickest pieces shrivel to tenderness and the small buds brown deeply. Do not let them burn. Remove from the oven. Cool for 5 minutes and taste again for salt. Serve hot, at room temperature, or even cold.

DRESSED ROASTED BROCCOLI, TWO WAYS

As soon as you take the broccoli out of the oven, toss it with ¼ cup **Roasted Lemon Dressing** (page 221). Let cool to just warm or room temperature, tossing occasionally, before serving. It will keep in a covered container in the refrigerator for 3 days. Bring back to room temperature before serving.

Or toss it immediately with up to ½ cup **Mustard Vinaigrette** (page 364). Let cool to just warm or room temperature, tossing occasionally. It will keep in a covered container in the refrigerator for up to 3 days. Bring back to room temperature, then refresh with more dressing. Top with shaved aged Gouda cheese before serving.

Roasted Broccoli Rabe

To my taste, blanching broccoli rabe makes it too bitter; as with broccoli, roasting is best.

for 4 SERVINGS

1 pound broccoli rabe (1 bunch)

¼ cup excellent olive oil

1 teaspoon coarse kosher salt

Preheat the oven to 450°F. Trim the ends of the broccoli rabe lightly. If any stems are thicker than ¼ inch, peel them lightly too. Toss with the oil and then the salt. Arrange in an even layer on a baking sheet. Roast until the leaves begin to brown and crisp and the stalks turn just tender, 8 to 10 minutes. Serve hot, at room temperature, or cold.

DRESSED ROASTED BROCCOLI RABE

While the broccoli rabe is still hot, transfer it to a bowl and toss with ¼ cup **Anchovy Dressing** (page 379) or **Mustard Vinaigrette** (page 364). Serve or cool to room temperature, tossing occasionally. Store in a covered container in the refrigerator for up to 2 days; it's good chilled.

Roasted Cauliflower

Roasted under high heat, cauliflower is as soft and comforting as potato, but often tastier, its florets toasted and salty.

Cutting cauliflower into "steaks" rather than separating the florets from the core yields wide, flat surfaces that brown well and cook evenly. Once roasted, the slices can be cut and folded seamlessly into dishes where whole florets might stick out. You can fold small, soft bites of cauliflower into a bowl of fregola in Roasted Cauliflower, Fregola, and Walnuts (page 106) or dress it with sweetly spiced maple currants (opposite).

I start with two heads of cauliflower; once roasted, they shrink considerably in size.

makes 4 CUPS, ENOUGH FOR ABOUT 4 SERVINGS

**2½ pounds cauliflower
(2 small heads)**

**2 tablespoons excellent
olive oil**

**1 to 2 teaspoons coarse
kosher salt, plus more
if needed**

Preheat the oven to 400°F. If necessary, trim the cauliflower stems flush with the bottom of the heads. Place the heads stem down on the cutting board. Cut through them crosswise into ¾-inch-thick slices, as if you were slicing a loaf of bread. If any whole florets fall away, cut them in half.

Brush the larger slices with most of the oil and arrange them in an even, single layer on a couple of baking sheets. Toss the smaller pieces and crumbles with the rest of the oil. Season all the pieces well with the salt, tasting a thicker piece raw to judge if it is sufficiently seasoned.

Roast until well browned on the bottom, 25 to 30 minutes. Only then should you flip the pieces over and roast until brown on the other side. The smaller pieces will crisp; the larger pieces will shrivel. Cook until the largest slices are completely tender, another 10 to 15 minutes. Cool for 5 minutes and taste again for salt. Serve or store in a covered container in the refrigerator for up to 3 days. When seasoned just right, roasted cauliflower is delicious cold.

MAPLE CURRANTS + ROASTED CAULIFLOWER + CUMIN-RAISIN VINAIGRETTE + shallot → ROASTED CAULIFLOWER & MAPLE CURRANTS WITH CUMIN VINAIGRETTE

Roasted Cauliflower and Maple Currants with Cumin Vinaigrette

This dish has so many wonderful flavors—toasty cauliflower, sweet currants, tart vinaigrette—that I almost hate to serve it alongside anything else. But it's particularly good with prosciutto or even a simple seared steak (page 280), for the fall or winter table.

⟶ FOR EACH SERVING

⅔ cup **Roasted Cauliflower** (opposite), slightly warm or at room temperature

2 to 3 teaspoons **Maple Currants** (page 368)

1 small shallot, thinly sliced

2 teaspoons **Cumin-Sherry Vinaigrette** (page 364), or to taste

Cut the cauliflower into bite-sized pieces and place in a bowl. Add the currants, shallot, and vinaigrette and toss well. Serve or store in the refrigerator for up to 2 days. Bring to room temperature before serving.

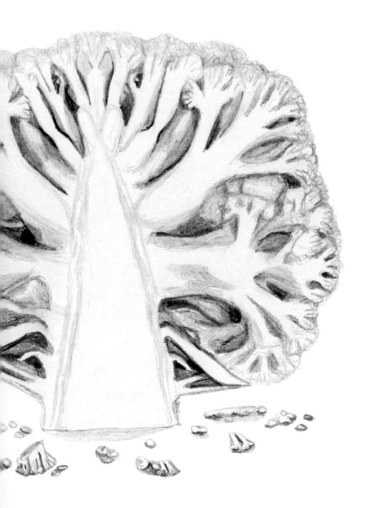

Roasted Cauliflower, Fregola, and Walnuts

Fregola is a small, round toasted pasta from Sardinia. I like it better than pearl couscous (aka Israeli couscous), but you can use either here as long as you are careful not to overcook it. Each forkful of fregola is interspersed with bits of cauliflower, raisin, lemon zest, and the occasional crunch of spice. For the best texture and flavor, I add the spiced salt in stages. This dish is great to serve for a filling lunch.

⟶ **FOR 4 SERVINGS**

8 cups water

3 tablespoons coarse kosher salt

1½ cups fregola or pearl couscous

1 recipe **Roasted Cauliflower** (page 104), cut in ½-inch pieces, at room temperature

2 recipes (2½ tablespoons) **Cumin-Coriander Salt** (page 372)

1 cup walnuts, toasted (page 368) and chopped

1¼ cups golden raisins

Grated zest of 2 lemons

Bring the water to a boil in a saucepan over high heat. Add 3 tablespoons of the kosher salt. Add the fregola or couscous and cook until tender but still chewy, 10 to 12 minutes for fregola, 7 to 8 minutes for couscous. Drain.

Place the cauliflower in a large bowl. Add half of the spiced salt and toss. Add the walnuts, raisins, lemon zest, cooked fregola, and the remaining spiced salt. Toss well. Serve warm or at room temperature. The cauliflower can be made up to 2 hours ahead and held at room temperature. It can be refrigerated for up to 3 days; bring to room temperature before serving.

Poached Cauliflower

Giardiniera is a traditional Italian condiment of pickled vegetables marinated in oil, often with herbs and spices. Typical giardiniera vegetables include sweet peppers, sliced carrots, celery, and cauliflower. I like my giardiniera more versatile, so I use only one vegetable—cauliflower—and poach it in a broth containing white wine, rather than brine it in vinegar. What I don't snack on straight from the container, I'll add to a salad with prosciutto, olives, and mustard (page 108), or a Cauliflower, Peanut, and Cheese Bisque (opposite).

makes ABOUT 4 CUPS PICKLES AND 5 CUPS BROTH

1 tablespoon coriander seeds, roughly crushed

6 garlic cloves, very thinly sliced

5 cups Quick Poaching Broth (page 360)

1 tablespoon coarse kosher salt

6 fresh thyme sprigs

1 tablespoon white wine vinegar

1 pound cauliflower (about half a head), stem trimmed, cut into 1-inch pieces (about 4 cups)

Toast the coriander seeds in a medium saucepan over medium-high heat until fragrant, about 1 minute. Add the garlic, poaching broth, salt, and thyme. Bring to a boil, cover, turn the heat down, and simmer for 5 minutes to infuse.

Add the vinegar and cauliflower. Bring back to a boil over high heat and cook uncovered until the cauliflower is just tender when pierced with a fork, 1 to 2 minutes. Turn off the heat and let cool in the broth.

Store the cauliflower and poaching broth together in a covered container in the refrigerator for at least 3 days and up to 5. Serve cold or at room temperature.

Poached Cauliflower, Peanut, and Cheese Bisque

This is a decadent, creamy soup. Peanuts lend weight to the light but pungent cheese stock; poached cauliflower brightens it. Remove the crust from a piece of day-old bread and use the "innards" for the bread crumbs here.

If you make a larger amount of this soup, you may need to blend it in batches.

→ **MAKES ABOUT 8 CUPS, FOR 4–6 SERVINGS**

4 cups **broth from Poached Cauliflower** (opposite)

1⅓ cups **Cheese Stock** (page 385)

¼ cup finely chopped roasted, unsalted peanuts

3 cups chopped **Poached Cauliflower**

Packed ¾ cup fresh coarse bread crumbs (preferably rye or sourdough)

1 cup heavy cream

Combine the cauliflower broth, cheese stock, and peanuts in a medium saucepan. Cover and bring to a quick boil. Turn the heat down and simmer until the peanuts are soft, about 10 minutes. Add the cauliflower to heat through and the bread crumbs to soften, about 1 minute.

Place in a blender in batches and puree well. (*If you want to make the soup in advance and serve it hot, don't add the cream. Reheat the puree and add the cream right before serving.*) Stir in the cream. Serve warm or cold. The soup will keep in the refrigerator for up to 5 days. Once the soup has been refrigerated, you should plan to serve it cold or at room temperature; the acidic cauliflower broth will cause the cream to curdle if reheated.

Poached Cauliflower with Prosciutto, Olives, and Mustard

In this dish, poaching broth and mustard make a light marinade for the cauliflower, which I then drape with thin slices of prosciutto. A great dish for a picnic, it's also terrific at the start of a winter meal, followed by Cheese Stock and Onion Jam Soup (page 35).

⟶ **FOR EACH SERVING**

1 tablespoon Dijon mustard

3 tablespoons **broth from Poached Cauliflower** (page 106)

½ cup chopped **Poached Cauliflower**

5 mild green olives (such as Picholine), pitted and chopped

Packed 1 tablespoon roughly chopped fresh flat-leaf parsley

1 small scallion, greens and white, cut into ¼-inch slices

5 teaspoons excellent olive oil

1 slice prosciutto

Place the mustard in a small bowl. Whisk in the broth to make a quick marinade. Mix in the cauliflower; let sit for 2 minutes, tossing once.

Remove the cauliflower from the marinade with a slotted spoon and place in a bowl. Set the marinade aside. Add the olives, parsley, and scallion to the cauliflower. Add 4 teaspoons of the oil and toss lightly. At this point, you can let the cauliflower rest at room temperature for up to 1 hour.

When you're ready to serve, plate the cauliflower and drizzle with the remaining 1 teaspoon oil and a few drops of the reserved marinade. (You can turn leftover marinade into a dressing for greens by whisking in more olive oil.) Drape with a piece of prosciutto and serve.

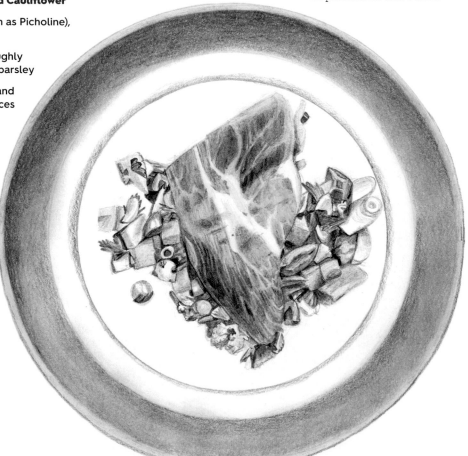

Fennel

starting point

Shaved Fennel

Even shaved thin, fennel has an assertive anise flavor that is able to frame other ingredients like fresh herbs or citrus zest without overpowering them. Shaved fennel can also marinate in oil without becoming too soft, making it a great stand-in for lettuce. Coring the fennel isn't necessary when it's thinly sliced.

makes **ABOUT 2 CUPS**

1 medium fennel bulb

Cut off the stalks and fronds from the fennel bulb. If the root end is discolored, trim it lightly. Cut the bulb lengthwise in half. Place each cut side down. Peel off the outer layers only if they are discolored or bruised. Cut crosswise through the bulb, as thinly as you can, or use a mandoline. The slices should be translucent.

Store the shaved fennel topped with a damp paper towel in a well-sealed container in the refrigerator for up to 5 days.

exploration

Fennel, Grapefruit, and Ricotta Salad

The texture of this refreshing winter fruit and herb salad is achieved by thoughtfully layering ingredients rather than tossing them all together. If you don't have great ricotta for this salad, one that tastes excellent on its own, use shavings of drier ricotta salata or Parmesan. In a multicourse meal, this salad nicely bridges savory and sweet courses.

→ **FOR EACH SERVING**

¾ cup **Shaved Fennel** (at left)

⅓ cup very thinly sliced red onion

Coarse kosher salt

⅓ cup **Parsley Vinaigrette** (made with lemon, page 69)

⅓ cup fresh ricotta cheese or **Savory Ricotta Custard** (page 386), or see headnote

1 small grapefruit, suprêmed (page 217)

1 small handful of torn mint

1 small handful of other soft fresh herbs, including fennel fronds

1½ teaspoons fresh lemon juice

Flaky sea salt and freshly ground black pepper

Combine the fennel, onion, a pinch of kosher salt, and the vinaigrette in a bowl. Let marinate for 5 minutes.

Arrange the ricotta, grapefruit wedges, and herbs on a plate. Lift the fennel salad out of the bowl and scatter over the top. Drizzle any dressing left in the bowl over the whole plate. Drizzle on the lemon juice, season with a bit of flaky salt and pepper, and serve.

Braised Fennel

Braised fennel is mellow, with the faintest hint of anise. It is stunning hot, warm, or cold. The fennel broth is delicious in place of stock in risotto or used to moisten bread for a Braised stuffing.

Braised fennel is best made 1 day in advance. Once I've finished it, I freeze any remaining broth in containers to use as a fragrant vegetable stock, or in ice cube trays to serve in Bloody Marys.

makes 6 CUPS FENNEL AND 2½ CUPS BROTH, ENOUGH FOR 4 TO 6 SERVINGS

3 medium fennel bulbs (about 3 pounds), stalks and fronds removed, bottom lightly trimmed, cut through the core into ½-inch-thick wedges

3 cups water

⅓ cup dry white wine

5 fresh thyme sprigs

1 bay leaf

1 teaspoon fennel seeds, crushed

3 garlic cloves, thinly sliced

1 tablespoon coarse kosher salt, plus more if needed

1 tablespoon excellent olive oil

Juice from 1 lemon, or to taste

Preheat the oven to 350°F. Place the fennel snugly in a 9-x-13-inch roasting pan or Dutch oven. Combine the water, wine, thyme, bay leaf, fennel seeds, garlic, salt, and oil in a saucepan over high heat; bring to a quick boil. Pour the braising liquid over the fennel. Cover tightly with foil or a lid. Place in the oven and braise until the fennel is translucent and quite tender at its core, but not falling apart, 30 to 40 minutes. Cool in the braising liquid, tasting and seasoning with lemon juice and salt as necessary, as it cools. Serve warm or cold. The fennel can be stored in the refrigerator in the broth for up to 5 days.

Braised Fennel Antipasto

This is a simple, elegant dish. Delicious on its own, the braised fennel is outstanding with good salty cheese and excellent olive oil (the olive oil is really key) as a light lunch or opener for a multicourse meal.

→ **FOR EACH SERVING**

¾ cup **Braised Fennel** (opposite), at room temperature

Excellent olive oil

Leaves from 2 fresh oregano sprigs

Flaky sea salt and freshly ground black pepper

8 to 10 shavings of excellent Parmesan cheese

Slice large wedges of fennel in half lengthwise through the core. Place on a plate, drizzle with oil and then sprinkle with oregano, salt, and pepper. Shave the Parmesan over the top. Serve at room temperature.

Braised Fennel, Brussels Sprout, and Goat Cheese Gratin

This quick gratin affirms a perfect partnership of fennel and cheese. It's a great dish for a fall holiday dinner or winter brunch. You can make the gratin in small ramekins for individual portions; assemble the gratin in advance and bake when you're ready to serve. Don't cook the Brussels sprouts beforehand, since the thin slices will steam while the gratin bakes. You'll want the bread crumbs to have crunch; use homemade if possible.

→ **FOR 4 SERVINGS**

1½ cups raw **Shaved Brussels Sprouts** (12 ounces; page 116)

1 recipe **Braised Fennel** (opposite), cut into 1-inch pieces

1 cup **broth from Braised Fennel**

1 teaspoon coarse kosher salt

½ teaspoon freshly ground white or black pepper

½ cup heavy cream

½ cup soft goat cheese (4 ounces)

½ cup freshly grated Parmesan cheese

½ cup **Toasted Bread Crumbs** (page 355); if using store-bought, toss with a little olive oil

Preheat the oven to 400°F. Mix the Brussels sprouts, fennel, broth, salt, pepper, cream, half of the goat cheese, and half of the Parmesan together in a bowl. Toss well.

Transfer to a small baking dish or individual ramekins. Top with the bread crumbs and the remaining Parmesan and goat cheese. Bake until the top is golden and crisp, 15 to 20 minutes. Serve hot.

Fennel Syrup

The infused honeys of Corrado Assenza of Caffe Sicilia in Noto, Italy, inspired this fennel-flavored simple syrup. A gin cocktail (at right) and Any-Herb Lemonade (page 71) are reason enough to keep some on hand.

makes 1½ CUPS

1 cup water

1 cup sugar

Packed ½ cup fennel fronds

½ cup thinly sliced fennel stalks

3 cardamom pods, crushed

Place the water and sugar in a saucepan over high heat. Bring to a boil and immediately add the fennel fronds, sliced fennel, and cardamom. Turn down to a simmer, cover, and cook for 3 minutes, until fragrant.

Remove from the heat and let steep until completely cool. If you'd like a stronger flavor, leave the solids in the syrup and refrigerate it, straining when you like how it tastes. Otherwise, strain now. Store in the refrigerator in a covered container for up to 2 months.

The Little Noto Cocktail

The fennel base of this cocktail complements the flavors of gin. The egg white is optional, but makes the drink velvety and light.

→ FOR 1 COCKTAIL

2 ounces gin

1 ounce fresh grapefruit juice

¾ ounce fresh lemon juice

1½ ounces **Fennel Syrup** (at left) *or* **Any-Herb Simple Syrup** (page 71)

1 large egg white (optional)

Fennel fronds, for garnish

If using the egg white: Combine the gin, grapefruit juice, lemon juice, fennel syrup, and egg white in a cocktail shaker or a jar with a tight-fitting lid. Close the lid and shake vigorously until the egg white becomes foamy, about 10 seconds. Fill the shaker halfway with ice and shake very gently until just chilled, 3 to 5 seconds. (If you overshake the egg white, it will deflate.) Strain into a cocktail glass. Garnish with fennel fronds.

If not using the egg white: Combine the gin, grapefruit juice, lemon juice, and fennel syrup in a cocktail shaker or a jar with a tight-fitting lid. Fill halfway with ice. Close the lid and shake vigorously for 10 seconds. Strain into a cocktail glass. Garnish with fennel fronds.

Cabbage

Shaved Raw Cabbage

exploration

Green cabbage is densely packed. Even one small head can feed four people. It stores well, and if a cut side of it begins to mold, you can just trim the bad part off and use the rest.

All it needs is a bit of salt to soften it when you're using it raw, especially if it is paired with ingredients that are already cooked, as in Shaved Cabbage and Braised-Leek Salad (at right) and Cabbage and Green Lentils with Orange Vinaigrette (page 345). Shaved cabbage also cooks in an instant, so it makes a good last-minute addition to soup. Try substituting it for the celeriac in Julienned Celeriac (page 168).

makes ABOUT 4 CUPS

1 small green cabbage
(1 pound)

Cut the cabbage in half through the stem with a sharp knife. Place both halves cut side down on the cutting board. Cut each half in half again through the stem; you'll have 4 wedges. Starting at the end opposite the stem, cut each wedge crosswise into thin slices, no more than ¼ inch thick, until you reach the core. Discard or nibble on the core.

Kept in a tightly sealed container in the refrigerator, shaved cabbage will last for up to 1 week.

Shaved Cabbage and Braised-Leek Salad

The combination of crème fraîche or sour cream and butter from the braised leeks makes for a creamy slaw, infinitely richer than one with mayonnaise. The slaw can be scaled up to use a whole small head of cabbage to serve four. Serve it with Salted Roast Chicken (page 253) and Roasted Sunchokes (page 183).

→ **FOR EACH SERVING**

1 cup **Shaved Raw Cabbage** (at left)

¼ teaspoon coarse kosher salt

⅓ cup **Wine-Braised Leeks** (page 28), cut into thin ribbons, warm or at room temperature

½ teaspoon fresh lemon juice

2 teaspoons crème fraîche or sour cream

Combine the cabbage and salt in a bowl. Toss lightly and briefly with your fingers to soften and season it; let sit for 10 minutes.

Pour off any water the cabbage may have released. Add the leeks, lemon juice, and cream, and toss to coat. The cabbage will continue to release water as it sits, so it's best to serve this salad immediately.

Shaved Cabbage with Bacon Vinaigrette and Rye Crisps

Made from day-old bread, rye crisps are a delicious snack. The key is to cut them thin so they toast quickly and are easy to break apart; using a dense loaf helps. I keep a batch of Bacon Vinaigrette around throughout cabbage season for this simple salad.

—> **FOR EACH SERVING**

3 thin slices day-old dense, dark rye bread

Excellent olive oil

Coarse kosher salt

1¼ cups **Shaved Raw Cabbage** (page 113)

1½ to 2 tablespoons **Bacon Vinaigrette** (page 296), slightly warm or room temperature

Preheat the oven to 300°F. Lay the bread out on a baking sheet. Brush lightly with oil on both sides and sprinkle with a little salt. Toast in the oven until the bread begins to brown and crisp, about 15 minutes. Remove from the oven.

Meanwhile, put the cabbage in a bowl. Add ½ teaspoon salt and toss lightly with your fingers to soften and season. Let sit for 10 minutes.

Stir the bacon vinaigrette to recombine it, add to the cabbage, and toss. Use your hands to break large pieces of the rye crisps into uneven shards. Combine with the cabbage. Serve immediately, or let sit for up to 15 minutes, allowing the crisps to soak up the flavor of the vinaigrette.

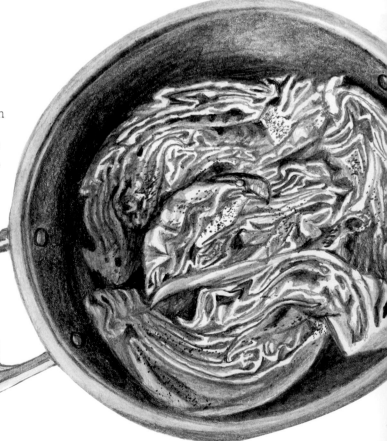

Spiced Braised Cabbage

Cabbage becomes soft and sweet when braised in wine and butter. Za'atar, both subtle and sufficient, is a suggested spice. You can substitute other spices or herbs if you like—caraway is really good.

for 4 SERVINGS

1 small or ½ large green cabbage (1 pound)

1 to 2 tablespoons grapeseed or canola oil

2 tablespoons unsalted butter

1 small shallot, thinly sliced

2 garlic cloves, thinly sliced

½ cup crisp white wine

1 teaspoon za'atar (see headnote)

1 teaspoon coarse kosher salt

Lightly trim the stem end of the cabbage and discard the outer leaves. Cut the cabbage in half through the core, then slice each piece in half again to make 4 equal wedges.

Heat 1 tablespoon of the oil in a wide, heavy-bottomed pot or a Dutch oven over medium-high heat. Sear the cabbage wedges, in batches, if necessary, browning both cut sides well, for a few minutes on each side. If the pan becomes too dry and risks burning, turn the heat down slightly and add a few more drops of oil. Transfer the seared cabbage to a plate.

Turn off the heat and let the pot cool for a minute or two. Add the butter, shallot, and garlic and turn the heat to low. Cook until the shallot is soft, about 2 minutes. Add the wine, ½ teaspoon of the za'atar, and ½ teaspoon of the salt. Return the cabbage to the pot, nestling the wedges in a single layer. Sprinkle on the remaining ½ teaspoon za'atar and ½ teaspoon salt and cover. Cook over medium-low heat for 8 to 10 minutes, until lightly browned. Turn the wedges over, re-cover, and cook until the cabbage wilts and the core is very tender, 8 to 10 minutes more.

Serve the cabbage with the braising juices. The cabbage will keep in the refrigerator for up to 3 days.

Serve

→ warm or cold, with a dollop of sour cream

→ under Orange-and-Fennel Pulled Pork (page 288)

→ in a sandwich on a baguette with mustard and slices of ham

Brussels Sprouts

Like little cabbages, Brussels sprouts are sweet when raw and shave nicely. For a beautiful warm salad, I also unravel the leaves (opposite).

Cooked, they are a bit trickier, for they lack the water that makes cabbage succumb so kindly to the heat. Roasted Brussels sprouts can be tasty, but they become hollow and papery. Blanched, they get waterlogged. Instead, I sear them (page 119); prepared that way, they can support condiments both salty and sweet.

starting point

Shaved Brussels Sprouts

1 pound Brussels sprouts gives you about 6¾ cups shaved

I don't like using a mandoline for Brussels sprouts; they are too small. To shave them by hand, first cut them in half through the core. Place each half cut side down on a cutting board and slice thinly crosswise, down to the core. Discard any tough remains of core.

Store the shaved sprouts in a closed, perfectly dry container for up to 5 days.

Use

—→ for Shaved Brussels Sprout and Swiss Chard Slaw (at right)

—→ in any soup

—→ as a bed for roasting fish (page 246)

SHAVED BRUSSELS SPROUT AND SWISS CHARD SLAW

You can substitute other greens for the Swiss chard and/or fold in chopped toasted walnuts (page 368) or sautéed shiitakes (page 199).

Toss 3 cups each **Shaved Brussels Sprouts** and **Raw and Ribboned Swiss Chard** (page 48) with 2 teaspoons fresh lemon juice and ½ teaspoon kosher salt. Let sit for 20 minutes. Stir in 3 teaspoons **Spiced-Apple-Cider-Honey Vinaigrette** (page 365).

Unraveled Brussels Sprouts

To "unravel" a Brussels sprout, you unfurl its leaves one by one, detaching them from the sprout's core. Cooked in a hot pan, the leaves are nothing short of elegant, and make a light vegetable dish.

1 POUND BRUSSELS SPROUTS GIVES YOU ABOUT 7 CUPS UNRAVELED LEAVES.
FIGURE ½ POUND SPROUTS PER PERSON.

Brussels sprouts

Unsalted butter, or
grapeseed or canola oil

Coarse kosher salt

Choose the largest Brussels sprouts you can find for unraveling. Cut each Brussels sprout in half through the core. If they are very large, cut in half again. Peel the leaves from each piece, one layer at a time. When the leaves resist and you can't tug them away, set the cores aside. After you have unraveled all of the leaves, gather the cores and slice thinly. Add these slices to the leaves.

Store the leaves in a covered container or a plastic bag with clean dry paper towels in the refrigerator for 3 to 5 days.

To cook, sauté the leaves in butter or oil over high heat, stirring constantly, until they turn a bright, shiny green, about 1 minute. You want them soft, but with some bite; taste to be sure. Season with salt and serve warm or at room temperature. The leaves will hold their crunch for several hours.

Use in

→ Sautéed Unraveled Brussels Sprouts with Caraway, Lemon, and Dill (page 118)

Cook and finish with

→ Whole-Grain Mustard Aioli (page 381)

Serve with

→ Stuffed and Seared Chicken Thighs (page 260)

Sautéed Unraveled Brussels Sprouts with Caraway, Lemon, and Dill

The sautéed leaves become silky smooth yet keep a little crunch. Because the leaves wilt slightly and quickly as they cook, you can make up to 4 servings at one time in one large pan. A wok works well for this too. Serve this as a warm side dish, or as part of a cold buffet. Once off the heat, the leaves will not wilt further.

—→ FOR EACH SERVING

2 teaspoons unsalted butter

1 teaspoon canola oil

1 small shallot, minced

1½ teaspoons caraway seeds

About 3 cups **Unraveled Brussels Sprouts** (page 117)

1 teaspoon coarse kosher salt

1 tablespoon chopped fresh dill

1 tablespoon fresh lemon juice

Freshly grated Parmesan cheese (optional)

Place the butter and oil in a skillet or wok over medium heat. Once the butter bubbles or the oil shimmers, add the shallot and caraway seeds. Cook, stirring continuously as the shallots soften and the caraway seeds turn fragrant, about 2 minutes. Do not let them burn.

Turn the heat to high; add the sprout leaves all at once. Toss to coat well with the fat. Add the salt and cook, stirring continuously, until the leaves turn bright, shiny green, about 1 minute. You want them soft, but with some bite; taste to be sure. Add the dill and lemon juice. Taste for salt. Serve warm or at room temperature, with a healthy dose of grated Parmesan, if you like. The leaves will hold their crunch for several hours.

Seared Brussels Sprouts

Brussels sprouts absorb a great deal of oil as they cook; the generous amount called for ensures they brown evenly, without drying out and burning. You'll need to sear them in batches. If possible, choose smaller Brussels sprouts, which are easy to cook thoroughly without burning. Cut larger Brussels sprouts in quarters, searing both cut sides before flipping them over.

for **4 SERVINGS**

½ cup or more high-heat oil (such as grapeseed or canola)

2 pounds small Brussels sprouts, ends lightly trimmed, halved through the core

1 teaspoon coarse kosher salt

If glazing the sprouts, make the glaze before you start cooking. Place a large, heavy skillet over medium heat; add ¼ cup of the oil. When the oil is hot, place half of the Brussels sprouts, cut side down, in the pan. Sprinkle with ½ teaspoon of the salt. Sear until the bottoms are a dark, nutty brown, about 2 minutes. Use tongs to flip them over individually, then brown them on the round side—this ensures they cook evenly. Taste one: It should be soft on the outside with only residual crunch inside. If some of the pieces are well browned but still too crunchy, cover the pan and continue to cook, lowering the heat if necessary to keep them from burning. Once done, transfer to a bowl. Repeat with the remaining oil, Brussels sprouts, and salt.

Serve the seared sprouts as is, or finish them with a quick glaze (see below). They're best the day they're made.

GLAZED SEARED BRUSSELS SPROUTS

Before you start the sprouts, make your choice of glaze.

Honey-Shallot (or Scallion) Glaze: Whisk 2 tablespoons fish sauce, 2 tablespoons water, and 4 teaspoons honey in a small bowl. To this, add ½ cup thinly sliced shallots or scallions and 2 tablespoons unsalted butter.

Balsamic–Onion Jam Glaze: Whisk 2 tablespoons balsamic vinegar, 2 tablespoons water, 6 tablespoons **Onion Jam** (page 34), and ½ teaspoon coarse kosher salt in a small bowl.

Once all the sprouts are seared, combine them in the pan. Turn the heat to medium. Add the glaze and cook, stirring, until thickened, about 1 minute. Turn off the heat, cover the pan, and let steam for 1 minute. Transfer to a bowl, spoon over any glaze, and serve.

Summer Fruits and Vegetables

Corn

Corn Off the Cob

If you don't think you'll use the corn you buy within a few days, cut it from the cob so it doesn't dry out. Save the leftover cobs to make stock for soup (page 124).

makes ¾ TO 1 CUP KERNELS PER EAR

Peel back the green husks from each ear of corn and break off the stem. Remove as much of the silk as you can with your fingers. Run the ear under cold water, rubbing to remove the rest. Place the ears on paper towels to drain for 5 minutes.

Lay the corn down on the cutting board. Drag a sharp knife down one side of the ear, slicing off three or four of rows of kernels at a time. Cut close to the cob, but without digging into it. Rotate the ear as you slice, removing all the rows in quick order. Because you are cutting close to the board, not standing the ear up and whittling off the kernels, you'll lose none to the floor.

Refrigerate the cut kernels, covered loosely with damp paper towels in an airtight container, for up to 5 days. You can freeze the kernels, but they will lose their crunch when thawed. You can wrap the shaved cobs in plastic wrap to use for soup and refrigerate for up to 3 days. Or, you can store them, tightly sealed in a freezer bag, for up to 3 weeks. A big batch of Green Beans and Corn with Ricotta Salata (page 96) yields enough cobs to make a batch of corn stock.

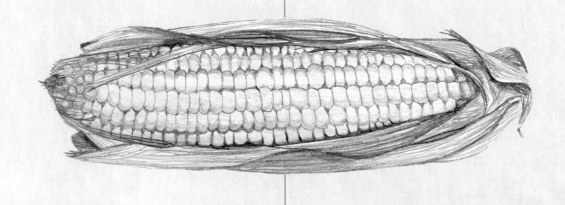

Corn and Potato Soup with Rosemary

For this delicate, fresher version of the standard corn chowder, I make a quick stock from the corn cobs. I add the corn kernels at the very end, giving them only enough heat to bring their flavor alive, and finish the soup with crisp bacon bits and rosemary.

I try to make and freeze corn stock whenever I accumulate enough cobs, whether or not I have immediate plans to make soup.

—→ **FOR 4 SERVINGS**

CORN STOCK

6 cobs from **Corn Off the Cob** (page 123)

10 cups water

2 bay leaves

1 wedge from a small onion

1 teaspoon coarse kosher salt

SOUP

½ pound sliced bacon, cut into ½-inch pieces

1 tablespoon unsalted butter

1½ cups chopped onions

¾ pound Yukon Gold or Red Bliss potatoes, unpeeled, cut into ½-inch pieces

4 to 5 cups **Corn Off the Cob**

2 fresh rosemary sprigs

1 cup whole milk

1 tablespoon coarse kosher salt, plus more to taste

Freshly ground black pepper

To make the corn stock: Place the corn cobs, water, bay leaves, onion wedge, and salt in a large saucepan over high heat. Bring to a quick boil, then turn down the heat and simmer until the stock tastes sweet and strongly of corn, 30 to 40 minutes. Skim off any foam that rises to the top; it will cloud the broth. Once the stock is done, strain it and return it to the pan. You'll have about 6 cups clear, light golden stock.

To make the soup: Meanwhile, cook the bacon in a large skillet over low heat, turning it, until the fat is rendered and the bacon is crisp, about 7 minutes. Remove the bacon from the pan and reserve. Discard all but 2 teaspoons of the bacon fat in the pan. Add the butter and chopped onions and cook over medium heat until mostly soft, about 10 minutes.

Add the onions to the stock, along with the fat and juices in the skillet. Add the potatoes. Bring to a quick boil, then turn down the heat and simmer until the potatoes are just tender, 5 to 6 minutes. *(To make the soup in advance, cook until the potatoes are tender, let them cool in the broth, and refrigerate for up to 5 days. Store the corn kernels and reserved bacon separately.)* Add the corn kernels and reserved bacon and bring the soup back to a simmer; cook just until the kernels have lost their starchiness, about 1 minute more. Turn off the heat and add the rosemary, milk, 1 tablespoon or more salt, and a couple of grinds of pepper. Let sit for 1 minute; the rosemary will infuse the broth almost immediately. Discard the rosemary and serve the soup hot.

Charred Corn

Charred corn tastes smoky, but the kernels still snap with juice. Don't brush the corn with oil or butter before charring it; either will burn. A close broiler works as well as a strong stovetop gas flame. A campfire is my preference, though you'll need a grate to rest on top of the flame and long tongs to turn the corn.

for **EACH EAR**

Shuck the corn, either pulling off the husks (if you are broiling the corn) or tying them back, but keep the stem on—this is your handle. Remove the silk, wash the ears, and drain well on paper towels.

Set the corn on the grate of a gas burner turned to high, with the kernels directly touching the flame, or directly under the flame of your broiler. When one section of kernels is charred, 2 to 3 minutes, use the stem to turn the ear and char the next section. If you are cooking many ears, use multiple burners. If you're charring a big batch of corn, keep the charred ears warm in a 250°F oven, or wrap each ear in foil to maintain the heat. Serve hot, right on the stem.

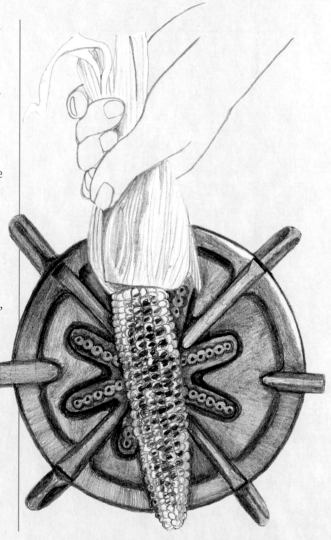

Sprinkle with

→ flaky sea salt

→ Bay Salt (page 374)

Rub with

→ cold seasoned butter, such as Green-Peppercorn Butter (page 378)

→ cold unsalted butter, then roll in raw Scallion-Sesame Magic Mix (page 40)

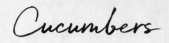

Cucumbers

Roasted Cucumbers with Caraway Seeds and Scallions

This dish surprises everyone. Remarkably, the cucumbers stay vibrant, even when softened by salt and heat. Use the best you can find; I prefer larger cucumbers here, especially since they are peeled. Garlic Yogurt Sauce (page 380), spooned on top, makes the buttered cucumbers richer still.

for 4 SERVINGS

1½ pounds cucumbers (about 2 medium; see headnote), peeled

1 teaspoon coarse kosher salt, plus more if needed

4 tablespoons (½ stick) unsalted butter

2 large scallions, greens and whites, cut into 1-inch pieces

½ teaspoon caraway seeds

2 teaspoons chopped fresh dill

Freshly ground black pepper

Preheat the oven to 400°F. Cut the cucumbers in half crosswise, then trim each half into quarters lengthwise. Very lightly trim away the most exposed cucumber seeds from each wedge. Slice each wedge lengthwise one more time; you should have 32 pieces. Put the cucumbers in a bowl and toss with the salt.

Melt the butter in a roasting pan, then add the cucumbers and scallions. Mix to coat well. Roast until every piece has dulled in color and softened completely, but still retains its shape, 30 to 35 minutes. The cucumbers should be pliable, yielding to the tines of a fork.

Meanwhile, toast the caraway seeds in a small dry skillet over medium heat, shaking the pan continuously to prevent them from burning, until brown and fragrant, 5 to 7 minutes.

Fold the toasted caraway seeds, dill, and pepper into the cucumbers. Let sit for 10 minutes. Before serving, taste again for salt: too little, the cucumbers taste flat; too much and the other seasonings get lost. Serve slightly warm straight from the pan or transfer to a serving dish and serve at room temperature. Store in the refrigerator in a covered container for up to 3 days. Rewarm gently before serving.

Save the peels for

→ Cucumber-Peel Kimchi (page 130)

Serve under

→ Poached Chicken Breasts (page 264)

Roasted Cucumbers and Red Onions

This dish is especially good served with poached, grilled, or smoked fish, or chicken. Or use it in Roasted Cucumber and Buttermilk Soup (page 128).

I season the cucumber and onion pieces separately, because the cucumbers pick up a disproportionate amount of the salt when they are seasoned together. Then I roast the vegetables together, and their juices combine to make a light sauce.

makes ABOUT 5 CUPS, ENOUGH FOR 4 SERVINGS

1½ pounds cucumbers (about 2 medium), unpeeled

1¾ pounds red onions (2 medium), unpeeled

6 tablespoons excellent olive oil

4 teaspoons coarse kosher salt

Cut the cucumbers in half crosswise. Cut each half again lengthwise. Cut each quarter into 4 even wedges. You'll have 32 pieces. Lightly trim away the most exposed cucumber seeds. Place the cucumbers in a bowl; toss with 3 tablespoons of the oil and 1 teaspoon of the salt.

Cut the onions in half through the stem. Trim the stem of the wiry roots, leaving it otherwise intact to hold the pieces together, and peel. Place the onion halves cut side down on a cutting board. Cut each half into 8 even wedges, each wedge sharing a bit of the root. You'll have 32 even wedges. Place in a bowl and toss with the remaining 3 tablespoons oil and 3 teaspoons salt. Marinate for 30 minutes.

Meanwhile, preheat the oven to 350°F. Line a baking sheet with parchment paper.

Spread the cucumbers and onions, and any accumulated juices and oils, on the baking sheet. Roast for 20 minutes, then lift up the sides of the parchment to gently redistribute the softening vegetables, being careful not to let any juices spill out into the pan. Continue to roast until the cucumbers dull completely in color and turn soft—they should be pliable, yielding to the tines of a fork, about 25 minutes more. If the onions begin to darken before they or the cucumbers are totally soft, pull up the sides of the parchment, allowing the vegetables and juices to fall toward the center. Bring the edges together and fold twice, to form a seam. (Tenting the vegetables shields them from direct heat.)

Once the cucumbers and onions are completely soft, let cool on the baking sheet for at least 10 minutes before serving; the flavors are best when not piping hot. This dish is also great at room temperature and even straight from the refrigerator. When serving and/or storing, remember to capture all of the vegetables' released juices. The cucumbers and onions will keep for 5 days in a covered container in the refrigerator.

Roasted Cucumber and Buttermilk Soup

This rich sipping soup is great for a summer lunch—refreshingly sour, a bit spicy from the raw garlic, and lightly creamy. Don't substitute standard vegetable stock for the Quick Spring Stock; it's too sweet.

   Make sure all the ingredients are cold or at room temperature, so the buttermilk doesn't separate when you add it.

—> FOR 4 SERVINGS

   2 cups **Roasted Cucumbers and Red Onions** (page 127), cooled

   2 cups **Quick Spring Stock** (page 88), cooled

   1 cup buttermilk, or plain whole-milk yogurt in a pinch

   2 small garlic cloves, peeled

   Coarse kosher salt (optional)

Combine the cucumbers, stock, buttermilk, and garlic in a blender, in batches if necessary, and puree until smooth. Taste for salt; it may not need any. Serve immediately, or chill in a covered container. The soup keeps for up to 2 days, although the raw garlic sometimes becomes more pungent as it sits.

Cucumbers, Raw and Ready

Height-of-season cucumbers are sweet, not bitter, and versatile. They pickle quickly and puree smoothly. You can leave them unpeeled or save the peels for kimchi (page 130). Store cut cucumbers in a covered container topped with a slightly damp paper towel for up to 3 days.

Sweet-and-Sour Cucumber Salad

This is a classic deli cucumber salad. Serve it alone or with Stuffed and Seared Chicken Thighs (page 260), grilled sausages, or shrimp.

→ **MAKES 4 CUPS, ENOUGH FOR 4 SERVINGS**

2 cups thinly sliced cucumbers, raw and ready, any variety

1 cup very thinly sliced onion

1 cup thinly sliced celery

1 teaspoon coarse kosher salt, plus more to taste

½ cup distilled white vinegar

2 teaspoons whole-grain mustard

2 tablespoons sugar

¼ cup coarsely chopped fresh herbs (such as flat-leaf parsley, chervil, or mint)

Toss the cucumbers, onion, and celery with the salt and let sit for 30 minutes to soften and season; they will release a good amount of water.

In a medium bowl, mix the vinegar, mustard, and sugar together. Drain the vegetables and add to the dressing. Add the herbs, toss well, and taste for salt. Serve, or store in the refrigerator for up to 3 days.

Cucumber-Melon-Cashew Drink

Use only the freshest cucumbers and melon. Save the cucumber peels to make kimchi (page 130).

→ **MAKES 9 CUPS, ENOUGH FOR 6 TO 8 SERVINGS**

Heaping ½ cup chopped unsalted cashews

1 cup water

3 pounds cucumbers, raw and ready, peeled and cut into 1-inch pieces

1 honeydew melon (about 5 pounds), peeled, seeded, and cut into 1-inch pieces

Place the cashews and water in a small saucepan over high heat. Cover and bring to a quick boil, then turn the heat down and simmer gently until soft, about 7 minutes.

Puree the cucumbers in batches in a blender. Strain through a sieve into a large pitcher. Set aside the blender; do not clean. Discard the cucumber pulp. You'll have about 3 cups juice.

In the same blender, puree the melon in batches until smooth. Do not strain. Add to the cucumber juice.

Lastly, place the cashews and water in the blender. Add as much cucumber-melon juice as the blender will allow and puree until very smooth. Pour back into the pitcher and stir. Chill before serving over ice. Store in the refrigerator for up to 2 days.

Cucumber-Peel Kimchi

Taking seasoning cues from kimchi, I pair cucumber peels with salt, garlic, rice vinegar, hot red pepper flakes, and scallion. The peels absorb the flavors quickly, but because they contain little water, they remain crisp, with a texture like seaweed. You can scale up the recipe to make a big batch.

—> **MAKES ½ CUP**

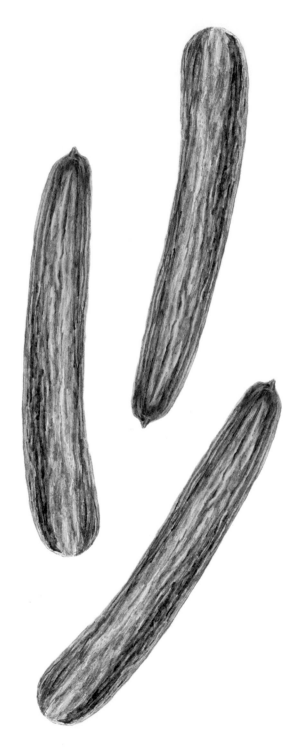

1 cup cucumber peels (from 1½ pounds cucumbers; about 2 medium)

1 teaspoon coarse kosher salt, plus more if needed

1 small garlic clove, minced and smashed to a paste or put through a press

1½ teaspoons rice vinegar

1 teaspoon hot red pepper flakes, crushed with your fingers

1 small scallion, greens and white, very thinly sliced

½ teaspoon toasted sesame seeds

Slice the cucumber peels into long ribbons about ⅛ inch thick. Place in a small bowl and toss with the salt—it will seem like a lot, but don't worry—and let stand for 10 minutes.

Combine the garlic, vinegar, red pepper, and scallion in another bowl. Add to the cucumber peels and toss well. Let stand for another 10 minutes. Taste for salt. Add the sesame seeds and toss. The kimchi is ready to serve, but will take on more flavor if left to sit overnight in the refrigerator. The peels will remain crisp and bright for a week.

Use in

—> Mussels Kimchi (page 235)

Cumin-Roasted Eggplant

Roasted properly and hit with vinegar while still hot, eggplant marinates, becoming a more ripened, realized version of itself. In this state, it is delicious to eat straight from the roasting pan, or cooled to room temperature.

makes 4 CUPS, ENOUGH FOR ABOUT 4 SERVINGS

1 tablespoon coarse kosher salt

2 pounds Japanese or other slender eggplants, trimmed, cut in half crosswise, then lengthwise into even 1½-inch-wide wedges

3 tablespoons excellent olive oil

1 teaspoon ground cumin

1 teaspoon sherry vinegar

Use 1½ teaspoons of the salt to season the cut sides of the eggplant wedges. Lay them skin side down on paper towels, to absorb any weeping water. Let sit at room temperature for 1 hour.

Preheat the oven to 375°F. When you're ready to roast, wipe the eggplant dry with clean paper towels (do not rinse) and place in a large bowl. Toss with 2 tablespoons of the oil, using your hands to coat the cut sides evenly. Arrange the eggplant wedges on a baking sheet, skin side down and close together for easy seasoning. Sprinkle with the cumin, rubbing it into the flesh. Season with the remaining 1½ teaspoons salt. Now move the eggplant pieces apart so they're no longer touching.

Roast until the flesh is brown, dry, and taut, and the inside pillowy, 30 to 40 minutes. While still warm, transfer the eggplant to a bowl. Sprinkle with the vinegar and the remaining 1 tablespoon oil and toss gently. Cover tightly with foil or plastic wrap to steam, and cool to room temperature. Serve or refrigerate for up to 5 days.

Use in

→ Roasted Eggplant and Braised Mushrooms with Walnut Oil (page 133)

→ Roasted Eggplant with Tomatoes and Garlic-Skin Vinegar (page 132)

→ Roasted Eggplant, Gruyère, and Cumin-Raisin Gratin (page 132)

→ Roasted Eggplant with Yogurt and Mint (page 133)

→ Roasted Radicchio, Fontina, and Eggplant Sandwich (page 61)

Dress with

→ Refrigerator-Door Vinaigrette (page 383) for a cold antipasto

Roasted Eggplant with Tomatoes and Garlic-Skin Vinegar

The flavors in this dish are classic Greek ones (garlic, red wine vinegar, tomatoes), and right for any summer table. Dress the tomatoes first, allowing them to develop their own flavor before folding in the boldly seasoned eggplant.

⟶ **FOR EACH SERVING**

1 small ripe round tomato, cut into 1-inch pieces

¼ teaspoon coarse kosher salt

1 tablespoon **Garlic-Skin Vinegar** (page 23)

1 fresh oregano sprig

1 small garlic clove, slivered

1 cup **Cumin-Roasted Eggplant** (page 131), cut into 1-inch pieces

1 tablespoon roughly chopped fresh mint

Excellent olive oil

Place the tomato in a salad bowl and add the salt, vinegar, oregano, and garlic. Let sit for 15 minutes. Remove and discard the oregano. Mix in the eggplant, toss with the mint and a drizzle of oil, and serve.

Roasted Eggplant, Gruyère, and Cumin-Raisin Gratin

Think of this as a grown-up eggplant Parmesan. A pungent, warm, sweet salad dressing becomes a sauce for the roasted eggplant, while Gruyère adds saltiness. Serve with crisp roasted potatoes to make a meal.

⟶ **FOR EACH SERVING**

1 cup **Cumin-Roasted Eggplant** (page 131)

1½ teaspoons **Cumin-Raisin Vinaigrette** (page 363) or good sherry vinegar

2 tablespoons grated Gruyère cheese

1½ tablespoons **Toasted Bread Crumbs** (page 355)

Preheat the broiler. For each serving, place the eggplant wedges in an individual gratin dish. Drizzle with the vinaigrette. Top with Gruyère, then the bread crumbs. Broil until brown and bubbly, about 3 minutes. Serve hot.

Roasted Eggplant with Yogurt and Mint

This is a great companion to Spiced Lamb Meatballs (page 297) or a starter before Lamb Shanks Braised in Two Vinegars (page 302). It looks nicer to spread the yogurt dressing onto the plate first instead of spooning it on top of the eggplant, and it encourages you to use the eggplant as a sauce mop. All of the ingredients can be prepared in advance, but you'll want to assemble the salad right before serving. Don't omit the mint; it is a great foil for the sweet pomegranate molasses.

—> FOR 4 SERVINGS

½ cup plain whole-milk yogurt

2 tablespoons excellent olive oil

1 small shallot, minced

2 tablespoons thinly sliced fresh mint

Coarse kosher salt and freshly ground black pepper

2 cups **Cumin-Roasted Eggplant** (page 131)

2 teaspoons pomegranate molasses

Whisk the yogurt, oil, shallot, and 1 tablespoon of the mint in a bowl. Season with salt and pepper. Spread the dressing on a plate. Arrange the eggplant on top. Drizzle with the pomegranate molasses, sprinkle with the remaining 1 tablespoon mint, and serve.

Roasted Eggplant and Braised Mushrooms with Walnut Oil

This dish ushers summer into fall. Use only excellent, fresh nut oil.

—> FOR EACH SERVING

¼ cup roughly chopped **Cumin-Roasted Eggplant** (page 131)

¼ cup **Triple-Braised Wild Mushrooms** (page 194), with some of their liquid

1 tablespoon minced fresh flat-leaf parsley

Walnut oil

Warm the eggplant and mushrooms together in a skillet over medium heat. Remove from the heat and stir in the parsley. Transfer to a plate, drizzle with walnut oil, and serve warm.

Pickled Eggplant

The brine for this pickle is straight-up Italian-American. The eggplant is cooked through, then saturated with vinegar and hot red pepper flakes. It turns soft enough to fold into a salad with tomato confit, contributing its own sharp dressing. But because it keeps its shape intact, it can be broiled with mozzarella for an antipasto.

makes **2 CUPS**

1 large eggplant (about 1 pound)

1 tablespoon coarse kosher salt

½ to ¾ cup excellent olive oil

¾ cup white wine vinegar

1⅓ cups water

½ teaspoon hot red pepper flakes

3 garlic cloves, sliced

½ teaspoon sugar

1 or 2 fresh oregano sprigs

Peel the eggplant. Cut in half lengthwise, then again lengthwise into long, ½-inch-thick strips. Put the eggplant in a bowl, sprinkle with the salt, and toss with your hands to coat evenly. Layer the eggplant in a colander placed over a bowl or plate. Lay plastic wrap directly on top of the eggplant slices, then put a heavy pot on top as a weight. Let sit for 30 minutes. Don't rinse the eggplant, but pat the slices dry with paper towels. Discard any liquid.

Put at least ¼ inch oil in a heavy-bottomed skillet over medium heat. Do not let the oil smoke. Carefully fry the eggplant strips in batches, as many as you can fit in one layer. Cook until very soft and translucent, but not very brown, 2 to 3 minutes per side. Remove with tongs or a slotted spoon and place in a heatproof 1-quart container, such as a canning jar. Repeat until all of the eggplant has been cooked, adding more oil if necessary.

Combine the vinegar, water, red pepper, garlic, sugar, and oregano in a small saucepan. Bring just to a bare simmer, stir to dissolve the sugar, and turn off the heat. Pour the hot brine over the eggplant pieces until they are totally submerged. Let cool to room temperature before covering with a lid. Refrigerate for at least 6 hours before serving. Pickled eggplant will keep in the refrigerator for several weeks.

Pickled Eggplant and Confit Tomato Antipasto

Sharp and sweet tomato juices balance the assertive eggplant brine, and onions provide crunch and bite—an unexpected and delicious contrast. Serve with cured meats such as prosciutto or salami or roasted fish, perhaps with bread to sop up the juices.

⟶ **FOR EACH SERVING**

½ cup **Pickled Eggplant** (opposite)

1 tablespoon **brine from Pickled Eggplant**

½ cup **Confit Tomatoes** (page 148)

1 tablespoon **juice from Confit Tomatoes**

1 tablespoon **torn fresh mint**

A few thin onion slices

Cut the eggplant into ½-inch cubes. Combine all the ingredients in a bowl, bursting a couple of the tomatoes to release more of their juices. Let marinate for 10 minutes before serving. This dish keeps for up to 2 days, covered and refrigerated. Bring to room temperature before serving.

Broiled Pickled Eggplant with Mozzarella

Broiling intensifies the pickle's sharp flavor. To tame it a bit, I rinse the eggplant under cold water and dry it before broiling. Then I match it with melty, milky mild cheese. It's terrific with beer.

⟶ **FOR 4 SERVINGS**

1 recipe **Pickled Eggplant** (opposite)

Excellent olive oil

8 ounces mozzarella cheese, coarsely grated

Preheat the broiler with a rack placed 6 inches below it. Run the eggplant slices under cold water to rinse off the excess brine. Place the slices between paper towels and press down to gently flatten them and draw out excess liquid.

Once they are dry, brush a thin coat of oil over both sides of each eggplant slice and arrange on an oiled baking sheet; the pieces should touch. Scatter the mozzarella evenly on top. Slide under the broiler and cook until brown, bubbly, and crisp at the edges, 2 to 4 minutes. Serve hot.

Green Bell Peppers

Best Roasted Green Peppers

Seasoned with olive oil, salt, and sugar, these are not your typical roasted peppers. But technique matters too: For the peppers to taste sweet, you need to brown them deeply, then steam them until soft. Parchment paper, used first to prevent the peppers from sticking to the baking sheet, serves as the steaming pouch, at once thoroughly cooking the peppers and trapping their delicious juices. These juices mingle with a late addition of vinegar, which parries with the salt and sugar to become a savory marinade.

makes **ABOUT 2 CUPS**

6 large green bell peppers, prepped (opposite)

2 tablespoons excellent olive oil

1¾ teaspoons coarse kosher salt

1¾ teaspoons sugar

1 tablespoon white wine vinegar, plus more if needed

Preheat the oven to 350°F. Line a baking sheet with parchment paper. Toss the peppers with the oil, salt, and sugar. Arrange the slices in a single layer on the baking sheet, skin side down. Roast until the edges brown, about 35 minutes; the peppers themselves will still be a bit stiff.

Carefully pull up the long edges of the parchment, letting the peppers fall toward the center. Fold the edges together twice to tent the peppers, then (carefully) tuck the unfolded ends of the parchment pouch underneath. Continue to roast until the peppers are meltingly soft, at least another 10 minutes.

Remove from the oven, open the pouch, and immediately sprinkle the peppers with the vinegar. Quickly refold the parchment and let the peppers cool completely in the pouch. Once the peppers are at room temperature, taste them; you may decide to add more vinegar. They are best served at room temperature, or even cold. Refrigerate for up to 5 days. They freeze well for up to 1 month.

Serve with

→ Whole-Grain Mustard Aioli (page 381), for a snack

→ Perfect Hard-Boiled Eggs (page 349)

→ Pickled Red Onions (page 36) and Cumin Vinaigrette (page 363 or 364)

Use in

→ Short-Rib Sandwich with Best Roasted Green Peppers (page 284)

PREPPING BELL PEPPERS

With a small knife, cut into the pepper "shoulders" and around the stem to pull out the core, seeds still attached. Save the cores and seeds to use in Roasted Green Bell Pepper Cores (page 138).

Cut the remaining pepper lengthwise in half. Cut each half along the ribs into curved segments. And most important: Trim each segment of all white pith.

Roasted-Pepper Breakfast Sandwich

This sandwich won recognition from *Time Out New York* magazine for Best Cheap Eats for a café I helped open in New York City's East Village. On good bread, and with the addition of egg—and even better, with warm shredded Confit Duck (page 276)—this is a favorite for brunch.

→ FOR EACH SERVING

2 slices toasted peasant bread or 1 toasted hard roll, split

Whole-Grain Mustard Aioli (page 381), or unsalted butter at room temperature

1 **Perfect Hard-Boiled Egg** (page 349), peeled and sliced

¼ cup **Best Roasted Green Peppers** (opposite)

Spread both slices of bread with aioli. Arrange the egg on one slice, then pile on the roasted peppers. Top with the other slice of bread and serve.

Roasted Green Bell Pepper Cores

Otherwise dense and tasteless green pepper cores roast to an unexpectedly bold condiment. The slightly bitter seeds turn savory under a bit of heat, seasoned with red pepper flakes, minced garlic, and cumin seeds. The stems soften too, leaving little to discard. Larger peppers have meaty cores and thick stems that need to be cut into small pieces before roasting.

makes ABOUT ¾ CUP

6 green bell pepper cores, seeds attached (page 137)

1 tablespoon excellent olive oil

½ teaspoon coarse kosher salt

White wine vinegar

Pinch of ground cumin

Pinch of hot red pepper flakes

1 small garlic clove, minced

Preheat the oven to 350°F. Line a small baking sheet with parchment paper. Trim away the toughest ends of the pepper stems. Slice thinly through the remaining stems and straight through the cores. Slice the cores into ¼-inch pieces; you should have about 1 cup. Toss the cores and any seeds with the oil and salt in a small bowl. Spread out on the baking sheet, seeds and all. Place in the oven and roast until the seeds are dark brown—make sure they don't burn—and the white part of the cores is tender to a knife, about 20 minutes.

Remove from the oven, and while they are still warm, transfer to a small bowl, carefully scraping the parchment with a thin spatula or knife blade to pick up every seed and bit of oil. Immediately add a splash of vinegar, the cumin, red pepper, and garlic. Toss well and cover tightly with plastic wrap so it will steam as it cools. Keep covered until the mixture is at room temperature, tossing once or twice to keep the flavors mixed. Store in a covered container in the refrigerator for up to 5 days.

Serve

→ on bread thickly spread with salted butter

→ layered in a sandwich with sharp cheese and mustard

→ finely chopped to relish consistency and mixed with chopped hard-boiled egg (page 349)

Lightly Pickled Summer Squash

The following recipe offers a middle ground for those who like their summer squash raw and fresh-tasting and those who want them cooked. The quick poaching broth softens and seasons the squash. You can customize the broth with herbs and spices you like. I choose the highly aromatic coriander and thyme. Take care to slice the squash thinly and evenly.

makes 3 CUPS PICKLES, 30 TO 35 PIECES, AND 2½ CUPS BRINE

1 pound yellow summer squash (about 2 medium)

4 teaspoons coarse kosher salt

1 tablespoon coriander seeds, roughly crushed

6 garlic cloves, very thinly sliced

2½ cups Quick Poaching Broth (page 360)

6 fresh thyme sprigs

1 tablespoon plus 1½ teaspoons white wine vinegar

Cut the squash in half lengthwise. Cut each half into long ⅛-inch-thick slices. Place in a large bowl and toss with 1½ teaspoons of the salt.

Toast the crushed coriander seeds in a medium saucepan over medium-high heat, shaking continuously, until very fragrant, about 1 minute. Add the garlic, poaching broth, remaining 2½ teaspoons salt, and the thyme. Bring to a quick boil, cover, then turn the heat down to low and simmer for 5 minutes.

Remove the broth from the heat, add the vinegar, and immediately pour over the squash. If necessary, weigh the squash down with another bowl to submerge. Cool to room temperature in the broth. Store in a covered container in the refrigerator for up to 5 days. The pickled squash is served best cold or at room temperature.

Use in

→ Summer Squash with Olives and Ground Pork (page 140)

Summer Squash with Olives and Ground Pork

A few olives and garlicky ground pork enliven fragrant, floral squash. Sour cream, lightened with some of the squash broth, brings the separate components together.

⟶ **FOR EACH SERVING**

1 teaspoon grapeseed or canola oil

1 small garlic clove, minced

½ cup (4 ounces) ground pork

12 long slices **Lightly Pickled Summer Squash** (page 139)

2 tablespoons **brine from Lightly Pickled Summer Squash**, with some of the garlic and thyme

4 Picholine or other mild green olives, pitted and roughly chopped

Up to 1 teaspoon sour cream

Heat the oil in a small skillet over medium heat. Add the garlic and cook for 30 seconds; don't let it brown. Add the pork and cook, stirring, until only slightly pink. Remove from the heat.

Meanwhile, gently warm the squash and brine in a saucepan over medium heat. Stir in the olives and sour cream. Transfer to a plate, spoon the pork on top, and serve.

Confit Zucchini Squash

Cooked slowly with cumin and salt to melting tenderness in plenty of oil, zucchini squash becomes one of my best condiments. Be sure to get the seasoning just right when you make this confit; otherwise, it risks being bland. The key is to let the squash cool before tasting. The flavors bloom as the oil cools.

makes 4 CUPS

1 pound (about 3 medium) zucchini squash, sliced crosswise very thinly

½ cup excellent olive oil

1½ teaspoons coarse kosher salt

½ teaspoon ground cumin

Place the squash in a large skillet or Dutch oven with the oil, salt, and cumin. Cook, uncovered, over low heat, stirring occasionally and gently, making sure it doesn't begin to brown, 25 to 30 minutes, until it is translucent and completely tender. The pieces will have broken up slightly. Let cool before tasting; the flavors are best at room temperature. Refrigerate in a covered container for up to 2 weeks.

Use in

→ Confit Zucchini Squash and Potato Soup with Rosemary (page 143)

→ Confit Zucchini Squash and Skillet Flatbread (page 142)

→ Tagliatelle with Confit Zucchini Squash, Oregano, and Crème Fraîche (page 311)

→ Spiced Eggs Baked in Confit Zucchini Squash (page 144)

Confit Zucchini Squash and Skillet Flatbread

Confit Zucchini Squash is best eaten slightly warm or at room temperature. A just-made flatbread will provide all the heat the toppings need. You can keep portions of flatbread dough in the freezer to cook only as many at a time as you want.

—→ **FOR EACH SERVING**

2 tablespoons Greek yogurt

1 tablespoon excellent olive oil

Packed ½ teaspoon chopped fresh oregano

Coarse kosher salt

1½ teaspoons fresh lemon juice

¼ cup **Confit Zucchini Squash** (page 141)

1 **Skillet Flatbread** (page 357), still warm

1 tablespoon freshly grated pecorino or Grana Padano cheese

Hot red pepper flakes

Freshly ground black pepper

Whisk the yogurt, oil, ¼ teaspoon of the oregano, a couple of pinches of salt, and the lemon juice together in a bowl.

Spread the confit on top of the warm flatbread, near to the edges. Top with dollops of the yogurt sauce and lightly it spread around. Sprinkle with the cheese, a pinch of red pepper, a grind or two of black pepper, and the remaining ¼ teaspoon oregano. Serve.

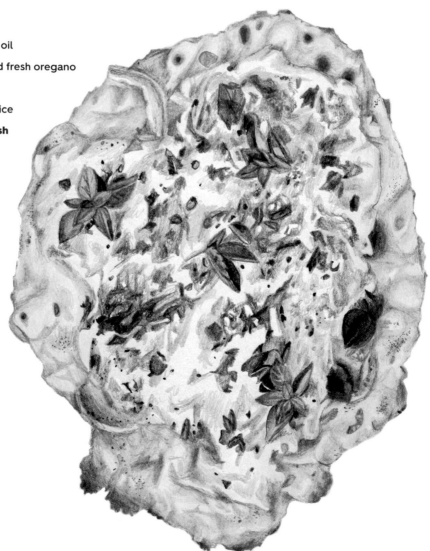

Confit Zucchini Squash and Potato Soup with Rosemary

You don't need a separate stock to make this flavorful, quick-to-assemble soup. The prepared zucchini turns the water in which the potatoes cook into a delicious broth. This is a good dish to use up the last little bit of confit.

—> **FOR EACH SERVING**

1¼ cups water

1 small potato (any variety), unpeeled and diced

1 teaspoon coarse kosher salt, plus more if needed

½ cup **Confit Zucchini Squash** (page 141), with some of its oil

1 fresh rosemary sprig

Freshly grated Parmesan cheese (optional)

Coarse kosher salt and freshly ground black pepper

Put the water, potato, and salt in a saucepan over high heat. Bring to a quick boil, then cover, turn the heat down, and simmer until the potato is just tender, 8 to 10 minutes.

Add the confit and rosemary. Cover and simmer until the potato is very soft, about 5 minutes more. Add cheese, if you like, and pepper to taste. Taste for salt.

The flavors will further develop as this soup cools, so wait about 10 minutes before serving. It is also surprisingly delicious eaten barely warm. Discard the rosemary before serving. Refrigerate, covered, for up to 2 days.

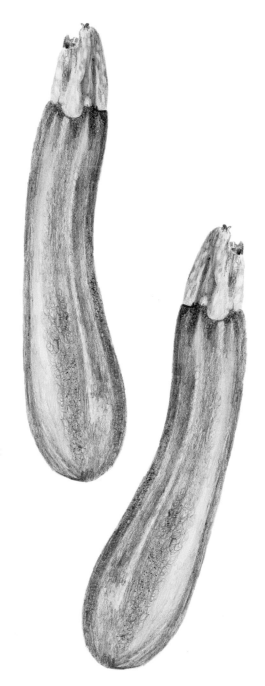

Spiced Eggs Baked in Confit Zucchini Squash

This is no ordinary vegetable-and-egg bake. Because the zucchini is already cooked and seasoned, you just need to layer the ingredients—including crunchy spice seeds—and allow mere minutes to cook the eggs. Serve with grilled bread.

→ **FOR EACH SERVING**

½ cup **Confit Zucchini Squash** (page 141), drained of most of its oil

¼ teaspoon hot red pepper flakes

¼ teaspoon coriander seeds, crushed

¼ teaspoon cumin seeds

2 large eggs

Sweet paprika

Flaky sea salt

1 fresh thyme sprig (optional)

Preheat the oven to 375°F. Stir the squash, red pepper, coriander, and cumin together in a bowl.

Place an ovenproof skillet over high heat. Once the skillet is very hot, add the spiced confit and quickly spread it out. Gently crack the eggs on top, being careful not to break the yolks. Sprinkle with a pinch each of paprika and sea salt. Top with the thyme sprig, if using. Transfer to the oven and bake until the egg whites turn just opaque but the yolks are still glossy and loose,

at least 5 minutes but no more than 10. Take out of the oven and spoon any oil released by the squash onto the eggs.

Allow the dish to sit for 10 minutes before serving; the oil needs to cool slightly while the flavors continue to develop.

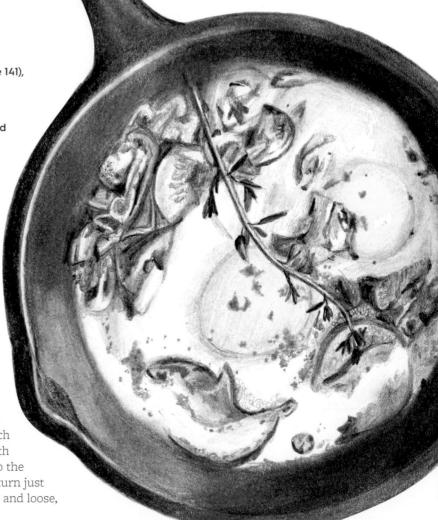

Green Tomatoes and Red Tomatoes

Sour Pickled Green Tomatoes

These versatile pickles are not sweet, but tart and crisp. How much water is given off by the tomatoes determines if your pickles will lean "half sour" or "briny." Both are good.

The thinner you cut the tomatoes, the faster they pickle. The best way to prepare them for this recipe is to cut them in half through the stem (no need to core). Place each half cut side down. Starting at the stem end, cut straight down through the tomato into ¼-inch-thick half-moons. Cut this way, the tomatoes stay intact better than if they were cut in wedges.

makes **ABOUT 3 CUPS**

1½ pounds green tomatoes, halved and cut crosswise into even ¼-inch-thick slices (see headnote)

2 garlic cloves, thinly sliced

2 teaspoons coarse kosher salt

½ teaspoon sugar

¼ cup white wine vinegar

Loosely packed ¼ cup fresh dill sprigs

Put the tomatoes and garlic in a wide bowl. Add the salt and sugar and toss lightly. Add the vinegar and dill and toss again. The tomatoes will not be completely submerged, but they will release a good deal of water as they pickle, and that will dilute the strong brine and increase its volume.

Cover the pickles and refrigerate for at least 4 hours, tossing occasionally. They are best after being brined for at least a day; toss them once or twice during that time.

Store in a tall, narrow container so the pickles remain submerged in the brine. If the brine does not completely cover the tomatoes, just mix them now and again. I like having a batch that ranges from half to full sour. Either way, the pickles will keep crisp in the refrigerator for months.

Serve with

→ Perfectly Poached Salmon (page 225) and Whole-Grain Mustard Aioli (page 381)

→ Salt-Roasted Potatoes with Smoked Trout (page 179)

→ buttered brown bread

→ ham or fried chicken on a picnic

Raw Tomatoes

Ripe tomatoes are the reward for waiting until the height of summer heat. The best, heavy with juice and fragile to hold, are sold close to where they are grown. Buy the ripest you can find and use them quickly. Keep them on your counter, not in the refrigerator, which alters their texture and deprives them of most of their taste. You can cut tomatoes in advance of when you need to use them, but season and dress them right before serving: They quickly weep and soften under salt and acid. When using fresh tomatoes in soup, I don't peel them. Instead, I grate them on the large holes of a box grater and eat the peels on buttered toast.

Cherry tomatoes can be particularly sweet, but stay away from the ones called "grape," which have less juice and flavor. Look for those that are plump, with thin skin.

Slowly cooking little tomatoes with good olive oil and lemon turns them into a sauce you'll never run out of ideas for.

Tomatoes with Red Onion and Beet-Peel Vinaigrette

The juices from the tomatoes, released by the salt, mix with the tangy citrus vinaigrette to form a dressing that is more than a sum of the salad's red and purple parts. Here, I use the beet peels put up from one season's produce for the next.

⟶ **FOR EACH SERVING**

1 cup cherry tomatoes, halved

Coarse kosher salt

A few slices red onion

2 tablespoons **Beet–Peel Vinaigrette** (page 164)

4 or 5 fresh basil leaves, torn

Freshly ground black pepper

Flaky sea salt

Sprinkle the cut sides of the tomatoes with kosher salt; let them sit for 5 minutes. Meanwhile, toss the onions with the vinaigrette in a bowl.

Add the tomatoes to the onions and toss. To serve, lift the tomatoes and onions out of the bowl and arrange on a plate. Drizzle the vinaigrette left in the bowl over the top, then finish with the basil, a few grinds of pepper, and some flaky salt.

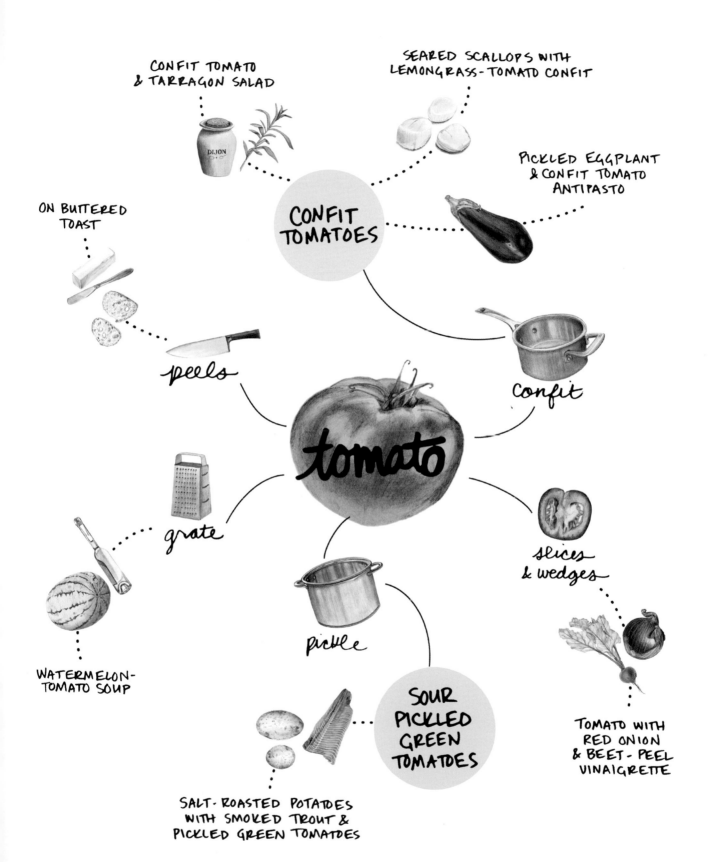

CONFIT TOMATO
& TARRAGON SALAD

SEARED SCALLOPS WITH
LEMONGRASS-TOMATO CONFIT

PICKLED EGGPLANT
& CONFIT TOMATO
ANTIPASTO

DIJON

ON BUTTERED
TOAST

CONFIT
TOMATOES

peels

confit

tomato

grate

slices
& wedges

pickle

WATERMELON-
TOMATO SOUP

SOUR
PICKLED
GREEN
TOMATOES

TOMATO WITH
RED ONION
& BEET-PEEL
VINAIGRETTE

SALT-ROASTED POTATOES
WITH SMOKED TROUT &
PICKLED GREEN TOMATOES

Confit Tomatoes

Though they are cooked, these cherry tomatoes stay remarkably fresh tasting; the juices they release, mixed with olive oil and lemon, become a ready-made sauce. They freeze well too. Come winter, I prefer these to canned tomatoes.

makes 1½ CUPS

1 small lemon

1 big fresh thyme or sage sprig

1 pint cherry tomatoes

3 tablespoons excellent olive oil

¼ teaspoon coarse kosher salt

Serve with

→ seared scallops (page 239)

→ Pickled Eggplant (page 134)

→ Many-Herb Salad (page 64)

Use in

→ Confit Tomato and Tarragon Salad (opposite)

Remove the zest from the lemon with a vegetable peeler and scrape away any white pith. Cut the lemon flesh into quarters.

Put the thyme, tomatoes, oil, and lemon zest in a small skillet over medium-low heat. Cover and cook, shaking the pan occasionally, until the tomato skins begin to split, 15 to 20 minutes. The tomatoes should sweat and swell, not sauté; if they start to brown, turn the heat down. With tongs, squeeze 2 or 3 split-skinned tomatoes to collapse them and release their juices. Stir, cover again, and cook a few minutes more to slightly thicken the juices. Remove from the heat and add the juice of 1 lemon quarter and the salt. Cool in the pan. Transfer to a covered container and refrigerate for up to 5 days. Freeze for up to 3 months.

Confit Tomato and Tarragon Salad

Lemon, oil, and tomato juices combine with vinegar, mustard, and shallots to make a dressing for tomatoes in the same bowl.

—> **FOR EACH SERVING**

½ teaspoon Dijon mustard

1 tablespoon minced shallot

1 tablespoon fresh tarragon leaves

4 teaspoons white wine vinegar

¼ teaspoon coarse kosher salt

1 recipe **Confit Tomatoes** (opposite), with all their juices

Combine the mustard, shallot, tarragon, vinegar, and salt in a bowl; whisk well. Add the tomatoes, breaking up one or two. Stir to coat the tomatoes with the vinaigrette. (*You can make this salad up to an hour in advance and let sit at room temperature for up to 30 minutes. Stir once before serving.*) Serve at room temperature.

Spoon over

—> garlic-rubbed grilled bread

Serve with

—> seared steak (page 280)

—> roasted sardines (page 246) or smoked sardines (page 242)

Molasses-Roasted Peaches

For times when peaches aren't at their best or when you've been overambitious at the market, roasting is a great save, giving the fruit enough edge to take on stronger flavors.

for 4 SERVINGS

2 pounds peaches
(about 4 large)

1 teaspoon coarse
kosher salt

1½ tablespoons
excellent olive oil

1 tablespoon molasses

Preheat the oven to 400°F. Cut each peach into 8 wedges. Discard the pits. With a small knife, scrape out any red, woody remains from the cavities. Arrange the peaches in a roasting pan, skin side down. Sprinkle lightly with salt and drizzle with the oil. Cover tightly with foil and place in the oven.

Check after 30 minutes. Roast until the peaches swell with heat, but remain intact. They should give in to a sharp knife without collapsing and the skins should brown lightly and begin to wrinkle, but won't slip off easily. Re-cover them and give them more oven time if necessary.

Remove from the oven and let rest for 5 minutes, covered. Drizzle on the molasses and stir gently with a spatula to mix the molasses with the peach juices and to coat the peaches with syrup. Cool to room temperature. Serve or refrigerate in a covered container for up to 5 days, after having scraped every last bit of syrup from the roasting pan. They will freeze for up to 1 month, but the texture will suffer, so use them thawed as a spread for toast or pancakes.

Use in

→ Escarole, Roasted Peach, and Tahini Salad (opposite)

→ Seared Peaches and Burrata Quinoa Crepes (page 333)

Serve with

→ Seared and Roasted Duck Breast (page 270)

→ Seared Kale with Garlic and Lemon (page 50), topped with prosciutto

→ ice cream or yogurt

CUTTING RAW PEACHES

Starting at the stem end, use a small knife to cut down along the seam and up the other side, back to the stem. Twist the two halves apart.

You can tell if a peach is really ripe by how easily you can do this, and how loosely the cavity cradles the pit. If the peach is too soft and juicy to separate, it is best eaten as is, without plate or pause. You can also place it alongside a wedge of radicchio dressed with **Green-Peppercorn Vinaigrette** (page 362).

If the peach is firm enough to slice, but still easily twists apart, it's sturdy enough to withstand some tossing and a coating of Buttermilk Dressing (page 380), or just some lemon juice and walnut oil. The less sweet the peach, the thinner you should slice it; one large peach can cover a salad for two.

If an underripe peach won't twist apart at all, abandon the effort—and the peach—entirely.

Escarole, Roasted Peach, and Tahini Salad

This is an impressive salad with assertive pantry items (molasses and tahini); bold, bitter crisp greens; and sweet plumped fruit. Pepitas give the salad the light crunch and balance of salt it needs.

→ FOR EACH SERVING

2 teaspoons tahini

2 teaspoons fresh lemon juice

2 teaspoons **syrup from Molasses-Roasted Peaches** (opposite)

Coarse kosher salt

1½ cups roughly torn escarole

8 wedges **Molasses-Roasted Peaches**, cut into ¾-inch pieces

1 tablespoon salted pepitas

Whisk the tahini, lemon juice, peach syrup, and a pinch or two of salt together in a bowl. Add the escarole and toss to coat. Fold in the peaches, sprinkle with pepitas, and serve.

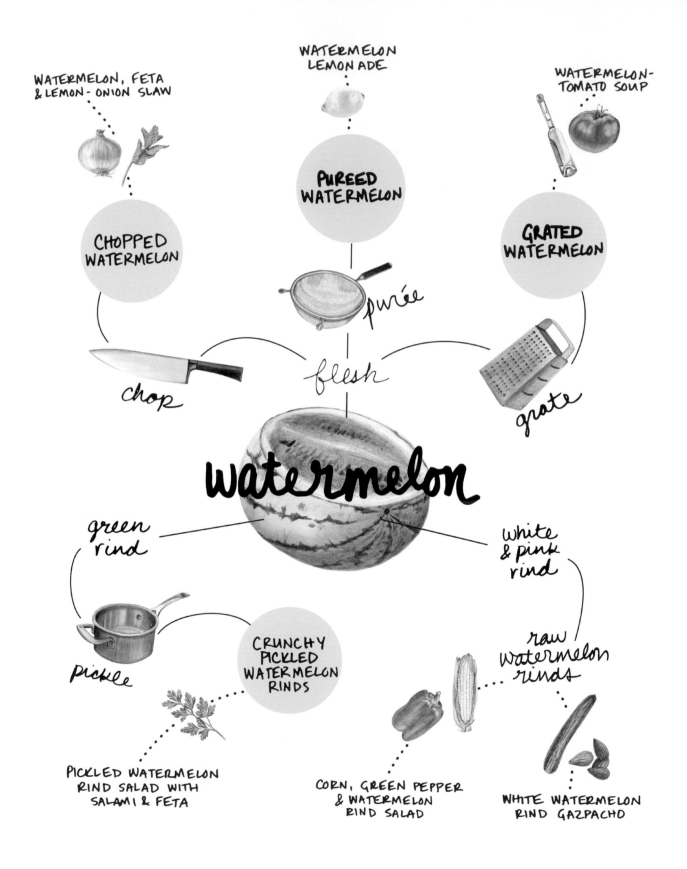

WATERMELON, FETA
& LEMON-ONION SLAW

WATERMELON
LEMONADE

WATERMELON-
TOMATO SOUP

CHOPPED
WATERMELON

PUREED
WATERMELON

GRATED
WATERMELON

chop

purée

flesh

grate

watermelon

green
rind

white
& pink
rind

pickle

CRUNCHY
PICKLED
WATERMELON
RINDS

raw
watermelon
rinds

PICKLED WATERMELON
RIND SALAD WITH
SALAMI & FETA

CORN, GREEN PEPPER
& WATERMELON
RIND SALAD

WHITE WATERMELON
RIND GAZPACHO

Watermelon

Watermelon, Chopped and Juiced

Avoid petite watermelons with tasteless, mealy flesh, and the precut wedges that have lost juices to the cutting board and plastic wrap, and go ahead and buy a big one. Use the juice to make a large pitcher of Watermelon Lemonade (page 154). The juice and pulp together combine with tomatoes for Watermelon-Tomato Soup (page 156).

ONE (10-POUND) WATERMELON WILL GIVE YOU 12 CUPS OF 1-INCH CUBES, OR 8 CUPS JUICE

Cut a watermelon into large chunks. Carve the flesh off the rind and break it into pieces over a large bowl, removing the obvious seeds with your fingers as you work. Grate the pieces through the large holes of a box grater or (preferably) pass through a food mill into another bowl.

Once the seeds are removed, you can puree the pulp into smooth juice, or leave as is.

Store pulp or juice in the refrigerator for up to 3 days, or in the freezer for months.

USING WATERMELON RINDS

Carving away the watermelon's pink flesh, you are left with a rind that consists of a crunchy white inner strip, sweet like a honeydew melon and vegetal like a cucumber; and a dark green, helmet-hard, crisp outer shell. After you've removed the flesh, you can keep these pieces intact in a covered container in the refrigerator for up to 5 days.

When you are ready to use them, carefully remove the white part with a paring knife—it's okay if there's a bit of pink flesh still—leaving only a ⅛-inch layer behind on the green. You can continue to store the white rind separate from the green rind for another few days.

Use the white and pale pink parts in Watermelon Rind, Corn, and Green Bell Pepper Salad (page 154) and White Watermelon-Rind Gazpacho (page 155), and the green part for Crunchy Pickled Watermelon Rinds (page 157).

Watermelon Lemonade

When the first watermelons come out, I buy the largest one to haul home for juice. I freeze the juice in quart and pint containers that I can grab as soon as the mood for lemonade strikes.

→ **MAKES ABOUT 7 CUPS, ENOUGH FOR 6 TO 8 SERVINGS**

1 cup fresh lemon juice

⅓ cup sugar

6 cups juiced watermelon, strained (page 153)

Combine the lemon juice and sugar in a small saucepan over medium heat. Gently warm the juice, stirring, just until the sugar dissolves. Remove from the heat and cool to room temperature.

Pour the lemon syrup into a large pitcher. Add the watermelon juice and stir. Chill well. Serve over ice. Store in the refrigerator for up to 3 days or in the freezer for up to 3 months.

Watermelon, Feta, and Lemon-Onion Slaw

Fresh, sweet watermelon marinates in a bright, spicy, sour slaw. Bulgarian feta, smooth and less salty than Greek feta, is layered between the chunks of fruit and pickle, providing creamy relief. Serve alongside Orange-and-Fennel Pulled Pork (page 288) sandwiches.

→ **FOR 4 SERVINGS**

4 cups ½-inch cubes watermelon (page 153)

2 teaspoons excellent olive oil

2 to 3 tablespoons roughly chopped fresh mint

4 ounces Bulgarian feta cheese, crumbled (about 1 cup)

½ cup **Spicy Lemon-Onion Slaw** (page 36)

Place the watermelon in a serving bowl. Toss with the oil and mint. Scatter on the feta, then top with the slaw. This salad can sit for up to 2 hours at room temperature but is best served immediately.

Watermelon Rind, Corn, and Green Bell Pepper Salad

This is a surprisingly terrific combination of ingredients. The rind macerates in vinegar; the corn is heated briefly, just to tenderness; and the pepper is charred to sweetness. A marinade of good olive oil and a bit of vinegar, cumin, and sugar brings everything together.

→ **FOR 4 SERVINGS**

2 cups ½-inch-chopped watermelon rind, white and pale pink parts only (page 153)

2 teaspoons white wine vinegar, plus more if needed

1½ teaspoons coarse kosher salt, plus more if needed

2 tablespoons excellent olive oil

2 cups raw **Corn Off the Cob** (page 123; from 3 ears of corn)

1 teaspoon ground cumin

2 cups diced (¼ inch) green bell peppers

½ teaspoon sugar

Loosely packed ¼ cup fresh cilantro leaves

Place the rind in a large bowl and sprinkle with 1½ teaspoons of the vinegar and a pinch of salt. Let sit, tossing occasionally, for 5 minutes.

Heat 1 tablespoon of the oil in a large skillet over high heat. Add the corn and toss well. Add 1 teaspoon salt and ½ teaspoon of the cumin and cook over medium-high heat, stirring frequently, until the corn is juicy but still a bit crisp, about 2 minutes. Transfer the corn to the bowl with the rind.

Wipe out the skillet and heat the remaining 1 tablespoon oil over medium-high heat. When it is hot, add the peppers and cook, tossing frequently, until they begin to char and are almost soft, 5 to 7 minutes. Season with the sugar and the remaining ½ teaspoon salt, ½ teaspoon vinegar, and ½ teaspoon cumin. Add the peppers to the corn and watermelon rind. Toss well. Add the cilantro and let sit at room temperature, stirring occasionally, for about 30 minutes. Taste for salt and vinegar. Serve at room temperature or chilled. Store in the refrigerator for up to 3 days.

White Watermelon-Rind Gazpacho

This "white" gazpacho is more vegetal and creamy than the red version, owing to the cucumber, watermelon rind, almonds, and bread. I use cherry tomatoes—which are super sweet— but in a small amount so they do not overwhelm the other ingredients.

I prefer the finer puree of a blender over the slightly coarser texture from a food processor. For the best consistency, I first make a paste primarily with the almonds, bread, and olive oil. Then I add watermelon rind and cucumber.

→ **MAKES 7 CUPS, ENOUGH FOR 6 TO 8 SERVINGS**

¾ cup slivered blanched almonds

Packed 1 cup mixed fresh flat-leaf parsley and mint leaves

1 celery stalk, coarsely chopped

½ cup cherry tomatoes

1 garlic clove

1½ cups 1-inch cubes good white bread (hard crusts removed)

5 tablespoons excellent olive oil

4 cups roughly chopped cucumbers, peeled (about 1 pound)

8 cups 1-inch cubes watermelon rind, white and pale pink parts only (about 2 pounds; page 153)

1 tablespoon plus 2 teaspoons balsamic or sherry vinegar, plus more if needed

1 tablespoon coarse kosher salt, plus more if needed

Combine the almonds, herbs, celery, tomatoes, garlic, bread, and oil. Use a blender or food processor (see headnote) to puree in batches, 2 to 3 minutes per batch. Transfer to a large bowl. Don't bother to clean out the blender or food processor.

Combine the cucumbers, watermelon rind, vinegar, and salt. Puree in batches. Add to the almond mixture and stir well. Taste for salt and vinegar. Chill before serving. The gazpacho will keep in the refrigerator, covered, for up to 2 days.

Watermelon-Tomato Soup

If you have fresh mint or jalapeño, add some to each bowl as you serve it. Refrigerator-Door Relish (page 382) makes a good stir-in too.

⟶ **FOR 4 SERVINGS**

3 tablespoons excellent olive oil, plus more if needed

½ cup finely diced red onion

1½ teaspoons coarse kosher salt, plus more if needed

About 2 pounds watermelon, cut into large wedges

About 2 pounds ripe tomatoes

1½ tablespoons sherry vinegar, plus more if needed

Heat 2 tablespoons of the oil in a medium skillet over medium-high heat. Add the onion and cook, stirring frequently, until completely tender and lightly browned, about 12 minutes. Season with ½ teaspoon of the salt.

As the onion cooks, pick out the easy-to-reach seeds from the watermelon and discard. Rest a box grater inside a large bowl, large holes facing up, and grate the watermelon flesh into the bowl. Fish out any remaining seeds. Measure out 2½ cups of the pulp and juice and transfer to another bowl. Save any extra for another use.

Cut the tomatoes in half through their midsections. With your fingers, scoop out the seeds. Place the grater back into the first bowl. With the cut side down, grate the tomato pulp into the bowl. You will be left with just the tomato skin—to snack on, if you like—and the white cores. Discard the cores. Measure out 3½ cups of the pulp and juice and add to the watermelon.

Add the cooked onion to the tomatoes and watermelon. Season with the remaining 1 teaspoon salt and the vinegar. Stir in the remaining 1 tablespoon oil. Let sit a few minutes, then taste and adjust the salt, vinegar, and oil, adding a bit more of each if necessary. Serve at room temperature or refrigerate, covered, for up to 3 days.

Crunchy Pickled Watermelon Rinds

The outer green skins of the watermelon make outstanding, forever-crisp pickles, unlike any you've ever had. Use the rinds from large watermelons only.

makes 1 QUART PICKLES AND 1½ CUPS BRINE

1 cup red wine vinegar

¼ cup chopped fresh flat-leaf parsley

8 garlic cloves, thinly sliced

2 tablespoons plus 2 teaspoons coarse kosher salt

2 teaspoons sugar

Tough green skin from 1 (7- to 8-pound) watermelon, cut into 1-inch-wide strips, 4 to 5 inches long (page 153)

½ cup excellent olive oil

Combine the vinegar, parsley, garlic, salt, and sugar in a large shallow bowl or baking dish. Stir to dissolve the salt and sugar. Add the rinds and toss well to coat. Let sit for 15 minutes at room temperature, tossing once or twice. Add the oil and toss again to coat all the rinds with oil.

Pack the rinds snugly in a 1-quart jar. Pour in enough brine so the rinds are submerged completely—you may have some brine left over. Cover the jar and let the rinds sit at room temperature for at least 6 hours, or in the refrigerator for 2 days. Store in the refrigerator for up to 4 months. Don't worry if the parsley darkens. Bring the pickles to room temperature to warm up the oil before serving.

Pickled Watermelon Rind Salad with Salami and Feta

This salad is bold, sharp, and crunchy. It keeps well at room temperature for a couple of hours, making it one of my favorite picnic dishes. Leftovers dull by the next day.

→ FOR 8 SERVINGS

12 pieces **Crunchy Pickled Watermelon Rinds** (at left)

3 ounces thinly sliced Italian salami, cut into ⅛-inch-wide strips

1¾ cups thinly sliced red onions

5 cups arugula

5 ounces feta cheese, preferably Bulgarian, crumbled (about 1¼ cups)

2½ tablespoons **brine from Crunchy Pickled Watermelon Rinds**

1 tablespoon plus 1 teaspoon excellent olive oil

Freshly ground black pepper

Cut the pickled rinds into ¼-inch dice. Place in a medium bowl. Add the salami and onions. Toss together well, using your fingers to separate the salami and break up the onion slices. Let sit at room temperature for up to 30 minutes or refrigerate for up to 4 hours.

When you're ready to serve, add the arugula, feta, pickle brine, oil, and pepper to taste. Mix the salad gently but thoroughly with your hands and serve.

Roots and Winter Squash

Beets

starting point

Roasted Beets

Keep two important rules in mind when roasting beets: 1) use a good-fitting roasting pan and 2) add water. You want to steam-roast the beets to loosen their skins and prevent them from drying out.

I cook an entire bunch of beets at one time so I can make other dishes. If you cut the recipe in half, scale down the size of your roasting pan; this helps prevent the water from evaporating too quickly.

I'm not a fan of beet greens. They usually suffer in transportation, and the stems have little flavor. Taste them yourself before putting in the effort to cook them.

makes 8 MEDIUM BEETS, 6 TO 8 CUPS WEDGES, AND 1½ TO 2 CUPS COOKING LIQUID

2¾ to 3 pounds beets (8 medium), scrubbed, both ends very lightly trimmed

1 tablespoon coarse kosher salt

Preheat the oven to 350°F. Place the beets in a baking dish just large enough to hold them snugly in a single layer. Sprinkle with the salt. Pour enough water into the dish to come up ½ inch. Cover very tightly with foil. Bake until very tender, slipping a sharp knife into the center of the biggest beet to make sure, about 1 hour. Watch that the water does not evaporate; the beets will burn. Remove from the oven and let sit for at least 10 minutes, covered.

If the beets are roasted sufficiently, the peels should just slip off with your thumbs. (Disposable gloves will protect your hands from beet stains.) Save the peels for Beet-Peel Vinegar (page 164); save the cooking liquid to store the beets or for Pickled Beets (page 162).

Cut into large wedges and serve warm or at room temperature.

If not serving the beets immediately, put them—whole or cut into wedges—in a container and strain the cooking liquid over them. Cover and refrigerate for up to 5 days. Or cool the beets completely, wrap individually, first in plastic wrap and then in foil, and freeze for up to 1 month. Freeze the cooking liquid in a pint container for up to 1 month.

Use in

$\longrightarrow$ Quick Borscht with Pulled Pork (page 163)

$\longrightarrow$ Roasted Beets and Pickled Onions with Pistachios and Bay Salt (page 162)

$\longrightarrow$ Pickled Beets (page 162)

Pickled Beets

Exceedingly sharp vinegar can easily override the beet's distinctive flavor. I prefer this sweeter pickling brine, tempered with the cooking liquid from the beets themselves.

The color of this brine—adapted from the Zuni Café's signature zucchini pickle by the late, great Judy Rodgers—is particularly suited to golden beets, but use any color beets you like. Feel free to halve or double the recipe.

—▶ **MAKES ABOUT 1 QUART PICKLES**

3 cups apple cider vinegar

1½ cups sugar

2¼ teaspoons powdered mustard

1 teaspoon ground turmeric

¾ teaspoon ground cumin

4 **Roasted Beets** (page 161), peeled and cut into ½-inch-thick wedges

⅓ cup **cooking liquid from Roasted Beets**

Bring the vinegar, sugar, mustard, turmeric, and cumin to a quick boil in a small saucepan over high heat. Turn the heat down and simmer for a few minutes to dissolve the sugar and develop the flavors.

Put the beets in a large bowl. Pour the hot brine over them and stir in up to ⅓ cup beet cooking liquid, to taste. Cool to room temperature. The beets will be ready to eat, but the flavor improves if they are left to sit, covered and refrigerated, overnight. Store in a covered container in the refrigerator for up to 2 months.

Serve with

—▶ Orange-and-Fennel Pulled Pork (page 288)

—▶ goat cheese, in a salad dressed with Green-Peppercorn Vinaigrette (page 362)

ROASTED BEETS AND PICKLED ONIONS WITH PISTACHIOS AND BAY SALT

Magic happens when you dust beets with Bay Salt.

Slice peeled **Roasted Beets** (page 161) and arrange them on a platter. Top with **Pickled Red Onions** (page 36) and sprinkle with chopped pistachios. Dust with **Bay Salt** (page 374) to taste. Serve at room temperature.

Quick Borscht
with Pulled Pork

When you have roasted beets and pulled pork on hand, you can make outstanding borscht in minutes.

⟶ **FOR 4 SERVINGS**

2 tablespoons unsalted butter

1 medium onion, thinly sliced

3 garlic cloves, thinly sliced

1 cup Shaved Raw Cabbage (page 113)

5 Roasted Beets (page 161), peeled and cut into ½-inch cubes

1½ cups cooking liquid from Roasted Beets

1½ cups water

¼ teaspoon ground allspice

1½ teaspoons coarse kosher salt

1½ cups Orange-and-Fennel Pulled Pork (page 288), large pieces pulled apart

1½ tablespoons red or white wine vinegar, or to taste

½ cup sour cream

Melt the butter in a heavy-bottomed pot over medium heat. Add the onion and garlic and cook until the onion is almost translucent, about 3 minutes. Add the cabbage and cook, stirring, until the cabbage wilts, about 2 minutes.

Add the beets, beet liquid, water, allspice, salt, and pork. Turn the heat up to high and bring to a simmer. Turn off the heat once the pork and beets are just warmed through. (*You can make this soup in advance and refrigerate or freeze it at this point. Reheat and finish seasoning just before you are ready to serve.*)

Off the heat, stir in the vinegar, adding more as you like. Ladle into four bowls, top each with sour cream, and serve.

Beet-Peel Vinegar

As I slide the peels off just-roasted beets, I submerge them in red wine vinegar. They sit, refrigerated, for a week, and the once-brassy red vinegar turns lipstick purple (or orange if I use golden beets). It tastes both sweet and sharp.

You can make the vinegar with raw or cooked beet peels. Use in Beet-Peel Vinaigrette.

makes ¾ CUP

Packed ⅓ cup beet peels, well scrubbed if raw

¾ cup red wine vinegar

Put the peels into a 1-pint canning jar or container and pour in the vinegar. Push down on the peels to make sure they're submerged. Cover and macerate in the refrigerator for 1 week before using. Leave the peels in for longer, if you like; remove them when the vinegar has mellowed sufficiently. Strained, the vinegar keeps, refrigerated, for months.

exploration

Beet-Peel Vinaigrette

Creamy but not heavy, this dressing is an excellent way to add the flavor and color of beets to a salad without their bulk.

You can reduce orange juice in a large batch and store it in the freezer in ⅓-cup portions to pull this vinaigrette together quickly. Drizzle over romaine lettuce and serve with crumbled hard-boiled egg (page 349), or use in a salad of Tomatoes with Red Onion and Beet-Peel Vinaigrette (page 146).

⟶ MAKES ABOUT 1 CUP

⅔ cup fresh orange juice

¼ cup **Beet-Peel Vinegar** (at left)

2½ tablespoons Dijon mustard

½ cup excellent olive oil

Place the juice in a small saucepan or shallow pan over very low heat. Cook slowly, until the juice is reduced by half. (If you rush this step, the juice may take on a beige color and caramel off-taste.) Let cool to room temperature.

Whisk together the vinegar, mustard, and reduced orange juice in a small bowl. Slowly drizzle in the olive oil, whisking continuously to make an emulsified dressing.

Store in a jar in the refrigerator for up to 1 month. Whisk again before using.

Carrots

starting point

Butter-Bathed Carrots

Some of the best carrots I've eaten were those I cooked at my first job behind the stove—a butter-and-herb-clad jumble of caramelized orange sticks, dusted with sage. I've adapted the preparation to the oven. The roasting takes longer but the process is largely hands-off, and the flavor is richer. And to keep the carrots tasty for days, I leave out the herbs.

The prolonged high heat turns a heap of prim, faintly sweet pale sticks into what resembles broken, bright orange pastels. If Willy Wonka had carrots, this is the candy he'd make.

makes 4 CUPS, ENOUGH FOR 4 SERVINGS

3 pounds carrots
(preferably thin)

4 tablespoons (½ stick)
unsalted butter

¼ cup excellent olive oil

2 teaspoons coarse
kosher salt

Preheat the oven to 425°F. Peel the carrots, leaving a bit of the pretty stems attached, if you like. If the carrots measure more than ½ inch at their thickest point, cut them lengthwise into pieces, each no more than ½ inch thick. In larger commodity carrots, the cores often have very little flavor, so you may want to trim any especially thick ones: Cut each carrot in half crosswise, then in quarters lengthwise. Carefully cut the core from each piece.

Melt the butter with the oil over medium-low heat in a large Dutch oven. Toss in the carrots and stir well. Season with the salt.

Transfer to the oven and roast, uncovered, turning them occasionally with a wide spatula. After 45 minutes, start checking: Roast until they begin to shrivel beyond the point of tenderness, brown deeply at the edges, and most important, bend or break easily. The longer they cook—well past the glazed stage—the tastier they will be, but make sure to pull them from the oven if they begin to burn. Let cool for 10 minutes before serving; these carrots are best warm or at room temperature.

Store the carrots along with the scraped-up juices and fat in a covered container in the refrigerator for up to 5 days. Even with the butter congealed, I like to eat these carrots cold too. If you prefer to warm them, do so gently in a covered pan over low heat.

Use in

⟶ Butter-Bathed Carrots with Balsamic-Poached Figs and Goat Cheese (page 166)

Serve with

⟶ Freekeh in Garlic Tea (page 337)

BUTTER-
BATHED
CARROTS + BALSAMIC-
POACHED FIGS + pistachios parsley salt soft goat cheese → BUTTER-BATHED CARROTS WITH BALSAMIC-POACHED FIGS & GOAT CHEESE

Butter-Bathed Carrots with Balsamic-Poached Figs and Goat Cheese

Gussy up the butter-rich carrots with balsamic figs, and keep their sweetness in check with salty goat cheese. This is an impressive salad.

→ **FOR EACH SERVING**

1 cup **Butter-Bathed Carrots** (page 165), slightly warm or at room temperature

2 tablespoons sliced **Balsamic-Poached Figs** (page 366)

4 teaspoons syrup from **Balsamic-Poached Figs**

2 tablespoons roughly chopped pistachios

2 teaspoons roughly chopped fresh flat-leaf parsley

Flaky sea salt

2 tablespoons soft goat cheese

Combine the carrots, figs, syrup, pistachios, parsley, and a pinch of sea salt in a bowl. Stir gently to avoid breaking all the carrots. Transfer to a plate or bowl, crumble the goat cheese on top, and serve.

PREPPING AND STORING RAW ROOT VEGETABLES

Raw vegetables are not just a rite of spring. Young parsnips with tiny cores and wispy ends; small turnips with bright, tender leaves; sunchokes with milky white, crisp flesh; thin carrots in bright colors: These are the unsung heroes of late-winter meals too.

Parsnips, celeriac, and sunchokes oxidize quickly when peeled. To avoid this, salt them lightly as you peel them. If you're using them immediately, adding an acid like lemon juice is usually not necessary. But keep an eye out for any possible discoloration and add a good squeeze if you are storing them beyond a few hours.

You can also store prepped root vegetables in water. Thinly cut parsnips will curl at the ends; sunchokes will get a last good rinse. Carrots dry out if cut and refrigerated for days, so it's good to give them a bath in which to laze. Turnips, however, typically preserve their freshness without a water soak, even after sitting cut for a few days. Radishes get waterlogged if submerged for long, so I usually rest a damp paper towel atop them instead. In fact, this is a good idea with any cut vegetable, to prevent them from drying out.

With all these vegetables, you'll want to thoroughly clean their leaves. If the leaves are flavorful (taste them first), you might serve them separately as a salad with Cumin-Raisin Vinaigrette (page 363) or sautéed with a pinch of minced garlic or slivers of Wine-Pickled Garlic Cloves (page 24). I often keep the leaves attached to their bulbs, as handles for nibbling.

The thinner you cut them, the sweeter raw vegetables seem to taste.

→ Cut parsnips lengthwise and remove the core. Then cut them into wedges, no more than ¼ inch thick.

→ Celeriac needs to be thinly cut, or it is difficult to chew and tastes of soap.

→ Cut small turnips and radishes in half or quarters through the leaves, allowing each part its share of greens.

Some raw root vegetables, such as parsnips and celeriac, benefit from a light seasoning of salt to make them more malleable and easier to dress and eat. Radishes often need a light salting but should be patted dry before dressing, because their cut surfaces become too slick.

Julienned Celeriac

Celeriac is a variety of celery cultivated for the root, which is usually large and knobby, with rough skin. Concealed inside is dense, white flesh with a mild and strikingly clean celery taste. I like to amplify this flavor with wine, garlic, and herbs—and just a bit of salt—rather than clobber it with oil and high heat.

Cutting celeriac into julienne is no easy affair, but bound tightly in plastic wrap, the raw slaw keeps for up to a week in the refrigerator. If you don't want to spend time cutting the entire celeriac, you can slice and julienne only a bit at a time; peel the unused portion in advance and wrap it well to store.

makes **ABOUT 4 CUPS**

1 (1-pound) celeriac

2 teaspoons
coarse kosher salt
(if serving raw)

If the celeriac is particularly dirty, roll it around in a dish towel to remove any loose dirt. Place it on a cutting board. With a large, sharp knife, cut off the root tendrils to create a flat side and expose the white flesh. Place the cut side down and follow the contours of the root with the knife, cutting from top to bottom and removing the peel in wide strips. You may notice crevices where brown peel seems to have wormed its way into the root; leave these and concentrate on just the outer peel. When you're done, clean the cutting board of tendrils, peel, and dirt.

Cut the celeriac in half through the top. Place each half on the cutting board, flat side down. Cut the celeriac in ⅛-inch-thick slices. Stack the slices a few at a time and slice again to make ⅛-inch-thick matchsticks (julienne).

How much celeriac you get varies by how much is lost to trimming. (*The cut celeriac, wrapped tightly in plastic wrap, will stay crunchy in the refrigerator for up to 1 week. It may turn slightly gray after 2 days; this is okay.*)

When you are ready to use it and if you are serving the celeriac raw, put it into a large bowl and use your fingers to rub in the salt. Let sit for 20 minutes, more if cut a bit thick. It should be pliable and still crisp and taste fresh. Before using, lift the celeriac out of any water it has expelled.

Use in

→ Seared Sea Bass with Creamy Brown Butter and Julienned Celeriac (page 240)

→ Seared Sausage with Julienned Celeriac (opposite)

→ Poached Chicken, Celeriac, and Asparagus Slaw with Buttermilk Dressing (page 265)

Seared Sausage with Julienned Celeriac

To pair with spicy sausage, I favor sturdy, crunchy celeriac, seasoned with an assertive spice rub I also use to braise pork. Try piling the celeriac on top of the sausage in a sandwich too.

⟶ **FOR EACH SERVING**

1 link Italian or Polish sausage

1 tablespoon excellent olive oil

1 cup **Julienned Celeriac** (opposite), unsalted

2 teaspoons **Pork Spice Rub** (page 373)

Whole-grain mustard, for serving

Prick the sausage in several places with the tip of a paring knife to help release excess fat. Cook it in a skillet over medium-low heat, browning it well on all sides and being careful not to burn it. Transfer the sausage to a plate.

Pour off the excess fat in the pan, leaving the caramelized sausage juices. Add the oil. When the oil moves easily in the pan, add the celeriac and spice rub. Cook briefly, stirring frequently and scraping up all browned bits. The celeriac should become pliable but remain crunchy.

Add the celeriac to the plate with the sausage and serve with mustard.

Celeriac Remoulade

Remoulade is like tartar sauce, usually an aioli or mayonnaise with relish-sized ingredients ranging from pickles to spices, even dried fruit. It is possibly the best dressing for celeriac. This dish is a cool accompaniment to any braised meat, and delicious spread on toast with a slice of ham.

⟶ **FOR EACH SERVING**

1 cup **Julienned Celeriac** (opposite), salted

1 tablespoon good-quality mayonnaise or **Whole-Grain Mustard Aioli** (page 381)

Coarse kosher salt

2 or 3 cornichons, finely diced

½ small radish, finely diced or julienned

Mix the celeriac and mayonnaise together in a bowl. Taste and, if necessary, add additional salt. Stir in the cornichons and radish.

The remoulade will keep overnight, though the vegetables will begin to release water and continue to soften. To freshen, drain the vegetables and toss again with a little more mayonnaise.

Celeriac Braised in White Wine and Coriander

I use coriander when I want a flavor that is slightly rounder and softer than black pepper. Here, I pair it with white wine, herbs, and garlic.

***makes* ABOUT 6 CUPS CELERIAC AND ABOUT 2⅔ CUPS BROTH, ENOUGH FOR 4 TO 6 SERVINGS**

2½ pounds celeriac, peeled (page 168)

3 cups water

⅓ cup crisp white wine

5 fresh thyme sprigs, or 1 or 2 fresh sage sprigs

1 dried bay leaf

1½ tablespoons coarse kosher salt

1 tablespoon excellent olive oil

3 garlic cloves, thinly sliced

½ teaspoon coriander seeds, roughly crushed with a mortar and pestle, spice grinder, or the side of a knife

Preheat the oven to 350°F. Cut the celeriac in half through the top. Place the flat side of each half on the cutting board and cut into ½-inch-thick half-moons.

Arrange the pieces snugly in a large Dutch oven, no more than two layers deep. Add the water; it should barely cover all the pieces. Add the wine, thyme, bay leaf, salt, oil, garlic, and coriander. Cover, bring to a quick boil over high heat, then place in the oven.

Braise until the celeriac is soft enough to be pierced easily with a fork, 30 to 45 minutes, depending on the size of the pan.

If you don't have a Dutch oven, place the celeriac in a roasting pan. Bring the water, wine, braising herbs and spices, and the oil to a boil in a separate pot before adding to the celeriac. Cover very tightly with foil and allow a little extra time to cook.

Let the celeriac cool in its broth for 5 minutes. Taste; if it needs additional salt, add it while still warm. Serve immediately, or cool in the braising liquid and store in the refrigerator for up to 5 days.

Braised Celeriac Gratin

I nestle tender pieces of celeriac into a shallow pan or ramekins, so they can cook in the thickening milk and cheese without steaming to mush. The celeriac is as filling as potato, but considerably lighter. I serve this dish for brunch alongside a salad, or at any winter meal.

→ **FOR 4 SERVINGS**

1 tablespoon cold unsalted butter, cut into bits, plus more for the pan

1 cup **broth from Celeriac Braised in White Wine and Coriander** (opposite)

1 teaspoon powdered mustard

½ cup whole milk

4 teaspoons all-purpose flour

Packed 2 tablespoons grated Gouda cheese

Packed ¼ cup freshly grated Parmesan cheese

Coarse kosher salt

2 cups **Celeriac Braised in White Wine and Coriander**, cut into 1-inch pieces

½ cup **Bread Crumbs** (page 355, or store-bought), untoasted

Preheat the oven to 425°F. Butter an 8-inch pie pan or four individual gratin dishes.

Combine the broth, mustard, and milk in a medium saucepan over medium-low heat. Warm through. Whisk in the flour, then add the Gouda and 2 tablespoons of the Parmesan and whisk until melted. Taste for salt. Stir in the celeriac. Spoon into the pie pan or divide among the gratin dishes. Top with the bread crumbs and the remaining 2 tablespoons Parmesan. Dot with the butter.

Place on a baking sheet and bake until the gratin is bubbling, brown, and beginning to thicken, 25 to 30 minutes. It will continue to thicken and set as it cools. Serve hot or warm. You can make the gratin up to a day in advance, reheating in a 350°F oven for about 10 minutes.

Braised Celeriac Soup

I thicken this highly aromatic soup with toasty Nut Cream for an unexpected, outstanding complement of tastes. If I don't have Nut Cream, I use plain heavy cream and serve a small bowl of toasted almonds on the side.

→ **FOR EACH SERVING**

1¼ cups **Celeriac Braised in White Wine and Coriander** (opposite)

½ cup **broth from Celeriac Braised in White Wine and Coriander**

½ cup **Quick Spring Stock** (page 88)

Coarse kosher salt and freshly ground white pepper

Fresh dill fronds

1 tablespoon **Nut Cream** (page 369) or heavy cream

Combine the celeriac, broth, and stock in a saucepan. Warm over medium heat. Transfer to a blender and puree until very smooth. Add a grind or two of white pepper, and salt if necessary. Serve, scattered with dill fronds and a drizzle of nut cream.

Parsnips Braised in White Wine and Cumin

Parsnips and carrots share silhouettes, but that's where their similarities end. Bitten into whole and raw, carrots crack and crunch; parsnips chew like a green branch. Yes, both are sweet, but carrots' flavors are accessible and convenient; parsnips' more elusive, remote.

Cook parsnips slowly with aromatics and wine, and you unlock a sweetness unmatched by their carrot cousins—and other winter vegetables. Cumin further emboldens the shy parsnip; lemon animates it. Parsnips match up with other naturally sweet ingredients, such as raisins in a salad with spinach and Cumin-Raisin Vinaigrette (page 363), or with scallops (page 239). They stand up to a bit of spice too, such as ginger, garlic, and chiles.

Be sure to core thicker parsnips. You can cut and core them in advance, storing them in cold water to prevent discoloration. And if the cores are sweet (taste them!), you can snack on them raw.

makes 4 CUPS, ENOUGH FOR 4 SERVINGS

2 pounds parsnips (about 10 medium)

¾ cup crisp white wine

¾ cup water

1½ teaspoons coarse kosher salt

1½ teaspoons ground cumin

Juice of ½ lemon (optional)

Preheat the oven to 350°F. Peel the parsnips and trim the ends lightly. Cut off any part of the parsnip less than ½ inch wide. Cut the remaining pieces of parsnip lengthwise into similar-sized sticks. Slice out the thickest part of any visible cores (they don't completely soften).

Put the parsnips in a Dutch oven or roasting pan. They should fit in a snug, mostly single layer. Stir the wine, water, salt, and cumin together and pour over the parsnips. Cover the pan (use a double layer of foil for the roasting pan) and braise until the parsnips are very tender, about 40 minutes, gently stirring once halfway through.

Let the parsnips cool in their braising liquid for 5 to 10 minutes, stirring once or twice. They will absorb a good deal of the liquid as they cool. Taste. Sometimes they invite a squeeze of lemon; add it now. Check for salt. Serve warm or at room temperature.

Store in the refrigerator for up to 5 days. Reheat, covered, in their braising juices. Freeze for up to 3 months; a parsnip's texture suffers when thawed, but the vegetables and braising liquid can still make an excellent soup.

Braised Parsnip Velouté

Serve this silky, slightly sweet soup plain in a mug with a slim pat of butter, chopped parsley, and flaky sea salt, or top it with Scallion-Sesame Magic Mix (page 40) or a pinch of Pork Spice Rub (page 373). You can serve it warm or cold for brunch, as a simple lunch in itself, or as part of a fall dinner.

—> **FOR 4 SERVINGS**

1 cup sliced onion

4 tablespoons (½ stick) unsalted butter

¼ cup all-purpose flour

½ teaspoon coarse kosher salt

4 cups boiling water, plus up to 1 cup warm water if needed

2 cups **Parsnips Braised in White Wine and Cumin** (opposite), with their braising liquid

Unsalted butter, chopped parsley, and flaky sea salt; **Scallion-Sesame Magic Mix** (page 40); *or* **Pork Spice Rub** (page 373), for serving (optional, but terrific)

Cook the onion in the butter in a medium saucepan over medium-low heat until very soft and translucent, 10 to 15 minutes. Add the flour and salt and stir to make a paste. Cook, stirring constantly, until the roux is light brown, about 5 minutes.

Add the boiling water, turn the heat up to high, and bring to a full boil, whisking constantly. Boil, whisking, until the sauce thickens slightly, about 1 minute. Turn off the heat. Add the parsnips and any braising juices and let rest for 5 minutes to heat through.

Transfer to a blender and puree in batches until smooth. If necessary, add warm water to bring the soup to the desired consistency. Thinner is better than thicker here. Taste for salt.

Ladle into four soup bowls, garnish if you like, and serve. This soup is also good at room temperature, and it will sweeten somewhat as it cools. Store in the refrigerator for up to 5 days.

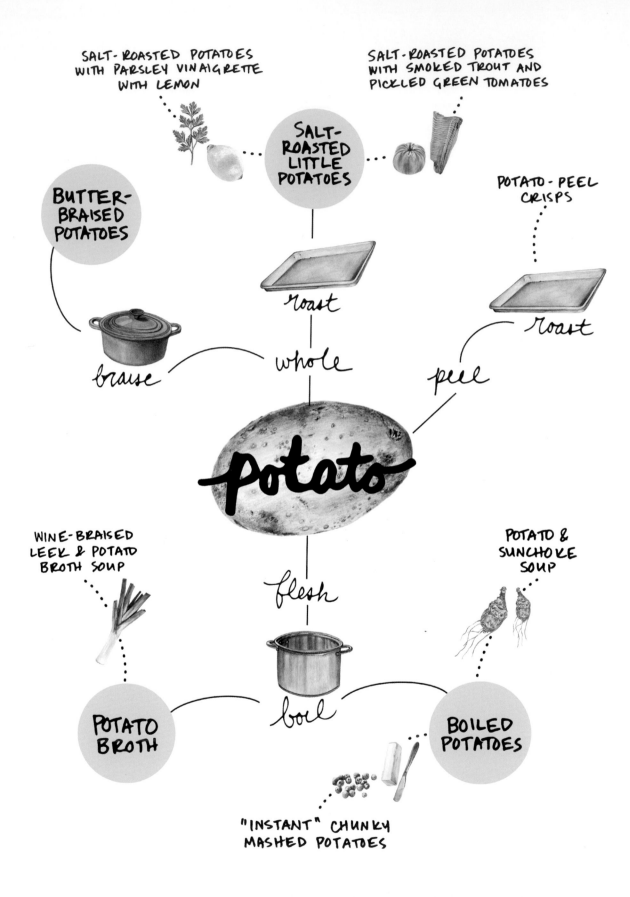

SALT-ROASTED POTATOES
WITH PARSLEY VINAIGRETTE
WITH LEMON

SALT-ROASTED POTATOES
WITH SMOKED TROUT AND
PICKLED GREEN TOMATOES

SALT-ROASTED LITTLE POTATOES

BUTTER-BRAISED POTATOES

POTATO-PEEL CRISPS

roast

roast

braise

whole

peel

potato

WINE-BRAISED
LEEK & POTATO
BROTH SOUP

POTATO &
SUNCHOKE
SOUP

flesh

boil

POTATO BROTH

BOILED POTATOES

"INSTANT" CHUNKY
MASHED POTATOES

Potatoes

starting point

Boiled Potatoes and Potato Broth

The quantities in this recipe are less important than the ratio of potato to water to salt. The creamy, salty potatoes are delicious with melted butter and black pepper, and the cooking broth is light, clean, and flavorful.

makes **6 CUPS POTATO BROTH, ENOUGH FOR 6 SERVINGS**

2 pounds Yukon Gold potatoes (all about the same size)

8 cups water

5 teaspoons kosher salt

Use Boiled Potatoes in

→ "Instant" Chunky Mashed Potatoes (page 176)

Use Potato Broth in

→ Wine-Braised Leek and Potato Broth Soup (page 30)

→ Potato and Sunchoke Soup (page 177)

Wash the potatoes well, scrubbing them to remove any dirt. Peel the potatoes in long, thick, even strips. Save the peels, wrapped in a tight bundle in plastic wrap, in the refrigerator for up to 2 days, to use for crisps (page 176).

Put the potatoes in a large saucepan and add the water and salt. The water should cover the potatoes by at least 1 inch. If it doesn't, add water by the cupful and another ¾ teaspoon salt per extra cup water. Cover and bring to a boil over high heat. Turn the heat down and cook at an assertive simmer until very tender, 20 to 30 minutes, depending on the size of the potatoes. Turn off the heat, uncover, and let the potatoes cool in the potato broth. Taste the water. If it's more salty than potato-y, break up a potato to release more starch and flavor.

Once they have cooled, store the potatoes in the refrigerator in the broth for up to 5 days. Potatoes don't freeze well, but the broth does. Strain it, if you like, and freeze in 2-cup containers.

"Instant" Chunky Mashed Potatoes

To turn Boiled Potatoes into quick mashed potatoes, you need just one saucepan, one spoon, and a few minutes. No food mill or grater necessary. I like to serve these in individual portions in a mug, with a pat of butter on top.

—> **FOR EACH SERVING**

¼ **cup heavy cream**

1 **tablespoon unsalted butter**

¼ **teaspoon coarse kosher salt**

Freshly ground white pepper

1 **cup quartered Boiled Potatoes** (page 175)

Put the cream, butter, salt, and a few grinds of pepper in a saucepan. Bring to a quick boil, stir once to melt the butter, and turn off the heat.

Use your hands to break the potatoes into small pieces, directly into the saucepan. Turn the heat to low, stir once, then cover and cook until the potatoes are just warmed through, about 1 minute. Uncover the pot and stir with a wooden spoon to break up any large pieces of potato and encourage them to absorb the cream. Taste for salt and serve.

POTATO-PEEL CRISPS

Potato peels make ideal chips. They crisp naturally in the oven with little oil, tangling and curling into a messy heap. They are quick to make and even quicker to eat.

Toss thick strips of potato peels with enough excellent olive oil to coat them lightly. Season with coarse kosher salt and lots of freshly ground black pepper. Spread the peels out on a baking sheet lined with parchment paper and place in a preheated 375°F oven. Bake until completely dry and crisp, stirring once or twice, testing a few larger pieces to ensure the whole batch is done, 10 to 15 minutes. Cool on the baking sheet; they will continue to crisp a bit as they cool.

You can eat them now or store them in an airtight container at room temperature for a couple of days. If they become chewy, recrisp them in a 300°F oven for about 10 minutes. They may shrivel a bit more, but will taste just as good.

Potato and Sunchoke Soup

A velvety, light, but rich pureed soup, this can be served hot or cold. The potato broth gives the soup sufficient flavor but not too much viscosity—a bonus, especially when you serve the soup chilled. It freezes beautifully.

—> **FOR EACH SERVING**

1 cup peeled and chopped sunchokes (page 167)

1½ cups **Potato Broth** (page 175)

1 small **Boiled Potato** (page 175), chopped

Coarse kosher salt

1½ teaspoons unsalted butter

Put the sunchokes and broth in a saucepan over medium-high heat. Bring to a simmer and cook, covered, until soft, about 10 minutes. Transfer the sunchokes and 1 cup of the potato broth to a blender. Add the potato, and puree. Thin with the remaining potato broth or water to the desired consistency; the soup will thicken as it cools. Taste for salt.

If serving the soup chilled, blend in the butter and refrigerate until completely cooled. If serving warm, pour the soup into a bowl or mug and top with the butter.

Salt-Roasted Little Potatoes

When I crave French fries, these salt-roasted potatoes step up to fit the bill. Small, creamy potatoes, peels left on, are baked buried in salt. Their insides turn fluffy; their skins are as salty as roasted nuts. They are great on their own or with Sour Pickled Green Tomatoes (page 145). You can reuse the salt several times for future batches of potatoes.

makes ABOUT 4 CUPS, ENOUGH FOR 4 SERVINGS

2 pounds baby Yukon Gold potatoes or fingerlings (measuring no more than 1 inch in diameter)

6 to 8 cups coarse kosher salt, enough to surround and bury the potatoes completely

Preheat the oven to 325°F. Wash the potatoes and dry them well.

Choose a roasting pan just large enough to accommodate all the potatoes in a single layer. Cover the bottom of the pan with an even ¼-inch layer of salt. Place the potatoes gently on top of the salt, touching.

Cover the potatoes completely with additional salt, making sure to fill the spaces in between, but leave a small naked spot on one or two of the largest potatoes to make it easy to test them for doneness without breaking the salt crust seal.

Roast until very tender, 30 to 45 minutes, depending on size. Test the largest potato with a sharp knife; it should slide in effortlessly. Some of the smaller potatoes, even if they are done earlier, will get increasingly tender with

additional time, and will shrivel and become deliciously chewy.

Remove the pan from the oven and let the potatoes cool in the salt. Once they are cool enough to handle, dig out the potatoes from under the salt crust and roll them one at a time between your hands to remove any excessive chunks of salt—they should still have a nice dusting, as if they dried in the sun after a day in the sea.

Serve warm or at room temperature. Store any leftover potatoes in the refrigerator for up to a week. They will need to be dried out, though, in a 325°F oven until hot and crisp again, about 10 minutes, before serving. Cool the salt completely before storing in a covered container or plastic bag at room temperature.

Toss with

→ Parsley Vinaigrette, with lemon (page 69)

→ Green-Peppercorn Vinaigrette (page 362)

→ Whole-Grain Mustard Aioli (page 381)

→ Chicken Salt (page 263)

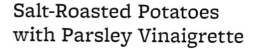

Salt-Roasted Potatoes with Parsley Vinaigrette

The key to this dish is to let the dressed, warm potatoes rest before serving. If you taste them immediately after dressing, you'll notice they will be too sharp and uneven. But after just 5 minutes, the seasoning settles in. The potatoes are great at room temperature, especially good on a buffet table. I like them the next day.

→ **FOR EACH SERVING**

1½ cups **Salt-Roasted Little Potatoes** (opposite), hot from the oven

2 to 3 tablespoons **Parsley Vinaigrette** (made with lemon; page 69)

Flaky sea salt and freshly ground black pepper

Put the hot potatoes in a bowl and smash roughly with a spoon or spatula. Toss with the vinaigrette while warm. Cover with plastic wrap and let rest for 5 minutes. Toss again. Season with salt and pepper. Serve warm or at room temperature.

SALT-ROASTED POTATOES WITH SMOKED TROUT AND PICKLED GREEN TOMATOES

You can combine these ingredients into an hors d'oeuvre, or serve them as a starter salad.

FOR AN HORS D'OEUVRE: Choose the smallest **Salt-Roasted Little Potatoes**. Recrisp them if necessary. Top each with a small amount of **Whole-Grain Mustard Aioli** (page 381) or sour cream and a bite-sized piece of smoked trout (page 242, or store-bought). Add a slice of **Sour Pickled Green Tomato** (page 145), along with some of the dill or garlic from the brine. Allow 3 potatoes per serving.

FOR EACH SERVING OF SALAD: Cut 1 cup **Salt-Roasted Little Potatoes** into bite-sized pieces. Recrisp if necessary. While still warm, toss with 2 tablespoons **brine from Sour Pickled Green Tomatoes**, 2 tablespoons sour cream, coarse kosher salt to taste, and a pinch of white pepper. Gently fold in ½ cup **Sour Pickled Green Tomatoes**, cut into bite-sized pieces if large, and a small smoked trout fillet broken into large pieces (½ cup), until just combined. Fold in some chopped fresh dill. Serve.

Butter-Braised Potatoes

These braised potatoes are intensely creamy, a result of absorbing a good deal of butter as they cook. Like roasted potatoes, they brown deeply on the cut sides, but stay tender and creamy even when cold. Capers added near the end punch up the salt, and fry until crisp.

Use small potatoes and a cast-iron pan. To double the recipe, use two 10-inch skillets and 2 pounds potatoes. If you happen to have individual cast-iron pans, you can cook and serve each portion of potatoes separately, at the end stirring in a spoonful of Confit Zucchini Squash (page 141) and/or topping with a poached or soft-boiled egg (pages 351 and 353). Serve the potatoes cold in a salad with Seared Kale (page 50), lemon, and red pepper flakes. In all cases, you'll need a lid to fit.

Credit goes to *Cook's Illustrated* for this braising method.

1 pound small (1-inch-diameter) red-skinned or baby Yukon Gold potatoes, scrubbed and cut in half

1¼ cups water

2 tablespoons unsalted butter, cut into bits

1 fresh thyme sprig

½ teaspoon coarse kosher salt

1½ tablespoons drained capers, chopped

Place the potatoes cut side down in a 10-inch cast-iron skillet. They should fit snugly in one layer.

Add the water, butter, thyme, and salt; the potatoes will not be entirely submerged. Cover and bring to a quick boil over high heat. Turn the heat down to medium-low and simmer, covered, until the potatoes are just tender enough to be pierced easily with a fork; check at 10 minutes.

Once they are tender—check the biggest piece—remove the lid and turn the heat to high, allowing most of the water to cook off. When the liquid has reduced to ¼ inch, about 5 minutes, add the capers, sprinkling them in between the potatoes.

Continue to cook until the potatoes have absorbed most of the butter and are crisp and brown on the underside.

Turn off the heat. Let the sizzling subside. Don't try to prematurely pry the potatoes from the pan. Once they crisp, they will release with gentle help from a thin spatula. Transfer the potatoes and capers to a bowl; toss gently. Serve hot or at room temperature.

To store, place in a covered container and refrigerate for up to 5 days. Serve cold, or reheat in a 400°F oven for 10 minutes.

Sunchokes (Jerusalem Artichokes)

Sunchokes taste like a cross of celery and pear, with the crunch of crisp apple. Their flesh is almost translucent when sliced extra thin, and they are delicious eaten raw in salad. Regardless of how they are cut, they cook quickly and make a nice complement to or substitute for potatoes in soup (page 177). Sunchokes pick up the taste of butter beautifully when sautéed.

starting point

Sunchokes, Raw and Ready

Unless the sunchokes are going to be roasted, the skin detracts from their delicate flavor, so I peel them. If the sunchokes are particularly warty, this can be tedious work; you may choose instead to just scrub them well under running water. In either case, you'll need to work quickly so the creamy flesh doesn't discolor as it makes contact with air. If serving sunchokes raw, try to choose large ones. Peel only what you need. If you won't be using them soon, keep peeled sunchokes in a bowl of water with some lemon juice to prevent them from turning pink-brown.

exploration

Sunchoke Salad with Apple and Red Onion

A raw sunchoke is crisp like an apple and, cut thinly, equally aromatic. Red onion brings additional crunch and necessary bite to this light, elegant composed winter salad drizzled with a dressing of nut oil, mustard, and crème fraîche.

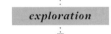→ **FOR EACH SERVING**

- 4 teaspoons crème fraîche
- 4 teaspoons hazelnut oil
- 4 teaspoons whole-grain mustard
- Several very thin rings of red onion
- 1 small sweet apple, very thinly sliced into rounds
- 6 small **sunchokes raw and ready** (at left), peeled, sliced paper-thin
- Flaky sea salt

Combine the crème fraîche, hazelnut oil, and mustard in a small bowl. Scatter the onions, apples, and sunchokes on a plate. Drizzle liberally with the dressing. Season with salt. Serve right away.

Roasted Sunchokes

I like to serve roasted sunchokes at room temperature with Whole-Grain Mustard Aioli (page 381), Dill-and-Leek-Greens Pesto (page 32), or Tahini Sauce (page 371). Or I'll scrape the hot sunchokes and any browned bits in the roasting pan into a bowl and finish them with black pepper or za'atar, a shower of good sherry vinegar, and a pat of butter. You can also simply toss them with sharp vinaigrette.

3 POUNDS SUNCHOKES MAKES ABOUT 5 CUPS, ENOUGH FOR 4 SERVINGS

THE FOLLOWING GUIDELINES WILL WORK FOR POTATOES TOO.

→ Start with double the amount of raw root vegetables than you'll need when they're roasted. Sunchokes shrink by half when cooked (potatoes shrink by a third).

→ Cut the pieces to an even size, about 1 inch thick, so they cook quickly and evenly but have time to brown.

→ Lightly coat the pieces with a high-heat oil such as grapeseed or canola, so they don't burn.

→ Salt liberally and evenly, about 1½ teaspoons for every pound.

→ Place directly on a metal roasting pan or baking sheet; do not overcrowd.

→ Roast at 425°F. Sunchokes and potatoes take about 25 minutes.

→ Don't stir haphazardly. Turn the pieces individually with tongs as they brown, or scrape them loose with a metal spatula.

Don't despair if some pieces stick; just scrape the pan well, incorporating any crisped bits into the mix.

ROASTING ROOT VEGETABLES

Not all root vegetables are best roasted. Large turnips become bitter; radishes turn watery. While potatoes become crisp outside and soft inside, parsnips and celeriac shrivel and turn chewy. And not all root vegetables should be roasted the same way. Beets need to be steam-roasted with water, so their peels slip off easily at the end.

So if you want to serve a combination of root vegetables, roast them separately. This way, you can brown the potatoes without burning the turnips and you won't crowd the pan, forcing some pieces of vegetable to steam while others brown. Plus, roasting root vegetables individually gives you more options for using each of them.

Roasted Sunchokes with Two Finishes

I prefer roasted sunchokes just out of the oven, hot and tender, finished with butter and salt, herbs and vinegar. But you can roast them in advance and reheat them to finish when you're ready to serve.

⟶ **FOR 4 SERVINGS**

5 cups **Roasted Sunchokes**, hot from the oven (page 183)

2 tablespoons cold unsalted butter, cut into bits

WITH ZA'ATAR SALT

2 teaspoons **Za'atar Salt** (page 373)

WITH SHERRY VINEGAR

4 teaspoons sherry vinegar

4 teaspoons roughly chopped fresh flat-leaf parsley

Flaky sea salt and freshly ground black pepper

Place the hot sunchokes in a bowl. Add the butter and the za'atar salt, or the vinegar and parsley. Toss continuously until the butter melts and coats the sunchokes evenly.

Season the vinegar version with salt and pepper. Serve warm.

Roasted Sunchokes and Steamed Mushrooms in Broth

Separate, distinct preparations of mushrooms and sunchokes give you a dish worlds better than one where these ingredients would just get cooked together in a pan. You can scale up this recipe to serve four, using a larger pan and a full batch of the mushrooms.

⟶ **FOR EACH SERVING**

½ cup **Wild Mushrooms Steamed in Their Juices** (page 198)

1 teaspoon excellent olive oil

½ cup **Roasted Sunchokes** (page 183)

2 teaspoons cold unsalted butter, cut into bits

2 teaspoons roughly chopped fresh flat-leaf parsley

Celery salt or coarse kosher salt and freshly ground black pepper

Gently press all of the broth out of the mushrooms; reserve the broth.

Heat the oil in a small skillet over medium heat. Add the mushrooms and sunchokes and cook, stirring, to just heat through, about 1 minute. Turn the heat down to low. Add the mushroom broth, gently shaking the pan to coat the vegetables.

Turn off the heat and add the butter and parsley. Season to taste with salt and pepper. Toss well to coat with the sauce. Taste for salt. Serve.

Wine-Poached Sunchokes

You can cook sunchokes in the same white wine–fortified broth you might use for fish or poultry. Poached sunchokes are fragrant and taste almost floral. I like them best in a bowl, warmed in their poaching broth and enriched with a bit of sour cream or butter, black pepper, and fresh herbs. Use extra sunchoke broth as a substitute for any vegetable stock or even some of the stock in Chicken Stock with Spring Vegetables and Parmesan (page 77).

Choose the largest sunchokes possible; by far, they are easier to peel.

makes ABOUT 5 CUPS, ENOUGH FOR 4 SERVINGS

8 cups **Quick Poaching Broth** (page 360)

2 pounds sunchokes, peeled (page 167) and cut into 1-inch pieces (about 2½ cups)

4 teaspoons coarse kosher salt

Put the broth in a large saucepan and bring to a boil over high heat. Add the sunchokes and salt. Cover and reduce to the barest simmer. Poach until the sunchokes are very tender, about 15 minutes. Serve, or let cool to room temperature.

Once cooled, you can store the sunchokes in a covered container in their broth for up to 5 days. They will recrisp when cold. Serve them at room temperature or reheat in their broth to soften.

Raw Turnips

Small turnips—called Japanese, Hakurei, or baby turnips—are creamy white, with thin, ropy roots and sprightly green leaves. They are moist and sweet and best to eat raw. Look for those with the sturdy leaves still attached—this will clue you to their freshness. The larger turnips, with a pale purple collar ringing tough, truncated stems, are bitter; I don't include them here.

To prepare the turnips, rinse them under cold water. Keep the tail on and lightly trim the top where the little whiskers around the stems grow. They are delicious whole, dipped in Anchovy Butter (page 378). Or you can thinly slice them for a salad with Anchovy Dressing and Walnuts (at right).

Spring Turnips with Anchovy Dressing and Walnuts

You can look to the pairing of the ingredients in this dish for ideas for other great dishes—use ras el hanout with walnuts in a chicken salad; toss turnips with whole anchovies and seared greens. Only use the turnip greens if they are fresh and tasty.

Ras el hanout is a spice mix from North Africa, often used in Moroccan cuisine.

⟶ **FOR EACH SERVING**

¼ cup roughly torn baby turnip greens (optional)

1 cup thinly sliced baby white turnips (at left)

1 tablespoon **Anchovy Dressing** (page 379)

1 tablespoon chopped toasted walnuts (page 368)

Pinch of ras el hanout

If you have turnip greens, toss them with the dressing and walnuts in a bowl. Arrange the turnips on a plate and place the dressed greens on top.

If you're not using the greens, toss the turnips, dressing, and walnuts together. Place on a serving plate.

Sprinkle with ras el hanout and serve immediately.

Roasted Glazed Turnips with Honey and Fish Sauce

Surprisingly, quiet-flavored turnips are not easily overrun by loud flavors, such as this sweet-and-salty butter, honey, and fish sauce glaze. (Don't let the fish sauce put you off; the turnips won't taste the slightest bit fishy.) They cook to tenderness without becoming mushy, and make for a rather light side dish. Serve alongside a bowl of toasty grains.

Choose smaller turnips over larger ones every time. For this recipe in particular, the smaller ones give off less water when they cook, which helps the honey and fish sauce form a robust, syrupy glaze.

for **4 SERVINGS**

2 tablespoons excellent olive oil

3 tablespoons unsalted butter, cut into bits

2½ pounds baby white turnips, 1 inch wide, well washed, cut in half through the stem

2½ tablespoons honey

1¼ teaspoons coarse kosher salt

1 tablespoon plus 2 teaspoons fish sauce

Preheat the oven to 450°F. Put the oil and butter in a 9-x-13-inch baking dish and place in the oven. When the butter has melted, add the turnips, honey, and salt. Stir well, then arrange the turnips in a single layer with their cut sides down where possible.

Roast until the turnips begin to brown and are just tender, 20 to 25 minutes. Stir in the fish sauce, rearranging most of the turnips cut side down. Roast until the sauce thickens to a glaze and the turnips are deep brown and a little wrinkled, about 10 minutes—the sauce will thicken somewhat as it cools too. Serve directly from the baking dish, stirring as you serve to continually recoat the turnips. They are delicious cooled to room temperature too. Refrigerate in a covered container for up to 5 days. Reheat in a covered pan over low heat.

Serve with

→ Seared Kale with Garlic and Lemon (page 50)

→ White Wine–Braised Duck Legs (page 273)

Roasted Butternut Squash Slices

You can roast squash in thin, unpeeled, unseeded slices for a playful, meaty, versatile "chip." Consider adding toasted, seed-full slices to crisp salad greens.

No two squash are the same size. To ensure you're seasoning them sufficiently, use about 1 teaspoon salt for every pound of squash.

makes 4 CUPS, ENOUGH FOR 4 SERVINGS

1 large butternut squash (about 2 pounds), scrubbed

Excellent olive oil

2 teaspoons coarse kosher salt

Preheat the oven to 350°F. Line two baking sheets with parchment paper. Trim each end of the squash slightly. Cut in half crosswise, separating the bulbous seed section from the neck of the squash. Cut each in half again, lengthwise this time. Place the flat side of each piece down on the cutting board. With a sharp, heavy knife, cut crosswise into half-moons no more than ¼ inch thick. You will cut through the seed cavity, keeping the seeds tethered to the flesh. (*You can cut the squash and store it raw, covered with a damp paper towel in a covered container in the refrigerator, for up to 5 days.*)

Use either a pastry brush or your hands to lightly paint each side of each slice of squash with olive oil, taking care not to push out any seeds. Season evenly with salt and arrange on the baking sheets.

Roast the squash for 15 minutes. The pieces should be tender and bright orange. Raise the oven temperature to 425°F and roast until the squash slices begin to brown, 7 to 10 minutes more. Use a wide spatula to carefully flip each slice. Roast until the slices appear slightly wrinkled and dry, another 5 to 7 minutes. Some pieces will look plumper than others.

The squash slices will keep for up to 2 days in the refrigerator. Stored cold, the seeds will get progressively chewier, but they will recrisp if you heat the squash slices in a preheated 300°F oven for 10 minutes.

Squash and Rosemary Compote with Honey and Cayenne

Squash should roast to this compote's level of richness on its own, but honey helps. To avoid cooking the squash to a mush, cut it carefully and roast the individual pieces first, before combining them with the honey-lemon dressing off the heat. The compote is as vegetal as it is sweet and versatile. Serve it next to Butter-Braised Potatoes (page 180) or Balsamic-Poached Figs (page 366) on the Thanksgiving table, or alongside Seared and Roasted Duck Breast (page 270).

makes **2 CUPS**

1 butternut squash (about 1½ pounds), peeled, seeded, and cut into ½-inch cubes

1 tablespoon excellent olive oil

2 teaspoons coarse kosher salt

2 tablespoons honey

1 tablespoon minced fresh rosemary

1 tablespoon fresh lemon juice

⅛ teaspoon cayenne

Preheat the oven to 425°F. Line a baking sheet with parchment paper. Toss the squash with the olive oil and 1½ teaspoons of the salt. Arrange in an even layer on the baking sheet. Roast until the squash looks a bit shriveled and is soft enough to pierce with a knife, 20 to 30 minutes. Don't let it get too soft, or the compote will turn to mush. Once tender, remove the squash from the oven to cool.

Stir the honey, rosemary, juice, cayenne, and the remaining ½ teaspoon salt together in a medium bowl. Use a rubber spatula or large spoon to gently fold in and coat the squash. Serve at room temperature. The compote will keep in the refrigerator for up to 1 week.

Pickled Acorn Squash

Winter squash—acorn squash, in particular—is difficult to cut and cook well. Most of us halve it and roast it, then turn leftovers into soup. But this strong pickle brine is a way for the squash to wear a different set of flavors without losing its great texture. The turmeric in the brine turns the squash jewel orange.

Steaming the slices first ensures that they are tender but stay sturdy, and that they will absorb the brine.

No need to peel the squash; the peel helps the flower-shaped slices that result from cutting the "wavy" sides of the squash crosswise stay intact, and is often tender enough to eat.

makes 1 QUART

1 large acorn squash (about 2 pounds), scrubbed

4 cups apple cider vinegar

2 cups sugar

1 tablespoon powdered mustard

1 tablespoon yellow mustard seeds

1½ teaspoons ground turmeric

1 teaspoon ground cumin

Pinch of hot red pepper flakes

Cut the squash in half lengthwise. Remove the seeds and fibers from the cavity, then cut each half crosswise into ½-inch-thick slices.

Fill a medium saucepan with just under 1 inch of water. Place a steamer basket on top and layer the squash in the basket. Cover the pan. Bring the water to a simmer over medium heat and steam the squash until knife-tender but not mushy, about 10 minutes.

Meanwhile, bring the vinegar, sugar, powdered mustard, mustard seeds, turmeric, cumin,

and red pepper flakes to a quick boil in a small saucepan over high heat. Turn the heat down and simmer for a few minutes to develop the flavors. Cover to keep warm and set aside.

Lift the steamer basket out of the pan. Discard the water and immediately put the squash back directly into the pan. Cover with the hot brine. Weight down any floating pieces of squash with a smaller pot lid or cover them with a piece of parchment paper. Let cool to room temperature.

You can serve the pickles right away. Or refrigerate in the brine in a covered container for up to 1 month.

Serve

⟶ in a sandwich with Orange-and-Fennel Pulled Pork (page 288)

⟶ alongside Salted Roast Chicken (page 253)

⟶ in a sandwich with roasted cauliflower and melted Gruyère cheese

Pickled Squash Spread

I like this spread on sandwiches on one slice of the bread, opposite mustard. (It's delicious on a warm sandwich with the Orange-and-Fennel Pulled Pork on page 288.) The smooth paste is intense and sharp, both sweet and sour. It is unlike any condiment you have on your shelf, and is one of my favorite host gifts. The paste keeps for months, and a little goes a long way. Textures of squash vary, so they will puree differently; in any case, I like my paste silky smooth. A long run in the food processor should achieve this, but you might like to use a fine-mesh strainer at the end too.

⟶ **MAKES 1 CUP**

1 cup **Pickled Acorn Squash** pieces (opposite), peel removed

2 tablespoons **brine from Pickled Acorn Squash**

2 tablespoons unsalted butter, at room temperature

Place the squash, brine, and butter in a food processor. Puree until completely smooth, at least 5 full minutes. If you like, push the spread through a fine-mesh strainer. Store in the refrigerator for up to 1 month.

Mushrooms

Mushrooms

Triple-Braised Wild Mushrooms

In this recipe, I cook a single batch of mushrooms in three rounds of wine and stock, each time letting the cooking liquids—including those released by the mushrooms themselves—reconcentrate their flavor. The mushrooms absorb it all, becoming tastier and more tender each time.

These mushrooms can stand up to heavier flavors. They fare equally well on their own too—even at room temperature—served with some of their juices and black pepper.

makes 2½ TO 3 CUPS

1 pound oyster, trumpet, or lobster mushrooms

1 to 1½ tablespoons grapeseed or canola oil

½ cup crisp white wine

1½ teaspoons coarse kosher salt

1½ cups excellent chicken stock (such as Worth-It Chicken Stock, page 267) or Garlic Stock (page 21)

1 fresh thyme sprig

Lightly trim the mushroom stems; oyster and lobster mushrooms might need more aggressive trimming. If they are dirty, wash under cold running water, cap up to prevent excess water from saturating the gills. Place on paper towels, cover with another layer of paper towels, and pat very dry. Cut into long ½-inch-thick slices, through the cap and stem where possible.

Heat a large skillet over high heat for 30 seconds. Add enough of the oil to just coat the pan, and immediately add half of the mushrooms, cut side down; they should fit snugly in the pan without overlapping. Turn the heat down to medium.

Place a heavy, smaller pan or pot directly on top of the mushrooms to weight them down and encourage a thorough sear. The mushrooms will begin to release their juices. Once they evaporate and the edges of the mushrooms turn caramel-brown, 2 to 3 minutes, remove the top pan and cook until the mushrooms are completely and evenly browned on the bottom, about 2 minutes more. Flip the mushrooms over, a piece at a time. Weight them down again and sear until the second side is browned, about 2 minutes. If the mushrooms begin to burn, add a bit more oil to the pan and turn the heat down. Once the mushrooms are seared on both sides, transfer them to a small bowl. Sear the remaining mushroom slices in the same manner, adding oil to the hot pan as necessary, 1 teaspoon at a time. The second batch of mushrooms will take less time to cook. Make sure they don't burn.

Once all of the mushrooms are seared, return them all to the pan. Turn the heat down to medium and add ¼ cup of the wine. While it simmers briskly, use a spatula to release any browned bits from the bottom of the pan. When the wine is almost completely reduced, add ½ teaspoon of the salt and ½ cup of the stock. Cover and simmer until the mushrooms have almost completely absorbed the stock, about 6 minutes. Add the remaining ¼ cup wine and cook until it is almost completely reduced. Add another ½ teaspoon salt and ½ cup stock. Cover again and simmer until the mushrooms have almost completely absorbed the stock, another 6 minutes. Add the remaining ½ teaspoon salt and ½ cup stock, cover, and cook until the mushrooms are very tender and the liquid is intensely rich, about 3 minutes.

Store in a covered container in the refrigerator for up to 5 days. You can freeze the mushrooms for up to 1 month, though their texture may suffer upon thawing.

Use in

→ Chicken Livers with Triple-Braised Wild Mushrooms (page 269)

→ Triple-Braised Wild Mushrooms with Quinoa and Pickled Asparagus (at right)

→ Triple-Braised Wild Mushrooms and Garlic-Skin Vinegar (page 196)

→ Triple-Braised Wild Mushroom, Bread, and Butter Soup (page 196)

→ Roasted Eggplant and Braised Mushrooms with Walnut Oil (page 133)

TRIPLE-BRAISED WILD MUSHROOMS WITH QUINOA AND PICKLED ASPARAGUS

For the nimble cook, a dish like this is either the reward for stocking up—or the impetus to do so. All the ingredients should be at room temperature.

FOR EACH SERVING

Arrange ¼ cup of the **Triple-Braised Wild Mushrooms** (opposite) on a plate along with a spear of chopped **Pickled Asparagus** (page 82) and a few slivers of the garlic from the asparagus brine. Scatter a spoonful of **Popcorn Quinoa** (page 329) or lightly toasted walnuts (page 368) or sesame seeds on top, followed by a drizzle of the **mushroom-braising liquid** and a few drops of excellent sesame oil.

Triple-Braised Wild Mushrooms and Garlic-Skin Vinegar

This dish makes a great antipasto, cold or warm. Garlic-Skin Vinegar is more mellow than red wine vinegar. Capers add back some sharpness, and salt and texture as well.

If you don't have the garlic vinegar, make a quick mock-up: Thinly slice 1 small garlic clove and combine it with 1 tablespoon red wine vinegar. Let sit for at least 10 minutes before using.

—⟶ **FOR EACH APPETIZER SERVING**

½ cup **Triple-Braised Wild Mushrooms** (page 194)

1 teaspoon **braising liquid from Triple-Braised Wild Mushrooms**, at room temperature

½ teaspoon **Garlic-Skin Vinegar** (page 23), or see headnote

Freshly ground black pepper

½ teaspoon chopped drained capers

Combine the mushrooms, braising liquid, vinegar, and a grind or two of pepper in a bowl. Let sit for 5 minutes, tossing frequently. Arrange the mushrooms on a plate, top with the capers, and serve.

Triple-Braised Wild Mushroom, Bread, and Butter Soup

I like the contrast of the mushrooms and good chicken stock, and prefer not to use mushroom stock here. The combination of chicken, mushroom, and butter in one bowl is familiar and satisfying.

—⟶ **FOR EACH SERVING**

1 thick slice peasant or sourdough bread, with crust, cut into 1-inch cubes

1 tablespoon excellent olive oil

1 small garlic clove, thinly sliced

½ cup **Triple-Braised Wild Mushrooms** (page 194), thinly sliced or chopped small

¾ cup excellent chicken stock (such as Worth-It Chicken Stock, page 267)

Coarse kosher salt

1 tablespoon cold unsalted butter

Preheat the oven to 400°F. Place the bread cubes on a baking sheet. Bake until evenly browned, about 5 minutes, turning once.

Meanwhile, place the oil in a saucepan over medium-low heat. Add the garlic and cook just to infuse the oil, no more than 1 minute; take care not to let the garlic brown. Add the mushrooms and stir to coat. Turn the heat up to medium, encouraging the mushrooms to brown, about 2 minutes. Add the stock; heat through and taste for salt. Turn off the heat and stir in the butter. Pour into a bowl and top with the toasted croutons. Serve immediately.

ROASTED EGGPLANT & BRAISED MUSHROOMS WITH WALNUT OIL

TRIPLE-BRAISED WILD MUSHROOMS & GARLIC-SKIN VINEGAR

TRIPLE-BRAISED WILD MUSHROOMS WITH QUINOA & PICKLED ASPARAGUS

CHICKEN LIVERS WITH TRIPLE-BRAISED WILD MUSHROOMS

TRIPLE-BRAISED WILD MUSHROOM, BREAD & BUTTER SOUP

TRIPLE-BRAISED WILD MUSHROOMS

STUFFED & SEARED CHICKEN THIGHS

INCOMPARABLY RICH MUSHROOM STOCK

braise

MUSHROOM DUXELLES

mushroom

boil

sauté

steam

WILD MUSHROOMS STEAMED IN THEIR JUICES

CRISP SAUTÉED SHIITAKES

MUSHROOM TOAST

ROASTED SUNCHOKES & STEAMED MUSHROOMS IN BROTH

MUSHROOM RISOTTO WITH NUT STOCK & ROASTED GARLIC

LINGUINE, SHORT RIBS & CRISP SAUTÉED SHIITAKES

FRIED RICE WITH SAUTÉED MUSHROOMS & SWISS CHARD STEMS JAM

Wild Mushrooms Steamed in Their Juices

While the mushrooms steam, their stems—along with garlic and onion—combine to flavor a delicate broth in the pan below. When reduced to a near syrup, the broth turns a bit sweet. I balance this sweetness with celery salt.

makes 2 CUPS

1 pound shiitake mushrooms

1 (1-inch) onion wedge, sliced

1 garlic clove, roughly chopped

Coarse kosher salt

½ teaspoon whole black peppercorns

Pinch of celery salt

Stem the mushrooms and rinse both caps and stems under cold water. Put the stems, onion, and garlic in a medium saucepan. Fit a steamer basket on top and add water until it comes to just below where the steamer sits. Fill the steamer with the mushroom caps, sprinkling them evenly with salt. Turn the heat to high to bring to a quick boil. Cover the pan and turn the heat down so the water simmers. Steam until the mushrooms are quite tender, about 10 minutes.

Carefully lift up the steamer basket and place it on a plate to catch any dripping juices. Add the peppercorns to the saucepan. Turn the heat up to high and boil until the liquid reduces to about ⅓ cup, adding any juices that

dripped from the mushrooms. Taste. It is a delicate stock, but should taste rich, not thin. Continue to reduce until the broth tastes right to you; it is better to store the mushrooms in just a few tablespoons of concentrated broth rather than submerge them in lackluster pot liquid. Once the broth is very flavorful, season it with the celery salt. Place the mushrooms in a serving bowl and strain the broth on top of them. Serve hot or let cool to store.

Store in the refrigerator for up to 5 days. You can freeze the mushrooms in their broth for up to 1 month, though their texture suffers a bit.

Use in

→ Roasted Sunchokes and Steamed Mushrooms in Broth (page 184)

Serve

→ on toast with pecorino, garlic, fresh herbs, and a Poached Egg (page 351)

→ topped with toasted pine nuts alongside blanched peas

Crisp Sautéed Shiitakes

I slice each mushroom into thin strips, giving the caramelizing heat more surfaces to hit.

makes **ABOUT 2 CUPS**

1 pound shiitake mushrooms, stems removed, caps cleaned and dried well

1 tablespoon plus 2 teaspoons grapeseed or canola oil

½ teaspoon coarse kosher salt

Freshly ground black pepper

Cut the shiitake caps into ⅛-inch-wide slices.

Place a large skillet over high heat for 30 seconds. Once hot, add 1 tablespoon of the oil, half of the mushrooms, and ¼ teaspoon of the salt. Stir to coat. Turn the heat down to medium. Let the mushrooms cook undisturbed, so the ones on the bottom begin to brown, about 2 minutes. Use a spatula to stir and release any stuck pieces and give the paler pieces on the top a chance to sear. As they cook, the mushrooms will release, then reabsorb, their own juices. Continue to cook until all the pieces are brown and begin to crisp at the edges, stirring and scraping only as needed to prevent any from burning. This will take 2 to 3 minutes, depending on the meatiness of your mushrooms. If they begin to burn, add a few drops more oil to the pan, scrape any pieces stuck to the bottom, and turn the heat down.

Transfer the cooked mushrooms to a bowl. Turn the heat back up to high for 30 seconds, add the remaining 2 teaspoons oil, the remaining mushrooms, and the remaining ¼ teaspoon salt; repeat the cooking. The second batch of mushrooms will take less time to cook. Combine both batches of mushrooms, season with pepper, and taste for salt. Serve warm or store in a covered container in the refrigerator for up to 7 days. These mushrooms do not freeze well.

Use in

→ Duck Breast, Crisp Sautéed Shiitake, and Scallion Soup (page 272)

→ Fried Rice with Sautéed Mushrooms and Swiss Chard Stems Jam (page 55)

→ Shaved Brussels Sprout and Swiss Chard Slaw (page 116)

Add to

→ linguine, along with bits of leftover Wine-Braised Short Ribs (page 283)

Drizzle with

→ good toasted sesame oil for a stand-alone small plate

Incomparably Rich Mushroom Stock

If reduced properly, patiently, this stock is as rich as the best meat broth. It is nothing like store-bought mushroom stock. You will know what to do with it once you taste it, though sipping it from a mug is a fine idea.

You don't need to use premium dried mushrooms, so long as the mushrooms are unseasoned and mostly intact. You can double the recipe for a greater yield, but expect a longer cooking time to get it to taste as rich.

makes ABOUT 3 CUPS

2 ounces assorted dried mushrooms (look for nice, whole pieces with little dust in the packaging)

8 cups cold water

1½ cups sliced shallots (about 6)

2 garlic cloves, thinly sliced

12 whole black peppercorns

8 fresh thyme sprigs

2 teaspoons coarse kosher salt

Put the mushrooms and water in a medium saucepan over high heat. Bring to a quick boil, cover, and turn the heat down. Simmer for 15 minutes. Add the shallots, garlic, peppercorns, and thyme. Simmer, covered, until the broth is reduced by at least half, to 3 to 4 cups, about 30 minutes. It will darken well past the color of packaged mushroom broth and taste sweet and rich. Strain through a fine-mesh strainer, then pass through a fine-mesh strainer lined with cheesecloth to remove any grit. Season lightly with salt.

Store in the refrigerator for up to 1 week, or in the freezer for up to 3 months.

Mushroom Duxelles

Finely chopped, cooked with butter, garlic, and shallots, then seasoned with nutmeg and sherry, these mushrooms are highly seasoned and have the convenience of a condiment, though they're delicious on their own.

If the mushrooms are particularly dirty, swish them quickly in tepid water. Break off and save the stems; drain the caps on towels, gill side down. Because you will cook the mushrooms until they are completely dry, don't worry about having trapped a bit of water in the caps.

The texture of hand-chopped mushrooms far surpasses those chopped in a food processor, but you can use a processor if you prefer. You'll need to work in batches, and stop if you see the mushrooms forming a paste.

makes 1¼ CUPS

2 shallots, diced

2 tablespoons unsalted butter

1 large garlic clove, minced

12 ounces button mushrooms, including stems, diced

¾ teaspoon coarse kosher salt

Freshly ground black pepper

1 tablespoon dry sherry

¼ teaspoon freshly grated nutmeg

Place the shallots and butter in a large skillet and cook over medium-low heat for 3 minutes, until the shallots absorb most of the butter. Add the garlic and cook until the shallots begin to soften and turn pale yellow, about 5 minutes more.

Stir in the mushrooms and turn the heat up to high. As they cook, the mushrooms will absorb the cooking juices already in the pan, then they will release their own juices back into it. Continue to cook, stirring frequently, until the mushrooms begin to darken and the pan becomes dry, about 5 minutes.

Remove from the heat. While warm, season with the salt, pepper, sherry, and nutmeg.

Refrigerate for up to 5 days or freeze for up to 3 months. Thaw in the refrigerator. Reheat gently to warm.

Add to

⟶ broth with greens and wild rice

⟶ scrambled eggs with fresh herbs and goat cheese

Serve over

⟶ roasted potatoes

Use in

⟶ Stuffed and Seared Chicken Thighs (page 260)

Apples, Oranges, and Lemons

Apples

Apples Roasted with Olive Oil

Roasting is a great way to hold the bushel of apples you brought back from the orchard, or the lackluster ones that have sat too long in your fridge. I don't add sweetener; apples' natural flavors concentrate in the oven's dry heat. They are mind-blowingly good straight from the fridge, but you can warm and serve them with sour cream. Or cut and mix into Wild Rice (page 326) with toasted pecans and onions sautéed in butter. You won't lack ideas for how else to use them.

Wash the apples well before peeling, so you can munch on the peels or make them into a slaw. See page 207 for the best way to slice apples evenly for roasting.

makes **ABOUT 2 CUPS**

1½ pounds (4 medium) fresh firm apples, peeled, cored, and cut into ½-inch-thick slices

2 tablespoons excellent olive oil

¾ teaspoon coarse kosher salt

Preheat the oven to 325°F. Line a baking sheet with parchment paper. Put the apples in a large bowl. Add the oil and toss to coat each slice lightly. Season evenly with the salt. Arrange the slices in neat rows on the baking sheet, not touching. Don't dump the apples directly onto the sheet; you risk pouring on excess olive oil that may have collected at the bottom of the bowl.

Roast until the apples are completely tender but not too soft, 30 to 40 minutes. I like them best when they maintain their light color and don't brown at all in the heat. If they begin to brown, turn down the heat. Caramelization tastes good, but it also dries out the fruit.

Store in a covered container in the refrigerator for up to 5 days.

Save the peels for

→ Apple-Peel Slaw (page 206)

Save the cores for

→ Apple-Core Agrodolce (page 210)

→ Apple-Core Agrodolce Old-Fashioned (page 211)

→ Apple-Core Mostarda (page 211)

→ Apple-Core Mostarda and Gorgonzola Flatbread (page 211)

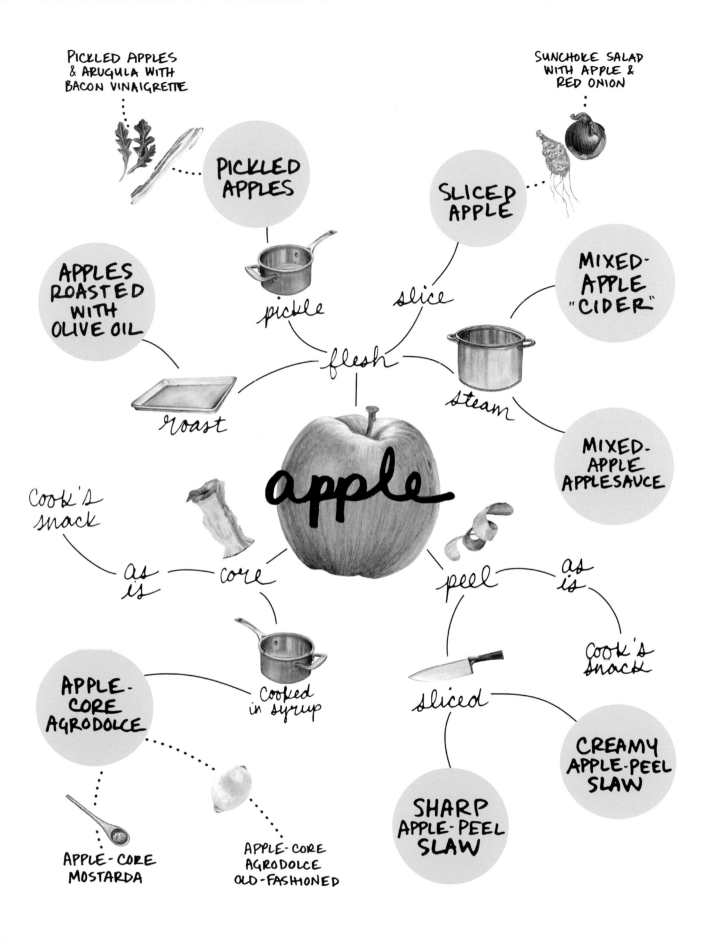

PICKLED APPLES
& ARUGULA WITH
BACON VINAIGRETTE

SUNCHOKE SALAD
WITH APPLE &
RED ONION

PICKLED APPLES

SLICED APPLE

APPLES ROASTED WITH OLIVE OIL

MIXED-APPLE "CIDER"

pickle

slice

flesh

roast

steam

MIXED-APPLE APPLESAUCE

apple

Cook's snack

as is

core

peel

as is

Cooked in syrup

Cook's snack

APPLE-CORE AGRODOLCE

sliced

CREAMY APPLE-PEEL SLAW

SHARP APPLE-PEEL SLAW

APPLE-CORE MOSTARDA

APPLE-CORE AGRODOLCE OLD-FASHIONED

Apple-Peel Slaw, Two Kinds

Any apple peel can work for these, but the skin from a crisp and tart apple, like a Gala, holds up best. These slaw recipes are interchangeable; both are delicious on toast with good cheddar cheese, alongside chicken salad, in a sandwich with grilled sausage, or any place you might serve a more typical cabbage slaw.

makes 2 CUPS

Peels from 3 pounds apples (page 207)

SHARP SLAW

1 tablespoon red wine vinegar

2 tablespoons capers, rinsed and minced

2 teaspoons Dijon mustard

Coarse kosher salt

¼ cup excellent olive oil

½ cup very thinly sliced red onion

CREAMY SLAW

1 large egg yolk

2½ tablespoons capers, rinsed and minced

1 teaspoon red wine vinegar

½ teaspoon Dijon mustard

Coarse kosher salt

¼ cup excellent olive oil

½ cup very thinly sliced red onion

Cut the peels into very thin strips.

To make the sharp slaw: Whisk the vinegar, capers, mustard, and a pinch of salt together in a small bowl. Whisk in the olive oil to make an emulsified dressing. Put the peels and onion in a large bowl and drizzle in the dressing bit by bit. Toss to coat, keeping the slaw light. You may have dressing left over. Taste for salt.

To make the creamy slaw: Whisk the yolk, capers, vinegar, mustard, and a pinch of salt together in a small bowl. Whisk in the oil, a drop at a time, to make a creamy dressing.

Put the peels and onion in a large bowl and drizzle in the dressing bit by bit. Toss to coat, keeping the slaw light. You may have dressing left over. Taste for salt.

Serve either slaw right away, or refrigerate, covered, for up to 2 days. If necessary, retoss with a little of the reserved extra dressing.

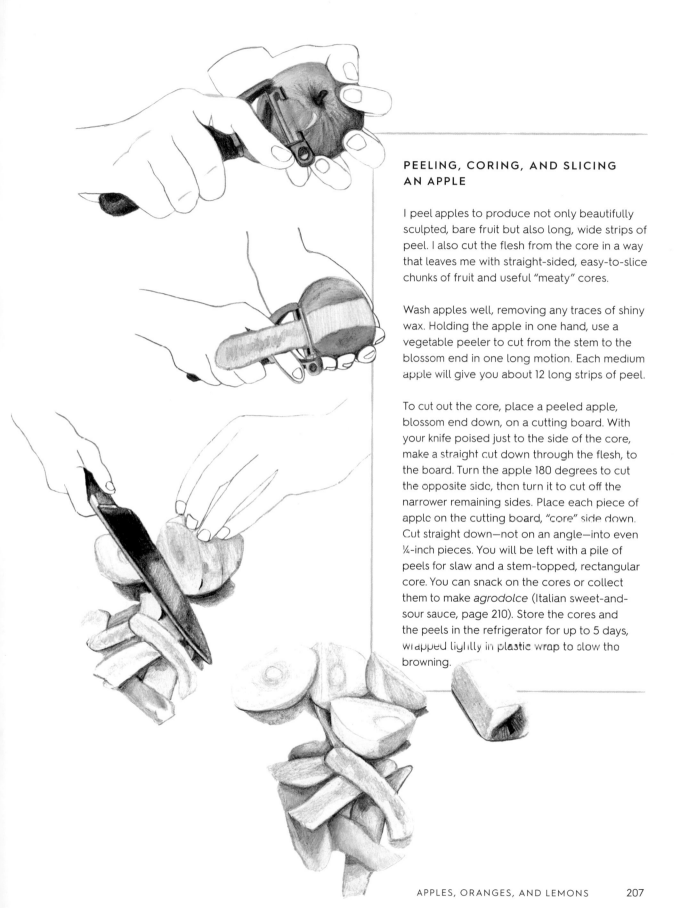

PEELING, CORING, AND SLICING AN APPLE

I peel apples to produce not only beautifully sculpted, bare fruit but also long, wide strips of peel. I also cut the flesh from the core in a way that leaves me with straight-sided, easy-to-slice chunks of fruit and useful "meaty" cores.

Wash apples well, removing any traces of shiny wax. Holding the apple in one hand, use a vegetable peeler to cut from the stem to the blossom end in one long motion. Each medium apple will give you about 12 long strips of peel.

To cut out the core, place a peeled apple, blossom end down, on a cutting board. With your knife poised just to the side of the core, make a straight cut down through the flesh, to the board. Turn the apple 180 degrees to cut the opposite side, then turn it to cut off the narrower remaining sides. Place each piece of apple on the cutting board, "core" side down. Cut straight down—not on an angle—into even ¼-inch pieces. You will be left with a pile of peels for slaw and a stem-topped, rectangular core. You can snack on the cores or collect them to make *agrodolce* (Italian sweet-and-sour sauce, page 210). Store the cores and the peels in the refrigerator for up to 5 days, wrapped lightly in plastic wrap to slow the browning.

Pickled Apples

An adaptation of the pickle brine the late chef Judy Rodgers used for her famous zucchini pickles at Zuni Café, this brine is especially assertive. Rather than dilute it, I simply slice the apples raw and let them pickle in it cold. The slices may pickle just at the edges, but even this is enough. The light pickling is a way for the apples to wear some flavor without losing much of their own. You'll need a little less than 1 cup brine for each medium apple.

I use any kind of apple for this recipe. I like them to be firm, although the softer ones pick up the brine more quickly.

makes ABOUT 4 CUPS APPLES AND ABOUT 2¼ CUPS BRINE

2 cups apple cider vinegar

1 cup sugar

1½ teaspoons powdered mustard

1½ teaspoons yellow mustard seeds (optional)

¾ teaspoon ground turmeric

½ teaspoon ground cumin

3 medium apples, peeled, cored, and cut into ¼-inch-thick slices

Bring the vinegar, sugar, mustard powder and seeds, turmeric, and cumin to a quick boil in a saucepan over high heat. Turn the heat down and simmer for a few minutes to intensify the flavors. Cool the brine completely. Refrigerate to chill.

Put the apple slices in a large bowl or heatproof container. Stir the brine to redistribute the spices, and pour it over the apples. Cover with plastic wrap and press it down on the surface to keep the apples submerged. Refrigerate. The apples will pick up the brine immediately, and will fully pickle after several hours. They will continue to absorb more brine as they sit. Keep refrigerated. They will keep for at least 3 days and up to 1 week if the apples are firm.

Use in

→ Pickled Apples and Arugula with Bacon Vinaigrette (opposite)

Serve with

→ Seared Chicken Livers (page 269)

Pickled Apples and Arugula with Bacon Vinaigrette

Salty, bitter, and sour, this salad is crunchy, chewy, and soft, and cannot be served with meek-flavored dishes. I think it stands best alone as a light lunch or a first course in a meal that includes Creamy Braised Celery (page 90) or Orange-and-Fennel Pulled Pork (page 288). If you must use baby arugula, please chop the apples small, or they will weigh down and overpower the less-flavorful little greens.

⟶ **FOR EACH SERVING**

2 cups arugula (preferably not baby arugula)

1½ teaspoons **Bacon Vinaigrette** (page 296), at room temperature

3 to 5 slices **Pickled Apples** (opposite)

Coarse kosher salt

Toss the arugula with the vinaigrette. Add the pickled apples, season with salt, and serve.

Apple-Core Agrodolce

Agrodolce is an Italian sweet-and-sour sauce, often made with cooked fruit. Agrodolce pairs well with caramelized shallots (page 41), or use it to glaze seared or roasted meats.

makes 1 CUP

10 meaty cores from red apples (page 207; seeds and stems are okay)

⅔ cup sugar

1 bay leaf

1 cup white wine vinegar

⅔ cup water

Put all the ingredients into a small saucepan. The liquid should just cover the apple cores. If it doesn't, choose a smaller pan.

Cover and bring to a boil over high heat. Once the liquid is boiling, turn the heat down to medium-low and simmer, covered, until the cores appear bloated and translucent, 25 to 35 minutes.

Use a fork or tongs to lift the cores out of the liquid, placing them in a strainer over a bowl. Measure the liquid in the saucepan, so you have a gauge for how much longer it should cook. It could take up to 30 minutes to reduce from 2 cups down to 1 cup.

Return the liquid to the saucepan and add any liquid accumulated in the bowl. Turn the heat to low and reduce the liquid, uncovered, until it measures 1 cup.

Return the cores to the syrup and let them cool together. Store together in the refrigerator for up to 2 months. Lift out the cores before using the syrup.

Use in

→ Apple-Core Mostarda (opposite)

→ Apple-Core Agrodolce Old-Fashioned (opposite)

Apple-Core Agrodolce Old-Fashioned

If you like cocktail sours and hard ciders, this is your drink. A bit of bitters prevents it from being too sweet. It's terrific iced or served warm.

⟶ **FOR EACH COCKTAIL**

2 ounces bourbon

1 ounce **strained syrup from Apple-Core Agrodolce** (opposite)

2 dashes of bitters

1 strip of lemon zest, white pith scraped away

Fill a rocks glass with ice. Add the bourbon, agrodolce syrup, and bitters. Stir for 10 seconds. Fold the lemon zest in half to release its oils and rub it around the rim of the glass before dropping it in the drink.

Apple-Core Mostarda

By adding mustard to the near-gelatinous, intensely sweet-and-sour flesh from the cores cooked for agrodolce, I make something delicious out of what would otherwise be trash.

Serve the mostarda with cheeses and cured meats, or spread on bread and pile with bacon and arugula.

⟶ **MAKES ABOUT ½ CUP**

4 cores from **Apple-Core Agrodolce** (opposite), cooled

1 tablespoon whole-grain mustard

Use your fingers to pull off all the flesh from the cores. Chop the flesh roughly. Put in a small bowl and stir in the mustard. Cover and chill. Store in the refrigerator for up to 3 weeks.

APPLE-CORE MOSTARDA AND GORGONZOLA FLATBREAD

Smear a couple of tablespoons of sweet Gorgonzola over warm **Skillet Flatbread** (page 357) or toast. Sprinkle with minced onion and fresh thyme leaves. Dollop with **Apple-Core Mostarda** and sprinkle with flaky sea salt and freshly ground black pepper.

SKILLET FLATBREAD + APPLE-CORE MOSTARDA + Gorgonzola Red onion thyme salt black pepper → APPLE-CORE MOSTARDA & GORGONZOLA FLATBREAD

Mixed-Apple Applesauce and "Cider"

Nimble cooks set out to cook one thing, but take away two.

I started with mixed apples picked from an orchard—Honeycrisp, Empire, Ginger Gold, McIntosh, Gala, Macoun, Braeburn, Red Rome, and Crispin—and cut them, unpeeled, into large chunks (cores and seeds and all), then piled them in a steamer basket over boiling water. Put through a food mill, the applesauce was good. But the magic was what was left in the pot: an astoundingly fragrant "cider" that—because of the variety of apples—was complex like fine sherry.

If you like applesauce on the sweeter side, you can add some sugar or honey after you've pureed it. How much depends entirely on your choice of apples and your taste. Red skins tint the sauce pink; green ones, yellow.

makes 4 CUPS APPLESAUCE AND ABOUT 1 CUP "CIDER"

3 pounds assorted apples, washed well

Place a steamer basket in a large pot. Add water; it should not rise much above the level of the basket. Cut the apples into quarters, or smaller chunks if they are large, and pile into the basket—seeds, stems, peels, and all.

Cover and bring to a boil over high heat. Turn the heat down and simmer until the apples are tender, about 30 minutes. Remove the basket with the apples from the pot and let the apples cool. Taste the cooking water. It will likely taste thin. Simmer over medium-low heat, uncovered, until it is fragrant and a bit syrupy, and reduced almost to 1 cup, about 35 minutes. Pour into a mug to serve immediately or cool to room temperature, then store in a covered container in the refrigerator. The cider is good hot or cold. If you choose not to drink the cider, let it cool and mix it into the applesauce.

Meanwhile, pass the cooked apples through a food mill; discard the peels, seeds, stems, and cores. Cool the applesauce to room temperature. If not serving the cider separately, mix it into the applesauce to taste. Store in a covered container in the refrigerator for up to 1 week, or freeze for up to 2 months.

Oranges

Roasted Orange Slices

Use these thinly sliced caramelized orange slices in salads, especially Arugula, Roasted Orange, Zucchini, and Blue Cheese Salad (page 214); Popcorn Quinoa and Oranges with Fig, Olive, and Walnut Relish (page 330); or just nibble on them as a snack.

makes 1 CUP

1 pound thin-skinned (juice) oranges, scrubbed

1½ tablespoons excellent olive oil

¼ teaspoon coarse kosher salt

1½ tablespoons white wine vinegar

Preheat the oven to 350°F. Line a baking sheet with parchment paper. Cut the oranges into quarters. Remove any seeds. Slice each quarter crosswise into triangles, no more than ⅛ inch thick. Put them in a bowl and toss with the olive oil and salt.

Spill the oranges onto the baking sheet, then spread them with your fingers into a single layer. Roast until they are soft and browning at the edges, about 45 minutes. Remove from the oven, but leave the oven on.

Carefully grab the long sides of the parchment and shake the orange pieces so they fall to the center. Sprinkle the pile of orange slices with the vinegar. Fold the edges of the parchment together several times to make a pouch and carefully tuck the open sides underneath. Roast for another 10 minutes to plump the caramelized slices.

Let the oranges cool inside the parchment pouch. Transfer to a container, scraping in anything left on the parchment, cover, and refrigerate for up to 1 week.

Arugula, Roasted Orange, Zucchini, and Blue Cheese Salad

I love this salad's mix of cooked and raw produce, ripe cheese, and fresh flavors. The assertive vinaigrette amplifies the sweet roasted oranges without silencing the zucchini.

⟶ **FOR EACH MAIN-COURSE SERVING, OR 2 SIDE SALADS**

3 tablespoons **Refrigerator-Door Vinaigrette** (page 383)

2 cups lightly packed arugula

1 teaspoon capers, rinsed and minced

½ cup **Roasted Orange Slices** (page 213)

½ cup thinly sliced height-of-season zucchini

2 ounces blue cheese, crumbled (about ½ cup)

Freshly ground black pepper

Place the vinaigrette in a large bowl. Spread it loosely around the bottom of the bowl with clean fingers. Place the arugula on top and use your fingers to mix the greens lightly, taking care not to bruise the leaves.

Add the capers, oranges, zucchini, cheese, and a few grinds of black pepper. Gently toss, then serve.

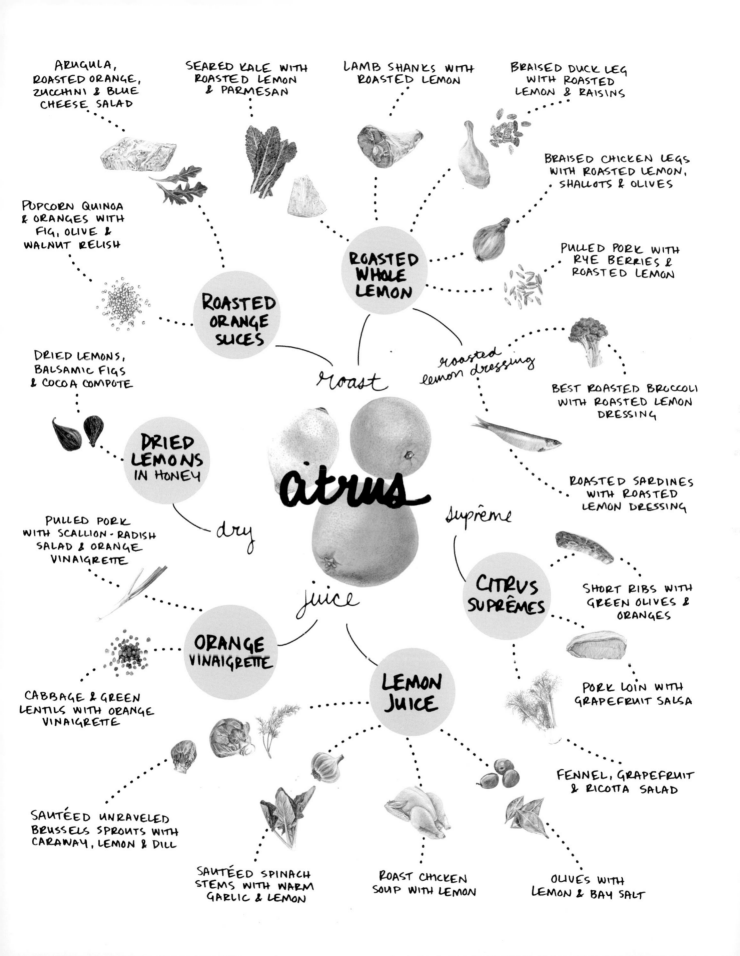

ARUGULA,
ROASTED ORANGE,
ZUCCHINI & BLUE
CHEESE SALAD

SEARED KALE WITH
ROASTED LEMON
& PARMESAN

LAMB SHANKS WITH
ROASTED LEMON

BRAISED DUCK LEG
WITH ROASTED
LEMON & RAISINS

BRAISED CHICKEN LEGS
WITH ROASTED LEMON,
SHALLOTS & OLIVES

POPCORN QUINOA
& ORANGES WITH
FIG, OLIVE &
WALNUT RELISH

ROASTED
WHOLE
LEMON

PULLED PORK WITH
RYE BERRIES &
ROASTED LEMON

ROASTED
ORANGE
SLICES

roasted
lemon dressing

DRIED LEMONS,
BALSAMIC FIGS
& COCOA COMPOTE

roast

BEST ROASTED BROCCOLI
WITH ROASTED LEMON
DRESSING

citrus

DRIED
LEMONS
IN HONEY

ROASTED SARDINES
WITH ROASTED
LEMON DRESSING

suprême

PULLED PORK
WITH SCALLION-RADISH
SALAD & ORANGE
VINAIGRETTE

dry

CITRUS
SUPRÊMES

SHORT RIBS WITH
GREEN OLIVES &
ORANGES

juice

ORANGE
VINAIGRETTE

LEMON
JUICE

PORK LOIN WITH
GRAPEFRUIT SALSA

CABBAGE & GREEN
LENTILS WITH ORANGE
VINAIGRETTE

FENNEL, GRAPEFRUIT
& RICOTTA SALAD

SAUTÉED UNRAVELED
BRUSSELS SPROUTS WITH
CARAWAY, LEMON & DILL

SAUTÉED SPINACH
STEMS WITH WARM
GARLIC & LEMON

ROAST CHICKEN
SOUP WITH LEMON

OLIVES WITH
LEMON & BAY SALT

Orange Vinaigrette

This vinaigrette is sweet, bright, and more intensely flavored than typical citrus sauces. The key is a very slow reduction of freshly squeezed juice, which fortifies the flavor without caramelizing it. If you squeeze your own oranges for juice, you get an extra flavor infusion from the zest. But if you don't want to juice your own fruit, buy a bottle of good fresh orange juice to reduce all at once, without any zest, then freeze the concentrate in suitable portions.

You can use capers instead of green peppercorns, or add a little lemon juice and salt so the vinaigrette isn't too sweet.

makes ABOUT 1¼ CUPS

Grated orange zest (optional, if squeezing your own juice; from about 8 oranges)

2 cups fresh orange juice (from about 8 oranges)

¼ cup champagne vinegar *or* white wine vinegar

2 tablespoons plus 2 teaspoons Dijon mustard

½ cup roughly chopped shallots

1 teaspoon green peppercorns in brine (see headnote)

¼ cup excellent olive oil

Coarse kosher salt

Put the zest, if using, and the juice in a small saucepan and cook at a bare simmer to reduce by half, about 30 minutes. Cool completely.

Put the vinegar, mustard, shallots, and green peppercorns into a blender and puree. Add the reduced orange juice and zest. With the blender running, pour in the olive oil in a thin stream until the dressing is emulsified. Taste if it needs salt.

Store in the refrigerator for up to 3 weeks. Whisk well before using.

Use in

→ Pulled Pork with Scallion-Radish Salad and Orange Vinaigrette (page 289)

→ Cabbage and Green Lentils with Orange Vinaigrette (page 345)

CUTTING AND USING CITRUS SUPRÊMES

Suprêming removes the peel, pith, membranes, and seeds of citrus fruit, leaving only the tender segments and juice. An average-size grapefruit gives you a scant ½ cup suprêmes; an orange yields about ⅓ cup.

1. Lightly trim each end of the fruit to reveal the barest amount of flesh. Place one flat side on a cutting board. Following the contours of the fruit, cut the peel and pith in long strips from top to bottom all around the fruit until you are left with a neatly trimmed ball of citrus flesh.

2. and 2a. Holding the fruit in one hand, and working over a small bowl to catch any juices, slide a sharp paring knife along each side of every membrane, cutting toward the center of the fruit; the segments will release where the cuts meet.

3. When all the segments have been released, squeeze all the juice out of the fruit's pulpy remains. Add the juice to the suprêmes.

Store the suprêmes in their juice for up to 5 days. If you're inclined, you can scrape the bitter pith from the peels so you have only zest; slice thin. Add this to the juice too, or freeze separately for later use.

Use Citrus Suprêmes in

GRAPEFRUIT SUPRÊMES

⟶ Pork Loin with Grapefruit Salsa (page 287)

⟶ Fennel, Grapefruit, and Ricotta Salad (page 109)

ORANGE SUPRÊMES

⟶ Short Ribs with Green Olives and Oranges (page 284)

⟶ a salad with Roasted Radicchio (page 60)

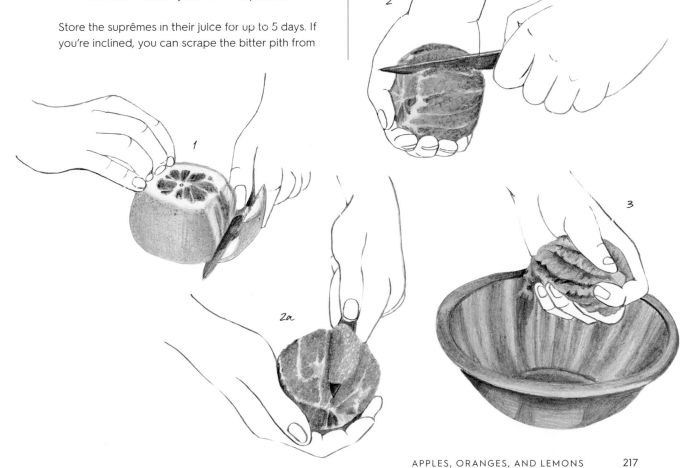

Lemons

starting point

Juiced Lemons

Whenever I have time to think ahead, I save the juice from extra lemon halves so I can always have lemonade on hand. Ice cube trays make neat work of freezing juice in small portions. Collect the frozen juice cubes in freezer bags to store. To save larger amounts of juice for a big batch of lemonade, pour into a pint container and freeze.

SIMPLE SYRUP

To make a generous 1 cup syrup, put ¾ cup water and ¾ cup sugar in a small saucepan over high heat. Bring to a boil, then turn off the heat. Stir to make sure the sugar is completely dissolved; let steep until completely cool. Store in the refrigerator in a closed container for up to 2 months.

exploration

Lemonade for One or More

You can make a "lemonade kit," freezing juice by the cupful (for a pitcher, to serve 6) or a few tablespoons (for a single serving) and keeping Simple Syrup on hand. Use plain syrup or infuse it with herbs (page 71).

—> **FOR EACH SERVING**

   3 tablespoons lemon juice

   3 tablespoons **Simple Syrup** (at left)

   1 cup water

—> **FOR 6 SERVINGS**

   1 cup fresh lemon juice

   1 cup **Simple Syrup**

   5 to 6 cups water

Place the juice and syrup in a glass or pitcher. If the juice is frozen, let it thaw. (To speed things up, you can warm the syrup and pour it over the frozen juice.) Add the water. Mix well and chill. Add ice when you're ready to serve.

Dried Lemons in Honey

Air-dried lemons take on qualities absent in their fresh counterparts: The desiccated white pith loses its bitterness, and the skin takes on both crunch and chewiness. In winter, when indoor heat makes the air extra dry, I place the lemon halves I've juiced cut side up on a rack. After a week, the residual juices turn amber and musky, the pulp shrinks and recedes. Yellow peels tint to orange, spotting brown, and become coarse and leathery, more shell than skin. Unwrapped lemon halves dry nicely perched on a refrigerator shelf too, and without risk of decay. In the refrigerator, they will take about 1½ weeks to dry. After they have dried, you can collect them in a jar and keep them refrigerated until you're ready to use them.

Save the juice for Lemonade (opposite), or anytime you need lemon juice. Steep the dried shells in honey for your next host gift.

6 lemon halves, juiced, then dried (see headnote)

6 allspice berries

1½ pieces star anise

1½ cups honey

6 tablespoons water

Carefully cut the lemon halves into 6 or 8 pieces with a serrated knife. Discard any seeds. Put the lemons in a small saucepan. Add the allspice, star anise, honey, and water. Cover and simmer for 10 minutes over very low heat, until the peels soften. Cool in the pan.

Store in a tightly closed container at room temperature. These will keep for up to 1 year.

Use in

→ Dried Lemon, Balsamic Fig, and Cocoa Compote (page 220)

Serve with

→ cured or braised meats

→ Savory Ricotta Custard (page 386)

→ sharp cheeses

→ ice cream, as a sauce

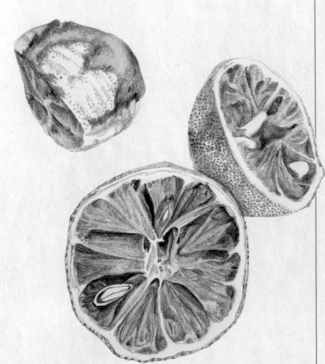

Dried Lemon, Balsamic Fig, and Cocoa Compote

This compote screams for chocolate ice cream, and it's also great served with sharp, hard cheeses or on top of Savory Ricotta Custard (page 386). Or serve it on its own in a demitasse cup, to end a meal. Unsweetened cocoa powder is key to keeping the compote from being cloyingly sweet.

→ **FOR 4 SERVINGS (ABOUT 1 CUP)**

1 cup **Balsamic-Poached Figs** (page 366), drained

2 pieces **Dried Lemons in Honey** (page 219), drained and diced

1 tablespoon or more **honey from Dried Lemons in Honey**

Coarse kosher salt

¼ teaspoon unsweetened cocoa powder

Combine the figs, lemon pieces, honey, and a few pinches of salt in a bowl and toss together well. Let sit for 30 minutes or more so the flavors mellow.

Just before serving, stir again and sprinkle with cocoa powder. The compote is best within a couple of hours, at room temperature.

Roasted Whole Lemons

Roasted whole lemons taste as bright as the sun, as rich as candy, and are to the palate what pastels are to pencils. Unlike preserved lemons, they are not salty, and you can use the entire lemon, not just the peel. They are intensely sour, but still acidic in one soft, delicious bite. Pair these lemons with salty ingredients (olives, capers, cheese), acidic ones (tomatoes and grapefruit), and sweet things (dates, shrimp). Or, rinse and dip in chocolate.

Roasting whole citrus requires nothing more than a pinch of salt, a shallot—which caramelizes and tames the pith's bitterness—a heavy lidded pot, and a bit of water.

Meyer lemons are well suited to roasting whole. However, this recipe succeeds with any lemon.

makes **2 CUPS**

2 pounds small lemons (preferably Meyer), stems removed, scrubbed, cut almost in half across the middle, exposed seeds discarded

2 large shallots, thinly sliced

½ cup water

2 pinches of coarse kosher salt

Preheat the oven to 375°F. Put the lemons, shallots, water, and salt into a Dutch oven or other snug-fitting, heavy-bottomed ovenproof pot with a tight-fitting lid. Cover, place in the oven, and roast for 1½ hours. Peek inside: The liquid in the pot will have taken on a golden hue and thickened slightly, the lemons will have begun to collapse, and the shallot will have melted into the liquid. Use tongs to grab a piece of a lemon and wipe down the glazed juices on the sides of the pot. Cover again and return to the oven.

Check every 15 minutes, stirring gently to coat the lemons with the sauce. Remove from the oven when the white pith of the lemons is completely translucent and the juices have turned syrupy and caramel brown. If the juices get too dark, turn the oven temperature down to 300°F to finish cooking. Remove from the oven and let cool.

Once the roasted lemons are cool, store them in the refrigerator for up to 1 month or in the freezer for up to 3 months.

Use in

⟶ Roasted Lemon Dressing (at right)

⟶ Seared Kale with Roasted Lemon and Parmesan (page 51)

⟶ Braised Chicken Legs with Roasted Lemon, Shallots, and Olives (page 258)

⟶ Pulled Pork with Rye Berries and Roasted Lemon (page 290)

exploration

Roasted Lemon Dressing

This bold dressing is sharp and sweet. Pair it with bitter greens or gamey meat.

⟶ **MAKES ABOUT 1 CUP**

¼ cup finely chopped **Roasted Whole Lemons** (opposite)

¼ cup golden raisins, finely chopped

2 tablespoons minced red onion

1 teaspoon coarse kosher salt

2 tablespoons sherry vinegar

Leaves from a few sprigs fresh thyme

½ cup excellent olive oil

Combine the lemon, raisins, onion, salt, and vinegar in a small bowl. Let macerate for 15 minutes. Add the thyme and mix well. Add the olive oil, whisking it in a little at a time. Let the vinaigrette sit for another 30 minutes before serving.

It will keep for weeks, refrigerated. Whisk again before using.

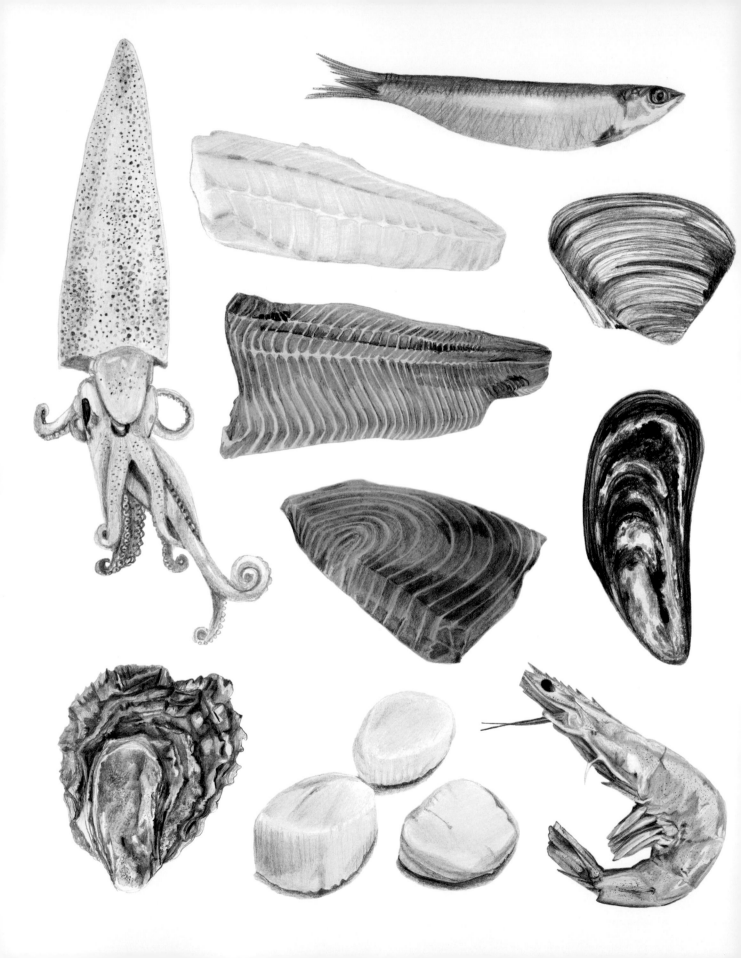

Fish and Shellfish

SERVING RAW FISH AND SHELLFISH

You can serve many fish and shellfish raw when you trust that they are exceedingly fresh. Thinly slice and arrange on a plate, or cut in small bites or large chunks for a small bowl. The thinner the slices, the lighter the dressing should be. The thicker the slices or richer the fish, the more dressing they can take.

Here are some combinations to get you started.

→ Sliced scallops with Scallion-Sesame Magic Mix (page 40) or Many-Herb Salad (page 64)

→ Small chunks of tuna with Parsley Vinaigrette (made with lemon; page 69)

→ Oysters with Wine-Pickled Garlic and Dill (page 25)

→ Sliced sea bass with lemon and Bay Salt (page 374)

→ Sliced salmon with Refrigerator-Door Vinaigrette (page 383)

→ Clams with Garlic-Skin Vinegar (page 23)

Perfectly Poached Fish or Scallops

Poached fish is easy to cook. Salting the poaching broth enough to season the fish will make the broth too salty to reduce for a sauce. Instead, I salt the fish in advance and allow it to cure for at least 30 minutes before cooking. Curing fish this way provides a broth worth saving. The amount of salt I call for will seem like a lot, but it is what you need to season the fish throughout—especially important if you serve it cold. Whether you poach one fillet or ten, keep the ratio of fish to salt the same (8 ounces fish to 1¼ teaspoons salt), and use only as much broth as you need to cover them by 1 inch. If you don't have Quick Poaching Broth on hand, you can make it first in the pan you'll use to cook the fish, and store any extra cooled broth in the freezer.

Leaving the skin on fish to poach helps keep the flesh intact. After cooking, remove it. You can stockpile skins in the freezer, first scraping off the fat from the underside with the back of a knife and laying them flat between layers of plastic wrap.

Poached fish always shines under a squeeze of lemon, but sometimes the richest pairings, including Whole-Grain Mustard Aioli (page 381), are the best.

makes **4 SERVINGS**

4 (8-ounce) skin-on fish fillets (such as halibut or king salmon) *or* 2 pounds large (2-ounce) dry-packed scallops, tough side muscle removed

3½ to 4 cups Quick Poaching Broth (page 360)

5 teaspoons coarse kosher salt

The right size pan makes all the difference, since you want to make sure you use enough broth to submerge the fish, but no more than you need. Put the fillets or scallops in a single layer in the smallest possible skillet with a tight-fitting lid. Pour in enough cold broth to cover the fish, ideally by ½ inch. Lift out the fish and place on a double-thick layer of paper towels. Leave the broth in the pan.

Pat the fish very dry with the paper towels and season all over with the salt. Use it all, and pay particular attention to the thicker parts of the fillets, including the sides. No need to salt the skin side. Let sit at room temperature for at least 30 minutes. (*You can salt the fish and refrigerate it up to 4 hours ahead; remove from the refrigerator 30 minutes before poaching.*)

Bring the poaching broth to a quick boil over high heat. Once it boils, turn the heat down to very low to let the simmer completely subside. Submerge the fish in the broth, skin side down. Cover with the lid. Keep the heat very low, and never let the broth more than quake at the surface—you can peek in if you need to. (A heat diffuser comes in handy for this.) If the heat isn't low enough, turn it off, then turn it back on only if the broth cools too much. (Stick a finger in after 5 minutes; it's good if it's still too hot to touch!) The fish will cook beautifully, though it may need a minute more.

As it poaches, the outside of the fish turns opaque; the once-glossy flesh fades to matte. The broth gently penetrates the fish until it breaks into large flakes. A 1-inch-thick 8-ounce fillet will take 5 to 6 minutes to poach to medium-rare; a large, 2-ounce scallop, about 3 minutes. To check the fish: Use a slotted spatula to lift the fillet out of the poaching broth. Use your fingers (it's hot, I know) or a pair of tongs to gently squeeze the sides of the fillet. If it separates easily into large flakes, it is done. To check the scallops: Rely on the timing rather than texture; aim for them to remain translucent in the center, a bit underdone on the inside. Remember that they will continue to cook as they rest off the heat.

With your fingers or the help of a small knife or thin spatula, peel off the skin of the fillets (see headnote) and set aside. Sometimes, there's a brown fatty layer left behind—scrape this off and discard. Serve the fish warm or at room temperature. Or cool, then cover and refrigerate it to serve cold. It will keep for 2 days.

Strain the poaching broth and, if not using right away, freeze for up to 3 months. You cannot reuse the broth to poach more fish, but you can strain and reduce it to a rich demi-glace (opposite). If you want to serve it over warm fish, tightly cover the just-poached fish while the broth cooks down to a sauce.

explorations

Crispy Fish Skin

Fish skin—crisp, crackly, salty—is a happy reward for poaching fish. Freeze scraped uncrisped fish skin, laid flat between pieces of wax paper or parchment paper, in a freezer bag. Thaw in the refrigerator before using.

→ **MAKES 4 CRISP SKINS**

4 pieces **skin from Perfectly Poached Fish (page 225)**

Coarse kosher salt

Preheat the oven to 275°F. Lightly oil a wire rack and set it on a baking sheet. If you haven't already done so, use the dull side of a small knife to carefully but diligently scrape all fat from the underside of the skin. This will make it nearly translucent.

Carefully lay the skins on the rack. Bake until crisp and lightly browned, 20 to 30 minutes. Sprinkle with salt to taste while still warm. Let cool to crisp fully before serving.

You can refrigerate the crisped skin, covered, in an airtight container for up to 2 days. If it softens, recrisp it in a 300°F oven for about 10 minutes.

Use as a topping for

→ A Single Deviled Egg (page 350)

→ Roasted Asparagus (page 80), doused with lemon

→ salad greens (arugula, spinach, watercress)

→ Poached Chicken Breasts (page 264)

→ plain or sticky rice

→ cooked eggs

Fish Demi-Glace and Butter Sauce

Beurre blanc is a silky sauce traditionally made by cautiously whisking cold butter into a concentrate of shallots and wine. Instead of wine, here I use the leftover fish poaching broth—now a rich brew—fortified not just with wine, but with lemon, herbs, and fish oils. Without the butter, the demi-glace is salty, robust, and delicious. With butter added, it's creamy and complex. Since the poaching liquid takes at least 20 minutes to reduce, if you want to serve either the demi-glace or butter sauce with the just-poached fish, you'll need to cover the fish tightly to keep it warm while the broth reduces.

You can also make the demi-glace in the same pan in which you cooked the fish, but strain the broth before reducing it.

$\longrightarrow$ **MAKES 2 TABLESPOONS DEMI-GLACE,
½ CUP BUTTER SAUCE**

2 cups broth from Perfectly Poached Fish (page 225), strained

8 tablespoons (1 stick) cold unsalted butter, cut into 8 pieces

Coarse kosher salt

For the demi-glace: Put the broth in a small saucepan and simmer over medium-low heat until it is reduced to just 2 tablespoons, about 20 minutes. You can freeze the demi-glace for up to 1 month. Reheat in a small saucepan before adding the butter to make the butter sauce.

For the butter sauce: After the broth has reduced, turn the heat down to very low and whisk in the cold butter, one piece at a time, to turn the sauce creamy. Season with salt, if necessary.

Serve immediately. Or transfer to a small bowl, cover, and refrigerate for up to 3 days. Freeze the butter sauce for up to 1 month. Once chilled, the butter sauce cannot be remelted. Use as a spread instead.

Use the demi-glace

$\longrightarrow$ Whisk into Whole-Grain Mustard Aïoli (page 381) or just whole-grain mustard, and serve it alongside the chilled fish

$\longrightarrow$ Mix into rice vermicelli and flake hot or cold fish on top

Use the butter sauce

$\longrightarrow$ Toss with warm Roasted Broccoli Rabe (page 103)

$\longrightarrow$ Chill and spread on grilled bread

Poached Shrimp

Poached shrimp are usually served cold, but they are outstanding warm. Despite convention, I don't clobber them with cocktail sauce. Instead I prefer to sprinkle them with a pinch of Bay Salt (page 374) and freshly ground white pepper. But should you want a sauce on the side, you can reduce the poaching liquid to a robust glaze and mix with softened butter, mayonnaise, or Whole-Grain Mustard Aioli (page 381). Or pile Spicy Lemon-Onion Slaw (page 36) on top.

Choose head-on shrimp if you can get them.

It's easy to poach a large amount of shrimp at a time. Follow the proportions of shrimp to salt and use only as much broth as you need to completely submerge the shrimp and allow them to move freely in the pot as they cook. The poaching broth is quick to make, if you don't have any on hand.

makes 4 SERVINGS, 4 TO 5 SHRIMP PER SERVING

1 pound large (16–20 count) shrimp, peeled (preferably leaving the tail attached) and deveined

1½ teaspoons coarse kosher salt

About 2 cups Quick Poaching Broth (page 360)

Pat the shrimp dry and toss them with the salt, making sure to season inside the cut where you cleaned out the vein. Let them quick-cure for 15 minutes at room temperature.

Bring the broth to a boil in a medium covered saucepan. If you are serving the shrimp cold, set up a bowl of generously salted ice water. Taste the ice water to be sure.

Once the broth comes to a boil, turn off the heat, add the shrimp, and cover the pan. Check after 3 minutes. If a shrimp is opaque in the center, it's done. If not, cover and poach for another minute. Once they're cooked, lift the shrimp out with a slotted spoon. Serve immediately. Or plunge into the ice bath to cool completely. Drain well. Serve cold, or store in the refrigerator in a covered container, lined with a paper towel, for up to 2 days.

Poached or Sautéed Shrimp with Peaches, Arugula, and Walnut Oil

This salad is fresh, herbal, and light, but not timid. However you prepare the shrimp—poached as on the opposite page or cooked quickly in oil as described here—they taste super sweet with height-of-season peaches. This can be scaled up easily for a crowd, but wait until right before serving to mix the ingredients together.

⟶ **FOR EACH SERVING**

½ cup thinly sliced red onion

Loosely packed ½ cup thinly **Shaved Fennel** (page 109)

1 cup thinly sliced peach or nectarine

1 tablespoon plus ½ teaspoon walnut oil, plus more if needed

½ teaspoon flaky sea salt, plus more for the shrimp and salad, if needed

1 teaspoon excellent olive oil (if sautéing the shrimp)

3 extra-large (16–20 count) shrimp, peeled and deveined, or cold **Poached Shrimp** (opposite)

Squeeze of lemon, plus more if needed

1 tablespoon loosely packed fresh tarragon leaves

Loosely packed ½ cup arugula

Toss the onion, fennel, peach, walnut oil, and salt together; let the salad marinate at room temperature for 10 minutes.

To sauté the shrimp: Heat a skillet over medium-high heat. Add the olive oil and cook the shrimp until just opaque in the middle, turning once, about 4 minutes total. Season with a bit of salt and the lemon juice.

Cut the sautéed or poached shrimp into ½-inch pieces.

Just before serving, toss the shrimp into the salad, add the tarragon and arugula, and toss lightly.

If necessary, adjust the flavors of the salad with a squeeze of lemon juice, a pinch of salt, and/or more walnut oil.

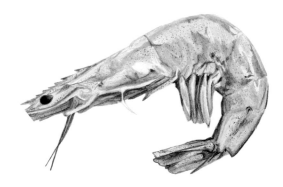

Wine-and-Tomato-Braised Squid

Serve this classic slow-cooked tomatoey squid stew with Rustic Polenta (page 314) or Butter-Braised Potatoes (page 180). Use it as a sauce for other shellfish, as in the Quick Shellfish Stew (opposite). Combine it with eggplant—great to serve over grilled toast. Use either red or white wine; they are interchangeable here.

makes 4 SERVINGS

¼ cup excellent olive oil

2½ cups thinly sliced onions

4 large garlic cloves, thinly sliced

2 teaspoons or more coarse kosher salt, plus more if necessary

½ cup dry red or white wine

1 (28-ounce) can whole tomatoes

4 fresh oregano sprigs

Zest of 2 lemons, removed in strips with a sharp peeler and scraped of white pith

2 pounds cleaned squid, tentacles halved lengthwise, bodies cut crosswise into ½-inch rings

Juice of ½ lemon, or more

Place the oil, onions, and garlic in a large saucepan over medium heat. Stir in the salt. Cook until the onion and garlic begin to soften, about 5 minutes. Add the wine. Simmer until almost completely evaporated, about 3 minutes.

Use your hands to crush the tomatoes directly into the pan. Pour in their juices, then add the oregano, lemon zest, and squid. Stir and bring to a simmer. Cover and cook until the squid is as tender as firm tofu, about 30 minutes. Taste the sauce; if it seems thin, remove the squid with a slotted spoon, then reduce the sauce until robust. You should have about 1½ cups sauce. Add the squid back to the sauce.

Finish with lemon juice and, if necessary, salt, to make the sauce more savory than sweet. Serve, store in the refrigerator for up to 5 days, or freeze for up to 3 months.

Squid and Eggplant Caponata

Like Italian vegetable caponata, this dish has distinct, sharp Sicilian flavors deepened by cumin, courtesy of the roasted eggplant. Serve warm or at room temperature with grilled bread to sop up all the sauce.

—> **FOR EACH SERVING**

½ cup **Cumin-Roasted Eggplant** (page 131), cut into 1-inch pieces, warm or at room temperature

½ cup **Wine-and-Tomato-Braised Squid** (opposite), warm or at room temperature

½ teaspoon red wine vinegar

2½ tablespoons excellent olive oil

1 teaspoon finely chopped drained capers

Fold the eggplant and squid together in a bowl. Drizzle with the vinegar, 2 tablespoons of the oil, and the capers.

Transfer to a plate, drizzle with the remaining ½ tablespoon oil, and serve.

Quick Shellfish Stew

A small portion of leftover braised squid justifies a run to the fish market for mussels—and when you want to feed a crowd, this dish scales up with little effort and time. You can substitute canned white beans for those you cook at home, adding a minced small garlic clove to the pot and a drizzle of red wine vinegar along with the lemon juice at the end.

—> **FOR EACH SERVING**

½ pound (about 20) mussels in the shell, cleaned (page 233)

1 cup **Wine-and-Tomato-Braised Squid** (opposite)

½ cup **White Beans with Garlic and Vinegar** (page 342), or see headnote

½ cup water

4 teaspoons fresh lemon juice

Coarse kosher salt

Combine the mussels, braised squid, beans, and water in a large saucepan. Cover and turn the heat to high. Shake the pan intermittently to jostle the mussels as they cook. Start checking at 3 minutes and remove from the heat as soon as the mussels steam open. Discard any that don't open.

Add the lemon juice and taste for salt. Serve immediately.

Steamed Mussels

Fresh herbs, seasoned butters, and cream make fine flavorings for steamed mussels. Potatoes or bread turn them into a meal.

Keep the proportion of wine to mussels the same and you'll easily riff on this basic recipe. If you like, add 3 tablespoons Refrigerator-Door Vinaigrette (page 383) after the mussels are steamed open; omit the salt. Toss in a handful of toasted bread crumbs (page 355) and serve warm.

You can also serve the mussels out of their shells. Once the mussels are cool enough to handle, pull the meat from the shells with your fingers.

for **EACH SERVING (ABOUT ¾ CUP SHUCKED MUSSELS)**

1½ pounds large mussels, cleaned (opposite)

3 tablespoons crisp white wine

3 tablespoons unsalted butter or Herb-Infused Butter (page 377)

¼ teaspoon coarse kosher salt

1 tablespoon chopped fresh herbs

Place the mussels, wine, and butter in a large pan with a lid. Turn the heat to high and cover. With one hand on the lid and the other on the handle, shake the pan back and forth over the heat for about 30 seconds. The mussels will begin to open. Continue to steam until all the shells open and the meat turns bright coral, 2 to 3 minutes more. Discard any mussels whose shells remain closed.

Season the broth with salt and add the herbs. Place the mussels and broth in a serving bowl and serve.

You can store shucked mussel meats in their broth in a covered container in the refrigerator for up to 1 day. Or you can freeze the meats in the cooled broth for up to 1 month. Thaw in the refrigerator before using.

USING SHUCKED MUSSELS

→ Grill a thick piece of bread. Rub the bread with garlic, then drizzle with mussel broth and a light squeeze of lemon. Toss the shucked mussels with a tangy mayonnaise, such as **Whole-Grain Mustard Aioli** (page 381), and pile on top.

→ Marinate the shucked mussels with **Cucumber-Peel Kimchi** (page 130) for a cold salad.

→ Combine the mussels and broth with roughly chopped **Boiled Potatoes** (page 175) and fresh herbs for a quick, delicious soup.

CHOOSING AND CLEANING MUSSELS AND CLAMS

Look for fresh shellfish without chips or cracks in their shells.

If you can, avoid buying shellfish in bulk bags, where you can't inspect the innermost pieces.

Search out large rope-grown mussels, such as blue mussels, and choose larger rather than smaller clams.

Wild or farmed, all mussels and clams need to be washed thoroughly, their shells wiped with a clean sponge under cold running water, to rinse any sand or grime.

Pull off the beard, the stringy, mossy part that peeks out of the inner crevice of each mussel. Some retail markets remove this beard before selling.

Large clams, such as cherrystones, often hold a good deal of sand in their shells; soaking them in cold salty water for an hour helps them discharge it: Place the clams in a large bowl with cold water to cover; add 3 tablespoons salt for every quart of water. Swish the clams around a few times, then let rest for 30 minutes. The water will turn murky as the clams expel their sand. Repeat this purging once more. Once they're clean, store the clams on ice, uncovered, until you're ready to cook them. If you want to avoid all grit in steamed clams, you should have cheesecloth on hand to strain the juices.

Mussels with Anchovy Butter

If you don't have Anchovy Butter on hand, slip a minced anchovy and 2 tablespoons of butter into the pan.

→ **FOR EACH SERVING**

1 pound large mussels, cleaned (at left)

2 tablespoons dry white wine

2 tablespoons **Anchovy Butter** (page 378), or see headnote

3 tablespoons **Toasted Bread Crumbs** (page 355)

2 tablespoons roughly chopped fresh flat-leaf parsley

Place the mussels, wine, and butter in a large saucepan. Turn the heat to high and cover. With one hand on the lid and the other on the handle, shake the pan back and forth over the heat for about 30 seconds. The mussels will begin to open. Continue to steam until all the shells open and the meat turns bright coral, 2 to 3 minutes more. Discard any mussels that remain closed.

Place the mussels and broth in a serving bowl. Sprinkle with the bread crumbs and parsley and serve.

Serve with

→ Salt-Roasted Little Potatoes (page 178)

→ Roasted Sunchokes (page 183)

→ Confit Tomatoes (page 148)

Mussels with Braised Fennel and Hazelnut Cream

This dish is an outstanding upgrade on classic mussels with wine and cream. The fragrant fennel broth stands in for wine, and Nut Cream for plain.

If you want to double this recipe but do not have a large enough pan to accommodate the full batch of mussels, you can warm the fennel in the pan first, then divide it between the serving bowls and steam the mussels in batches afterward.

—→ **FOR EACH MAIN-COURSE SERVING OR 2 APPETIZER SERVINGS**

1 tablespoon excellent olive oil

1 cup **Braised Fennel** (page 110), cut into ½-inch pieces

1 pound mussels, cleaned (page 233)

1 cup **broth from Braised Fennel**

1½ teaspoons chopped fresh tarragon or dill

Pinch of freshly ground white pepper

1 tablespoon **Nut Cream** (page 369) made with hazelnuts, *or* heavy cream

Place the oil in a large skillet with a lid. Turn the heat to high and add the fennel. Cook for 1 minute.

Add the mussels and cover. With one hand on the lid and the other on the handle, shake the pan back and forth over the heat for about 30 seconds. The mussels will begin to open up. Once they have mostly opened, remove the lid and add the fennel broth, tarragon, and pepper.

Cook for another minute, allowing the broth to reduce and the mussels to finish cooking. When the mussels are done, they will open fully and their meat will turn coral. Discard any that remain closed. Stir in the nut cream. Transfer to a serving bowl or bowls and serve.

Mussels Kimchi

Mussels taken out of their shells and marinated in Cucumber-Peel Kimchi recall a traditional seaweed salad. Serve this chilled, alongside a bowl of steamed rice with Scallion-Sesame Magic Mix (page 40), or on its own as a shared starter to a meal with Whole Roasted Fish (page 246). This is a great use for a few leftover mussels, and it's also a good excuse to buy more mussels than you need, saving any extra cooked mussels for this salad. The yield of mussel meat will vary. By my measurement, 1 pound mussels yields about ½ cup mussel meats.

—→ **FOR EACH SERVING**

½ cup shucked **Steamed Mussels** (page 232)

¼ cup **Cucumber-Peel Kimchi** (page 130)

Toss the mussels and kimchi together. Cover and refrigerate for at least 6 hours, or ideally overnight. Toss once again before serving.

CUCUMBER-PEEL KIMCHI + mussels

↓

MUSSELS KIMCHI

Steamed Cherrystone Clams

Cherrystone clams are meaty, briny, and most satisfying for a meal, but they can be full of sand. Leave yourself an hour to soak and clean them, as described on page 233. They release acutely salty brine, so you only need to use a portion of it for a sauce. If using other clams, taste the broth for salinity.

To steam, you'll need a medium saucepan with a lid, a strainer, and cheesecloth. If you don't have cheesecloth, use a soaked and squeezed-dry coffee filter or non-bleached paper towels.

for **EACH SERVING**

1 tablespoon excellent olive oil

2 garlic cloves, thinly sliced

¼ cup dry white wine

12 cherrystone clams, cleaned (page 233)

4 tablespoons (½ stick) unsalted butter

2 pinches freshly ground white pepper

Grated zest of 1 lemon

1 teaspoon fresh lemon juice

2 tablespoons chopped assorted fresh herbs (such as oregano, parsley, thyme, sage, cilantro, and mint)

Set a fine-mesh strainer over a heatproof measuring cup; line the strainer with cheesecloth.

Heat the oil in a medium saucepan over low heat. Add the garlic and cook until translucent, about 5 minutes. Turn the heat up to high and add the wine and clams. Cover and steam, shaking the pan intermittently, until the clams have mostly all opened, about 8 minutes.

Use a slotted spoon or tongs to lift the opened clams out of the broth and place in a serving bowl. Cover the pan again and steam any unopened clams another minute or two. If they haven't opened by then, toss them out.

Pour the broth through the cheesecloth into the measuring cup. Rinse any grit out of the pan. Return ¼ cup of the broth to the pan. (If you don't have enough broth, top it off with water.) Turn the heat to medium and add the butter, pepper, and lemon zest. Cook for 1 minute, then turn off the heat and add the lemon juice and herbs. Taste. Add the clams back to the pan just to rewarm. Serve.

Remove clams from their shells and serve on

→ thick slices of grilled buttered bread, with some of the broth

Add to

→ Sausage-and-Any-Bean Soup (page 343), with some of the broth

→ From-Scratch "Two-Minute" Risotto (page 322), with a little of the broth for the rice

Seared Fish Fillets with Brown Butter

A fish fillet with moist flesh and crisp skin, paired with an impossibly good, quick classic pan sauce.

Allow 30 minutes for the fish to cure with salt before searing. Not only does it season the fish, but it gives time for the fish to come to the ideal temperature for cooking. Use this recipe as a guide to cook any number of fillets, including one just for yourself. Keep the proportions of ingredients the same and adjust the pan size accordingly. Note the size fillets you have, so you can salt and cook them accurately: For every 8 ounces fish, use 1¼ teaspoons salt.

When buying fish fillets, look for those that appear plump but not waterlogged, and whose flesh is taut and intact, not flaking apart.

makes 4 SERVINGS

4 (8-ounce) skin-on fish fillets

5 teaspoons coarse kosher salt

Grapeseed or canola oil

8 tablespoons (1 stick) unsalted butter, cut into pieces

4 teaspoons spice seeds (such as coriander, cumin, or caraway), crushed, *and/or* 4 teaspoons chopped fresh herbs (such as thyme or oregano), *or* 4 teaspoons chopped rinsed cornichons, *or* 4 teaspoons **Refrigerator-Door "Salt"** (page 382)

Preheat the oven to 400°F. Note the thickness of the fillets. This will come in handy for timing. Place the fish, skin side down, on a plate and season each fillet with 1 teaspoon of the salt, paying particular attention to the thicker parts, including the sides of the fillets. Let the fish sit at room temperature to cure for

20 minutes; let fillets thicker than 2 inches sit for 30 minutes.

Searing demands high heat and totally dry skin. After the fillets rest, wrap each one in a paper towel to dry the flesh, then scrape the skin with the back of a knife to "squeegee" tucked-away moisture. Again, pat the entire fillet very dry. Right before you're ready to cook, season just the skin side of each fillet with ¼ teaspoon salt.

Heat a large, heavy ovenproof skillet over high heat for a full minute. Add just enough oil to coat the pan lightly but evenly. The oil should heat through immediately and, with a couple of tilts, run loosely across the pan.

Gently lay the fish in the pan, skin side down. It will sizzle loudly. Give the pan a little tug; if it is hot enough, the fillet should unstick itself. If it doesn't, just leave the fillet in place to cook. As it sears, the skin may begin to retract, which makes the fillets buckle upward. When this happens, press down gently on the top of the fish with a spatula to connect all the skin to the hot pan (otherwise, you'll just crisp the edges), then remove the spatula; the fish should now be flat.

Turn the heat down to medium, letting the fillets sear, undisturbed, until the edges of the skin begin to look brown and crisp. The fish skin may render a good deal of fat. As it accumulates, carefully pour or spoon off the fat and discard. Lift up and peek underneath the fish to make sure the entire skin side is crisp. Only after it is completely crisp, about 5 minutes, place the pan in the oven, without turning the fish over, to finish cooking, another 5 minutes per inch of thickness. Thinner tail-end pieces will take less time.

The fish is done when it is opaque and flakes easily when you gently squeeze it from the sides. It may still be a bit translucent inside.

Remove the pan from the oven and carefully pour out any excess fat. Place the pan over low heat. Add the butter and the spices, herbs, and/or other flavorings to the pan. The butter will melt and begin to brown immediately. Remembering that the pan handle is very hot, carefully tilt the pan toward you so the butter pools and the fish is not sitting over the direct heat. While the pan is tilted, use a large spoon to continuously baste the fish with the melted butter, being careful not to let the butter turn too dark, for about 30 seconds.

Use a spatula to transfer each fillet, skin side up, to a plate. Spoon on the browned butter and serve.

SEARING FISH STEAKS AND SCALLOPS

The proportion of salt to fish for searing fish steaks and scallops is the same as for skin-on fillets—1 teaspoon salt per 8 ounces fish—but the technique is slightly different. Choose thicker 8-ounce steaks and larger 2-ounce dry-packed scallops, which allow more time to sear without overcooking. You'll need 4 large scallops per serving.

Heat a heavy skillet over high heat for a full minute. Add just enough oil to coat the pan lightly but evenly. The oil should heat through immediately, and with a couple of tilts run loosely across the pan.

Season the steaks or scallops (tough side muscle removed) all over with salt. Unlike with skin-on fillets, you do not need to let them cure—I like the difference in flavor between the salty edges and sweeter interior that you get from cooking fish steaks right away.

Place the steaks or scallops in the pan (do not crowd) and cook undisturbed until the underside is brown and the flesh turns opaque no more than one-third of the way up the sides. Then turn over and sear the other side. Add a drizzle of oil to the pan if it appears dry.

Serve as is. Or, to make a pan sauce as for Seared Fish Fillets with Brown Butter, add the butter and spice and baste off the heat until the butter melts and browns, about 30 seconds.

Seared Sea Bass with Creamy Brown Butter and Julienned Celeriac

The addition of egg yolk to brown butter helps this sauce cling not only to the fish but also to the accompanying celeriac. Don't let the equipment setup deter you; it's an extraordinary dish, and once you're organized, easy to make and adjust to as few or as many fillets as you have.

⟶ **FOR 4 SERVINGS**

4 cups **Julienned Celeriac** (page 168), salted

2 tablespoons plus 2 teaspoons rice vinegar

5 teaspoons coarse kosher salt

4 (8-ounce) skin-on sea bass fillets

Grapeseed or canola oil

10 tablespoons (1¼ sticks) unsalted butter, cut into pieces

4 teaspoons caraway seeds

4 large egg yolks

Put the celeriac in a bowl and toss with the vinegar. Set aside.

Preheat the oven to 400°F. Use the salt to cure the fish as directed on page 238. Sear the fillets as directed, finishing with the butter and caraway seeds. Set a heatproof measuring cup near the stove; it will hold the hot brown butter from the pan.

Meanwhile, place the egg yolks in a heatproof medium bowl. Add a drop or two of water and whisk well. Set aside, leaving the whisk in place. Toss the seasoned celeriac again and place on serving plates.

When the fish is cooked and basted and the butter browned, remove the pan from the heat.

Place the fish on top of the celeriac, skin up. Immediately pour the browned butter into the measuring cup to stop the cooking. Drizzle the hot butter into the egg yolks, a few drops at a time, whisking continuously. After you've added about half of the butter, you can pour it in a thin stream; do not stop whisking or you'll likely curdle the egg.

When all the butter has been added, taste for salt. Pour the sauce over the fish and slaw and serve.

Seared Tuna with Anchovy Butter and Oregano

This quick, pungent sauce pairs Anchovy Butter with lemon and oregano to mimic a *bagna cauda* (a warm dip for vegetables), without the intensive prep the traditional Italian sauce requires. This recipe will yield enough sauce for 2 servings. I encourage you to douse the fish liberally or serve additional sauce as a dip for bread or grilled vegetables.

⟶ **FOR EACH SERVING**

1 (8-ounce) **seared tuna steak** (page 239), without sauce

1 tablespoon excellent olive oil

1 tablespoon **Anchovy Butter** (page 378)

1 large fresh oregano sprig

1 teaspoon fresh lemon juice

Freshly ground black pepper

Once the tuna is seared, transfer it to a plate. To the same pan, add the olive oil, anchovy butter, and oregano. Warm on low heat just to melt the butter and wilt the oregano. Off the heat, add the lemon juice and lots of pepper. Whisk to combine. Pour on top of the warm tuna and serve.

Seared Scallops with Ginger and Braised Parsnips

Ginger emboldens the cumin in the parsnips, and its bite wakes the dish from its comforting creaminess.

---> **FOR EACH SERVING**

Grapeseed or canola oil

4 large (2-ounce) dry-packed scallops, tough side muscle removed

1 teaspoon coarse kosher salt

2 tablespoons dry white wine

2 tablespoons **braising liquid from Parsnips Braised in White Wine and Cumin** (page 172)

1 teaspoon grated fresh ginger

1 teaspoon heavy cream

10 pieces **Parsnips Braised in White Wine and Cumin**

Heat a heavy skillet, large enough to fit the parsnips in roomy fashion, over high heat for 1 full minute. Add just enough oil to coat the pan lightly but evenly. It should heat through immediately, and with a couple of tilts run loosely across the pan's surface.

Season the scallops on both sides with salt, then place carefully in the pan. Leave them to sear until deep brown, about 2 minutes. Turn the scallops over and add the wine, braising liquid, and ginger. Turn the heat down to medium. Baste the scallops until the sauce thickens slightly, 1 to 2 minutes. They should be only just cooked through.

Transfer the scallops to a serving plate. Add the cream to the pan and swirl. Add the parsnips and cook over low heat until warm. Serve the parsnips alongside the scallops, with the sauce over everything.

Seared Scallops with Lemongrass-Tomato Confit

Instead of scallops, you can use large shrimp (8 ounces per serving) or skin-on fish fillets (page 238).

---> **FOR EACH SERVING**

1 tablespoon grapeseed or canola oil

4 (2-ounce) dry-packed scallops, tough side muscle removed

1 teaspoon coarse kosher salt

1½ teaspoons unsalted butter

1 teaspoon grated fresh ginger

½ tablespoon minced lemongrass *or Parsley! 1ts*

1 teaspoon seeded, minced jalapeño chile

½ cup **Confit Tomatoes** (page 148), with their juices *= Canned ½ c chopped Tomatoes*

1 teaspoon fresh lime juice *- lemon juice*

2 teaspoons roughly chopped fresh cilantro

Flaky sea salt

Heat a skillet over high heat. Add the oil; it should heat through immediately, and with a couple of tilts run loosely across the pan's surface. Quickly season the scallops on both sides with the kosher salt, then place carefully in the pan. Sear, untouched, until well browned on the bottom, about 2 minutes. Flip and cook the other side for 2 minutes more. Remove the scallops from the pan and let them rest on paper towels.

Turn off the heat and pour off any excess oil from the pan. Add the butter, ginger, lemongrass, and jalapeño to the still-hot pan. Stir for 30 seconds, then add the tomatoes with their juices and the lime juice. Fold in the cilantro.

Spoon the tomatoes and sauce into a serving bowl. Top with the scallops; finish with flaky salt.

Stovetop Smoked Fish or Shellfish

Smoking fish and shellfish at home is quick and easy. You need nothing more than a stovetop, wood chips (which you can find wherever grills are sold), foil, a metal roasting pan, a metal rack—and, importantly, good ventilation.

I think the best smoked fish are those you serve rare (like tuna), or that have more assertive flavors (like salmon, mackerel, and—by far my favorite—sardines). You can even smoke salt cod, once you've cooked it.

How much smoke is a personal preference. I like just a touch. Be conservative at first; you can always return the fish to the smoker for more.

You don't need to poach fish first, although mild, flakier varieties like cod or shellfish like scallops benefit from that initial step. You can poach seafood a day in advance, to divide the work. If you have poached it (page 225) and if you reduce the poaching broth to a glaze, you can add this glaze to aioli (page 381), which you'll serve alongside. (Worth it!)

You can serve the fish hot from the smoker, but any smoked fish is terrific cold.

¼ cup wood chips

Heavy-duty aluminum foil

Metal roasting pan

Vegetable oil

Rack to fit inside pan

Coarse kosher salt, 1 teaspoon for every 8 ounces fresh fish or shellfish (do not add salt to salt cod)

Fish or shellfish to smoke, raw or poached (see headnote)

If you're smoking a fish that you will finish in the oven (see box), preheat the oven to 450°F.

Make a smoking packet: Place the wood chips near one of the shorter ends of a 6-x-12-inch piece of foil. Fold the opposite end of the foil over the chips to enclose them. Fold in the three open sides of the packet twice to seal the pouch. With a utility knife or fork, poke a bunch of holes in the top of the foil for the smoke to escape.

Place the smoking packet at one end of the roasting pan. Lightly grease the rack with oil. Place the rack in the pan; it can rest directly on top of the smoking packet. Salt the fish or shellfish—lightly, if it's already been poached—then place it on the rack at the end farthest from the wood chips, for indirect smoke. Cover the entire roasting pan tightly with foil, tenting the foil if necessary, so it doesn't rest directly on the seafood. Position the whole pan so that a burner sits just below the smoking packet.

Turn the heat to high and watch the pan closely. The first wisps of smoke come quickly. Once you see the smoke start, turn the heat down to medium-low. Smoke until the fish or shellfish is light amber outside; start checking after 5 minutes. Don't peek into the pan too often—and stand back when you do to avoid smoke in your eyes—but you do need to check the fish or shellfish, and even taste a bit, along the way. You don't want to smoke it too dark. If you can, use tongs to turn the fish or shellfish once halfway through. The smoking may take up to 8 minutes total. Once you get the smokiness you like, lift up the fish or shellfish on its rack and, if necessary, place it in the oven to finish cooking. The amount of time in the oven will depend on the size of the fish. Large shrimp may need 3 minutes. Small whole fish or fillets will take about 5 minutes;

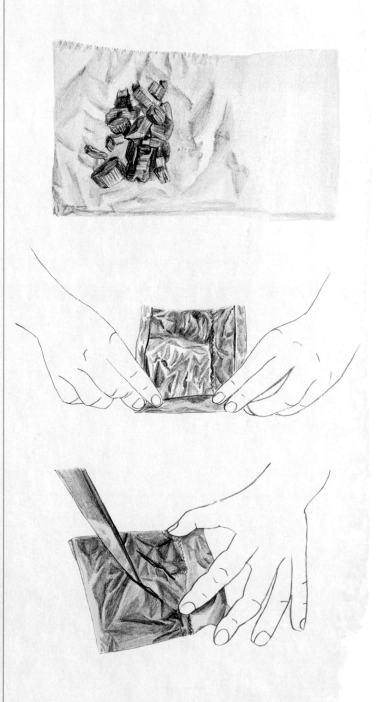

SMOKING FISH OR SHELLFISH

Smoke, and serve rare

> Tuna steaks
>
> Swordfish steaks
>
> Salmon fillets or steaks
>
> Trout fillets

Smoke, then finish in oven

> Whole large or small fish
>
> Large shrimp, peeled and deveined

Poach, then lightly smoke

> Mild, thick white fish fillets, such as cod, halibut, bass, or even salt cod
>
> Scallops

larger fish will need more time. Peek inside: For fish, the flesh should flake easily and be completely opaque at the backbone; shellfish should be opaque. Soak the chips with water to make sure they aren't still smoldering before throwing them away.

Serve the fish or shellfish hot, warm, or cold.

Serve with

⟶ Garlic Yogurt Sauce (page 380)

⟶ Whole-Grain Mustard Aioli (page 381)

⟶ Poached-Garlic Scrambled Eggs (page 353)

⟶ Sour Pickled Green Tomatoes (page 145)

⟶ Pickled Asparagus (page 82)

⟶ Parsnips Braised in White Wine and Cumin (page 172)

⟶ Confit Tomatoes (page 148)

SMOKED TROUT WITH DILL-AND-LEEK-GREENS PESTO AND WINE-PICKLED GARLIC

This dish is a brunch menu headliner. It's beautiful as a single plate or large platter. You can eyeball quantities of each ingredient—there are no wrong proportions. And if you don't want to smoke your own fish, excellent smoked trout is easy to buy. In addition to thick brown bread, you might serve mustard and sour cream on the side.

Arrange smoked trout (page 242, or store-bought) in large pieces on a plate. Whisk a little **brine from Wine-Pickled Garlic Cloves** (page 24) into **Dill-and-Leek-Greens Pesto** (page 32), to loosen it into a sauce. Spoon this on top of the trout. Sprinkle with slivered **Pickled Garlic**.

Whole Roasted Fish, Big and Small

Roasting fish is pretty foolproof, assuming the oven is hot and you moisten the skin with oil. Stuff the fish with herbs, citrus, and spices, or nothing at all. I like to roast fish in a compact roasting pan. A small pan ensures that whatever juices the fish releases—which I love to mop up—won't evaporate too quickly.

Sometimes it's nice to create a bed of thinly sliced vegetables that will cook in these same juices, as I suggest with the onions here. You can also set up for a quick pan sauce with some ripe tomatoes, herbs, and a splash of white wine—watch the tomatoes burst open slightly as the fish cooks. After the fish comes out, pour whatever is in the pan right on top of the fish, or serve it alongside. Sometimes I'll save this sauce for toast and eggs the next day.

You can tell if a whole fish is cooked all the way through by gently opening the cavity, with an eye to the backbone, being careful not to split the flesh. Because the fish cooks from the thinnest part (its belly, where it's gutted) to the thicker meat at its back, you can determine by the change in flesh how far it has cooked, and gauge how much longer it has to go. If the flesh around the backbone has turned opaque, the fish is done. Translucent, it needs a little more time. You can also pierce the skin just under or above the backbone to check.

The recipe is written for 1¼ pounds of fish—a single large fish to serve one or two, or a collection of small ones, such as sardines, as an appetizer for four. I salt the fish right before it goes in the oven, so the salt itself browns a bit for crunch.

1 (1¼-pound) whole fish (such as branzino) *or* 12 to 15 whole sardines, scaled and gutted

2 teaspoons coarse kosher salt

1 cup thinly sliced red onion

2 teaspoons excellent olive oil

¼ lemon, washed well and thinly sliced

Top with

—→ lemon juice and more coarse kosher salt

—→ Refrigerator-Door Vinaigrette (page 383)

—→ Coriander Vinaigrette (page 362)

—→ Green-Peppercorn Vinaigrette (page 362)

Preheat the oven to 475°F for a single whole fish or 500°F for smaller fish. Pat the fish dry inside and out. Wrap each fish individually in dry paper towels to absorb excess moisture; let sit for 10 minutes at room temperature.

Right before you are ready to roast, season the fish, inside and out, with 1¾ teaspoons of the salt. Place the onions in the roasting pan and season with the remaining ¼ teaspoon salt. Drizzle some of the oil over the onions, then lay the fish right on top. Place the lemon slices in the fish cavity. Drizzle the fish with the remaining oil. Roast just until completely opaque at the backbone, 15 to 20 minutes for a single, larger fish; 10 minutes for small ones. To serve, slide a wide spatula—or two if the fish is large—under the fish and transfer it to a platter. Scrape the juices and caramelized onions on top and serve.

Whole Roasted Fish with Wine-Pickled Garlic and Bay Salt

The garlic pickle brine is a good slightly sweet finishing vinegar for fish, and the Bay Salt is terrific on anything fresh from the sea.

→ **FOR 1 OR 2 SERVINGS**

¼ cup thinly sliced **Wine-Pickled Garlic Cloves** (page 24)

¼ cup **brine from Wine-Pickled Garlic Cloves**

3 tablespoons excellent olive oil

2 tablespoons roughly chopped fresh dill

1 teaspoon **Bay Salt** (page 374)

Freshly ground black pepper

1 recipe **Whole Roasted Fish** (page 246)

Combine the garlic, brine, oil, dill, salt, and a grind or two of pepper in a bowl. Once the fish is done, transfer it and the onions to a plate. Spoon the dressing on top, or serve it on the side as a dipping sauce.

WHOLE ROASTED FISH WITH TAHINI SAUCE

Tahini, lightened with lemon, is a creamy, nutty, unexpectedly elegant dressing for delicately flavored **Whole Roasted Fish** (page 246).

As soon as the fish comes out of the oven, transfer it to a plate. Scrape up the onions and combine them in a bowl with ½ cup **Tahini Sauce** (page 371). Drizzle over the fish or serve as a dipping sauce on the side, along with a wedge of lemon.

WHOLE ROASTED FISH + WINE-PICKLED GARLIC CLOVES + BAY SALT + olive oil dill black pepper → WHOLE ROASTED FISH WITH PICKLED GARLIC & BAY SALT

Roasted Sardines with Roasted Lemon Dressing

The combination of lemons, raisins, and sardines is a Sicilian favorite. It's best to make this a day in advance, marinating the fish right after they roast. You can smoke the sardines instead (page 242), and sauté a little sliced red onion to add to the dressing.

—→ **FOR EACH SERVING**

3 **whole Roasted Sardines** (page 246; about ¼ pound)

1 to 2 tablespoons **onions from the roasting pan**

1 to 2 tablespoons **Roasted Lemon Dressing** (page 221)

Pull off the fins and carefully lift off the top fillet of the fish. Use the tail to lift off the backbone and release the bottom fillet. (Leave the skin on.) Place the sardine fillets, onions, and dressing in a bowl; fold together gently to combine, being careful not to break the fish. Refrigerate overnight. Bring to room temperature before serving.

If you'd like to eat this the day you make it, allow at least 3 hours for the fish to marinate in the refrigerator, or 1 hour at room temperature.

Poultry

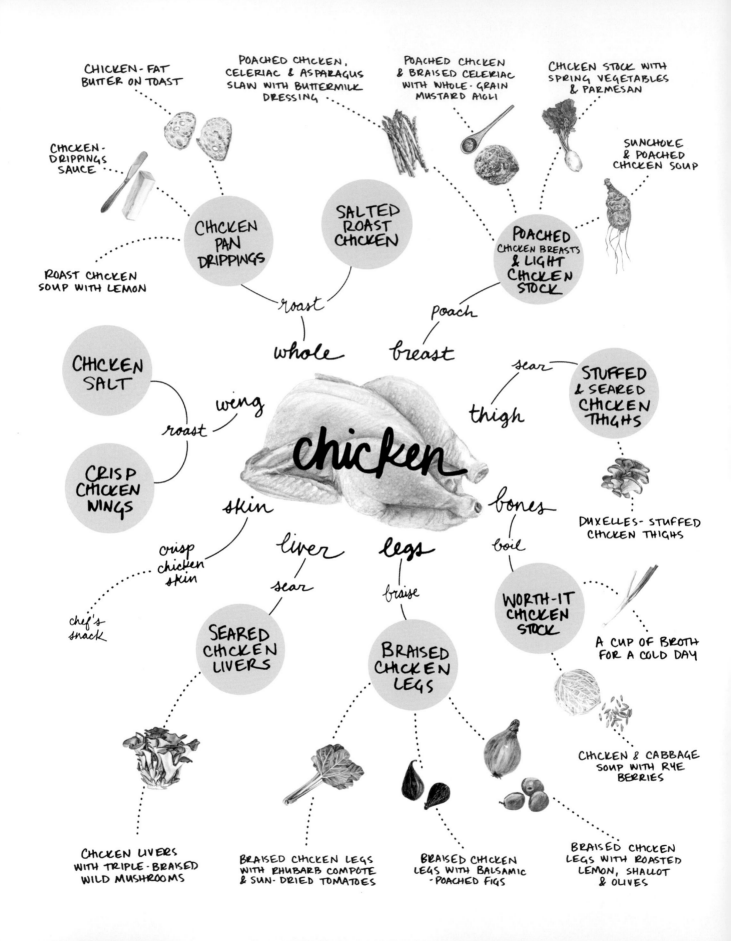

CHICKEN-FAT BUTTER ON TOAST

POACHED CHICKEN, CELERIAC & ASPARAGUS SLAW WITH BUTTERMILK DRESSING

POACHED CHICKEN & BRAISED CELERIAC WITH WHOLE-GRAIN MUSTARD AIOLI

CHICKEN STOCK WITH SPRING VEGETABLES & PARMESAN

CHICKEN-DRIPPINGS SAUCE

SUNCHOKE & POACHED CHICKEN SOUP

CHICKEN PAN DRIPPINGS

SALTED ROAST CHICKEN

POACHED CHICKEN BREASTS & LIGHT CHICKEN STOCK

ROAST CHICKEN SOUP WITH LEMON

roast

whole

poach

breast

sear

STUFFED & SEARED CHICKEN THIGHS

CHICKEN SALT

wing

thigh

roast

chicken

CRISP CHICKEN WINGS

skin

bones

DUXELLES-STUFFED CHICKEN THIGHS

crisp chicken skin

liver

legs

boil

WORTH-IT CHICKEN STOCK

chef's snack

sear

braise

A CUP OF BROTH FOR A COLD DAY

SEARED CHICKEN LIVERS

BRAISED CHICKEN LEGS

CHICKEN & CABBAGE SOUP WITH RYE BERRIES

CHICKEN LIVERS WITH TRIPLE-BRAISED WILD MUSHROOMS

BRAISED CHICKEN LEGS WITH RHUBARB COMPOTE & SUN-DRIED TOMATOES

BRAISED CHICKEN LEGS WITH BALSAMIC-POACHED FIGS

BRAISED CHICKEN LEGS WITH ROASTED LEMON, SHALLOT & OLIVES

Salted Roast Chicken

Here is a recipe for roasted chicken with tight, crisp skin and juicy, flavorful flesh, yielding rich, salty pan juices that chill to jelly.

Don't be put off by the quantity of salt I use. You'll be happy at how well it seasons the meat and keeps it tender and juicy. Try to allow 24 hours to let the chicken cure before cooking. If you don't have a full day, any number of hours is better than none.

I remain hands-off while the chicken roasts, and I do not reposition the bird for equal cooking of dark and white meats. Nor do I lift the bird onto a rack, hoping to crisp all sides of the skin. I stick it in the hot oven and let it go, happy with the chicken's resulting range of textures, from the soft, juice-soaked skin underneath to the crisped wing tips.

makes 1 WHOLE CHICKEN

1 (4-pound) chicken

1 to 1½ tablespoons coarse kosher salt

2 teaspoons grapeseed or canola oil

Rinse the chicken well and pat dry with paper towels. Save any innards, the neck, and if you're lucky enough to have them, the feet (collect them in the freezer for when you make Worth-It Chicken Stock, page 267). Season the chicken liberally with salt all over, paying particular attention to the thicker parts—the breasts and the front and back sides of the thighs. Toss any remaining salt inside the cavity. Set the chicken, breast up, on a plate, rest a paper towel loosely on the bird, and refrigerate for at least 4 hours, ideally for 12, and up to 24.

Preheat the oven to 450°F. Place the chicken directly in a roasting pan only slightly bigger than the bird itself. (The juices you'll collect in this snug pan are delicious. You'll want little of them to evaporate, and they are worth sacrificing a crisp underside.) Scatter the liver, gizzard, and heart around; they will crisp in the oven's high heat. Season them lightly with salt. Place the neck in the pan; it will add flavor to the accumulating juices. Coat the chicken lightly but evenly with oil.

Place in the oven. After 40 minutes, tip the bird up, lifting it carefully with tongs poked into the neck end; let any cavity juices spill into the roasting pan. Check for doneness after another 20 minutes: The cavity juices should run brown, the thighs should wiggle loosely in their sockets, and, when pricked, the meat juices should run yellow or clear (see the box on page 254). The top skin should be quite crisp. Remove the bird from the oven and transfer to a plate to rest for a full 5 minutes before serving. Do not cover or the skin will turn limp.

I like to serve the chicken cut into small pieces—the wings separated from the breast, the breast meat cut off the bone in thick slices, the legs cut in half, the back meat plucked off the bones, all parts served together right in the roasting pan with all the juices and fat. Don't forget the roasted chicken innards and neck too.

When it's perfectly cooked, it's easiest to break the chicken apart with your hands: Don some disposable gloves, if you want; grab the bird with your hands and pull it apart over the roasting pan so you don't lose any juices from the cavity. First wrest the legs from the hip joints, taking with them any skin from the back of the bird. Twist the thighs from the drumstick unless you want to leave the legs whole. Gently tear off the wings, pulling with them any crisped bits of the collar. Loosen the breast meat from its breast plate and pop loose pieces of back meat clinging to the bones, leaving the carcass completely clean.

In even the short time the chicken rests, the fat will separate from the juices, making it easier to spoon off and discard. If you want to save the drippings for another use or make them into a finished sauce (opposite), scrape all of the fat, brown bits, and juices from the bottom of the roasting pan into a heatproof bowl or container. If using the juices for sauce, skim off the fat that rises to the top and reserve to store for "butter" (page 256) or discard. If not using the drippings for sauce, let them cool before refrigerating. The fat and jus will separate completely; each is delicious on its own.

Use the chicken fat in

⟶ Chicken-Fat Butter (page 256)

Use the jus in

⟶ Roast Chicken Soup with Lemon (page 256)

⟶ Roast Chicken in Pan-Drippings Sauce (opposite)

Serve the meat with

⟶ Wine-Braised Leeks (page 28)

⟶ Confit Zucchini Squash (page 141)

DETERMINING DONENESS

Most recipes tell you that a chicken is done when a thermometer inserted into the thickest part of the thigh reads 165°F, but I prefer to rely on other cues. Pull at a leg to see how loose the bird's hip joint is; you may even want to cut the skin between the leg and the breast with a sharp knife for a better view. Once the skin is cut, the thigh should relax toward the pan a bit, pulling away from the breast. Examine the meat near the thigh joint, and be wary of any spots that look glossy. Prick the meat with a thin knife, catching the released juices with a spoon to examine them. I keep a white plastic spoon handy for accurate appraisal: Yellow juices that blush a bit pink are okay; anything the color of rosé is not done.

Roast Chicken in Pan-Drippings Sauce

The best way to reheat leftover roast chicken is to separate the meat and skin, treating each on its own. I pull the meat off the bone and bathe it in a sauce made from the chicken's pan drippings.

Use the unsalted butter or substitute Prune Butter (page 376) or Herb-Infused Butter (page 377). Anchovy Butter or Green-Peppercorn Butter (page 378) are delicious, but use them cautiously or they will make the sauce too salty.

—→ FOR EACH SERVING

2 tablespoons **jus from Salted Roast Chicken** (page 253)

2 teaspoons dry white wine

2 tablespoons water, plus more if needed

1 tablespoon or more unsalted butter, or see headnote

½ cup **shredded meat from Salted Roast Chicken**

Packed 1 tablespoon roughly chopped fresh oregano

Place the chicken jus, wine, 2 tablespoons water, and 1 tablespoon butter in a saucepan over medium heat. Bring to a simmer and stir. Cook until reduced by about half. Taste—if it is too salty, add a bit more water or unsalted butter. Stir in the chicken and cook just to heat through. Remove from the heat and fold in the oregano. Serve immediately.

Roast Chicken Soup with Lemon

This soup, which gets a lift from lemon juice at the end, uses every part of the chicken from the roasting pan, including the drippings and chicken skin. If you roast a whole chicken, you'll have enough drippings, meat, and skin to make soup for eight.

> **FOR EACH SERVING**

1¼ cups excellent chicken stock (such as Worth-It Chicken Stock, page 267)

½ cup chopped turnips, rutabaga, or parsnips

½ cup chopped potatoes (any kind), unpeeled

2 garlic cloves, thinly sliced

½ cup **shredded meat from Salted Roast Chicken** (page 253)

1½ teaspoons **jus from Salted Roast Chicken**

Packed ¼ cup torn kale or other sturdy greens

1 tablespoon fresh lemon juice

Coarse kosher salt and freshly ground black pepper

1 lemon slice, cut crosswise

1 large piece **Crisp Chicken Skin** (page 262; optional)

Pour the stock into a saucepan. Add the turnips, potatoes, and garlic and bring to a boil. Turn down the heat and simmer, covered, until the vegetables are tender, about 10 minutes.

Add the chicken meat and jus and the kale. Cover and simmer for 30 seconds to warm everything through. Taste, adding lemon juice, salt (if needed), and lots of pepper.

Serve immediately, with the lemon slice slipped into the broth and the skin on top, if you like.

Chicken-Fat Butter

If you save the chicken fat from your pan drippings, it's easy to put together this butter. Your toast will be happy you did.

> **MAKES 6 TABLESPOONS**

4 tablespoons (½ stick) unsalted butter, at room temperature

2 tablespoons **fat from Salted Roast Chicken** (page 253), chilled

¾ teaspoon coarse kosher salt

Combine all the ingredients in a bowl and mash together with a fork or a whisk. Initially, the butter and fat won't want to combine, but persevere. After a few minutes, everything will come together. Scrape into a small mold or ramekin and chill. Store in the refrigerator for up to 5 days or freeze for up to 1 month. Serve at room temperature.

Braised Whole Chicken Legs

Braising is a slow cooking process that typically calls for stock, along with aromatics (vegetables, herbs, and spices) and often wine. Here, I omit the stock and let the chicken's own juices fortify the resulting simple, perfect sauce.

Consider braising a large batch of legs and freezing them individually to reheat and tailor to your preference. You can also substitute any combination of thighs or drumsticks for the whole legs.

for 4 SERVINGS

2 pounds whole chicken legs (4 thighs with drumsticks attached)

2¼ teaspoons coarse kosher salt, plus more if needed

2 tablespoons canola oil

1 large onion, sliced

5 garlic cloves, sliced

6 large fresh thyme sprigs

1 cup crisp, floral white wine

Choose a Dutch oven or other heavy lidded pot wide enough to fit the chicken pieces in a single layer, but small enough that they fit snugly.

Pat the chicken dry all over. Season with the salt on both sides and let stand at room temperature for 30 minutes.

Place the pot over high heat. Once hot, add the oil; it should rapidly coat the pan. Place the chicken pieces, skin side down, in a single layer in the pot. Let them cook, without moving, until the skin is crisp and deep brown, 2 to 3 minutes. Do not let them burn. Transfer the pieces to a plate as they are finished.

Pour out all but 1 tablespoon of the fat from the pot. Add the onion and cook over medium-low heat until it begins to soften, 2 to 3 minutes, stirring frequently. Add the garlic, thyme, and wine. Put the chicken back in the pot, skin side up, and pour in any juices that accumulated on the plate. Bring to a quick simmer, then cover. Turn the heat down to low and cook, turning the chicken pieces every 15 minutes, until the meat pulls effortlessly from the bone, about 45 minutes total. (You can instead cook the chicken in a preheated 300°F oven, for about 1 hour.)

If you're not serving the chicken immediately, let it cool in its juices. As it cools, taste for salt. If it needs more, add it directly to the warm juices, and the cooling chicken will absorb it. Once cooled, remove the chicken pieces, strain the juices, and store the onion and garlic with the chicken pieces, separate from the juices. Discard the thyme. Refrigerate the chicken and the juices. As the juices chill, the fat will rise and set so you can easily skim it; add the skimmed juices to the chicken.

continued ↘

Store in the refrigerator for up to 5 days. Freeze in appropriate portion sizes—sauce and onions and garlic equally divided—for up to 1 month.

To reheat, preheat the oven to 400°F. Place the thawed chicken pieces with their juices in a snug Dutch oven or other heavy-bottomed ovenproof pot. Bring to a simmer on the stovetop, then cover and place in the oven. Bake until the juices have reduced slightly and the chicken is warmed through, 15 to 20 minutes. Serve hot.

Use in

→ Braised Chicken Legs with Roasted Lemon, Shallots, and Olives (at right)

→ Braised Chicken Legs with Balsamic-Poached Figs (opposite)

→ Braised Chicken Legs with Rhubarb Compote and Sun-Dried Tomatoes (opposite)

BRAISED CHICKEN LEGS WITH ROASTED LEMON, SHALLOTS, AND OLIVES

You can use lemon juice, or even toss lemon wedges in with the braising juices, but there is no real replacement for the concentrated bite of roasted lemon. Warm as many pieces of chicken as you want, as long as you do so in a snug-fitting pan, so the juices don't evaporate and burn.

FOR EACH SERVING

In a snug, heavy-bottomed ovenproof saucepan with a lid, combine ¼ cup each of **braising juices from Braised Whole Chicken Legs** (page 257), chopped pitted green olives, chopped **Roasted Whole Lemons** (page 220), and **Shallots Roasted with Sugar and Vinegar** (page 41) for each **Braised Whole Chicken Leg**. Add a pinch of hot red pepper flakes. Bring to a simmer, stir once, then cover and place in a preheated 400°F oven. Bake until the juices have reduced slightly and the chicken is warmed through, 15 to 20 minutes.

Braised Chicken Legs with Balsamic-Poached Figs

This dish partners slightly candied figs with rich, salty chicken juices. Serve it with a contrastingly simple salad, using Mustard Vinaigrette (page 364) or Bacon Vinaigrette (page 296). Warm as many pieces of chicken as you want, as long as you do so in a snug-fitting pan, so their juices don't evaporate and burn.

⟶ **FOR EACH SERVING**

1 **Braised Whole Chicken Leg** (page 257)

¼ cup **braising juices from Braised Whole Chicken Legs**

1 tablespoon **syrup from Balsamic-Poached Figs** (page 366)

6 halves **Balsamic-Poached Figs**

1 tablespoon fresh tarragon leaves

Preheat the oven to 400°F. Place all the ingredients in a snug, heavy-bottomed ovenproof saucepan with a lid. Bring to a simmer on the stovetop, stir once, then cover and place in the oven. Bake until the juices have reduced slightly and the chicken is warmed through, 15 to 20 minutes. Serve hot.

Braised Chicken Legs with Rhubarb Compote and Sun-Dried Tomatoes

This dish matches two concentrated fruits—one tart and one sweet—with rich chicken juices for a sauce. If you have Rhubarb Compote in the freezer and sun-dried tomatoes in your pantry, this is a quick-to-assemble dish. Warm as many pieces of chicken as you want, as long as you do so in a snug-fitting pan, so their juices don't evaporate and burn.

⟶ **FOR EACH SERVING**

1 **Braised Whole Chicken Leg** (page 257)

¼ cup **braising juices from Braised Whole Chicken Legs**

1 tablespoon thinly sliced sun-dried tomatoes

1 tablespoon **Rhubarb Compote** (page 98)

1 tablespoon unsalted butter

1 fresh oregano sprig

Coarse kosher salt

1 teaspoon grated lemon zest

Preheat the oven to 400°F. Place all the ingredients *except* the salt and lemon zest in a snug, heavy-bottomed ovenproof saucepan with a lid. Bring to a simmer on the stovetop, stir once, then cover and place in the oven. Bake until the juices have reduced slightly and the chicken is warmed through, 15 to 20 minutes. Taste for salt and stir in the zest. Serve hot.

Stuffed and Seared Chicken Thighs

Searing and stuffing a boneless thigh is one of the best ways to enjoy this cut. The key is to fold the thigh onto itself so its skin wraps entirely around the outside of the parcel. This way, you get a nice sear all around, while the meat inside—pressed together and insulated from direct, drying heat—stays tender. You can stuff the thigh with anything—from minced garlic and herbs to dried fruit—as long as your filling is fully cooked or quick-to-cook and won't burn easily if it spills out onto the hot pan. I prefer to eat dark meat warm, so I suggest serving these thighs as soon as you cook them.

If you cannot find boneless thighs with skin, ask your butcher to remove the single bone from the meat—or do it yourself (opposite).

for 4 SERVINGS

4 boneless, skin-on chicken thighs (about 1⅓ pounds)

2 teaspoons coarse kosher salt

4 tablespoons filling, such as **Mushroom Duxelles** (page 201), **Dill-and-Leek-Greens Pesto** (page 32), *or* **Refrigerator-Door Mustard** (page 383)

1 teaspoon grapeseed or canola oil

1 fresh thyme or oregano sprig (optional)

2 tablespoons cold unsalted butter (optional)

Season the skin side of the chicken with 1 teaspoon of the salt. Flip over and season the flesh side with the remaining salt. Let cure for 30 minutes before stuffing.

Preheat the oven to 400°F. Place 1 tablespoon of the filling down the center of each thigh. Bring one side of the thigh over the other to enclose the filling. Stretch the skin so it covers all the meat and secure the seam with a toothpick.

Heat an ovenproof medium pan over medium-high heat for 30 seconds. Add the oil and tilt the pan to coat the surface. Add the thighs, seams facing to one side. Turn the heat down to medium; cook until the skin is deeply golden and crisp, 6 to 7 minutes. Turn to sear the other side, about 5 minutes more.

Once both sides are seared, carefully pour the excess fat out of the pan. Place the pan in the oven and roast until the chicken is fully cooked, 5 to 7 minutes. Place the thighs on a serving plate. Add the thyme and cold butter, if using, to the still-hot pan. Swirl to infuse the butter and combine it with the other bits in the pan. As soon as the butter melts, spoon it liberally over the chicken. If you want, discard the thyme sprig. Serve immediately.

Serve with

→ a simple green salad

→ "Instant" Chunky Mashed Potatoes (page 176) and Swiss Chard Stems Jam (page 54)

BONING A CHICKEN THIGH

Lay the thigh skin side down on your cutting board. With a thin, sharp knife, trace the full length of the bone to expose it fully. Next, scrape along one side of the bone, from joint to joint, to release the meat. If you focus on carefully cleaning the bone, rather than cutting at the meat, you'll leave the chicken nicely intact. As you continue to scrape and loosen the bone from the meat—don't forget to cut around the joints—you'll be able to roll it over and cut it out.

Crisp Chicken Skin

I stockpile skin from poached chicken breasts, separating the strips with parchment paper and storing them in the freezer. Once I accumulate a few, I crisp pieces to break up for seasoning or to enjoy whole as a secret snack.

You can rush the crisping by drying at a higher temperature, but you risk burning the skin. Since it takes a little while to crisp, I like to do several at once.

Raw chicken skin,   **Coarse kosher salt**
thawed if frozen

Preheat the oven to 300°F. Lay the skin on a cutting board, flesh side up. Use a dull knife, such as a butter knife, to carefully scrape away excess fat. The fat might lie in a thin, even layer or collect as a bulbous deposit. You don't have to be meticulous with scraping, but the smoother and thinner the skin, the crisper it will be; aim for translucence. Place the skin, scraped side down, on a lightly oiled wire rack, stretching it so it lies flat. Set the rack over a baking sheet and sprinkle the skin lightly with salt. Bake until completely crisp, about 45 minutes. Once crisp, place the skin on paper towels to absorb excess rendered fat.

Cool completely, then place in an airtight container. Store in the refrigerator for up to 1 week. To recrisp, warm on a baking sheet in a preheated 300°F oven for about 10 minutes.

Serve over

→ Roast Chicken Soup with Lemon (page 256)

→ A Single Deviled Egg (page 350)

→ Parsnips Braised in White Wine and Cumin (page 172)

→ steamed white rice

Crisp Chicken Wings, Chicken Salt

Chicken wings, roasted on high until caramel-colored and completely crisp all over—even charred at the tips—leave behind crusty, browned bits. This is Chicken Salt. Get in the habit of scraping your pan for it each time, no matter how many wings you make. Parchment paper tears easily after prolonged high heat, so I don't use it here.

Crumble the salt over melted Gruyère cheese or Roasted Sunchokes (page 183), or salt the rim of a tomato cocktail.

Cook as many or as few wings as you like. If you want extra-crispy wings, follow the method of J. Kenji López-Alt and sprinkle the wings with salt and baking soda. (This will yield less chicken salt.)

for 4 SERVINGS WINGS AND 2 TABLESPOONS CHICKEN SALT

4 pounds chicken wings

1 or 2 tablespoons coarse kosher salt

1 tablespoon baking soda (optional)

¼ cup grapeseed or canola oil

For extra-crispy wings, toss them with 1 tablespoon salt and the baking soda. Place them on a rack and refrigerate, uncovered, for at least 12 hours and up to 18.

Preheat the oven to 425°F. Toss the wings with the oil and 1 tablespoon salt until evenly coated. Place the wings directly on a baking sheet, meaty side down. Don't crowd them; you may need to use two sheets.

Roast until the wings are caramel brown and very crisp on the bottom, about 20 minutes. Use a thin spatula to pry the wings off the baking sheet and turn them over. Don't worry if the skin sticks. Roast until the entire wing is caramel brown and crisp, another 20 to 25 minutes. If they are cooked through before they are deeply browned, return them to the oven. A bit of chew in the meat is fine, but not flabby skin.

Remove from the oven and transfer the wings to a serving plate. Serve the wings hot or cold.

Pour off the fat on the pan. While the pan is still hot, use a sturdy, heatproof spatula or pastry scraper to lift every bit of stuck-on chicken skin and desiccated juices from the pan. This may amount to no more than a few tablespoons. Transfer these scrapings to a plate lined with a few layers of paper towels to drain. Most of the fat will run off the scrapings, and they will crisp while they cool.

Once dry, store the chicken salt in a covered container in the refrigerator for up to 5 days, bringing to room temperature before using. Freeze for up to 1 month.

Poached Chicken Breasts, Light Chicken Broth

Poaching is the best way to cook a chicken's tender, mild white meat. A quick cure in salt before poaching properly seasons it without oversalting the broth itself.

Remove all skin and excess fat from the chicken before you poach, so the fat doesn't cloud the poaching liquid. Save the skin to crisp (page 262). The poaching liquid becomes its own light, flavorful chicken stock. If you use only as much as you need to cook the chicken, you'll get the most concentrated results. If you don't have Quick Poaching Broth on hand, you can make it first in the same pot you use to cook the chicken.

makes 4 SERVINGS CHICKEN AND ABOUT 2 CUPS BROTH

4 (8-ounce) boneless, skinless chicken breasts

1 tablespoon coarse kosher salt

2 cups **Quick Poaching Broth** (page 360), or see headnote

Place the chicken breasts on a plate, smooth side down. Carefully loosen the long tenderloin from the back of the breast, folding it back to lie next to the rest of the breast; it's okay if it comes loose.

Trim any large pockets of fat from the breasts. Salt generously on all sides. Let stand at room temperature for 30 minutes.

Choose a pot that fits the chicken breasts snugly in one layer; too wide a pot will require more broth. Add the broth and bring to a simmer. Submerge the chicken gently in the broth. Cover and cook, making sure the broth doesn't rise to more than a gentle simmer, until the meat is opaque all the way through, 8 to 10 minutes; the tenderloins may cook in as

little as 5 minutes. Pull the chicken pieces out as soon as they are done. Serve warm or cold, sliced thinly on the bias.

If you're not using the broth immediately, cool it, then strain and store in the refrigerator for up to 3 days, or in the freezer for a few months. You can keep the cooked chicken in the refrigerator, well wrapped, for up to 5 days.

Use the broth in

→ Chicken Stock with Spring Vegetables and Parmesan (page 77)

→ Sunchoke and Poached Chicken Soup (page 266)

Use the meat in

→ Poached Chicken and Braised Celeriac with Whole-Grain Mustard Aioli (opposite)

→ Poached Chicken, Celeriac, and Asparagus Slaw with Buttermilk Dressing (opposite)

Poached Chicken and Braised Celeriac with Whole-Grain Mustard Aioli

This is a lovely, easy, healthful, and beautiful dish. Wine and herbs amplify the quiet yet congruous flavors of the white meat and the celeriac. I like the crunch of coriander seeds at the end.

—> **FOR EACH SERVING**

1¼ cups **Celeriac Braised in White Wine and Coriander** (page 170), at room temperature

½ **Poached Chicken Breast** (opposite), thinly sliced or shredded

2 tablespoons **Whole-Grain Mustard Aioli** (page 381), thinned with a few drops of water or **Light Chicken Broth** (opposite)

A few coriander seeds, toasted and crushed

A few fresh tarragon leaves

Arrange the celeriac on a plate. Scatter the chicken on top, then spoon the aioli all over. Top with coriander seeds and tarragon and serve.

Poached Chicken, Celeriac, and Asparagus Slaw with Buttermilk Dressing

Get a jump on spring with this salad, just when asparagus comes into season and is sweet enough to eat raw. It's great for company and scales up easily. It makes a light lunch on its own or, in slightly smaller portions, with a warm baguette or a grain like Freekeh in Garlic Tea (page 337). Toss with the dressing right before serving or the salad will become watery.

Substitute the breasts from Salted Roast Chicken (page 253), if you want.

You can keep julienned celeriac and buttermilk dressing in the refrigerator for days, making this dish quicker to put together.

—> **FOR EACH SERVING**

1 cup **Julienned Celeriac** (page 168), salted and drained

1 cup thinly sliced asparagus

1 tablespoon minced fresh flat-leaf parsley

1 cup scallions (greens and whites), thinly sliced

¼ cup **Buttermilk Dressing** (page 380)

1 **Poached Chicken Breast** (opposite), warm or at room temperature

Mix the celeriac, asparagus, parsley, scallions, and dressing together in a bowl. Use your fingers to tear the chicken into small pieces. Add to the salad and toss well. Serve.

Sunchoke and Poached Chicken Soup

If you don't have cooked chicken for this light, bright soup, you can poach it in one pot while you start the vegetables for the soup in another. To serve four, you'll need to double the Poached Chicken recipe to get the amount of broth you need. You'll be happy for any extra chicken.

→ **FOR EACH SERVING**

2 teaspoons excellent olive oil

⅓ cup chopped onion

⅓ cup chopped sunchokes, peeled if you like (page 167)

1 cup **Light Chicken Broth** (page 264), or see headnote

Coarse kosher salt

⅓ cup shredded **Poached Chicken Breast** (page 264), or see headnote

Freshly ground black pepper

Chopped fresh flat-leaf parsley

Heat the oil in a pot over medium-high heat, add the onions, and cook until they begin to soften, about 5 minutes. Add the sunchokes and cook for 2 minutes more to flavor the oil. Add the broth and bring to a boil. Reduce to a simmer, cover, and cook until the vegetables are tender, 5 to 7 minutes. Taste for salt.

Turn off the heat and add the chicken. Cover and let sit, just to warm through. Add black pepper and chopped parsley to taste and serve.

MAKING GREAT STOCK

→ Use good ingredients—not wilted vegetables, nor freezer-burned vegetables or poultry parts, nor leftover bones from dinner.

→ Use bones with joints and cartilage (to give the stock body) and a bit of meat on them (for flavor).

→ Use just enough but not too many vegetables; it's mostly about the chicken.

→ Use filtered water; if you don't like the taste of your water, you won't like the taste of your stock.

→ Cook the stock slowly—you want to extract all the flavor you can from the bones, without reducing the yield. Also, simmering too strongly will cloud the stock and muddy the appearance and taste.

→ Taste continuously to see how the flavor develops and to know when the stock is done: Dip a large spoon into the stock, pulling from the broth beneath any fat floating on the surface. Sprinkle in the tiniest bit of salt, then taste. Initially, the stock will taste thin. Simmer until the stock tastes chicken-y on the tongue and rich in your throat.

→ Cool the stock quickly over ice water, but do not stir it much as it cools, or the fat will emulsify into the stock, masking how it looks and tastes.

Worth-It Chicken Stock, Summer and Winter

This stock is rich, clean, and gelatinous. Whether you make it on the stove or in the oven, it is largely a hands-off process. It's delicious as it is, but you can also infuse it while it's still warm with seasonings perfect for summer or winter.

Stock takes at least 3 hours to make, but it involves almost no hands-on time. (You can even make it in the oven, which simulates the roasted flavor of browned chicken bones.)

makes **ABOUT 6 CUPS**

5 pounds raw chicken wings, backs, necks, and feet (if you have any)

8 cups water (preferably filtered)

1 carrot, peeled and cut in half

1 celery stalk, cut in half

1 small onion, peeled and cut in half

FOR SUMMER STOCK

Strips of zest from 1 lemon (white pith removed)

5 fresh oregano or thyme sprigs

1 teaspoon whole white peppercorns

FOR WINTER STOCK

8 whole cloves

1 teaspoon whole black peppercorns

7 cardamom pods, cracked open

If you plan on using the oven, preheat it to 350°F. Choose a pot just big enough to hold everything with at least 1 inch clearance at the top. Add the bones and water.

Bring to a boil over high heat. Use a ladle or fine-mesh strainer to thoroughly and continuously skim off the foam as it rises, taking care not to remove too much water. When no more foam appears, add the carrot, celery, and onion. As soon as the stock comes back to a simmer, turn the heat down to very low or move the pot to the oven. Let the stock cook at a quiet, gentle simmer, skimming as necessary, about 3 hours. Taste to see when it's done (see Making Great Stock, opposite).

Strain the stock into a metal bowl—metal transfers heat quickly, so the stock will cool faster.

For summer or winter stock: If you are infusing the stock, add the seasonings now. Place the bowl of stock inside a larger bowl or container filled with a great deal of ice water. Cool completely, undisturbed.

The fat will rise to the top, and the seasonings will likely be trapped in this fat. Once completely cool, refrigerate the stock overnight. Spoon off the fat and seasonings before using and/or freezing the stock. The stock will keep for up to 5 days in the refrigerator and up to 3 months in the freezer.

A Cup of Broth for a Cold Day

Seasoning good chicken stock with this pork rub makes a warming soup to sip from a mug. I like the simple addition of scallions at the end.

→ **FOR EACH SERVING**

> 1½ cups excellent chicken stock (such as Worth-It Chicken Stock, page 267)
>
> ¾ teaspoon **Pork Spice Rub** (page 373)
>
> 1 tablespoon sliced scallion whites

Warm the stock in a saucepan over medium-high heat. Add the spice rub and turn off the heat. Cover and let the spices infuse for 3 to 5 minutes. Place the scallions in the bottom of a bowl or mug, pour the broth on top, and serve.

CHICKEN AND CABBAGE SOUP WITH RYE BERRIES

You can vary the contents of this meat-vegetable-grain soup as long as you start with excellent, rich stock, season it sufficiently with salt, and choose herbs you like. Instead of chicken, use pulled pork or little pieces of pork loin. Instead of cabbage, try **Julienned Celeriac** (page 168) or romaine lettuce. Instead of rye berries, add quinoa, freekeh, or wild rice.

Bring 1½ cups excellent chicken stock such as Worth-It Chicken Stock (page 267) to a quick boil. Add ¼ cup each **Shaved Raw Cabbage** (page 113), shredded **Poached Chicken** (page 264), and **Toasted Rye Berries** (page 334). Bring back to a simmer and taste for salt. Add chopped fresh herbs, such as oregano or tarragon, a grind of black pepper, and a drizzle of excellent olive oil.

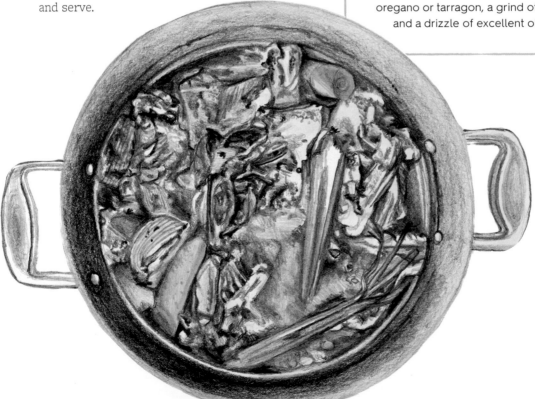

Seared Chicken Livers

Seared livers stay pink inside, and the browned bits left behind in the pan give you a chance to make a little sauce. In lieu of sauce, I sometimes dress the livers with a small pat of Green-Peppercorn Butter (page 378) or Herb-Infused Butter (page 377).

for EACH SERVING

3 chicken livers	1 tablespoon canola oil
1 teaspoon coarse kosher salt	1 tablespoon unsalted butter

Examine the livers for discoloration; they should be a uniform burgundy color. Cut away any dark or off-color spots. Trim any clinging fat and rinse the livers well under cold water. When you're ready to sear them, pat very dry and season on both sides with the salt.

Place a skillet over high heat and add the oil. When the oil runs loosely in the pan, but before it begins to smoke, lay down the livers and cook, without disturbing, until browned, 1 minute. Flip the livers over and cook for 1 minute more. Add the butter, immediately turn the heat down to low, and use a spoon to baste the livers for 20 seconds—the butter will melt and brown. Remove the livers from the skillet and let rest a few minutes. Serve the livers whole or thinly sliced, drizzled with the brown butter.

Chicken Livers with Triple-Braised Wild Mushrooms

I like richly flavored braised wild mushrooms for this take on a classic dish. Chewy oyster mushrooms are particularly good. You'll use the butter from cooking the livers in the sauce, so leave it in the pan.

⟶ FOR EACH SERVING

Butter and browned bits from Seared Chicken Livers (at left), still in the pan

1 fresh thyme sprig

1 tablespoon dry sherry

½ cup **Triple-Braised Wild Mushrooms** (page 194), with any juices

1 recipe **Seared Chicken Livers**, hot

Add the thyme and sherry to the butter in the hot pan in which you seared the livers. Turn the heat to low. Scrape up any browned bits stuck to the pan. Once the sherry has cooked off, about 1 minute, add the mushrooms with their juices. Toss and just warm through.

Spoon the mushrooms onto a plate. Slice the livers and place them on top. There should be a glaze left in the pan; scrape it over the livers. Serve.

Duck

Seared and Roasted Duck Breast

Start the duck breasts in a cold pan to slowly render the most fat possible from beneath the skin. This slow rendering will eventually crisp the skin. Duck renders a considerable amount of fat; you'll want to carefully pour it off as it accumulates. You can collect it in a heatproof container, and once it's cooled, freeze it. Use it to fry thinly sliced potatoes or stockpile it for Confit Duck (page 276). To discard the fat, set up a wad of crumpled newspaper in a heatproof bowl and pour the hot fat directly on top. When it cools, discard the paper.

You can sear 1 to 6 breasts at a time in a 10-inch cast-iron pan. Use 1 teaspoon salt per 8-ounce breast.

for 4 BREASTS

4 (8-ounce) duck breasts

4 teaspoons coarse kosher salt

Grapeseed or canola oil

Preheat the oven to 450°F. Use a paper towel to pat the duck dry all over. Use a sharp knife to score the skin, making crosshatch cuts about ½ inch apart. Cut through the fat but not into pink flesh. Season both sides of the breasts with the salt, rubbing it into the cuts.

Drizzle a slick of oil into a heavy ovenproof skillet. Add the duck breasts, skin side down. Turn the heat to medium-low. Cook, patiently waiting, until the skin is an even, deep brown and the fat layer between the skin and the meat disappears, about 10 minutes. Pour off the excess fat each time it begins to pool in the pan, and also again once the skin is finally crisped.

Once the skin is crisp and the fat is poured off, flip the breasts over and place in the oven. Cook to just medium-rare, 2 to 3 minutes. Transfer the duck breasts to a plate and let them rest for 5 minutes before serving or slicing.

Serve with

→ Squash and Rosemary Compote with Honey and Cayenne (page 189)

→ Glazed Seared Brussels Sprouts (page 119) and Onion Jam (page 34)

Use in

→ Duck Breast, Molasses-Roasted Peaches, Tamarind, and Basil (opposite)

→ Duck Breast, Crisp Sautéed Shiitake, and Scallion Soup (page 272)

Duck Breast, Molasses-Roasted Peaches, Tamarind, and Basil

There are few substitutes for the flavor of tamarind, a pod-like fruit from Africa and Latin America, packaged commonly as a burgundy-colored paste with a taste of dried sour cherries. Roasted peaches and fresh basil keep the balance on this rich, beautiful plate. You could make this dish into a fantastic salad, adding radicchio leaves dressed with lemon, olive oil, and salt.

—> **FOR EACH SERVING**

4 wedges **Molasses-Roasted Peaches** (page 150), each wedge sliced into 3 even pieces

2 tablespoons **syrup from Molasses-Roasted Peaches**

2 teaspoons tamarind paste

Packed 1 tablespoon torn fresh basil leaves

1 Seared and Roasted Duck Breast (opposite), warm or cold, cut into ¼-inch-thick slices

Flaky sea salt

Combine the peaches and their juices, the tamarind paste, and basil in a bowl.

Arrange the duck on a plate and sprinkle with salt. Spoon the peach compote over the meat, and serve.

Duck Breast, Crisp Sautéed Shiitake, and Scallion Soup

Thin slices of duck and mushrooms float in a clear, strong broth. The scallions are essential; don't skip them. I like the long strips of breast meat in this soup—they remind me of the pieces of pork in a wonton broth—but you can use shredded, defatted White Wine–Braised Duck Legs (opposite) too. Don't skimp on the stock; if you haven't made your own, use the best you can buy.

→ **FOR EACH SERVING**

¼ cup thinly sliced **Seared and Roasted Duck Breast** (page 270)

¼ cup **Crisp Sautéed Shiitakes** (page 199)

1 cup excellent chicken stock (such as Worth-It Chicken Stock, page 267)

Coarse kosher salt and freshly ground black pepper

2 tablespoons or more sliced scallions, greens and whites

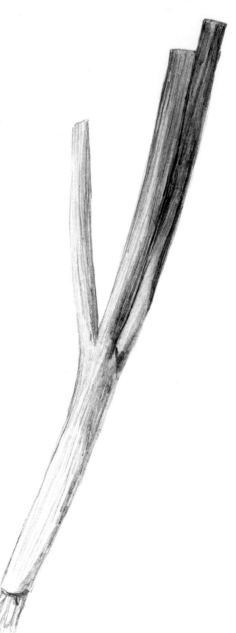

Put the duck, mushrooms, and stock in a saucepan over medium-high heat. Once the stock is warm, season with salt and add the scallions and lots of pepper. Serve.

White Wine–Braised Duck Legs

Braised duck leg meat is rich, and in this recipe, it's assertively seasoned but versatile. The braised meat is wonderful to have on hand and freezes beautifully. I suggest freezing the duck legs individually, with the braising juices evenly divided.

There's no stock in this recipe, but the duck's juices merge with white wine to make a lovely little sauce. To prevent unnecessary evaporation, cook the duck in a pot with a heavy, tight-fitting lid, such as a Dutch oven, only just large enough to hold all the legs. If you can, start this a day ahead.

for 4 LEGS

4 whole duck legs (legs and thighs; about 2¼ pounds total)

1¾ teaspoons coarse kosher salt, plus more if needed

1 tablespoon grapeseed or canola oil, plus more if needed

1 small onion, thinly sliced

2 small garlic cloves, thinly sliced

½ cup crisp white wine

Preheat the oven to 325°F. Rinse the duck with cold water and pat very dry. Season the legs with the salt, more heavily on the skin side. Refrigerate, uncovered, overnight, or leave at room temperature for 1 hour.

Heat the oil in an ovenproof pot just large enough to hold the duck snugly over medium-high heat, until it flows loosely. Pat the duck dry again and place the legs in the pot, skin side down. Sear until the skin is deep brown, about 5 minutes. Do not let it burn. Typically, duck renders sufficient fat to make additional oil unnecessary, but if the pot seems dry, add a few drops to prevent the skin from burning. As each leg is browned, transfer it from the pot to a plate.

Once all the legs are seared, pour out the excess fat in the pot but do not wipe it out. Return the duck legs to the pot, skin side up. Scatter the onion and garlic around the duck; add the wine. The duck will not be submerged.

Cover the pot and place in the oven. After 25 minutes, give everything a stir. Return to the oven and continue to check on the progress of the duck every 15 minutes, stirring each time. As the duck cooks, it will deepen in color and the sauce will turn creamy. It is done once the meat pulls easily from the bone, 45 to 60 minutes total.

Remove the pot from the oven, give the contents one last good stir, and allow to cool, covered, for 20 minutes.

continued ↘

Taste the sauce and a bit of the meat for salt. If it needs some, add it while still warm. Serve immediately. Or allow the duck to cool completely and refrigerate for up to 5 days. Freeze in individual portions with sauce for up to 2 months. Thaw in the refrigerator before reheating.

To reheat, put the legs and sauce in a snug saucepan or skillet with a lid. Cover and place on the stove over low heat or in a 400°F oven for 10 to 15 minutes.

Serve with

—→ Popcorn Quinoa (page 329) or Manny's Brown Rice (page 320)

Use in

—→ Braised Duck Leg with Roasted Lemon and Raisins (opposite)

—→ Braised Duck Leg with Saffron and Green Olives (opposite)

—→ Braised Duck Leg Crepes (at right)

—→ Duck Breast, Crisp Sautéed Shiitake, and Scallion Soup (page 272), instead of the duck breast

BRAISED DUCK LEG CREPES

For each serving, shred the meat from a **White Wine–Braised Duck Leg** (page 273); you can chop the skin and mix it in with the meat or discard, along with the bones. Reheat the meat/skin with its sauce. In another pan, reheat 3 **Brown-Rice Crepes** (page 321). Fill with the duck and serve.

WHITE WINE-BRAISED DUCK LEG + ROASTED WHOLE LEMONS + *raisins* *thyme* → BRAISED DUCK LEG WITH ROASTED LEMON & RAISINS

Braised Duck Leg with Roasted Lemon and Raisins

I like game meat with dried fruit, though I am cautious about how much I use. Here, concentrated roasted lemon prevents the classic combination from being too sweet.

→ **FOR EACH SERVING**

1 **White Wine–Braised Duck Leg** (page 273)

¼ cup **braising juices from White Wine–Braised Duck Legs**

¼ cup chopped **Roasted Whole Lemons** (page 220)

¼ cup golden raisins

Leaves from 1 fresh thyme or oregano sprig

Preheat the oven to 400°F. Combine the duck, braising juices, lemon, and raisins in a snug, heavy-bottomed ovenproof saucepan. Bring just to a simmer over medium heat, then cover and place in the oven. Bake until the duck is warmed through, 10 to 15 minutes.

Remove from the oven and fold in the herbs. Let rest for 2 minutes and serve.

Braised Duck Leg with Saffron and Green Olives

This is a simple but stunning dish, with an aroma to match.

→ **FOR EACH SERVING**

1 **White Wine–Braised Duck Leg** (page 273)

¼ cup **braising juices from White Wine–Braised Duck Legs**

1½ tablespoons roughly chopped pitted green olives

8 strands saffron

Preheat the oven to 400°F. Combine the duck, braising juices, olives, and saffron in a snug, heavy-bottomed ovenproof saucepan. Bring just to a simmer on the stove over medium heat, then cover and place in the oven. Bake until the duck is warmed through, 10 to 15 minutes. Remove from the oven. Let rest for 2 minutes, then serve.

Confit Duck

Decadence is confit duck. The term "confit" means the meat is cooked slowly in fat. Using lard—which is more flavorful than duck fat—makes this confit less expensive. Moulard is the traditional type of duck for confit, since their legs are large and meaty. If moulard is hard to find, adjust the salt to the size leg you have.

It's crucial to salt the duck legs well in advance. However, if you plan to cure the duck for longer than 12 hours, use 2 tablespoons total, instead of 3 tablespoons.

You can double or triple the recipe—it's a two-day process, so you might as well make it worth your while. The more legs you put in one pan, the less lard you'll need per pound of duck.

for 4 SERVINGS

4 whole (8-ounce) duck legs, preferably Moulard

2 or 3 tablespoons coarse kosher salt (see headnote)

1 teaspoon freshly ground black pepper

3 fresh thyme sprigs

3 bay leaves (fresh if possible), broken in pieces

1 tablespoon canola oil

3 pounds lard

Rinse the duck legs and pat very dry. Rub the legs all over with 1 tablespoon of the salt and place in a container. Sprinkle with the pepper, thyme, bay leaves, and 2 tablespoons of the remaining salt if curing for less than 12 hours; 1 tablespoon if curing for more. Refrigerate, covered, for 10 to 12 hours or overnight, turning once.

Rinse the duck under cool running water, saving the thyme and bay leaves, and pat dry. (*If you're not cooking it right away, store it in*

the refrigerator with the herbs, covered with plastic wrap, for up to 1 day.)

Preheat the oven to 300°F. Heat the canola oil in a large skillet over medium-high heat. Add the duck legs, skin side down, and cook until the skin is an even, deep brown, 15 to 20 minutes. As the legs brown, place them in a heavy ovenproof pot, just large enough to hold the legs snugly.

Pour any fat out of the skillet, wipe it out, and melt 2½ pounds of the lard. Pour it over the legs. If it doesn't completely cover them, melt and add the remaining lard. Add the reserved bay leaves and thyme. Cover and place in the oven. Cook until the meat falls from the bone, 2 to 2½ hours.

Remove from the oven and let the legs cool in the fat. If you'll be serving the duck soon, store in the refrigerator as is in the pot. Or transfer the legs to a container, cover them completely with the fat, cover the container, and refrigerate. Once you have eaten all the duck, reuse the fat for another batch of confit, combining it with half as much fresh lard. To freeze, wrap each leg in plastic wrap, then place them together in a freezer bag. Freeze for up to 3 months.

To reheat just the meat: Remove the skin. Pull the meat from the bones; leave in large pieces or shred it. Put it in a small saucepan and heat slowly. There's no need to add oil; whatever fat clings to the meat is enough to keep it from drying out. You might want to turn the heat up to high at the end to crisp some pieces.

To reheat a whole leg: Preheat the oven to 400°F. Use your fingers to wipe away excess fat from the leg. Carefully loosen the skin from the meat, keeping it attached near the bone. Place the leg skin side down in a cold ovenproof pan. The now loosened skin should lie mostly flat in the pan (it will crisp better than if left gripping the leg). Place in the oven until the skin is completely crisp and the meat is heated through, 12 to 15 minutes.

Use in

—→ Roasted-Pepper Breakfast Sandwich (page 137)

—→ Confit Duck Salad with Buttermilk Dressing (at right)

Serve with

—→ White Beans with Garlic and Vinegar (page 342)

—→ "Instant" Chunky Mashed Potatoes (page 176)

—→ Rhubarb Compote (page 98)

exploration

Confit Duck Salad with Buttermilk Dressing

Of all the dishes in this book, this might be the one I'd request as a last meal. You can add raw radishes to the plate, and small pickles, even a spoon of Rhubarb Compote (page 98). It requires little more than fresh, crisp lettuce—not the flavorless baby kind.

You can follow this method and serve the shredded duck on or alongside a salad of frisée with Green-Peppercorn Vinaigrette (page 362).

—→ **FOR EACH SERVING**

3 to 4 tablespoons **Buttermilk Dressing** (page 380)

½ head butter or red leaf lettuce (8 to 10 leaves)

1 **Confit Duck** leg (opposite), whole or shredded, reheated

Place the dressing in a bowl. Tear any large lettuce leaves in half and add to the bowl. Use your hands to gently swirl the leaves around, lightly coating the leaves. If using shredded meat, add it and toss again. Or serve the salad alongside the warm, crisp whole leg. Serve immediately.

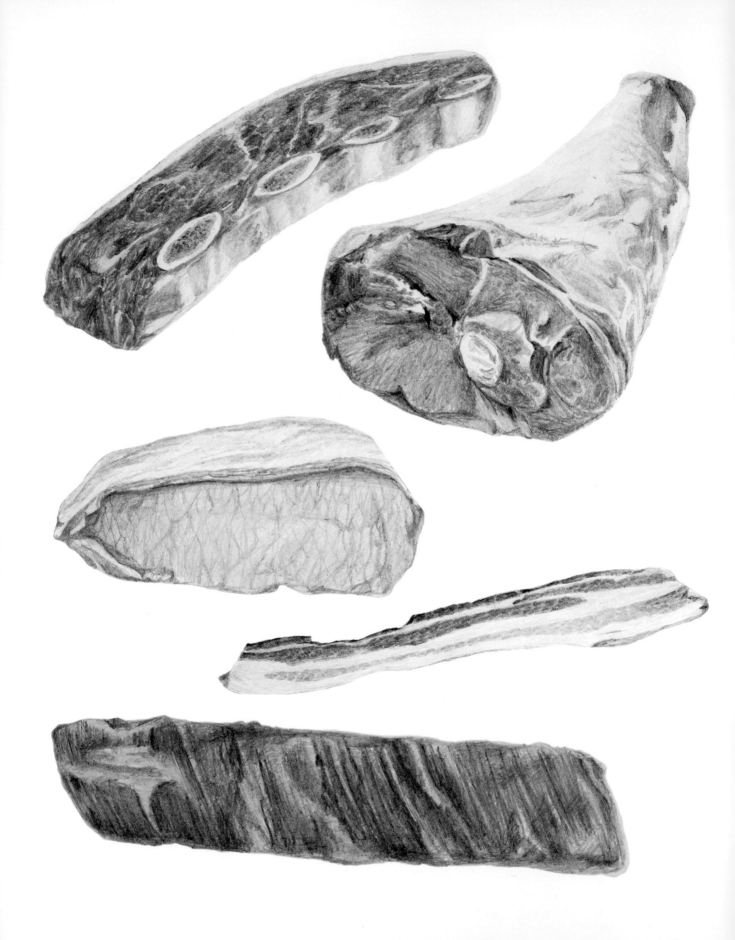

Meat

COOKING MEAT

Salt is important when you cook meat, whether you add it well in advance to season the muscles of the meat or at the last minute to make a deeply flavorful exterior sear. Don't skimp on it.

If you can, salt dense bone-in meats like lamb shanks and short ribs 24 hours in advance of cooking. If you don't have time, make the recipe anyway, knowing you can pull the meat from the bone once it's cooked and marinate it in the rich braising juices at the end.

Beyond the occasional marinade, searing requires little planning. An instant-read thermometer is a helpful aid for both searing and roasting. Braising takes more time and benefits from a little organization, such as freezing a quick kit of premeasured stock and wine. Freezing raw meat in seasoned individual portions makes sense too. Roll a package of ground meat into small meatballs, so you can pull out only the amount you want to cook. Break down a package of bacon into individual bundles, so you don't have to wrestle with a whole pound. Freeze several slices on waxed paper in a freezer bag, or in bundles of ½-inch pieces (page 295).

You can also freeze extra braising juices, as well as the smaller scrapings and juices left behind in a sauté or roasting pan: Use chicken stock to make a pan sauce with roast pork drippings, or stir reserved pork pan drippings into chicken broth to fortify a soup.

SEARING BONELESS STEAKS

Searing is a fantastic technique to completely cook all cuts of leaner beef, including skirt, flank, and rib eye.

→ Use 1 teaspoon salt for every 5 ounces of steak.

→ Before cooking, allow the salted meat to sit at room temperature for up to 30 minutes.

→ When you're ready to cook, get the pan very hot and pat the meat very dry.

→ Use oil with a high smoking point, such as grapeseed or canola oil.

→ Salt the meat very well again right before it goes into the pan.

→ Cook it until it's slightly underdone and let rest.

Searing times for different steaks don't differ much. With the meat at room temperature and the pan very hot, you'll get a nice sear in 2 or 3 minutes on each side. But to cook thicker steaks beyond rare, you'll want to finish them in the oven. Here are some guidelines to get you started.

→ **For boneless rib eye or New York strip,** 1½ inches thick, sear for 2 to 3 minutes per side and finish in a preheated 450°F oven for 5 minutes.

→ **For flank and skirt steak,** sear for about 1½ minutes per side, without oven time.

Beef

Seared Skirt Steak

Skirt steak is a long, winding cut of meat from the cow's belly; its gathered muscles give the meat a crinkly look. It marinates and cooks quickly. Seared in a hot, heavy, evenly heated pan, such as cast iron, a well-seared and seasoned piece of skirt steak is chewy and caramelized on the outside, juicy and tender inside.

Season the beef in advance of searing and let it sit on the counter to take the chill off it. Then hit it with salt again right before it goes into the pan. The recipe is written for one steak, but you can sear several to serve at once or to keep and eat cold and sliced.

for EACH SERVING

Scant 1½ teaspoons coarse kosher salt

1 (8-ounce) skirt steak

Grapeseed or canola oil

Rub ¾ teaspoon of the salt over both sides of the steak and let it sit at room temperature for 30 minutes. As the salt dissolves, wrap the steak well in paper towels to absorb all moisture.

Heat a cast-iron skillet over high heat for 1 full minute. Add just enough oil to coat the pan.

Unwrap the steak and season with the remaining scant ¾ teaspoon salt. Place the steak carefully in the skillet. Sear each side until well browned, about 1½ minutes per side for rare, 2 minutes for medium-rare. Transfer the steak to a cutting board and let it rest for up to 5 minutes: Rare will become medium-rare; medium-rare will become medium.

If you are serving it now, slice the steak on the bias into ½-inch-thick slices. If you are making the steak in advance, hold it at room temperature to serve within an hour, or store in the refrigerator in a covered container for up to 2 days and serve cold.

Use in

→ Seared Skirt Steak with Charred Tomatillos, Green Grapes, and Purslane (page 282)

→ a sandwich with Shallots Roasted with Sugar and Vinegar (page 41)

Serve with

→ Many-Herb Salad (page 64) and sliced avocado

→ a salad of crisp greens and Mustard Vinaigrette (page 364)

Seared Skirt Steak with Charred Tomatillos, Green Grapes, and Purslane

This salad makes a meal, and not just because of the filling meat, but for its variety of textures and temperatures. I love purslane—a beautiful, trailing, pea-sweet succulent with edible stems, flowers, and leaves—but it is often hard to find outside of a farmers' market. You can substitute sturdy, peppery watercress.

Pepitas are hulled, roasted pumpkin seeds.

→ **FOR EACH SERVING**

3 tablespoons excellent olive oil

10 tomatillos, outer husks removed, washed, and cut in half through the stem (about 1 cup)

Coarse kosher salt

1 cup seedless green grapes, quartered

¼ cup fresh cilantro leaves

½ small jalapeño chile, seeded and minced

2 cups purslane leaves and stems, or see headnote

¼ cup fresh mint leaves, torn

¼ cup pepitas (see headnote)

Juice of 1 lime

1 **Seared Skirt Steak** (page 281), warm or at room temperature

Flaky sea salt and cracked black pepper

Heat a cast-iron skillet over medium heat. Pour in 1 tablespoon of the olive oil. While the oil is heating, season the cut sides of the tomatillos with a light but even sprinkle of kosher salt. Once the pan is hot and the oil runs loosely, place the tomatillos cut sides down—they should sizzle—and let them sear until evenly golden, 4 to 5 minutes. If the tomatillos are small, cook them only on their cut side; they should soften sufficiently. If they are large and still firm after searing, flip them over to cook for an extra minute until just tender all the way through. Transfer to a bowl and let cool slightly. Sprinkle again with kosher salt.

Add the grapes, cilantro, jalapeño, purslane, mint, and pepitas to the tomatillos. Add the lime juice and remaining 2 tablespoons olive oil. Toss the salad lightly and taste for salt. Arrange the salad on a plate. Cut the steak on the bias into ½-inch-thick pieces and place over the salad. Finish with a little flaky sea salt and pepper.

STEAK WITH ANCHOVY BUTTER

The salty seared steak is a good match for the formidable flavor of anchovy. You'll love **Roasted Sunchokes** (page 183) on the side.

Follow the instructions on pages 280 and 281 to sear the steak of your choice. Transfer to a serving plate and let it rest. Top it with up to 1 tablespoon **Anchovy Butter** (page 378), grind on plenty of black pepper, and garnish with a big handful of chopped fresh parsley.

Wine-Braised Short Ribs

This braise is straight-up simple. The short ribs are fantastic with "Instant" Chunky Mashed Potatoes (page 176) and the vegetables from the braise.

If you can, salt the meat the day before you cook it.

makes 4 CUPS MEAT AND 4 CUPS BRAISING JUICES, PLUS VEGETABLES; ENOUGH FOR 4 TO 6 SERVINGS

3 pounds bone-in short ribs

1 tablespoon coarse kosher salt, plus more if needed

2 tablespoons grapeseed or canola oil

2 medium onions, cut Into 1-inch wedges (root ends trimmed but intact)

4 medium carrots, cut in half crosswise, then into ½-inch-thick batons

6 celery stalks, cut in half crosswise, then into ½-inch-thick batons

6 garlic cloves, sliced

1 (750-ml) bottle dry red wine

4 fresh thyme sprigs

3 cups excellent chicken stock (such as Worth-It Chicken Stock, page 267)

Lay the short ribs out on a baking sheet and season with the salt. Refrigerate, uncovered, for up to 24 hours. If you haven't planned in advance, let them sit at room temperature for 1 hour. When you are ready to cook, pat the meat very dry.

Preheat the oven to 350°F. Heat the oil in a Dutch oven over high heat. Sear the ribs until well browned on all sides, 4 to 5 minutes per side. If necessary, work in batches so the ribs aren't crowded. Transfer the ribs to a plate as they're done. Pour off all but 1 tablespoon of the fat in the pot.

Add the onions, carrots, celery, and garlic to the remaining fat. Turn the heat down to medium and cook until the vegetables begin to soften and brown lightly, about 5 minutes. Add the wine and thyme and bring to a boil, scraping up any browned bits stuck to the pan. Add the ribs and chicken stock; bring to a boil once again.

Cover, place in the oven, and cook until the meat is quite tender, about 1½ hours. Uncover and continue to cook, turning the ribs once or twice, until the meat begins to tear easily and the sauce has reduced by half, about 45 minutes more. If the ribs are done but the braising juices taste thin, remove the ribs from the pot. Short ribs release a good deal of fat, which will separate from the braising juices as the meat rests. Remove and reduce this fat, then reduce the juices on the stovetop over medium heat until deep and delicious. Taste the braising juices for salt, then return the ribs to the pot, turning them to coat well. Let the meat soak up the flavors of the juices for

5 minutes before serving. To serve, spoon the braising juices over the meat.

To store, use a slotted spoon to remove the ribs and then the vegetables from the braising juices. Store the vegetables and meat together in individual portions, if you like, in the refrigerator for up to 5 days. Strain the braising juices into a heatproof container. Cool completely before refrigerating. Once the juices have chilled, you can either discard any remaining fat that rises to the top or, if soft enough, stir it back in. Freeze the meat along with its juices in suitable portions for up to 3 months. The vegetables won't freeze very well, so eat them on their own.

To reheat, place the thawed meat and juices in a small ovenproof saucepan. Cover and place in a preheated 400°F oven until hot, stirring occasionally, about 10 minutes.

Use in

→ Short Ribs with Green Olives and Oranges (at right)

→ Short-Rib Sandwich with Best Roasted Green Peppers (at right)

Add to

→ linguine mixed with Crisp Sautéed Shiitakes (page 199)

exploration

Short Ribs with Green Olives and Oranges

I love briny and sweet ingredients with wine-rich beef. Use this dish as a template: Instead of green olives, you can add capers or pickles. Rather than oranges, try very ripe peaches.

→ **FOR EACH SERVING**

1 cup **meat from Wine-Braised Short Ribs** (page 283)

1 cup **braising juices from Wine-Braised Short Ribs**

1 tablespoon roughly chopped pitted green olives

1 tablespoon fresh orange juice

½ medium orange, cut into suprêmes (page 217)

Combine the meat, its juices, the olives, and the orange juice in a pan. Bring to a simmer over medium heat and reduce the liquid by half, to about ½ cup. Add the orange slices and heat them until just warmed through, 30 seconds. Serve.

SHORT-RIB SANDWICH WITH BEST ROASTED GREEN PEPPERS

Slather mustard on 2 slices of rye toast. Pile on **Best Roasted Green Peppers** (page 136), warmed **Wine-Braised Short Ribs** (page 283), and raw red onion or **Pickled Red Onions** (page 36).

Pork

Pork Loin with Fennel and Thyme

Don't overcook this cut. Use carefully sourced meat, and if possible, an instant-read thermometer. Especially with the loin, great flavor and texture depend on perfectly cooked meat. The fennel-thyme salt is great for leg of lamb too.

for 4 SERVINGS

1½ pounds boneless pork loin

3 small garlic cloves, slivered

1½ tablespoons excellent olive oil

2 tablespoons fennel seeds, crushed

1 tablespoon dried thyme

2 teaspoons coarse kosher salt

½ cup excellent chicken stock (such as Worth-It Chicken Stock, page 267; optional)

Preheat the oven to 375°F. Use a thin knife to make ½-inch-deep incisions, about 1½ inches apart, all around the loin. Use the side of the knife as a guide to slide a single garlic sliver into each cut. Don't worry if any slices stick out of the loin, or if you have any slices left over. Rub the loin all over with the oil.

Combine the fennel, thyme, and salt. Pat the pork with a thick coating of spice salt on all sides, including the ends. Place the loin in a roasting pan. Roast until medium, 145°F on an instant-read thermometer, about 45 minutes. The loin should give slightly when pressed.

Let the loin rest for at least 5 minutes before slicing. The meat should be light pink, not white.

Use a spatula to scrape the pan drippings into a small container to store in the refrigerator for up to 1 week, or in the freezer for up to 1 month. Or make them into a quick sauce: Place the roasting pan on the stovetop over high heat. Immediately add the chicken stock and scrape up the drippings, deglazing the pan. Turn the heat down to low and cook to reduce and concentrate the flavor of the sauce to your taste. Spoon on top of the pork or save for another use, such as enriching a future soup or even spooning onto a different cut of meat. Freeze the sauce in an airtight container for up to 1 month.

Use in

→ Pork Loin and Seared Kale in Broth (page 287)

→ Pork Loin with Grapefruit Salsa (page 287)

Serve with

→ a salad with Cumin-Raisin Vinaigrette (page 363)

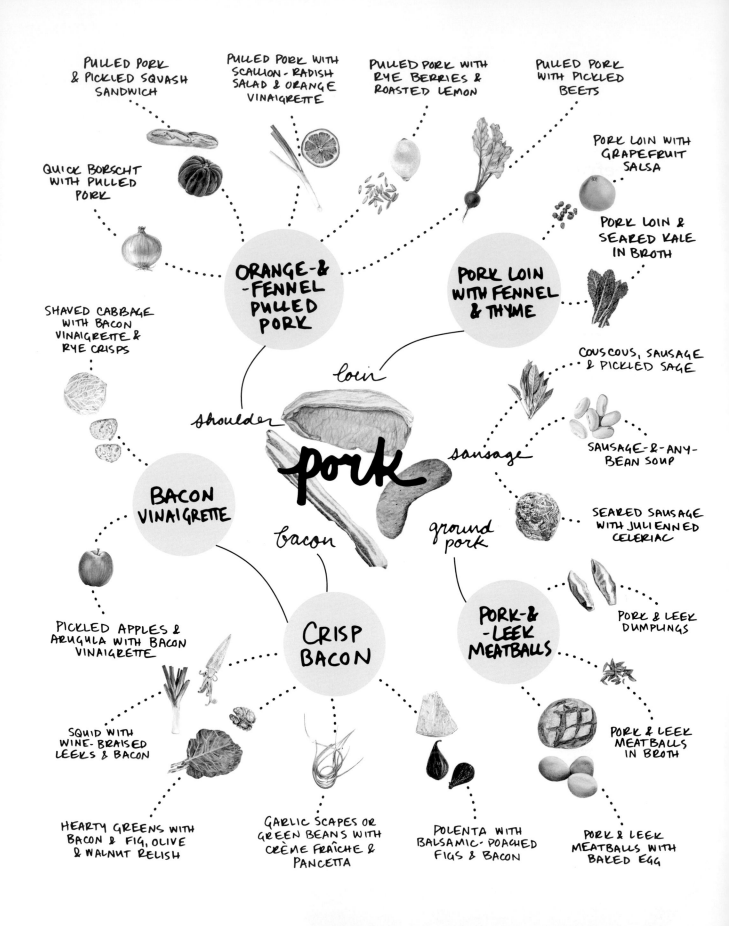

PULLED PORK
& PICKLED SQUASH
SANDWICH

PULLED PORK WITH
SCALLION-RADISH
SALAD & ORANGE
VINAIGRETTE

PULLED PORK WITH
RYE BERRIES &
ROASTED LEMON

PULLED PORK
WITH PICKLED
BEETS

QUICK BORSCHT
WITH PULLED
PORK

PORK LOIN WITH
GRAPEFRUIT
SALSA

PORK LOIN &
SEARED KALE
IN BROTH

SHAVED CABBAGE
WITH BACON
VINAIGRETTE &
RYE CRISPS

ORANGE-&
-FENNEL
PULLED
PORK

PORK LOIN
WITH FENNEL
& THYME

loin

COUSCOUS, SAUSAGE
& PICKLED SAGE

shoulder

pork

SAUSAGE-&-ANY-
BEAN SOUP

sausage

BACON
VINAIGRETTE

SEARED SAUSAGE
WITH JULIENNED
CELERIAC

bacon

*ground
pork*

PICKLED APPLES &
ARUGULA WITH BACON
VINAIGRETTE

CRISP
BACON

PORK-&
-LEEK
MEATBALLS

PORK & LEEK
DUMPLINGS

SQUID WITH
WINE-BRAISED
LEEKS & BACON

PORK & LEEK
MEATBALLS
IN BROTH

HEARTY GREENS WITH
BACON & FIG, OLIVE
& WALNUT RELISH

GARLIC SCAPES OR
GREEN BEANS WITH
CRÈME FRAÎCHE &
PANCETTA

POLENTA WITH
BALSAMIC-POACHED
FIGS & BACON

PORK & LEEK
MEATBALLS WITH
BAKED EGG

Pork Loin with Grapefruit Salsa

Even if you opt to make a smaller serving of this fresh dish—great for a light winter lunch—it is worth making the full batch of salsa and spooning any extra over slices of avocado.

⟶ **FOR 4 SERVINGS**

4 teaspoons whole-grain mustard

6 tablespoons excellent olive oil

½ teaspoon coarse kosher salt

2 tablespoons fresh lemon juice

4 teaspoons capers, rinsed and chopped

¼ cup grapefruit suprêmes (½ grapefruit; page 217), roughly chopped

¼ cup sliced scallions, greens and whites

2 tablespoons roughly chopped fresh flat-leaf parsley

1 recipe **Pork Loin with Fennel and Thyme** (page 285), warm or at room temperature

Whisk the mustard, oil, salt, and lemon juice together in a bowl. Gently stir in the capers, grapefruit, scallions, and parsley.

Cut the pork loin into ¼-inch-thick slices. Serve with the salsa spooned on top.

Pork Loin and Seared Kale in Broth

This quick-to-assemble soup marries the salty, herbal flavors from the pork roasting juices with bright, lemon-dressed cooked kale. I sometimes use raw kale and add lemon juice to the flavorful broth, and in both cases, a lemon slice, for a quieter aromatic infusion. Each spoonful of broth tastes a bit different than the last. You can cut down the amount of stock if you want a chunkier soup.

⟶ **FOR EACH SERVING**

½ cup **Seared Kale with Garlic and Lemon** (page 50) *or* 1 cup **Raw and Ribboned Kale** (page 48)

2 cups excellent chicken stock (such as Worth-It Chicken Stock, page 267)

1 tablespoon plus 1 teaspoon **pan juices from Pork Loin with Fennel and Thyme** (page 285)

¼ teaspoon coarse kosher salt (optional)

⅓ cup cubed (¼-inch) **meat from Pork Loin with Fennel and Thyme**

Juice of ½ lemon, if using raw kale

1 thin slice lemon

Place the kale in a saucepan. Add the stock and warm over medium heat. Add the pork pan juices and add the salt if necessary.

Turn off the heat and add the pork. Cover and let it sit for a minute or so, just to warm the meat through. If using raw kale, squeeze in the lemon juice. Place the lemon slice in a bowl, pour in the soup, and serve.

Orange-and-Fennel Pulled Pork

I love the combination of spices in this rub, together with the orange juice, which I use instead of stock. The reduced juice and caramelized shallot make up for any richness lost by not searing the meat. The pork is outstanding paired with sweet-and-sour pickles, such as squash, rhubarb, and beets.

for **4 TO 6 SERVINGS**

2½ pounds boneless pork shoulder

1 recipe (4 to 5 tablespoons) Pork Spice Rub (page 373)

¾ cup fresh orange juice

1 shallot, thinly sliced

Preheat the oven to 300°F. Pork shoulder has generous marbling and heavier pockets of fat. Leave most of this on the meat, but if an obviously thick (more than ½ inch) area of fat bothers you, you can trim it a bit. Use a small knife to make incisions all over the pork, including the ends. Press the spice mixture into these cuts and spread the rest of it over every part of the meat.

Place the pork in a small Dutch oven or other heavy, covered ovenproof pot that holds it rather snugly. Add ¼ cup of the orange juice and the shallot to the pot. Cover and place in the oven. Braise, checking every 45 minutes or so and using tongs to lift the meat and mop the glazed sides of the pot before laying the meat back into the braising juices. Braise until the pork falls apart with little resistance and has browned well, up to 4 hours. Once the

meat is tender and pulls apart easily, add the remaining ½ cup orange juice, cover, and cook another 20 minutes. Remove from the oven and shred the meat with tongs or two forks.

If you're not serving right away, let the pork cool to room temperature in the pot—it will continue to absorb flavor. When the meat is cool, drain and place the meat in a covered container in the refrigerator, separate from the juices. As the juices cool, the fat will gather at the surface; spoon it off before recombining the meat and juices to store. Refrigerate for up to 5 days. Freeze in appropriate portions for up to 4 months.

Use in

→ Pulled Pork with Pickled Beets (opposite)

→ a sandwich with Pickled Acorn Squash (page 190)

Serve with

→ Pickled Rhubarb (page 99)

→ slices of fresh watermelon

→ Rustic Polenta (page 314)

Pulled Pork with Pickled Beets

Cold butter thickens the pork braising juices to make a creamy sauce for peppery pork and warm, sharp pickled beets.

⟶ **FOR EACH SERVING**

1 cup **Orange-and-Fennel Pulled Pork** (opposite)

2 or 3 wedges **Pickled Beets** (page 162)

1 tablespoon **brine from Pickled Beets**

1 teaspoon cold unsalted butter

Coarse kosher salt and freshly ground black pepper

Chopped fresh dill

Reheat the pork in a covered saucepan over low heat until warm. Do not let it dry out. Add the beets so that they heat up a little too.

Transfer the pork and beets with a slotted spoon to a serving plate. Leave the pan over low heat, caramelizing any bits stuck to the bottom. Turn off the heat, then add the pickle brine, scraping up all bits with a wooden spoon or heatproof spatula. Stir in the butter to build a creamy sauce. Taste and season with salt.

Drizzle the sauce on the pork and beets, top with pepper and dill to taste, and serve.

Pulled Pork with Scallion-Radish Salad and Orange Vinaigrette

A fresh orange dressing reinforces the sweet, concentrated flavors of the orange-braised pork. Thickened with mustard, it clings to the radishes. The salad is sweet, herbal, slightly bitter, and light, and—as you'd expect—great on its own without the pork.

⟶ **FOR EACH SERVING**

1 cup **Orange-and-Fennel Pulled Pork** (opposite)

1 scallion, greens and white, thinly sliced on the bias

3 small radishes, cut into thin wedges

1 tablespoon **Orange Vinaigrette** (page 216)

½ to ¾ teaspoon whole-grain mustard

2 or 3 leaves Bibb or other soft green lettuce, torn

Warm the pork in a covered saucepan over low heat.

Meanwhile, toss the scallion and radishes together in a bowl. Add the vinaigrette and ½ teaspoon of the mustard and mix. The dressing should coat the radishes well. If it slides too easily off their slick, cut surfaces, add a bit more mustard to the bowl to thicken it. Add the lettuce and gently fold to dress evenly. Serve alongside the warm pork.

TOASTED RYE BERRIES + ORANGE-&-FENNEL PULLED PORK + ROASTED WHOLE LEMON → PULLED PORK WITH RYE BERRIES & ROASTED LEMON

Pulled Pork and Pickled Squash Sandwich

The sweet, sharp, dense pickle is a perfect foil for a sandwich dripping with rich, spicy meat.

⟶ **FOR EACH SERVING**

1 small baguette (about 6 inches), sliced in half lengthwise

Whole-grain or Dijon mustard

1 tablespoon **Pickled Squash Spread** (page 191) *or* 1 or 2 slices **Pickled Acorn Squash** (page 190), peel removed

½ cup **Orange-and-Fennel Pulled Pork** (page 288), warm

Preheat the oven to 450°F. Place the bread in the oven and toast until light brown and crisp, 3 to 4 minutes. Slather mustard on one half and the squash spread on the other, if you're using it. If not, slather mustard on both sides. Add the pork and its juices. Pile on the pickles, if that's what you're using. Serve.

PULLED PORK WITH RYE BERRIES AND ROASTED LEMON

This assertively flavored dish is delicious warm or at room temperature. For each serving, gently warm together ⅓ cup **Toasted Rye Berries** (page 334), ½ cup **Orange-and-Fennel Pulled Pork** (page 288), and 1 tablespoon diced **Roasted Whole Lemons** (page 220).

Pork and Leek Meatballs

Seared, these meatballs ooze with braised leek butter and melting Fontina cheese. This meat mixture is much looser than for most meatballs, and it can be a bit tricky to work with. But the less you fuss with it, the more tender the meat will be. It is worth the delicate care. Because it doesn't have many fillers or binders, it is not sturdy enough for burgers.

makes **ABOUT 32 MEATBALLS OR 64 DUMPLINGS**

1 teaspoon ground cumin

1 teaspoon ground coriander

2 teaspoons coarse kosher salt

½ cup torn pieces day-old bread, without crusts

¼ cup whole milk

1 large egg yolk

1 cup finely chopped Wine-Braised Leeks (page 28; discard the whole spices)

1 cup diced (¼-inch) Italian Fontina cheese

12 large garlic cloves, minced

1 pound ground pork

Grapeseed or canola oil, for cooking

Mix the cumin, coriander, and salt together in a small bowl.

Mix the bread, milk, and egg yolk together in another bowl. Let sit for 5 minutes to soak. Add the braised leeks, Fontina, and garlic to the bread and mix well.

Spread the meat onto a large baking sheet, using your fingertips or the edge of a spatula to poke it out into an even ½-inch-thick layer; do not push or press the meat—this will overwork it, making it tough.

Spread the leek-and-bread mixture in an even layer over the pork, all the way to the edges. Sprinkle the spice mix evenly over the top.

Use a spatula to scoop up half the meat from the baking sheet and flip it over onto the other half. Poke with your fingers or the edge of the spatula to spread the mix out into a ½-inch-thick layer again. Repeat one or two more times, flipping and poking, until the ingredients are well distributed.

Heat a bit of oil in a small pan over medium heat. Cook a tablespoon of the meatball mix and taste it—this is your chance to make any adjustments in seasoning.

You can store the loose pork mixture as is, covered, in the refrigerator for up to 3 days, or freeze it. You can divide the meat mixture into ½-cup portions for single servings of pasta or to stir into rice (page 320). Or freeze it in two large portions, each enough for 4 servings of dumplings. Place in airtight freezer bags, pressed flat so you can thaw it quickly.

Or, you can form the mixture into meatballs (1½ tablespoons) or dumpling portions (1 tablespoon) instead. Do this quickly and lightly; do not vigorously roll them together. Settle for irregular shapes over overworked meat. The meatballs are best frozen uncooked. Arrange them on a baking sheet and freeze. When they're solid, transfer them to a freezer bag and return to the freezer for up to 3 months. Thaw in the refrigerator on a paper towel–lined plate before cooking.

To cook the meatballs right away, place a cast-iron pan large enough to hold them in a single layer in the oven, then preheat the oven to 450°F. Meanwhile, place the meatballs in the refrigerator for at least 15 minutes to firm slightly. When they are firm, pull out the hot pan and lightly coat it with oil. Carefully, but quickly, place the meatballs in the pan. Drizzle lightly with additional oil. Place back in the oven and cook until they are barely pink in the center, 10 to 15 minutes. Transfer to a platter to serve, spooning any pan juices on top.

Use in

→ Pork and Leek Meatballs in Broth (opposite)

→ Pork and Leek Meatballs with Baked Egg (opposite)

→ Pork and Leek Dumplings (page 294)

Pork and Leek Meatballs in Broth

Lemon zest provides a bit of lift to this intensely rich dish. Combined with good chicken stock, the meatballs make a delicious quick soup.

⟶ **FOR EACH SERVING**

2 teaspoons grapeseed or canola oil

6 uncooked **Pork and Leek Meatballs** (page 291), thawed if frozen

¾ cup excellent chicken stock (such as Worth-It Chicken Stock, page 267)

Grated zest of ¼ lemon

Heat the oil in a saucepan over medium-high heat. Add the meatballs and brown well all over. The Fontina in the meatballs melts easily and may cause the meatballs to break apart a bit. This is okay—there will be more surfaces of meat to brown and build flavor for the broth.

Once the meatballs are browned, carefully pour off any fat. Add the stock and cook at a hearty simmer until the meatballs are just cooked through, 3 to 4 minutes, scraping the bottom of the pan to mix any browned bits into the stock. Once the meatballs are cooked, taste; the broth should be deep and rich. If it is not, continue to reduce it. Sprinkle the lemon zest on top and serve.

Pork and Leek Meatballs with Baked Egg

This is a one-pan dish—great for brunch—for as few or as many meatballs as you have. If you don't have individual baking dishes, arrange the leeks and meatballs snugly in an ovenproof skillet and crack the eggs on top to cook.

⟶ **FOR EACH SERVING**

¼ cup roughly chopped **Wine-Braised Leeks** (page 28)

3 uncooked **Pork and Leek Meatballs** (page 291), thawed if frozen

1 large egg

Freshly ground black pepper

Preheat the oven to 450°F. Place the leeks in a ramekin or individual gratin dish. Nestle the meatballs in the leeks. Crack the egg right on top, ideally not breaking the yolk. Bake until the egg white is just set but the yolk is still bright and loose, 10 to 15 minutes. At this point, the meatballs should be fully cooked. Let rest for 5 minutes. Grind over pepper and serve.

Pork and Leek Dumplings

Fatty pork, melting cheese, and butter keep these dumplings extra moist, so they don't require a dipping sauce. As with any dumplings, making a batch requires time. But if you have the filling ready—and especially if it's frozen in dumpling-size amounts—you can make as few as you want, for the time you have and number of people you need to feed.

For a smaller batch, use a snug-fitting pan and adjust the water accordingly.

→ **FOR 4 SERVINGS**

20 dumpling-sized portions uncooked **Pork and Leek Meatballs** (page 291), *or* 1¼ cups of the mixture, thawed if frozen

20 round dumpling wrappers

1 to 2 tablespoons canola oil

¼ to ⅓ cup water

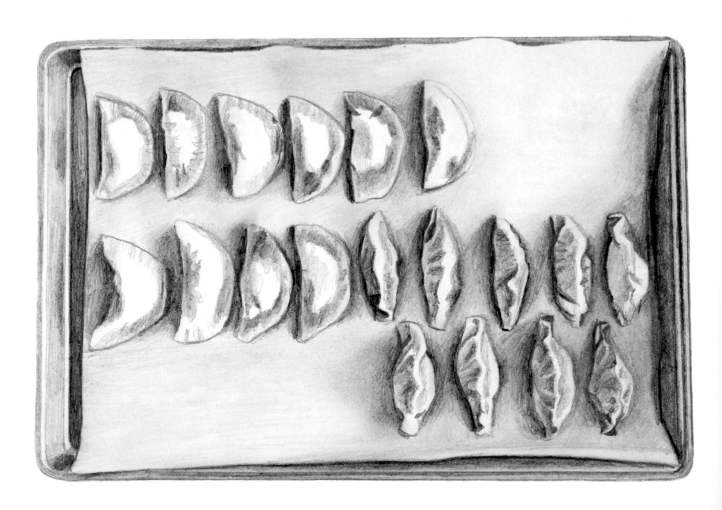

If the meatball mixture was not portioned, form it into 1-tablespoon balls (page 292).

Set up a small bowl of warm water on the counter. Use your finger to wet one side of a dumpling wrapper. Place a meatball in the center. Fold the edges together and seal well, pushing out any trapped air. Stand the dumpling upright on a baking sheet, seam up, gently pushing the bottom flat.

Heat the oil in a heavy 10-inch skillet, preferably cast iron, over medium heat. Repeat with the remaining meatballs and wrappers.

Once the oil is hot and shimmering, quickly and carefully place the dumplings in a snug spiral around the pan, starting from the outside and filling in to the center. Be deliberate where you place them, since as soon as they hit the pan they will stick. They can touch, but not overlap. Fry until deep golden on the bottom, about 2 minutes.

Remove the skillet from the heat and immediately add enough water to come one quarter of the way up the sides of the dumplings. Return the skillet to medium-low heat, cover, and cook for 2 minutes. Break open a dumpling to test if the meat is just cooked through. Once the dumplings are cooked, remove the lid and turn the heat to medium-high to evaporate the remaining water. Do not try to pry the dumplings off prematurely. Once the water is gone, they will begin to resear, recrisp, and release. Check them individually, lifting them with a spatula, and remove each one as soon as it is crispy and unstuck. Serve immediately.

Crisped Bacon

I've made a habit of cutting sliced bacon into small squares to store in individually wrapped parcels. That way, even when the bacon is frozen, I can grab only the amount I want to cook. I'll add a few tablespoons to Corn and Potato Soup with Rosemary (page 124), Polenta with Balsamic-Poached Figs and Bacon (page 317), or Squid with Wine-Braised Leeks and Bacon (page 30).

You can cook frozen bacon without thawing first. Just give it a few more minutes in the pan, breaking the pieces apart with tongs.

Choose all-natural bacon, preferably thick cut. Twelve ounces of bacon will give you about 1 cup chopped, crisped bacon and ½ cup fat.

Cut bacon strips in half lengthwise. Then cut crosswise into ½-inch squares. Place the bacon in a large skillet and turn the heat to low. After about 5 minutes, the fat will begin to render and the bacon will move freely in the pan. Turn the heat to medium to crisp the meat, stirring frequently, about 10 minutes. Once crisp, lift the bacon out of the pan with a slotted spoon and drain on paper towels. Save the amber-colored fat. Once cooled, you can store both separately in the refrigerator for up to 1 week. The fat can be frozen for months.

Bacon Vinaigrette

Packed with bacon and aided by sharp vinegar and strong mustard, this dressing transforms a humble cabbage into amazing slaw (page 114). It's also great with frisée, where the pieces of bacon tangle in the curly leaves. You can use it on any sturdy green, or alongside a Perfect Hard-Boiled Egg (page 349) or Salt-Roasted Little Potatoes (page 178). I also like it warm, on seared fish like halibut or bass, or mixed with a grain like rye berries or farro.

Make this while the bacon fat is still a little warm.

→ **MAKES ⅔ CUP**

2 tablespoons red wine vinegar

4 teaspoons whole-grain mustard

¼ cup excellent olive oil

¼ teaspoon coarse kosher salt

2 tablespoons **rendered fat from Crisped Bacon** (page 295), slightly warm

⅔ cup **Crisped Bacon**

Whisk the vinegar and mustard together in a small bowl. Whisk in the olive oil and salt, then the bacon fat, and finally the bacon pieces.

Store in the refrigerator for up to 1 week. Bring it to room temperature or warm slightly and whisk well before using.

Lamb

Spiced Lamb Meatballs or Patties

Cumin and paprika, vinegar-soaked raisins, herbs, and lemon brighten and lighten the lamb and make it stretch further—the final mixture is one and a half times as much as the original amount of meat. Make sure your spices are fresh, and don't skimp on the large amount of lemon zest.

Be careful how you cook ground lamb. It has less fat than other ground meat and, without warning, becomes crumbly and tastes muddy. To prevent this, I cook the lamb either as little meatballs or in large patties. Both shapes pick up great seared flavor but stay pink and moist inside.

makes ABOUT 40 (1-OUNCE) MEATBALLS OR 8 (5-OUNCE) PATTIES

1 cup raisin-sized pieces day-old white bread, without crusts

½ cup whole milk

2 large egg yolks

1 cup chopped golden raisins

2 teaspoons sherry vinegar

2 tablespoons ground cumin

1 tablespoon sweet paprika

2 teaspoons coarse kosher salt

2 teaspoons freshly ground black pepper

1½ teaspoons hot red pepper flakes

¼ cup coarsely grated onion (1 small)

Packed ¼ cup minced fresh oregano

4 small garlic cloves, minced

Packed 4 teaspoons grated lemon zest

2 pounds ground lamb

Grapeseed or canola oil, for cooking

Soak the bread with the milk and egg yolks in a large bowl. Combine the raisins and vinegar in a separate small bowl and macerate for 5 minutes. Combine the cumin, paprika, salt, black pepper, and red pepper flakes in a third bowl.

Once the bread is completely saturated, add the onion, oregano, garlic, lemon zest, and the raisins and vinegar. Mix well.

Spread the lamb onto a large baking sheet, using your fingertips or the edge of a spatula to poke it out into an even ½-inch-thick layer; do not push or press to flatten the meat—this will overwork it, making the cooked meat tough.

Spread the bread mixture in an even layer over the lamb, all the way to the edges. Coat with the spice mix evenly.

Use a spatula to scoop up half the meat from the baking sheet and flip it over onto the other half. Poke with your fingers or the edge of the spatula to spread the mix out into a ½-inch-thick layer again. Repeat one or two more times, flipping and poking, until the ingredients are well distributed; they may not be uniformly mixed.

Heat a bit of oil in a small pan over medium heat. Cook a tablespoon of the mix and taste it—this is your chance to make any adjustments in seasoning.

You can store the lamb mixture as is, covered, in the refrigerator for up to 3 days, pulling from it only what you need to cook. Or gently shape the mix into 1-ounce meatballs (about 1 tablespoon), working quickly and lightly; do not vigorously roll them together. Or press them lightly into patties, ¾ cup of the mixture per patty, pressed to ¾ inch thick. In all cases, settle for irregular shapes over overworked meat. (*You can freeze the raw meatballs or patties on a parchment paper–lined baking sheet. When they're solid, transfer them to a freezer bag and return to the freezer for up to 3 months. Thaw completely before cooking.*)

To cook, heat a skillet over medium-high heat; add enough oil to just coat the pan. Once the oil begins to ripple and run loosely, add the meatballs or patties, in batches if necessary, and leave them undisturbed to cook. Cook until the bottoms turn dark brown, about 2 minutes, being careful not to let any exposed raisins burn. Turn the meatballs or flip the patties over, reduce the heat to medium, cover the pan, and continue to brown, 1 to 2 minutes more. Once the outsides are brown but the insides remain a bit pink in the center, remove from the heat and let rest in the pan for a few minutes before serving.

If you want to break up the meat, use a spatula to cut the cooked patties or meatballs into pea-sized pieces (searing the meat in larger pieces first keeps it from drying out). If the broken-apart meat is bit underdone, cover the pan to trap the last bit of heat and rest for another minute. Save the browned bits and pan drippings for a quick, rich sauce.

Use meatballs in

→ Spiced Lamb Meatballs with Sautéed Kale and Walnuts (page 301)

→ Spiced Lamb Meatballs with Chickpeas, Pickled Parsley, and Yogurt (page 300)

→ Spiced Lamb Meatballs with Pan Sauce (opposite)

Use patties in

→ Spiced Lamb with Cherry Tomatoes and Rye Berries (opposite)

→ a sandwich on a bun, with spicy mayonnaise

Spiced Lamb Meatballs with Pan Sauce

The pan sauce for these lamb meatballs is a simple, quick reduction of lemon juice and chicken stock, fortified with browned bits of seared lamb. You can spoon the sauce over any heavy starch such as couscous or polenta, but the meatballs are satisfying on their own. In any case, sear as many as you want at a time, making sure the pan is hot and you don't crowd them too closely together. For several portions, cook the meatballs in a larger pan or in batches, as necessary, making the pan sauce only after the last round has seared.

—→ **FOR EACH SERVING**

> 6 to 8 **Spiced Lamb Meatballs** (page 297), cooked as directed on page 298, hot
>
> ½ cup excellent chicken stock (such as Worth-It Chicken Stock, page 267)
>
> Coarse kosher salt (optional)
>
> 1 teaspoon fresh lemon juice
>
> 1 tablespoon roughly chopped fresh herbs (such as thyme or oregano)

Place the meatballs on a serving plate and cover with foil to keep warm. Pour off any fat in the pan and place the pan over medium-high heat. Add the stock. Reduce by half, scraping up any browned bits on the bottom of the pan, to form a rich sauce. Taste for salt, then add the lemon juice and fresh herbs. Pour over the meatballs. Serve.

Spiced Lamb with Cherry Tomatoes and Rye Berries

The spiced lamb and hay-scented rye berries come together in an unexpected dish for late summer when sweet cherry tomatoes reach their seasonal peak. I use parsley, but you can substitute mint or cilantro.

—→ **FOR EACH SERVING**

> 1 teaspoon excellent olive oil
>
> 1 uncooked **Spiced Lamb Patty** (page 297), thawed if frozen (see headnote)
>
> ⅓ cup **Toasted Rye Berries** (page 334)
>
> ⅓ to ½ cup plump cherry tomatoes, cut in half
>
> 1 tablespoon roughly torn fresh flat-leaf parsley
>
> 1 lemon wedge

Follow the instructions for cooking lamb patties on page 298, using olive oil. Once the patty is brown, use a spatula to chop it into pieces the size of the cut tomatoes. Continue to cook for a minute longer to incorporate any juices that run out. Pull off the heat before the meat loses all its pink.

Transfer the lamb to a serving bowl. Add the rye berries to the pan, stirring to warm them and pick up the delicious bits of browned meat. Once warm, add the berries to the bowl with the lamb. Add the tomatoes and parsley and squeeze in the lemon juice. Toss again and serve.

Spiced Lamb Meatballs with Chickpeas, Pickled Parsley, and Yogurt

Pickled-parsley brine and the pan juices from the lamb meatballs make a sweet-and-sour pan sauce for the lamb and chickpeas, then additional pickle brine is whisked into yogurt for a cool, creamy dressing.

You can substitute drained canned chickpeas for the Salt-and-Pepper Chickpeas. Serve alongside or stuffed into a warm pita.

—> **FOR EACH SERVING**

Excellent olive oil

6 uncooked **Spiced Lamb Meatballs** (page 297), thawed if frozen

2 tablespoons plus 1 to 2 teaspoons **brine from Pickled Parsley** (page 66)

½ cup **Salt-and-Pepper Chickpeas** (page 340), or see headnote

¼ cup whole-milk Greek yogurt

Coarse kosher salt

Packed 1 tablespoon chopped **Pickled Parsley**

Oil your hands lightly and press gently on the meatballs to flatten slightly. Heat a skillet over medium-high heat; add enough oil just to coat the bottom. Once the oil begins to ripple and run loosely, add the meatballs, flat sides down, in batches if necessary. Cook until very brown underneath, about 2 minutes. Flip over each meatball and turn the heat down to medium. Cover the pan and cook until the second side is deep brown, 1 to 2 minutes more. Transfer to a bowl.

Place the skillet back on the stove over medium heat. Add 2 tablespoons of the pickle brine and scrape the stuck, browned bits in the pan with a flat, heatproof spatula or wooden spoon. Reduce the sauce by half to a glaze, then add the chickpeas, stirring to coat and warm them through. Scrape into the bowl with the lamb. Mix well. Transfer to a serving plate.

Mix the yogurt with the remaining pickle brine and a pinch of salt in a small bowl. Drizzle on top of or serve alongside the lamb and chickpeas. Scatter the pickled parsley on top. Serve.

Spiced Lamb Meatballs with Sautéed Kale and Walnuts

The lamb may be the star in this dish, but the lemon and walnuts make it shine. Use whatever sturdy greens you have on hand, and make sure the walnuts are fresh. I stir them into the sauce rather than sprinkle them on top of the dish at the end. Double the recipe for an impressive warm appetizer for four.

⟶ **FOR EACH SERVING**

Excellent olive oil

6 uncooked **Spiced Lamb Meatballs** (page 297), thawed if frozen

Packed 2 cups torn kale leaves

¼ teaspoon coarse kosher salt

⅓ cup excellent chicken stock (such as Worth-It Chicken Stock, page 267)

3 tablespoons chopped toasted walnuts (page 368)

2 teaspoons fresh lemon juice

Oil your hands lightly and press lightly on the meatballs to flatten slightly. Heat a skillet over medium-high heat; add enough oil just to coat the bottom. Once the oil begins to ripple and run loosely, add the meatballs, in batches if necessary. Cook until very brown underneath, about 2 minutes. Flip over each meatball and turn the heat down to medium. Cover the pan and cook until the second side is deep brown, 1 to 2 minutes more. Transfer to a plate and cover with foil to keep warm.

Return the skillet to the stove, turn the heat up to high, and add the kale and salt. Cook, tossing to wilt and barely color the kale, about 3 minutes. Add the stock. Use a wooden spoon or heatproof spatula to scrape up any browned bits from the bottom of the pan. Reduce the stock to a couple of tablespoons, then turn off the heat and add the walnuts and lemon juice. Toss to warm through. Scrape everything over the meatballs and serve.

Lamb Shanks Braised in Two Vinegars

A combination of sharp red wine vinegar and sweet balsamic vinegar creates a more vibrant, versatile sauce for rich lamb shanks. If you prefer sweet tastes to sharp ones, increase the balsamic vinegar by ¼ cup and decrease the red wine vinegar by the same amount.

If you have the time, it is worth salting the shanks a day in advance, instead of just before cooking. If serving the shanks the day you make them, leave time for a quick cure and for the braising juices to reduce at the end.

makes ABOUT 4 CUPS PULLED MEAT AND 3½ CUPS BRAISING JUICES, ENOUGH FOR 4 SERVINGS

4 large lamb shanks (about 5 pounds total)

Coarse kosher salt

1 tablespoon grapeseed or canola oil

2 cups sliced red onions

5 garlic cloves, peeled and smashed

3 cups excellent chicken stock (such as Worth-It Chicken Stock, page 267)

½ cup balsamic vinegar (see headnote)

½ cup red wine vinegar

Freshly ground black pepper

Season the lamb shanks well on all sides, including the cut ends, with 3½ teaspoons salt. If possible, let rest uncovered in the refrigerator for 24 hours. Otherwise, leave at room temperature for 1 hour before cooking.

Preheat the oven to 350°F. Wrap each shank in a paper towel to absorb all moisture. Heat the oil over medium-high heat in a large Dutch oven. Unwrap the shanks. Sear very well on all sides, in batches if necessary to give each shank space to lie flat in the pan. Transfer the shanks to a plate as they are done.

Add the onions and garlic to the pot. Cook for 5 minutes, stirring occasionally, to coat well and infuse the oil. Add the chicken stock and both vinegars. Stir to combine, then bring to a simmer.

Return the shanks and any accumulated juices to the pot; it's okay if they are not submerged. Cover the pot and place in the oven. Braise, turning the shanks every 30 minutes, until the meat turns a deep purple-brown and pulls away from the bone, 2 to 2½ hours. While the shanks cook, you'll notice the braising juices begin to coat the sides of the pot. When this happens, grab a shank with tongs and use the meat to wipe the sides clean and bring this concentrated flavor back into the sauce.

If serving right away, transfer the shanks from the pot to a plate and cover with foil to keep warm. Strain the braising juices into a tall heatproof container, such as a measuring cup. Return the onions and garlic to the pot. As fat collects on the top of the juices, spoon off as much as you can. Return the skimmed juices to the pot and bring to a simmer over medium-low heat. Reduce until they are rich and deep brown and taste as sweet as they do sharp, perhaps 20 minutes. The more you reduce the braising juices, the richer they become. When the juices are to your taste, season with pepper. Return the shanks to the braising juices, turning to coat them well, and gently reheat to serve.

If preparing the shanks in advance, do not reduce the juices. Instead, strain them, let them cool, then refrigerate for up to 3 days. The fat will rise and solidify for easy removal. Refrigerate the onion and garlic with the shanks separately from the juices. You can freeze the shanks individually with their braising juices, once defatted. Thaw in the refrigerator before reheating.

To reheat, preheat the oven to 400°F. Place the shanks with one quarter of the onion and garlic and one quarter of the juices per shank, in a pot. Cover and place in the oven. Heat until the shanks are warm and the meat is very tender, turning once or twice, about 15 minutes. The juices will have thickened slightly. Taste for salt, add pepper, and serve.

Use in

→ Flatbread with Lamb Shanks, Pine Nuts, and Mint (page 305)

→ Lamb Shanks with Roasted Lemon (page 304)

→ Lamb Shanks with Apple-Endive Slaw (page 304)

Serve with

→ Braised Celeriac Gratin (page 171)

→ Triple-Braised Wild Mushrooms (page 194)

→ Rustic Polenta (page 314)

Lamb Shanks with Apple-Endive Slaw

The apple-endive slaw is fresh and bright, crunchy yet creamy, bitter, a bit spicy, and tart—a perfect counterpoint to the rich lamb. Prepare the slaw ingredients, except the apple, ahead of time. Cut the apple and dress the slaw right before serving.

⟶ **FOR EACH SERVING**

1 **Lamb Shank Braised in Two Vinegars** (page 302), on or off the bone

⅓ cup **braising juices from Lamb Shanks Braised in Two Vinegars**

1½ tablespoons Dijon mustard

2 pinches of coarse kosher salt

1 cup julienned Belgian endive (1 small head)

½ cup thinly sliced red onion

1 tablespoon minced fresh oregano

½ green apple

Warm the lamb in the braising juices (page 303). Transfer the lamb to a plate and cover with foil to keep warm.

Whisk the braising juices with the mustard and salt in a large bowl. Add the endive, onion, and oregano and toss well. Julienne the apple, add to the slaw, and toss well. Transfer the slaw to a plate and serve the warmed shank on top.

Lamb Shanks with Roasted Lemon

Roasted lemon and a splash of vinegar punch up the lamb's already robust braising juices. Don't skip the pepper—and consider sneaking in pitted, halved green olives when reheating everything, if you have them.

⟶ **FOR EACH SERVING**

1 **Lamb Shank Braised in Two Vinegars** (page 302), on the bone

¾ cup **braising juices from Lamb Shanks Braised in Two Vinegars**

2 tablespoons chopped **Roasted Whole Lemons** (page 220)

Coarse kosher salt and freshly ground black pepper (optional)

Red wine vinegar or fresh lemon juice (optional)

Preheat the oven to 400°F. Put the lamb, braising juices, and lemon in a snug ovenproof pot. Cover and place in the oven. Heat, turning once, until the shank is warm and the braising juices have reduced, about 15 minutes. Taste; to balance the sweetness, you may need to add a bit of salt and pepper and a tiny splash of red wine vinegar or fresh lemon juice. Serve.

Flatbread with Lamb Shanks, Pine Nuts, and Mint

Citrus meets braised lamb as lime enlivens the rich meat, which is then scattered with fresh mint and pine nuts on top of warm, yogurt-slathered flatbreads.

You'll want to assemble the flatbreads at the last minute, but you can prepare all the ingredients for them separately ahead of time, keeping the lamb warm in a pot and the flatbreads warm in a low oven.

—→ FOR 4 APPETIZER SERVINGS OR
2 MAIN-COURSE SERVINGS

4 **Skillet Flatbreads** (page 357), cooked

About 1 cup **shredded meat from Lamb Shanks Braised in Two Vinegars** (page 302)

¾ cup **braising juices from Lamb Shanks Braised in Two Vinegars**

3 tablespoons water

⅓ cup Greek yogurt

¾ teaspoon ground cumin

1 teaspoon hot red pepper flakes

Small handful of fresh mint leaves, torn

1½ tablespoons toasted pine nuts or peanuts (page 368)

1 lime, cut into quarters

Flaky sea salt

Preheat the oven to 250°F. Cover the flatbreads and keep them warm. Combine the lamb, braising juices, and water in a small saucepan over low heat. Cover and cook until the lamb is completely warm and has absorbed some of the juices, about 5 minutes.

Spread a generous tablespoon yogurt on each flatbread, followed by one quarter of the meat and juices. Sprinkle the cumin, red pepper flakes, mint, and pine nuts on top. Squeeze with the lime and finish each flatbread with a healthy pinch of flaky sea salt. Serve.

Pasta and Polenta

Pasta

Cooking Pasta

Artisanal brands of pasta are made with nuttier, more freshly milled flours. They are sturdier, they chew better, and they often have deeper grooves and slightly uneven edges that catch and hold sauce. Choose these when possible.

My advice for cooking pasta goes against common wisdom about doing so in vast quantities of water. I suggest, instead, you use only the amount of water you need to keep the noodles loose in the pot—particularly thin ones like pappardelle—to better concentrate the starch they release. This starch is key to an excellent pasta dish.

Starch thickens a sauce and makes it stick. Even when the sauce is nothing more than good butter, the starch will bind the water and butter together to form a creamy blanket for the noodles. Without this starch, butter will merely grease the pasta, then pool at the bottom of the bowl.

Salt is crucial too. Bland pasta undermines even the most flavorful sauce. Well-salted pasta carries the dish and often needs little more than excellent olive oil, lemon zest, a fresh herb, and flaky salt to finish it. Most cooks don't use enough salt, and few taste their cooking water to see if it's salty enough.

The Only Pasta Recipe

Whether you reheat precooked pasta or cook it all at once from scratch; serve the pasta with a prepared sauce or make a quick sauce right in the pan; or are cooking for four people or just yourself, you'll sauce and finish the pasta the same way. This is the only recipe you need.

For each serving of pasta (¼ pound uncooked, 2 cups precooked), you'll need ½ cup prepared ingredients for the sauce, or 2 cups for a full pound.

If you need to make the sauce and it will take longer to prepare than the pasta takes to cook, start the sauce first. You want have the sauce in the pan when you're ready to put them together.

Pasta that will be served cold or at room temperature is better sauced first in a hot pan, then spread out on a baking sheet to cool. Most cold pasta dishes are best sauced and then eaten the same day they are made, whereas sauced pasta that will be reheated can hold for up to 2 days.

makes ABOUT 8 CUPS PASTA, ENOUGH FOR 4 SERVINGS

FOR SAUCING THE PASTA

Ingredients for sauce of your choice (see box, page 310), *or* 2 cups store-bought sauce

FOR THE PASTA

8 cups water

2 tablespoons plus 1 heaping teaspoon coarse kosher salt, plus more if needed

1 pound dried pasta

Excellent olive oil (optional)

Additional finishing ingredients (optional; see box for suggestions)

To make the sauce: You'll need a skillet large enough to hold all the pasta (not a saucepan), such as a 12-inch skillet for 1 pound pasta. If making your own sauce, cut the ingredients to match the appropriate size and shape of the pasta: Thinly slice mushrooms for linguine, chop onions and tomatoes for orecchiette, and so on. Cook these ingredients as necessary, salting cautiously; the pasta water you'll add brings a lot of salt with it. Quickly brown the mushrooms in butter; slowly stew the onions and tomatoes with olive oil. Many Starting Points in this book make great "instant" sauces—for example, Braised Fennel (page 110) in its braising broth or Wine-and-Tomato-Braised Squid (page 230). Simply place them in the pan to warm.

To cook the pasta: Bring the water to a rolling boil in a large, wide pot. Add the salt and then the pasta, swishing it about until the pieces get caught up in the boil and stay separate on their own.

If you are precooking the pasta to serve at another time: Place a strainer on top of a heatproof bowl large enough to catch the pasta water. Set out a large baking sheet, to allow the cooked pasta to cool quickly.

Drain the pasta well *before* it is al dente—it will be pliable, but still taste a bit raw.

To drain and store the pasta: Immediately pour the pasta into the strainer/bowl setup, then lift the strainer up out of the bowl and shake off the excess water. Quickly spill the pasta onto the baking sheet to cool. Drizzle the cooling pasta very lightly with oil and toss gently with tongs. Let the pasta and pasta water cool completely. You'll notice how the starch will turn the pasta water cloudy as it cools. Store the cooled pasta and pasta water in separate covered containers for up to 5 days.

If you are planning to serve the pasta right away: Continue cooking the pasta until *just shy of* al dente—taste a piece for that identifiable bite of resistance at the center. Don't rely on the package to tell you when the pasta is done; it will get overcooked. Because the pasta will continue to cook in the pan with its sauce, it will go limp if fully cooked from the start. You'll need a ladle or heatproof measuring cup to grab some pasta water from the pot to bind the sauce, and a spider to transfer the pasta to the sauce in the skillet. (If you don't have a spider, follow the instructions above for draining pasta and catching the pasta water.)

To finish the pasta: Heat the pasta in the skillet. When it is almost done—or if you are using precooked pasta—add about 1 tablespoon pasta water for each ½-cup serving of sauce, or ¼ cup for 4 servings, to the sauce. Turn the heat to high and bring to a strong simmer. Swirl the skillet to incorporate the water into the sauce. Add the pasta and toss continuously to coat well, about 30 seconds, adding more pasta water if the sauce becomes tacky or the pasta becomes too dry. Remove it from the heat, fold in any additional ingredients, and serve immediately. If you are serving the pasta at room temperature or cold, spill it onto a baking sheet to stop the cooking and let it cool before serving or storing for later use. (Leftovers can be refrigerated, covered, for up to 2 days.)

FAVORITE PASTA PAIRINGS

→ Penne with sliced Braised Fennel (page 110) and mashed Poached Garlic (page 20), finished with fresh lemon zest and chopped fresh oregano

→ Spaghetti with Crisp Sautéed Shiitakes (page 199), finished with Toasted Bread Crumbs (page 355) and hot red pepper flakes

→ Pappardelle with Seared Chicken Livers (page 269), finished with assorted bitter greens

→ Orecchiette with Onion Jam (page 34), finished with freshly grated Parmesan and thinly sliced prosciutto

Tagliatelle with Confit Zucchini Squash, Oregano, and Crème Fraîche

The sauce is made by combining Confit Zucchini Squash with just enough pasta water to warm it through, then adding cheese and crème fraîche to thicken it. Don't overheat the zucchini.

—→ FOR 4 SERVINGS

1 pound tagliatelle or spaghetti, cooked as directed in **The Only Pasta Recipe** (page 309)

Up to ½ cup **pasta cooking water from The Only Pasta Recipe**

2 cups **Confit Zucchini Squash** (page 141), with its oil

Up to 2 teaspoons coarse kosher salt

1½ cups or more finely grated pecorino cheese

¼ cup crème fraîche

¼ cup chopped fresh oregano

Grated lemon zest

Freshly ground black pepper

Place ¼ cup of the pasta water in a skillet large enough to hold all the pasta over high heat. Once it is hot, add the squash and toss quickly and continuously to combine.

Once the squash and pasta water begin to come together as a sauce, add the pasta, tossing well. If the pasta seems to absorb too much of the sauce, add more pasta water, a tablespoon at a time, until loose again. Add salt to taste.

Off the heat, add the pecorino, crème fraîche, oregano, and lemon zest and pepper to taste. Toss well again. Serve immediately.

Spring Vegetable and Herb Pasta

This sauce begins as a fragile emulsion of olive oil and pasta water. It is then enriched with herb butter—added cold, so it stays creamy—and seasoned with lemon zest and herbs. Make the vegetable medley first. If the vegetables aren't blanched already, you can steam them first in the skillet in which you'll make the pasta sauce.

—→ FOR 4 SERVINGS

¼ cup excellent olive oil

1 pound pasta (such as orecchiette), cooked as directed in **The Only Pasta Recipe** (page 309)

Up to ½ cup **pasta cooking water from The Only Pasta Recipe**

2 cups **Spring Vegetable Medley** (page 75), blanched, or a single vegetable

Grated zest from 4 lemons

4 tablespoons (½ stick) cold **Herb-Infused Butter** (page 377) or unsalted butter, cut into small pieces

Loosely packed 1 cup roughly chopped assorted fresh herbs (dill, tarragon, parsley, and chives)

Flaky sea salt and freshly ground black pepper

½ cup freshly grated Parmesan cheese, for serving

Heat the oil over high heat in a skillet large enough to hold the pasta. Once it is sizzling, add ¼ cup of the pasta water, swirling them together to distribute the oil through the water. In seconds, it will turn into a creamy, light green sauce. Add the vegetables and pasta and cook for another 30 seconds, tossing continuously to warm. Add 2 more tablespoons pasta water; make sure it heats through.

continued ↘

Without mixing, add the lemon zest and butter to the pasta. Remove from the heat. Toss continuously, until the now-forming sauce coats everything evenly. If it appears dry, add more pasta water, 1 tablespoon at a time. Once well coated, add the herbs, black pepper to taste, and, if necessary, salt. Toss again. Let the pasta sit off the heat for a few minutes for the flavors to meld. Serve warm or at room temperature, with grated Parmesan.

Linguine, Short Ribs, and Crisp Sautéed Shiitakes

Lemon and fresh herbs bring this traditional combination of mushrooms and meat together in a dish as delicious as it is filling. Make sure the shiitakes are sliced neatly and well browned. In small bites, they mingle nicely with the noodles. The short ribs are so filling that you'll need only 8 ounces of pasta for 4 servings.

—> **FOR 4 SERVINGS**

¾ cup **Crisp Sautéed Shiitakes** (page 199)

1 cup **shredded meat from Wine-Braised Short Ribs** (page 283)

1 cup **braising juices from Wine-Braised Short Ribs**

Freshly ground black pepper

½ pound linguine, cooked as directed in **The Only Pasta Recipe** (page 309)

Up to ½ cup **pasta cooking water from The Only Pasta Recipe**

2 tablespoons chopped fresh tarragon or oregano

Grated zest of 2 lemons

Combine the mushrooms, meat, and braising juices in a skillet large enough to hold the pasta over medium-high heat. Add lots of pepper.

Once the mixture is hot, add ¼ cup of the pasta water. Turn the heat up to high to bring the sauce together. Once it simmers, add the pasta and toss continuously until hot and flavorful, 30 seconds to 1 minute. If the sauce seems too thick or the noodles too dry, add more pasta water, 1 tablespoon at a time. Stir in the tarragon and lemon zest. Divide among four plates and serve immediately.

Linguine with Braised Leeks and Ricotta Custard

If you don't have Savory Ricotta Custard on hand, use fresh ricotta seasoned well with salt, pepper, and pecorino cheese. This dish can be served at room temperature too, but like all great cold pastas, it should be assembled warm before being cooled to serve.

—> **FOR 4 SERVINGS**

1½ cups **Wine-Braised Leeks** (page 28) with braising liquid

1 pound linguine, cooked as directed in **The Only Pasta Recipe** (page 309)

Up to ½ cup **pasta cooking water from The Only Pasta Recipe**

1½ tablespoons cold unsalted butter, cut into pieces

¾ cup **Savory Ricotta Custard** (page 386), or see headnote

Freshly ground black pepper

Cut the leeks into long, thin ribbons to mimic the shape of the pasta. Warm the leeks and braising liquid in a skillet large enough to hold the pasta over medium-high heat. Add ¼ cup of the pasta water and bring to a simmer. Add the linguine and toss to heat through and coat well, about 1 minute. If the pasta absorbs all of the liquid, add more pasta water, 1 tablespoon at a time. Off the heat, stir in the butter to melt and coat the noodles, then fold in the ricotta custard. Add black pepper to taste. Serve immediately, or let cool to room temperature, tossing once again before serving.

Tagliatelle with Poached Garlic and Egg Yolk

Here's a dish that is fast, rich, delicious, and always right. Once you see pasta water and egg yolk transform simple poached garlic into a rich, silky sauce, you'll be able to make this egg sauce with other prepared ingredients—Confit Tomatoes (page 148), Mushroom Duxelles page 201)—and for any amount of pasta you want to eat.

You may notice that I use more pasta water in this recipe than others. The thickening egg yolks require the extra liquid to cook to creaminess. The technique for saucing the pasta is the same no matter what shape you use. I like long noodles.

If you have stored Poached Garlic in oil, you can use that oil in place of the olive oil called for.

—> FOR 4 SERVINGS

4 large egg yolks

½ teaspoon cold water

¼ cup excellent olive oil or **oil from Poached Garlic** (page 20)

20 cloves **Poached Garlic**

1 pound tagliatelle, cooked as directed in **The Only Pasta Recipe** (page 309)

½ cup or more **pasta cooking water from The Only Pasta Recipe**

Flaky sea salt and freshly ground black pepper

Freshy grated Parmesan cheese

Whisk the egg yolks and cold water together in a small bowl.

Gently warm the oil in a skillet large enough to hold the pasta over medium-low heat. Add the garlic, mashing the cloves lightly with the back of a spoon. Once warm, turn the heat to medium-high.

Add ½ cup of the pasta water to the skillet and bring to a strong simmer. Add the pasta, tossing with tongs, until heated through. Turn off the heat and drizzle in the yolk mixture, tossing the pasta continuously as you do. If the sauce seems tacky or appears to congeal, quickly add a couple of teaspoons more of the pasta water as you toss the noodles. Season with flaky sea salt, pepper, and Parmesan to taste. Divide among four plates and serve immediately.

POACHED GARLIC + long noodles olive oil egg yolks salt pepper Parmesan → TAGLIATELLE WITH POACHED GARLIC & EGG YOLK

Polenta

Rustic Polenta

Polenta does not require an hour of continuous attention, as many recipes suggest. Rather, five minutes at the start pays off in a preparation that is otherwise hands-free. Cook polenta in a large nonstick pot, if you have one; you'll lose less cornmeal to the sides of the pot as it cooks down. But any good heavy pot will do. The quantity of water in this recipe yields a soft, spoonable polenta that can be eaten immediately or kept warm in the covered pot for up to 20 minutes. If you're making it ahead or you have leftovers, pour the still-hot polenta into a greased pan and refrigerate. It can be softened later with milk, stock, oil, or butter and a few minutes on the stove, or it can be cut and browned in the oven.

Although the cheese is optional, I strongly recommend it—especially if you plan on making polenta slices. If you omit the cheese, you'll want to add salt at the end.

for 4 MAIN-COURSE SERVINGS OR 6 SIDE SERVINGS

8 cups water

2 teaspoons coarse kosher salt, plus more if needed

1¾ cups stone-ground coarse polenta (not instant)

¼ pound Parmesan or pecorino cheese, finely grated (about 1½ cups loosely packed; optional)

Pour the water into a heavy pot, preferably nonstick. Cover and bring to a boil over high heat. Add the salt. Use a large whisk to stir the water to a whirlpool in the center of the pot. Add the polenta in a slow stream, pouring directly over the moving whisk and whisking continuously, until it is evenly suspended in the water to the very edges of the pot and begins to resemble porridge, about 5 full minutes. You'll know it's ready to cook on its own when you can leave the pot undisturbed for a couple of minutes and the polenta remains uniform throughout.

Turn the heat down to very low and continue to cook, uncovered. The polenta will turn thick in little time and form a thin skin on the surface, with occasional bubbles poking through. As it cooks, you may notice cornmeal sticking to the sides of the pot; stir occasionally, scraping the sides and bottom of the pot, to mix it all in. Cook until the polenta breaks down completely, about 45 minutes; it will still have a coarse texture, but it will taste creamy and soft.

Stir in the Parmesan. If you're not adding cheese, taste for salt. You can serve immediately or keep it warm for 20 minutes by covering it and turning the stove to its lowest setting. Stir well before serving.

To store, pour the hot polenta into a 9-x-13-inch greased baking pan; it should settle to at least 1 inch thick. Smooth the top. Once the polenta is cool and firm, store in the pan, covered, in the refrigerator. You can also cut the polenta into portions, so you can crisp or resoften as much or as little as you need, until you use it up. It will keep for up to 5 days in the refrigerator. It does not freeze well.

Soft creamy polenta

→ Season with Herb-Infused Butter (page 377) and freshly grated Parmesan cheese

→ Top with Seared Kale with Garlic and Lemon (page 50)

→ Serve under or alongside Whole Roasted Fish (page 246)

Firm polenta (from Rustic Polenta, opposite, or Baked Polenta, page 316)

→ Use in Polenta with Balsamic-Poached Figs and Bacon (page 317)

→ Top with a poached egg (page 351) and Confit Tomatoes (page 148)

REHEATING POLENTA FOR SOFT, CREAMY POLENTA

Because of its high water-to-cornmeal ratio, this polenta is easily resoftened. A dish that takes an hour to cook can reheat in under a minute. You can also vary how you finish the polenta, reheating it with stock and stirring in pan drippings, or adding warm milk and ricotta cheese.

For each serving, place a generous 1 cup polenta in a snug saucepan. Mash well with a fork. Add 2 tablespoons heavy cream, milk, or broth and 1½ teaspoons unsalted butter. Cook, covered, over low heat for a few minutes, stirring once or twice, until puffed up and very hot. Taste for salt. Stir in extra cheese, black pepper, honey, or fresh herbs, if you like.

Baked Polenta

Unlike most baked or grilled polenta, this version crisps nicely on the outside while turning creamy again on the inside. If you've let the polenta set in a baking pan, it will be easy to cut evenly. Though you can cut it in whatever shapes you want, the pieces should be about 1 inch thick, which will ensure they heat through in the time it takes for them to brown. You can also cut it into bite-sized pieces and serve as a snack or hors d'oeuvre.

⟶ **FOR 4 TO 6 SERVINGS**

Excellent olive oil

1 recipe **Rustic Polenta** (page 314), set

Loosely packed 2 cups freshly grated Parmesan or pecorino cheese (optional)

Preheat the oven to 500°F. Brush a large baking sheet with oil. Pat the polenta dry with paper towels, then turn it out in one piece onto a cutting board. Pat this side dry too. Cut the polenta into 4 to 6 even portions.

Arrange the pieces directly on the baking sheet and brush the top and sides lightly with more oil. If you like, sprinkle grated cheese on the top of each piece.

Slide the baking sheet into the oven. Once the top has nicely browned, flip over and bake until the other side is also brown and crisp, 20 to 25 minutes total. Serve hot.

Polenta with Balsamic-Poached Figs and Bacon

I have served this combination of ingredients baked and stacked, as suggested here, and also reheated and mixed together. As recrisped, bite-sized pieces, the polenta also skewers prettily for an hors d'oeuvre; these are especially easy to assemble when I have a stash of never-spoil Balsamic-Poached Figs on hand and bacon preportioned in the freezer (page 280). You can top the polenta with a few slices of pecorino cheese instead of the bacon.

→ FOR EACH SERVING

2 ounces (2 or 3 slices) thick-cut bacon, cut into ½-inch squares (about 3 tablespoons) *or* **Crisped Bacon** (page 295)

¼ cup **Balsamic-Poached Figs** (page 366)

1 teaspoon **syrup from Balsamic-Poached Figs**

2 tablespoons water

Freshly ground black pepper

1 main-course serving **Baked Polenta** (opposite), hot from the oven

If using uncooked bacon, place it in a cold skillet and turn the heat to low. As the fat begins to render, turn the heat up a bit to crisp the meat. Once it is crisp, pour off the fat but keep the bacon in the pan. Turn the heat down to low. If using precooked bacon, just place it in the pan. Add the figs, syrup, and water and stir. Cook until the figs are heated through and the water has been incorporated to make a sauce, about 2 minutes. Finish with black pepper to taste, pour over the polenta, and serve.

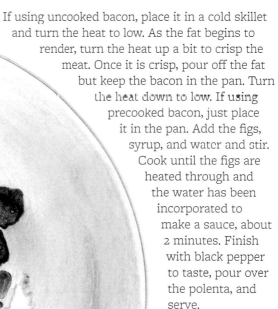

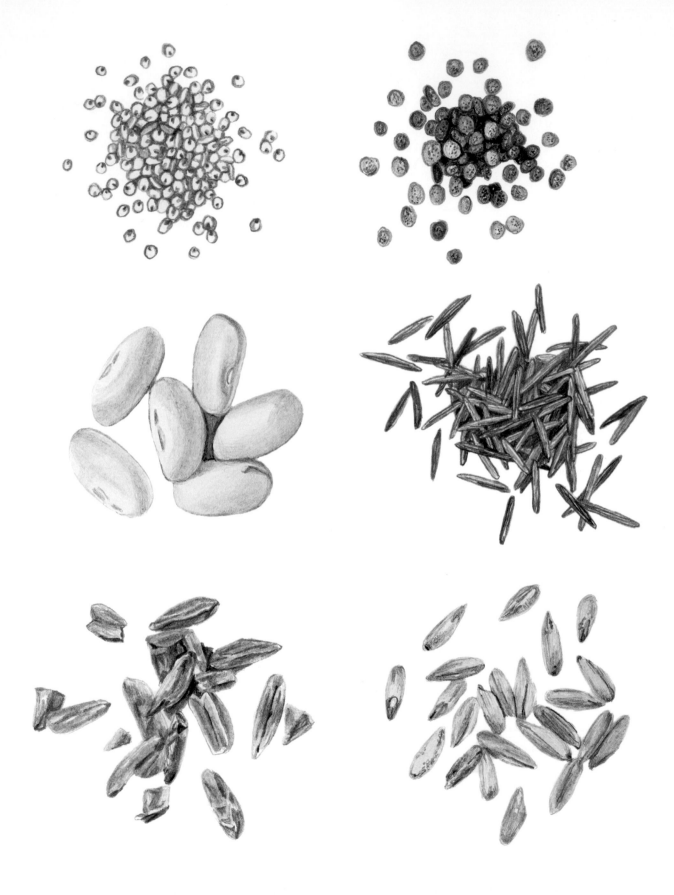

Rice, Other Grains, and Dried Beans

starting point ··

Manny's Brown Rice

I learned how to make rice from a talented cook from Puebla, Mexico—one of thousands who prop up New York restaurant kitchens—who would resist taking credit for this bastardized recipe, and especially for the use of brown rice instead of white.

I use a generous amount of olive oil, onions, water, and salt so that the cooked rice stays moist and flavorful for days. It's even good eaten cold. I get as many compliments on this simple recipe as any other.

makes **6 CUPS, ENOUGH FOR 6 SERVINGS**

6 tablespoons excellent olive oil

1¾ cups chopped onions

2½ teaspoons coarse kosher salt

4 cups water

2 cups short-grain brown rice

Heat the oil in a heavy-bottomed medium saucepan over medium heat. Add the onions and cook, stirring, until totally translucent, 10 to 12 minutes. If the onions begin to brown, turn the heat down and cover the pot. Add the salt and stir.

Meanwhile, bring the water to a boil in a kettle or covered pot (you don't want it to evaporate).

Just as the water begins to boil, add the rice to the onions and cook over medium heat, stirring for 1 minute to coat the rice well. When the water boils, add it to the rice. Scrape the sides of the pan and stir once to make sure all the grains are submerged. Once the water comes back to a boil, cover and reduce to a quiet but frisky simmer. As it cooks, steam may escape the pot, but the lid should not move.

Cook until the rice becomes chewy and has lost all its bite, about 40 minutes. If the rice is almost done when you taste it, turn off the heat and leave it to steam for 5 minutes. The rice will likely not have absorbed all of the water; this keeps it moist and flavorful for storage. Drain to serve. Or if you are not serving the rice immediately or anticipate having leftovers, spill the rice and its cooking water onto a baking sheet, scraping the sides of the pot to release all of the rice's starch. Whatever you don't serve immediately, let cool to room temperature. Use a rubber spatula to transfer the rice and all of its thickened cooking water from the baking sheet to a container. Store in the refrigerator for up to 5 days.

Serve with

⟶ Lamb Shanks Braised in Two Vinegars (page 302)

Use in

⟶ Brown-Rice Crepes (opposite)

Brown-Rice Crepes

These crepes are distinctive for their slight sour taste from fresh yogurt.

→ **MAKES ABOUT 10 CREPES**

1¼ cups **Manny's Brown Rice** (opposite)

¼ cup plus 2 tablespoons all-purpose flour

¾ teaspoon coarse kosher salt

3 large eggs

¾ cup milk

6 tablespoons 2% or whole-milk plain Greek yogurt

¼ teaspoon ground allspice

Unsalted butter

Stir all the ingredients *except* the butter together. Refrigerate for 15 minutes, or up to overnight.

Heat ½ tablespoon butter in a 10-inch cast-iron skillet or nonstick crepe pan over medium heat. Pour a generous ¼ cup batter into the pan; quickly tilt the pan to distribute the batter into a thin circle. Cook until the crepe's surface begins to bubble and the edges become yellow and crisp, about 1 minute. Flip with a spatula and finish cooking on the other side until dry and lightly browned, about 30 seconds more. Repeat with the remaining batter. You can stack the crepes on top of each other, separated by parchment paper, while warm.

Refrigerate the stacked crepes on the plate, covered, for up to 2 days. Freeze in a freezer bag for up to 1 month. Thaw in the refrigerator before reheating. Cook in a dry pan over medium heat to warm through.

Use in

→ Brown-Rice Crepes with Sweet Farmer Cheese (below)

→ Braised Duck Leg Crepes (page 274)

Brown-Rice Crepes with Sweet Farmer Cheese

Olive oil keeps these crepes from becoming too sweet, though they work as well for dessert as for breakfast.

→ **FOR EACH SERVING**

½ cup farmer cheese

½ teaspoon minced fresh thyme leaves

1 teaspoon sugar, plus more if needed

2 teaspoons excellent olive oil

Flaky sea salt

Grated lemon zest

2 **Brown-Rice Crepes** (at left) or **Quinoa Crepes** (page 332), thawed if frozen

Jam, for serving (optional)

Mix the cheese, thyme, sugar, and oil together in a small bowl. Season with a couple of pinches of salt and a bit of lemon zest. Taste for sugar. You want it to be on the sweet side, and fragrant with olive oil and lemon.

Warm the crepes in a pan over medium heat, one at a time, then divide the filling between the two, spreading it over half of the crepe. Fold the crepes into half-moons. Serve with jam, if you like.

From-Scratch "Two-Minute" Risotto

Start with this basic recipe, noting where you can make changes: Vary the wine you use to cook the rice, from a crisp white to sherry. Use different broths, such as Nut Stock or Garlic Stock. Finish the risotto with a different cheese or stir in olive or nut oil instead of butter.

You can even experiment with how much you precook the rice. I typically remove it from the pot just before the grains lose their crunchy center, but you can cook it for even less time. Either way, you want to quickly pour the rice onto a baking sheet to stop its cooking, and reserve any extra broth for when you're ready to finish it and serve.

This recipe makes enough for 4 small servings with mix-ins. Double the recipe to feed 4 to 6 people if you are serving the risotto plain.

When it's time to serve, you'll restart the process where you left off, with the parcooked risotto warmed a bit in one pot and the remainder of the stock heated in the other.

makes 4 CUPS RICE, ENOUGH FOR 4 SMALL SERVINGS WITH MIX-INS OR 2 SERVINGS WITHOUT

6 cups excellent stock, such as Worth-It Chicken Stock (page 267), Garlic Stock (page 21), *or* Quick Spring Stock (page 88)

3 tablespoons unsalted butter

2 large shallots, diced

1½ cups Arborio rice

1 teaspoon coarse kosher salt

½ cup acidic and floral white wine (such as Vinho Verde)

Bring the stock to a simmer. Turn the heat down to very low and cover to keep it hot.

Melt the butter in a heavy medium saucepan over medium-low heat. Add the shallots and cook, stirring, until they are translucent but without color, about 5 minutes. Stir in the rice and salt. Cook, stirring, until the rice becomes translucent at its edges, another few minutes.

Add the wine and cook, stirring frequently, until it's mostly absorbed. Turn the heat up to medium-high and add the stock about ¼ cup at a time. The rice will look saucy, but will not be submerged. Stir continuously between additions, replacing the stock only as the rice absorbs most of the previous amount. Continue in this manner until the rice still has a bit of raw bite, 10 to 12 more minutes.

Immediately pour the rice onto a baking sheet, scraping out every bit of starchy stock, and spread it out to cool. Once cool, transfer the risotto and its thickened stock to an airtight container and store in the refrigerator for up to 5 days. You will have 2 to 3 cups of stock left over; let it cool and store separately to finish the risotto when you're ready to serve.

To finish cooking the risotto, see Risotto, with Mix-Ins (page 324).

Use in

→ Risotto, with Mix-ins (page 324)

→ Mushroom Risotto with Nut Stock and Roasted Garlic (page 325)

→ Quick Spring-Stock Risotto with Herb Butter (page 325)

→ Cheese-Stock Risotto with Spring Vegetables (page 325)

PRECOOKING RISOTTO

There are different ways to precook risotto. If you want to cut down on the time it takes to finish the dish when you're ready to serve, parcook it to within minutes of being done (as described at left). Store in a covered container in the refrigerator for up to 5 days.

If you're short on prep time, you can cook the risotto just until the rice has absorbed all the wine. Cool the parcooked rice, then store in a covered container in the refrigerator for up to 5 days. When you are ready to finish it, spread the rice into a pan, separately heat your choice of stock, and cook as directed. You'll need more time to finish the dish, but you'll have more ways to vary it.

Or, you can cook the shallots and rice only up until you add the wine. Cool in a covered container in the refrigerator for up to 5 days, then cook as directed.

Risotto, with Mix-Ins

This recipe is for one portion of risotto to serve as a side or as a main dish with ingredients mixed in. But you can finish many servings the same as one; adjust the pan size to fit the rice in a layer ideally no more than 1 inch thick.

It is worth dirtying separate pans to warm the mix-ins rather than warming them in the rice directly. Once the rice is cooked, remove the pan from the heat, then stir in in the butter, cheese, and mix-ins. The ratio of rice to mix-ins is a matter of preference, but unless I'm serving risotto plain, I prefer it chock-full.

You'll use about ¾ cup stock to finish each serving of risotto. If you are short on reserved stock, bump it up with water.

⟶ **FOR EACH SERVING**

1 cup **From-Scratch "Two-Minute" Risotto** (page 322)

Up to ¾ cup mix-ins (see box)

¾ cup stock left over from the risotto

1 tablespoon unsalted butter *or* **Herb-Infused Butter** (page 377)

¼ cup freshly grated Parmesan or pecorino cheese

Coarse kosher salt, if needed

If possible, let the precooked risotto stand at room temperature for 10 minutes to come to room temperature. Warm the mix-ins separately. Heat the stock and keep it over very low heat.

Choose an appropriately sized pan—not too big or the cooking liquid you add to it will prematurely evaporate, and not too small lest you risk drowning the rice with stock. Spread the risotto out in the pan and turn the heat to medium-high. Add enough hot stock to barely cover the rice. Stir to rejuvenate the grains and release the flavorful starch. Once this stock is absorbed, continue adding more stock in batches, ¼ cup at a time, to finish cooking the risotto. Once the grains are of uniform texture but still somewhat firm—this takes just a couple of minutes—remove from the heat. Stir in the butter and cheese and taste for salt. Add any mix-ins. Cover the risotto and let it settle into itself, 1 minute. Serve immediately.

MIX-INS FOR RISOTTO

Add up to ¾ cup of any of these per serving of risotto.

⟶ Roughly chopped Seared Kale with Garlic and Lemon (page 50)

⟶ Chopped Wine-Braised Leeks (page 28)

⟶ Chopped Roasted Cauliflower (page 104)

FAVORITE RISOTTOS FROM THE NIMBLE PANTRY

MUSHROOM RISOTTO WITH NUT STOCK AND ROASTED GARLIC

Make the **From-Scratch "Two-Minute" Risotto**, using **Nut Stock** (page 370) for the stock and substituting dry sherry for the white wine. For each serving, finish with ½ cup **Crisp Sautéed Shiitakes** (page 199) and a few cloves of mashed **Roasted Garlic** (page 27), along with a pinch of **Bay Salt** (page 374) if you have it.

QUICK SPRING-STOCK RISOTTO WITH HERB BUTTER

Make the **From-Scratch "Two-Minute" Risotto**, using **Quick Spring Stock** (page 88) for the stock. For each serving, finish with 1 tablespoon each of **Herb-Infused Butter** (page 377) and freshly grated Parmesan cheese.

CHEESE-STOCK RISOTTO WITH SPRING VEGETABLES

Make the **From-Scratch "Two-Minute" Risotto**, using **Cheese Stock** (page 385) for the stock and using caution with salt. For each serving, finish with ¾ cup chopped **Spring Vegetable Medley** (page 75), 1 to 2 tablespoons roughly chopped fresh herbs, and freshly grated Parmesan cheese.

FROM SCRATCH "TWO-MINUTE" RISOTTO + CHEESE-STOCK + green beans Parmesan fresh herbs → CHEESE-STOCK RISOTTO WITH SPRING VEGETABLES

Wild Rice

Wild rice is delicious on its own or tossed with Spiced-Apple-Cider-Honey Vinaigrette (page 365), lemon juice, and toasted walnuts for a cold salad. Reduce the excess cooking broth for a start to soup.

Don't store the cooked wild rice in its broth; it bloats easily.

makes 4 CUPS WILD RICE AND 3 CUPS BROTH, ENOUGH FOR 4 SERVINGS

1½ cups wild rice

8 cups water

1 teaspoon coarse kosher salt, plus more as needed

Place the wild rice, water, and salt in a large saucepan. Bring to a quick boil, then reduce to a simmer and cook, covered, until the wild rice is tender but still chewy and bursts at the ends, 25 to 30 minutes.

Meanwhile, set up a large fine-mesh strainer over a large bowl. When the wild rice is done, immediately pour it into the strainer. Lift the strainer up over the bowl to let the last of the cooking water pass through. The wild rice will need more salt, so add it now. Spread the wild rice out on a baking sheet to cool.

Return the broth to the pot and simmer until it is reduced to 3 cups.

Refrigerate the wild rice and broth separately in airtight containers for up to 5 days. You can freeze the broth (in ¾-cup portions, if you like) for soup. Reheat the wild rice in a bit of its broth in a pot over low heat on the stove.

Use in

→ Wild Rice, Sunchoke, and Spring Greens Soup (opposite)

→ Wild Rice with Swiss Chard and Balsamic-Poached Figs (page 328)

BROTH FROM WILD RICE + olive oil · onion · wild rice · arugula · sunchoke · potato · thyme · lemon · black pepper → WILD RICE, SUNCHOKE & SPRING GREENS SOUP

Wild Rice, Sunchoke, and Spring Greens Soup

Despite containing both wild rice and potatoes, this soup remains brothy and light.

→ FOR EACH SERVING

1 tablespoon excellent olive oil

⅓ cup chopped onion

½ cup peeled, diced sunchokes (page 167)

½ cup peeled, diced Yukon Gold potatoes

¾ cup **broth from Wild Rice** (opposite)

1 fresh thyme sprig

1 (1-inch wide) strip lemon zest, white pith scraped away

Coarse kosher salt and freshly ground black pepper

¼ cup delicate spicy greens (such as arugula or baby mustard)

¼ cup cooked **Wild Rice**

Heat the oil in a medium saucepan over medium heat. Add the onion and cook until it begins to soften, about 5 minutes. Add the sunchokes and potatoes and cook for 2 minutes more, stirring frequently. Add the broth, thyme, and lemon zest. Cover, turn the heat down to medium-low, and simmer until the potatoes and sunchokes are tender, 15 to 20 minutes. Taste for salt.

To serve, put the greens and wild rice in a bowl and ladle in the hot broth. Season with pepper and serve.

Wild Rice with Swiss Chard and Balsamic-Poached Figs

Butter is key to tying the ingredients of this earthy, sweet vegetable dish together and keeping the grains moist. Lemon zest brightens the easily muted greens. Save the Swiss chard stems for Swiss Chard Stems Jam (page 54). I like to serve the relish and jam on the table in the same meal.

⟶ **FOR 4 SERVINGS**

1 tablespoon excellent olive oil

1 cup thinly sliced onion

1 teaspoon minced garlic

1 teaspoon coarse kosher salt, plus more if needed

1 bunch Swiss chard (about 12 leaves), stemmed and cut into 1-inch ribbons (page 48; about 6 cups)

½ cup finely chopped **Balsamic-Poached Figs** (page 366)

3 tablespoons unsalted butter

Grated zest of 1 lemon

1 recipe cooked **Wild Rice** (page 326)

Heat the oil in a large saucepan over medium heat. Add the onion, garlic, and salt and cook until the onion begins to soften, about 2 minutes. Add the chard and toss frequently to wilt. Mix in the figs and butter. Toss to heat through. Add the lemon zest and wild rice and cook, stirring often, until the rice is warm. Taste for salt. It's best served warm.

Popcorn Quinoa

Toasting quinoa, then cooking it with onions and a good amount of olive oil, makes it taste like tiny bits of popped corn. Be sure to chop the onion fine, so when it cooks, it disappears into the little grains.

I prefer red quinoa to the more common white. Red quinoa keeps its shape and chew better, and it carries the toasted taste far. If you can't find red, use white, but steam it for 5 minutes instead of 10.

makes **4 TO 5 CUPS, ENOUGH FOR 4 SERVINGS**

3 tablespoons olive oil

1½ cups red or white quinoa (see headnote)

½ cup finely chopped onion

1 teaspoon coarse kosher salt

2½ cups water

Heat 1½ tablespoons of the oil in a medium saucepan over medium heat. Add the quinoa and stir well. As it crackles and toasts, stir more frequently, until it becomes very fragrant, 5 to 6 minutes. Watch carefully so it doesn't burn. Scrape the quinoa into a heatproof bowl.

Pour the remaining 1½ tablespoons oil into the same pan and turn the heat to medium-low. Add the onion and cook until translucent, 10 to 15 minutes. Once the onion is tender, sweet, and buttery yellow, stir in the salt and turn off the heat. Return the quinoa to the saucepan.

Meanwhile, bring the water to a boil in a kettle or covered pan, so it doesn't evaporate while heating. Once boiling, pour the water into the quinoa, cover, and bring to a low simmer over low heat. Cook, stirring only occasionally, until the grains begin to swell and their "tails" (the germ) unwind, about 10 minutes. Turn off the heat and steam, covered, for another 10 minutes. (If you're cooking white quinoa, steam it for only 5 minutes.) The grains will have absorbed all the water but still be very moist.

Serve immediately. Or pour onto a baking sheet to cool quickly. Taste for salt and add more if necessary. Store in a covered container in the refrigerator for up to 5 days or freeze up to 3 months.

Use in

→ Popcorn Quinoa and Oranges with Fig, Olive, and Walnut Relish (page 330)

→ Quinoa Crepes (page 332)

Popcorn Quinoa and Oranges with Fig, Olive, and Walnut Relish

This is a terrific fall side dish. The amount of butter called for is essential, and enriches the whole dish. Don't shy from using it all.

You can substitute Roasted Orange Slices for the sautéed oranges.

⟶ **FOR 4 SERVINGS**

½ small juice orange, scrubbed, *or* ½ cup **Roasted Orange Slices** (page 213)

4 tablespoons (½ stick) unsalted butter, cut into pieces

Rounded ½ teaspoon coarse kosher salt

½ teaspoon hot red pepper flakes

3 cups **Popcorn Quinoa** (page 329)

1 cup **Fig, Olive, and Walnut Relish** (page 367)

If using the orange half, put it cut side down on a cutting board and cut it in half again. Remove any seeds. Slice each quarter crosswise, as thinly as you can, into triangle-shaped pieces.

Arrange the orange slices in a single layer in a large skillet. Add the butter, salt, and red pepper flakes. Cook over low heat until the butter melts. Turn the heat up to high. Cook until the edges of the orange slices begin to brown, turning once. Immediately remove the pan from the heat and stir in the quinoa and relish. Serve warm or at room temperature.

QUINOA CREPES

GREEN LENTIL
& BREAD SALAD
WITH OLIVES

CABBAGE &
GREEN LENTILS
WITH ORANGE
VINAIGRETTE

BITTER GREENS,
PICKLED CHICKPEAS
& SARDINES

GREEN
LENTILS WITH
CARDAMOM

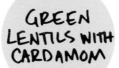

POPCORN
QUINOA

WINE-
PICKLED
CHICKPEAS

beans & grains

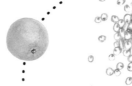

POPCORN QUINOA &
ORANGES WITH FIG,
OLIVE & WALNUT
RELISH

SALT-&-PEPPER
CHICKPEAS

MANNY'S
BROWN RICE

WHITE BEANS
WITH GARLIC &
VINEGAR

SPICED LAMB
MEATBALLS WITH
CHICKPEAS, PICKLED
PARSLEY & YOGURT

BROWN-RICE CREPES
WITH SWEET FARMER
CHEESE

WITH SCALLION-SESAME
MAGIC MIX

SAUSAGE-&-ANY
-BEAN SOUP

Quinoa Crepes

These are worlds better than crepes made from quinoa flour, which lacks the sweetness of softened onion and richness of toasted grain. Because there is wheat flour in the batter, these are not gluten-free.

The timing and method for cooking the crepes will vary depending on the thickness and temperature of the batter and the type of cooking pan. If you don't have a crepe pan, use a well-seasoned cast-iron skillet. A pastry brush helps you quickly refresh the butter in the pan. Use the first crepe as a test for heat and timing. Most recipes recommend high heat, but I find cooking over medium heat works best.

→ **MAKES 4 TO 6 (9-INCH) CREPES**

Packed 1 cup **Popcorn Quinoa** (page 329)

½ cup all-purpose flour

¼ teaspoon coarse kosher salt

1½ teaspoons sugar

¾ cup whole milk

2 large eggs

2 tablespoons unsalted butter, at room temperature, plus more for cooking

¼ cup water

Put all the ingredients in a blender. Blend until creamy and smooth. (*The batter can be refrigerated for up to 2 days.*)

Heat a 10-inch nonstick crepe pan or cast-iron skillet over medium heat for 1 minute. Brush the pan lightly with softened butter. Pour ½ cup batter into the center of the pan, then immediately lift and tilt the pan to guide the batter into a circle that fills the pan. If the batter is cold and thick—or the pan is too heavy—use a small, buttered offset spatula to help shape it.

Once the crepe firms and begins to look leathery, and pinhole bubbles appear at the edges, slide a thin spatula underneath to check for light, even browning. Flip over and cook until the second side is lightly browned. You can stack the crepes on top of each other, separated by parchment paper, while warm. They will separate with ease when you're ready to use them. The pan will retain good heat, so each subsequent crepe will require less time in the pan.

Refrigerate the stack of crepes and parchment on a plate, covered, for up to 2 days. Freeze in a freezer bag for up to 2 months. Thaw before reheating in a dry pan over low heat.

Use in

→ Peanut-Butter-and-Honey Quinoa Crepes (opposite)

→ Seared Peaches and Burrata Quinoa Crepes (opposite)

→ Braised Duck Leg Crepes (page 274) instead of Brown-Rice Crepes, or fill with any kind of braised meat and some Pickled Acorn Squash (page 190)

→ Brown-Rice Crepes with Sweet Farmer Cheese (page 321) instead of Brown-Rice Crepes

Seared Peaches and Burrata Quinoa Crepes

This is breakfast, dinner, or dessert, and a good use for peaches that aren't quite ripe.

Burrata is an Italian cow's milk cheese similar to mozzarella, but with a soft, creamy curd at its center. If you can't find it, use fresh ricotta cheese.

⟶ **FOR EACH SERVING**

2 **Quinoa Crepes** (opposite)

2 tablespoons excellent olive oil

Leaves from 4 fresh thyme sprigs

1 slightly firm peach, cut into ¼-inch-thick wedges

Flaky sea salt and freshly ground black pepper

3 tablespoons burrata cheese, or see headnote

Heat a 10-inch nonstick crepe pan or well-seasoned cast-iron skillet over low heat. Add the crepes, one at a time, to heat through. Set aside, stacking them on a plate, and cover to keep warm. Turn the heat up to medium and add the oil and thyme. Place the peaches in the pan and season with salt and pepper. Sear the peach slices until golden brown, then flip and season again.

Spread the warm crepes out on the work surface. Divide the peaches between the bottom halves of each of the crepes. Drizzle with some of the oil and fried thyme. Add one last sprinkle of sea salt. Top with the burrata and the rest of the herb oil, and fold over the other half of each crepe to cover. Use a wide spatula to carefully transfer the crepes to a serving plate. Serve hot.

PEANUT-BUTTER-AND-HONEY QUINOA CREPES

Spread peanut butter on a warm **Quinoa Crepe** (opposite) while you're making them and drizzle generously with honey. Fold the crepe in half and set aside, covered with foil, as you make and fill the rest.

Toasted Rye Berries or Farro

I use a generous amount of olive oil, onions, water, and salt to keep the grain moist and flavorful even after it's been refrigerated for days, as I do with other grains. I like rye berries better than farro, which is too similar to the plainer barley for my taste.

makes 4½ TO 5 CUPS, ENOUGH FOR 4 SERVINGS

6 tablespoons excellent olive oil

2 cups rye berries or farro

1¾ cups diced onions

2½ teaspoons coarse kosher salt

4 cups water

2 to 3 tablespoons unsalted butter, for serving

Heat 3 tablespoons of the oil in a heavy-bottomed medium saucepan over medium heat. Add the rye berries and cook, stirring constantly, until the grain begins to hiss and crackle. Monitor the grain closely as it starts to smell toasty. As soon as it deepens uniformly in color and smells of popcorn, about 5 minutes, pull the saucepan from the heat and transfer the grain—making sure to get every last bit—to a heatproof bowl.

Add the remaining 3 tablespoons oil and the onions to the saucepan. Turn the heat to medium-low and cook until the onions have lost their crunch and turned butter yellow, about 10 minutes. If the onions begin to brown, lower the heat and cover with a lid. Do not rush this step. Once cooked, add the salt.

Meanwhile, bring the water to a boil in a kettle or covered pot.

Just as the water comes to a boil, add the toasted grain to the onions, then carefully—it may splatter!—pour in the water all at once. Scrape the sides of the pan and stir to make sure all the grains are submerged. Maintain the heat until the water comes back to a quick boil. Once it does, cover the pot and reduce the heat to maintain a quiet but frisky simmer. Steam may well escape, but the pot lid should not dance. Turn the heat down, if necessary.

Cook until the grain still has just a bit of chew, about 35 minutes for farro, 40 for rye berries. Taste for salt. If you are serving right away, scoop out the grain, leaving behind any excess cooking water, which you can discard or save to use for soup, as you would the broth from wild rice (page 326). Serve the warm grain with a pat of butter.

If you are not serving the grain immediately, spill it and the cooking water onto a baking sheet. Once cool, use a rubber spatula to transfer the grain and all of its thickened, starchy cooking water to a covered container. Store in the refrigerator for up to 5 days. While the texture may suffer a bit upon thawing, you can freeze the cooked, cooled grain in its cooking water for up to 1 month.

Use in

→ Pulled Pork with Rye Berries and Roasted Lemon (page 290)

→ Spiced Lamb with Cherry Tomatoes and Rye Berries (page 299)

Rye Berry, Date, and Pistachio Pilaf

Although it's a great year-round side dish, this is particularly good in cold weather. It pairs well with game meat.

⟶ **FOR EACH SERVING**

1 cup **Toasted Rye Berries** (page 334)

½ cup finely chopped Medjool dates (about 3)

1 tablespoon unsalted butter

¼ cup roughly chopped unsalted pistachios

A pinch of grated orange zest

Coarse kosher salt

Warm the rye berries, dates, and butter together in a saucepan over low heat, just until the butter melts.

Cool almost to room temperature. Add the pistachios, orange zest, and salt to taste. Serve.

Freekeh in Garlic Tea

Freekeh is the whole kernel of a Mediterranean wheat, picked green, smoked, then subsequently dried. The grain is gray-green in color, chewy (typical for whole grains), and with a taste evoking smoke, leather, and stone. It is also one of the few whole grains that cook pretty quickly, which makes it useful to have around. Freekeh is easy to season just with salt but improves with slivers of garlic. It's delicious cooked in Quick Spring Stock (page 88) too. If you use that, leave out the garlic called for below.

You'll find freekeh packaged as whole kernels or milled into smaller, uneven pieces. Choose whole kernels, when available. Before cooking, spread the freekeh on a baking sheet and examine it for stones and bits of grass.

makes 6 CUPS, ENOUGH FOR 4 TO 6 SERVINGS

2 cups freekeh

4 cups water or stock
(see headnote)

1½ teaspoons coarse
kosher salt

4 garlic cloves, very
thinly sliced

Unsalted butter
(optional)

Put the freekeh, water, and salt in a heavy-bottomed saucepan and bring to a quick boil over high heat. Turn the heat down to medium-low and cook at a slow simmer, stirring occasionally, until the grains are just tender but still chewy, about 10 minutes. There should be plenty of cooking liquid left in the saucepan. Turn off the heat, add the garlic slices, and stir once. Cover and let sit for a few minutes to infuse. Serve warm as is, or with a pat of butter stirred in.

To store, pour the freekeh and garlic tea onto a baking sheet and spread out to cool quickly. Once the freekeh has cooled, store with its broth in a covered container in the refrigerator for up to 5 days. Stored this way, the grains continue to take on flavor. Freeze the freekeh in its cooking water for up to 1 month.

Use in

→ Freekeh with Onion Jam (page 338)

Mix with

→ Pickled Apples (page 208) and diced celery

→ Many-Herb Salad (page 64)

Freekeh with Onion Jam

Though simple, this dish is rich, filling, and delicious. The jam and freekeh are stalwart partners, and you can vary the kind of nut, citrus juice, and herb you use.

⟶ **FOR EACH SERVING**

¼ cup **Onion Jam** (page 34)

1¼ cups **Freekeh in Garlic Tea** (page 337), drained

3 tablespoons chopped toasted hazelnuts (page 368)

1 to 2 teaspoons minced fresh flat-leaf parsley

Fresh lemon juice

Gently warm the onion jam in a pan over medium heat. Add the freekeh and stir, coating it with the onions, until warm.

Off the heat, toss in the hazelnuts and parsley. Add a healthy squeeze of lemon juice. Serve immediately, or hold at room temperature for several hours.

Serve alongside

⟶ Perfectly Poached Salmon (page 225) and Whole-Grain Mustard Aioli (page 381)

⟶ Lamb Shanks Braised in Two Vinegars (page 302)

⟶ Seared Kale with Garlic and Lemon (page 50)

Dried Beans

SOAKING AND SEASONING BEANS

It's a good idea to soak your beans, if only because you ensure more even cooking and can better predict the time they will take to cook. Soaked uncooked beans are great candidates for long-term storage in the freezer. This discovery has changed how I shop for, store, cook, and use beans. I now soak the whole package at once—even if I don't plan to cook them soon—and freeze the soaked beans, along with the soaking water, in an airtight container in portions aligned with how I might cook them—individual servings for a bowl of soup, large batches for a side of refried beans for the table. Once thawed, the beans take under 45 minutes to cook. I've turned homemade beans into a more convenient pantry item that is tastier, more versatile, and cheaper than canned.

TO SOAK ANY BEAN: Use 3 cups water for every cup of dried beans, and soak for at least 8 hours or overnight. The beans will typically double in size once they are soaked (1 cup chickpeas becomes 2 cups soaked), and will double again once cooked (2 cups soaked chickpeas become 4 cups cooked). This helps you estimate how much to buy and how to portion what you soak. When you're ready to cook them, drain the beans and discard the soaking water.

Seasoning Beans

The best way to season beans is to season the liquid in which they've cooked. I use more water than the beans will absorb (1½ cups for every cup of soaked beans), and season the water (and thus, the cooked beans) at the end, while they're still warm. Because the age of the beans, the size and heaviness of the pot, and the heat they're cooked on will affect how much water they absorb, I adjust the seasoning to the amount of bean broth left at the end, not to the amount of beans I have. Once the broth is seasoned, I add it back to the beans and steep.

Salt-and-Pepper Chickpeas

Garlic makes a savory enough bean broth, but white peppercorns make it outrageously good. Serve the chickpeas in their warm broth as a side to grilled sausage, or in Spiced Lamb Meatballs with Chickpeas, Pickled Parsley, and Yogurt (page 300).

makes 4 CUPS, ENOUGH FOR 4 SERVINGS

2 cups soaked chickpeas (page 339), drained

3 cups water

¼ onion, cut in a wedge

Coarse kosher salt

1 tablespoon whole white peppercorns, tied in a cheesecloth sachet

3 garlic cloves, thinly sliced

Place the chickpeas, water, and onion in a medium saucepan. Cover and bring to a boil over high heat. Skim off any foam. Turn the heat down to low and simmer, covered, stirring occasionally, until completely tender, about 45 minutes, tasting from the bottom and top of the batch to make sure all are well cooked.

Drain the chickpeas over a heatproof measuring cup or bowl to collect the broth. Add up to 1½ teaspoons salt for every cup of bean broth. Return the beans and still-hot bean broth to the cooking pot, bury the peppercorn sachet in the beans, and stir in the garlic. Cover to steep for 5 minutes, then taste and adjust the salt if necessary. Cover and steep for 5 minutes more. Taste again. Discard the peppercorns. Serve, or pour the chickpeas onto a baking sheet to cool. Store the chickpeas with their broth in a covered container in the refrigerator for up to 5 days. Do not freeze.

Wine-Pickled Chickpeas

You can pickle all kinds of beans, using up leftovers from larger batches you've made—or even using unseasoned canned. They keep for weeks and lend more to a salad than plain, undressed ones. I often combine bitter spring greens and mineral-rich canned sardines with pickled chickpeas for staff lunch.

⟶ **MAKES 2 TO 2½ CUPS**

2 to 2½ cups cooked chickpeas, such as **Salt-and-Pepper Chickpeas** (opposite)

2 cups distilled white vinegar

1 cup dry white wine

1 tablespoon coarse kosher salt

1 tablespoon sugar

Drain and rinse the chickpeas. Set aside in a heatproof container.

Combine the vinegar, wine, salt, and sugar in a small pot and bring to a quick boil. Once the salt and sugar are dissolved, pour the hot brine over the chickpeas. Let cool to room temperature before serving. Or store in the refrigerator in a covered container for up to 1 month.

Bitter Greens, Pickled Chickpeas, and Sardines

You can compose this salad on a platter as directed, or mix it together to a tasty mess, which I prefer.

⟶ **FOR 4 SERVINGS**

¼ cup **brine from Wine-Pickled Chickpeas** (at left)

1 teaspoon whole-grain mustard

3 tablespoons excellent olive oil

1 bunch dandelion greens or watercress, roughly chopped

Flaky sea salt

1 cup drained **Wine-Pickled Chickpeas**

4 **Perfect Hard-Boiled Eggs** (page 349), peeled and halved

1 (4- to 5-ounce) can sardines in water, drained and filleted

Whisk the brine and mustard together in a large bowl. Pour in the oil in a thin stream, whisking, to make a thickened dressing. Spread the dressing around the inside of the bowl. Add the greens and use your fingers to stir gently to coat. Season with salt. Add the chickpeas and toss lightly.

Arrange the dressed greens and chickpeas on a serving platter or individual salad plates. Decorate with the egg halves and sardine fillets. Drizzle any remaining dressing over the top.

White Beans with Garlic and Vinegar

Garlic, vinegar, and salt are all you need to make white beans taste really good. Onion adds sweetness and viscosity to the broth, which the vinegar is happy to cut through. The broth is still nice and clear, though, because the beans—while completely soft—haven't messily broken down. You can go as heavy or light on the vinegar as you want; the hot beans will absorb and mellow the vinegar as they cool.

makes **4 CUPS, ENOUGH FOR 4 SERVINGS**

2 cups soaked white beans (page 339), drained

3 cups water

1 medium onion, thinly sliced

4 garlic cloves, thinly sliced

Coarse kosher salt

Red or white wine vinegar

Place the beans, water, onion, and garlic in a medium saucepan. Cover and bring to a boil over high heat. Skim off any foam. Turn the heat down to low, cover again, and simmer until completely tender, 40 to 50 minutes, tasting the beans from the bottom and top of the batch to make sure.

Drain the beans over a heatproof measuring cup or bowl to collect the broth. Add up to 1½ teaspoons salt and ½ teaspoon vinegar for every cup of bean broth. Return the beans and broth to the cooking pot and cover. Steep for 5 minutes, taste, and adjust the salt and vinegar if necessary. Cover and steep for 5 minutes more. Taste again. Serve or spill the beans and their broth onto a baking sheet to cool completely before storing. The beans will keep in the refrigerator, in their broth, for up to 5 days.

Serve with

⟶ Stovetop Smoked Fish (page 242), preferably sardines

⟶ Confit Duck (page 276)

⟶ Roasted Broccoli Rabe (page 103)

⟶ a big piece of toast with Green-Peppercorn Butter (page 378)

Sausage-and-Any-Bean Soup

This is a great recipe to have in your back pocket. Its winning flavor comes from ginger, hot pepper, bay leaf, garlic, and cheese.

 Use the instructions below as a template for any legume or bean soup. When your legumes or beans are precooked, the broth—just warmed through—stays light and clear. This soup is not a stew, but it fills and warms just as well.

→ **FOR 4 SERVINGS**

1 (4-ounce) sweet or hot Italian sausage

1 tablespoon excellent olive oil

1 tablespoon finely minced ginger

2 garlic cloves, thinly sliced

2 cups excellent chicken stock (such as Worth-It Chicken Stock, page 267)

1 cup cubed (½-inch pieces) Yukon Gold potato

½ teaspoon coarse kosher salt

1 bay leaf

Pinch of hot red pepper flakes

2 cups **Green Lentils with Cardamom** (page 344), **Salt-and-Pepper Chickpeas** (page 340), *or* **White Beans with Garlic and Vinegar** (opposite), drained

1 or 2 kale, collard, or Swiss chard leaves, stemmed and cut into ½-inch ribbons (page 48)

¼ cup chopped fresh flat-leaf parsley

Freshly grated Parmesan cheese

Freshly ground black pepper

Cut the sausage into ½-inch slices. Heat the oil in a pot over medium heat and add the sausage. Cook, stirring occasionally, until well browned all over, about 4 minutes. Add the ginger and garlic and cook, stirring frequently, until the ginger just starts to brown, about 2 minutes more.

Add the stock, potato, salt, bay leaf, and red pepper flakes. Bring to a simmer and cook, uncovered, until the potatoes are just tender, about 5 minutes. Stir in the lentils, greens, and parsley. Bring the soup back to a simmer and turn off the heat. Taste for salt. Serve with Parmesan and black pepper to taste.

Green Lentils with Cardamom

This recipe relies on slowly cooking a traditional mirepoix of carrot, onion, and celery. The mirepoix turns the water into a balanced broth that animates the tiny legumes; it's worth the effort to dice the vegetables small and evenly, so they don't upstage them. Cardamom and lentils go so well together that it's hard to tell where the taste of one ends and the other begins. Make sure the pods are fresh, a deep army green, and carry a strong perfume.

The lentils are delicious straight out of the pot, especially the day you make them. Or toss with sausage and feta cheese.

makes 6 CUPS, ENOUGH FOR 4 TO 6 SERVINGS

3 tablespoons excellent olive oil

½ cup finely diced carrot

½ cup finely diced celery

1¼ cups finely diced onion

3 cups French green lentils

9 green cardamom pods, crushed with the side of a knife

1½ tablespoons coarse kosher salt

6 cups water

Combine the oil, carrot, celery, and onions in a medium saucepan over medium-low heat. Cook, stirring frequently, until the vegetables are tender, 10 to 15 minutes. Do not let them brown. If they begin to pick up color, turn the heat down and/or cover the pan.

Once they are tender, add the lentils, cardamom, and salt. Stir well. Add the water and stir again. Partially cover the pan, turn up the heat, and bring to a quick boil. Then turn the heat down to low and simmer, still partially covered, stirring occasionally, until the lentils are tender, 30 to 40 minutes. Remove the cardamom husks and discard. Serve.

To store, pour the hot lentils and their cooking broth onto a baking sheet to cool. Once cooled, store both together in the refrigerator for up to 5 days. Do not freeze.

Use in

→ Green Lentil and Bread Salad with Olives (opposite)

→ Cabbage and Green Lentils with Orange Vinaigrette (opposite)

→ Sausage-and-Any-Bean Soup (page 343)

Green Lentil and Bread Salad with Olives

Lentils and olives mix with sharply seasoned, saturated bread. If you have a stash of bread cubes in the freezer, this is the time to use it. Consider making a full batch of dressing in any case, even if you're just making a meal for one. You'll be happy to have extra on hand.

→ **FOR 4 SERVINGS**

1½ cups **Cubed Bread** (page 354), toasted

3 cups **Green Lentils with Cardamom** (opposite), drained

Heaping ⅓ cup pitted green olives, roughly chopped

Heaping ⅓ cup thinly sliced red onion

⅓ cup excellent olive oil

3 tablespoons white wine vinegar

3 anchovy fillets, finely chopped

1½ tablespoons Dijon mustard

Combine the bread, lentils, olives, and onion in a large bowl; mix well.

Whisk the oil, vinegar, anchovies, and mustard together in a small bowl until emulsified. Pour the dressing over the salad and toss well. Let stand at room temperature for at least 15 minutes before serving. The bread will begin to soften; how much is your preference.

Cabbage and Green Lentils with Orange Vinaigrette

Cardamom and orange are good partners for legumes, game meat, and even fish. In this salad, the vinaigrette keeps the cabbage tasting fresh and light and brightens the otherwise muted lentils. The cabbage will release water as it continues to sit. Toss the salad right before serving.

→ **FOR 4 SERVINGS**

6 cups **Shaved Raw Cabbage** (page 113)

1½ teaspoons coarse kosher salt

¾ cup **Green Lentils with Cardamom** (opposite), drained

¼ cup plus 2 tablespoons **Orange Vinaigrette** (page 216)

Toss the cabbage and salt together in a large bowl. Use your fingers to lightly massage the salt into the cabbage. Let sit for 5 minutes. Add the lentils and vinaigrette. Toss well. Taste for salt and serve.

CUBED BREAD + GREEN LENTILS WITH CARDAMOM + green olives red onion olive oil vinegar Dijon anchovy → GREEN LENTIL & BREAD SALAD WITH OLIVES

The Pantry

Perfect Hard-Boiled Eggs

A hard-boiled egg should have some give on the outside and be creamy orange-yellow inside. The short and precise cooking time protects the yolk from overcooking to chalkiness. An ice bath stops the eggs from cooking further, and often makes them easier to peel.

makes **AS MANY LARGE EGGS AS YOU WANT TO COOK**

Place the eggs in a snug-fitting pot. Cover with cold water by 1 inch. Bring to a quick boil over high heat. As soon as the water boils, reduce to a steady simmer. Cook for exactly 1 minute. Cover, remove from the heat, and let rest for 4 minutes.

While the eggs rest, fill a bowl large enough to hold all the eggs with ice water. Lift each egg from the hot water with a slotted spoon and place in the ice bath. Let cool completely before peeling or storing in the refrigerator for up to 3 days.

To peel: Once the egg has cooled completely, lay it on its side on the work surface. Rest your palm on top of the egg and press gently to crack the underside against the work surface. With light but continuous pressure, roll the egg back and forth under your palm to crack the middle completely. The shell will now release easily.

Use in

→ Roasted-Pepper Breakfast Sandwich (page 137)

→ Many-Herb Salad (page 64)

→ Bitter Greens, Pickled Chickpeas, and Sardines (page 341)

→ A Singled Deviled Egg (page 350)

A Single Deviled Egg

As long as you have an egg—even better, a hard-boiled one—and standard condiments, you can make a pair of deviled eggs faster than you can prepare egg salad. Of course, the recipe scales up for a crowd.

Deviled eggs are fun to embellish and give us good reason to have spice salts and crisped chicken or fish skin on hand.

⟶ **FOR EACH SERVING**

1 **Perfect Hard-Boiled Egg** (page 349), peeled

1 teaspoon **Whole-Grain Mustard Aioli** (page 381) or mayonnaise

½ teaspoon Dijon mustard

Pinch of coarse kosher salt or **Bay Salt** (page 374), *or* ¼ teaspoon **Pork Spice Rub** (page 373)

Dash of distilled white vinegar or pickle brine (page 365; optional)

1 (1-inch) piece **Crisp Chicken Skin** (page 262) *or* **Crispy Fish Skin** (page 226), broken in half (optional, but worth it)

Cut the egg in half vertically; if you are making more than one egg, wipe the knife on a clean towel between cuts. Carefully pop out the yolk into a small bowl. For just an egg or two, mashing the yolks with a fork works fine. For a larger batch, pushing the yolks through a fine-mesh strainer nicely "powders" the yolks, making the filling lighter.

Add the aioli, mustard, salt, and vinegar. Combine well and taste. Divide the filling between the egg white halves. If you like, top with a piece of chicken or fish skin right before serving.

Poached Eggs

White vinegar added to the poaching water helps the egg whites set, without tainting the taste of the eggs. Use fresh eggs, which have "thicker" whites, and cook them cold, straight from the refrigerator, when they best hold their shape. Strain off any runny egg white before cooking—the thin, looser white makes a mess in the pan and always overcooks. Use a skillet rather than a high-sided pot.

I omit salt from the cooking water, because it does little to season the egg. It's better to top the egg with good, flaky sea salt just when you're ready to serve.

makes 1 TO 4 EGGS

1 quart water

1 tablespoon distilled white vinegar

1 to 4 large eggs, cold

Flaky sea salt

Cover a small plate with a double thickness of paper towels. Pour the water and vinegar into a skillet just large enough to hold all of the eggs. Cover and bring to a quick boil.

Meanwhile, crack each egg, one at a time, into a fine-mesh strainer over the sink. Do not shake the strainer but let any runny egg white pass through. Carefully place the strained eggs in a measuring cup or spouted bowl and place in the refrigerator. The chill helps the eggs stay intact, both when they are transferred to a cooking spoon and again when they are released into the water.

Once the water comes to a boil, remove the lid and turn down the heat so you have a very gentle simmer. Carefully pour 1 egg from the bowl into a large cooking spoon. Hover the spoon over the water, just inside the edge of the pan. Then, as you fully submerge the spoon, quickly turn it to face the side of the pan, trapping the egg. This helps the egg white neatly encircle the yolk. Hold for 5 seconds, then finish turning the spoon over to release the egg into the water. If the egg white sticks to the side of the pan, gently nudge it loose with the tip of the spoon. Repeat with all the eggs, adding them one at a time and turning the pan, if necessary, to position the spoon each time just at the pan's edge. Don't worry if a bit of the egg white sticks to the spoon.

Depending on the number of eggs you cook, you may need to adjust the heat to raise the water back to a very gentle simmer. As the eggs cook, use the spoon to nudge them around, making sure none stick to the bottom of the pan. Cook just until the whites closest to the yolks turn opaque but remain soft, 2 to 3 minutes. Lift out an egg with the slotted spoon to test one with your finger. The white should be neither gushy nor bouncy; tender is just right. The egg should keep a slim oval shape, the bright yellow yolk still visible through a milky new "shell."

Once done, rest the spoon, still cradling the egg, on the plate with the paper towels briefly to drain. Transfer to a serving plate, sprinkle with salt, and serve.

If you want to store the eggs for later, plunge them into an ice bath to cool as soon as they're removed from the pot. Once cool, drain well in a strainer or with a slotted spoon and store in a covered container in the refrigerator for up to 5 days. Reheat in a pot of simmering water only until the yolks are hot, about 30 seconds.

Silky Scrambled Eggs

You can make a big batch at once; just use a larger pan to maintain a shallow pool of egg "batter."

for EACH SERVING

2 large eggs

¼ teaspoon coarse kosher salt

Freshly ground black pepper

1½ tablespoons unsalted butter

Crack the eggs into a bowl. Add the salt and a grind or two of pepper. Whisk together, making sure to break up the yolks.

Heat a cast-iron or nonstick skillet over medium heat. Add 1 tablespoon of the butter. Spread it quickly over the surface of the pan with a heatproof spatula; do not let it brown.

Pour the beaten eggs into the middle of the pan in a swift, steady stream. Allow the eggs to cook, untouched, for about 10 seconds. The bottom layer will begin to bind, much like a crepe, but the top will remain bright yellow and runny.

Place the remaining butter on top of the eggs. Working quickly, fold the "crepe" onto itself, just a few times, stirring cooked eggs into uncooked. Do not overmix; you want folds of eggs, not tight little curds. Once the eggs have just folded together, about 15 seconds, slide them onto a plate—they will be silky and delicious. Serve immediately.

POACHED-GARLIC SCRAMBLED EGGS

Creamy, custard-like eggs, swirled with poached garlic, finished with butter, are a far cry from the typically dry, tight curds. They're more filling too.

For each serving, add to the whisked mixture of eggs, salt, and pepper 2 or 3 **Poached Garlic Cloves** (page 20), mashed with a fork; 1 additional pinch of salt; and 1 teaspoon roughly chopped dill. Cook as for **Silky Scrambled Eggs**, opposite, and serve immediately.

Instead of poached garlic, you can add **Dill-and-Leek-Greens Pesto** (page 32), **Confit Tomatoes** (page 148), and **Savory Ricotta Custard** (page 386) or seasoned fresh ricotta cheese to the eggs.

Soft-Boiled Egg

Tender whites, just set to spoon cleanly from their shells, protect orange-yellow custardy yolks thick enough to coat a spoon or finger of toast but runny enough to sauce anything they top.

makes 1 EGG

1 large egg

Place the egg in a small saucepan, cover with water by 1 inch, and bring to a quick boil over high heat. Immediately turn the heat down and simmer for 1 minute. Cover, remove from the heat, and let rest for 2 minutes more. Lift out with a slotted spoon. Serve immediately.

Top with

→ Herb-Infused Butter (page 377) and flaky salt

Bread

Cubed Bread

A bag of cubed bread in your freezer gives you a head start on a Braised Celeriac Gratin (page 171), Green Lentil and Bread Salad with Olives (page 345), Roasted Shallot and Bread Salad (page 42), or Triple-Braised Wild Mushroom, Bread, and Butter Soup (page 196). You can even toss the cubes with butter and sugar and toast them for ice cream.

Cut leftover or day-old bread, with or without the crusts, into approximately 1-inch cubes. Store in a freezer bag, pressing out as much of the air as you can before sealing. To prevent freezer burn, place this bag inside another one. Freeze for up to 1 month. Ideally, you'll want the cubes to thaw before toasting—this happens quickly. But you can also toast the cubes straight from the freezer, checking that no moisture remains inside the cubes, even after they appear sufficiently toasted. I reuse the freezer bags for subsequent batches of frozen bread.

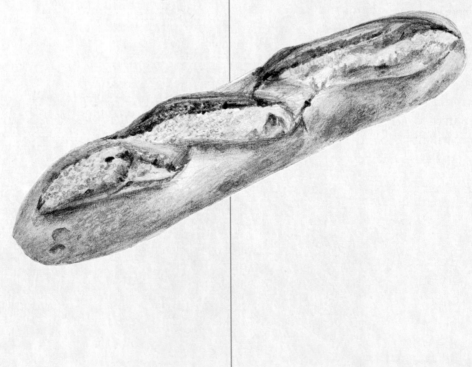

Bread Crumbs, Untoasted or Toasted

You can't do much with store-bought bread crumbs. The fine, sandy crumbs might thicken and bind, but they add no crunch. Panko crumbs, coarse as they are, keep deep-fried food light and crisp but lack flavor. To make great bread crumbs, you need great bread. Olive oil and salt help too.

Toasted fully, bread crumbs last for months. You'll reach for them when you want crunch but not something as heavy as a nut, or when you want to add bulk without cooking a grain. You can grind day-old artisan bread into crumbs and store them in the freezer, first trimming the sturdy crusts to save for croutons if you want. Both are a quick toast away from being ready to use.

makes **3 TO 3½ CUPS**

6 ounces bread, including crusts

¼ cup or more excellent olive oil

1 teaspoon coarse kosher salt

Preheat the oven to 300°F. Cut or tear the bread into 1-inch chunks. Pulse in a food processor until most pieces are the size of peas. They will not all be the same size. Make sure not to pulse the bread to dust.

To toast, place the crumbs in a bowl and lightly moisten with the oil. They do not need to be saturated but should feel like damp sand. Season with the salt. Spread on a baking sheet and toast until golden and completely crisp and dry, stirring occasionally, 20 to 30 minutes.

Once the crumbs are cool, store them in an airtight container at room temperature for up to 1 month. If they become chewy, recrisp them by throwing them back in a 300°F oven for 5 minutes.

Add rye or sourdough crumbs to

→ Ricotta Dumplings with Spring Stock and Seasonal Vegetables (page 78)

→ Mussels with Anchovy Butter (page 233)

Add peasant bread crumbs to

→ Tagliatelle with Poached Garlic and Egg Yolk (page 313)

→ Celery Gratin (page 91)

Crostini and Crisps

Instead of throwing away nubs of good bread, slice them for future crostini or toast crisps and freeze. Then when you need a cracker, you can pull a few of the slices out of a freezer bag and toast them. This is especially helpful if you have to wrangle a last-minute hors d'oeuvre.

Especially dense loaves, a day or two old, cut nicely into thinner slices to become crisps. Tossed in salads, these shards soak up dressings and give welcome crunch.

Day-old good bread of any kind, for crostini

Day-old good dense bread (like a moist dark rye), for crisps

Excellent olive oil

Coarse kosher salt

Preheat the oven to 300°F.

To make crostini: Slice the bread ¼ inch thick.

To make crisps: Slice the bread no thicker than ⅛ inch.

Arrange the slices on a baking sheet. Brush lightly with oil on both sides and sprinkle lightly with salt. Toast in the oven until the bread begins to brown lightly and crisps completely, 10 to 15 minutes, depending on the thickness and density of the bread. Remove from the oven but leave it on.

As the crostini or crisps cool, check that they have crisped well; if they are at all chewy, put them back in the oven to dry further. Store, cooled completely, in an airtight container at room temperature for up to 1 week.

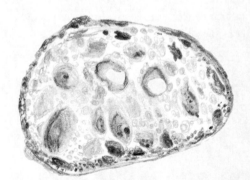

Skillet Flatbread

Everyone should have this recipe on hand. There is no better shortcut to a meal than a quick-to-put-together—or easy-to-keep-on-hand—warm, fragrant flatbread. It's a canvas for many ingredients in this book, or other ingredients in your pantry—I love it with canned sardines.

You can only make one flatbread at a time in a single skillet, but you can keep them warm, covered, in a low oven. They freeze beautifully in single portions, so you can make a full batch to keep on hand and cook only as few or as many at a time as you want.

Credit goes to the test kitchen at King Arthur Flour for the framework of this recipe. The ingredients and ratios are the same as theirs, but I've changed the preparation for a slightly less doughy bread.

makes 10 FLATBREADS

3 cups all-purpose flour, plus more for rolling

2 teaspoons baking powder

2 teaspoons coarse kosher salt

3 tablespoons excellent olive oil

1 cup ice water

Grapeseed or canola oil, for cooking

Mix the flour, baking powder, and salt together in a large bowl. Add the oil and ice water all at once and mix lightly with a large spoon until the dough is shaggy. Use your hands to bring the dough together into a soft ball. Do not knead. Transfer to a clean bowl and cover with plastic wrap; let rest at room temperature for 10 minutes.

Divide the dough into 10 equal pieces, each the size of a large egg. (*You can individually wrap and refrigerate the dough balls for up to 24 hours. Bring to room temperature for 20 minutes before rolling. Or freeze the individually wrapped portions in a freezer bag for up to 3 months. Thaw in the refrigerator and bring to room temperature for 20 minutes before rolling.*)

If you are cooking more than one flatbread, preheat the oven to 300°F to keep them warm. Line baking sheets with parchment paper and sprinkle lightly with flour. Sprinkle a little flour on the work surface and rolling pin, then roll each piece of dough into a ⅛-inch-thick round. Transfer to a baking sheet. Do not stack the uncooked flatbreads directly on top of each other; layer parchment paper in between.

Heat a cast-iron skillet over high heat. Once it is very hot, add 2 teaspoons oil; it should shimmer in the pan and coat the entire surface. Carefully lay a flatbread in the skillet and cover. (The lid will help the heat circulate and add air to the dough.)

Once the bottom of the flatbread is golden brown, after about 2 minutes, flip it over and cook, uncovered, on the other side until brown, checking that all shiny raw spots are cooked through, another 1 to 2 minutes. If you're cooking more breads, transfer the finished flatbreads to a clean baking sheet and keep in the oven until all are done.

Repeat with the remaining pieces of dough, adding oil to the pan only as necessary and lowering the heat if the flatbreads begin to burn. Serve warm.

Top with

→ olive oil, Za'atar Salt (page 373), and feta cheese

Use in

→ Confit Zucchini Squash and Skillet Flatbread (page 142)

→ Flatbread with Lamb Shanks, Pine Nuts, and Mint (page 305)

→ Apple-Core Mostarda and Gorgonzola Flatbread (page 211)

Wine and Vinegar

ABOUT WINE

Wine is to a dish what a frame is to a house; it provides structure and support to other ingredients. In braised chicken, short ribs, and duck, wine gives the cooking juices mature expression. With garlic and herbs, white wine amplifies the singular voice of otherwise quiet but fragrant vegetables—leeks (page 28), celery (page 90), and fennel (page 110). Wine's presence is something you notice most when it's absent: A sauce from meat pan drippings made without wine is like a Bloody Mary without Worcestershire.

Cook with the wine you drink. I keep a robust red, like a Syrah, and for white, a grassy, acidic Vinho Verde. With these two bottles, you can make any of the recipes in this book that call for wine.

You should not have to open a bottle of wine just to cook. You can freeze wine in portions ready to use for poaching broth, braising meat or vegetables, or for making sangria. Of course, this works best if you always freeze any remains of a bottle you start!

Freezing Wine

When you discover how useful it is to have wine on hand, you'll begin to look at a partially drunk bottle as a future ingredient. Rather than let a semi-used bottle of wine spoil, pour it into a container and freeze. You can accumulate small amounts of wine from various bottles over time, even adding them to the same large container in the freezer, until you have enough for a sangria batch (page 99).

WHITE WINE

Freeze ⅓-cup portions for braising celeriac, leeks, or fennel.

Freeze 1-cup portions for making Wine-Pickled Garlic Cloves (page 24), for braising celery (page 90) or chicken (page 257), for a double batch of White Wine–Braised Duck Legs (page 273), or for Quick Poaching Broth (page 360).

RED WINE

Freeze ½-cup portions for Wine-and-Tomato-Braised Squid (page 230).

Freeze 2-cup portions for sangria.

Quick Poaching Broth

This is a riff on classic court bouillon—a poaching stock for fish—that I also use for chicken breasts and select vegetables like cauliflower and summer squash. It's a quick-cooking vegetable broth with extra acidity—here, from both lemon and wine. This broth is one of the best reasons to freeze leftover white wine (page 359).

You can double or triple the recipe, which I highly recommend. Having a poaching broth on hand brings seemingly ambitious dishes quickly, easily together. These include poached salmon (page 225) and Sunchoke and Poached Chicken Soup (page 266).

makes ABOUT 7 CUPS

2 quarts water

1 cup dry white wine

Juice of 1 lemon

12 or so whole peppercorns (white or black)

2 garlic cloves, thinly sliced

1 cup thinly sliced carrots

2 cups thinly sliced onions

2 small handfuls of assorted fresh herbs (thyme, bay leaves, parsley, fennel fronds)

Combine all the ingredients in a saucepan, preferably one that is taller than it is wide. Bring to a quick boil, then turn the heat down to low. Simmer, uncovered, for 15 minutes. Taste a few pieces of the sliced vegetables to make sure they've released all their flavor. If they haven't, simmer for a few minutes more. Taste the broth again. It should taste light, acidic, and fresh.

You can strain and use the broth immediately. Or allow it to cool completely in the pan before straining, then store in the refrigerator for up to 5 days or in the freezer for several months. Consider storing the broth in multiple portions so you don't have to thaw an entire container for just a few cups.

Simple Vinaigrettes

A simple vinaigrette wakes up the palate to different tastes, an especially important role in a long, rich meal. Vinegars help spices bloom and give them a means of pairing with ingredients they could not otherwise cling to: Cumin piggybacks on sherry vinegar to dress roasted cauliflower; coriander marries with white wine vinegar to coat cucumbers and ramp leaves. You can use vinaigrettes to sauce warm and cold salads and grains, as well as raw and cooked meats, fish, and vegetables.

My rule for making a simple vinaigrette is to combine the best olive oil and the best vinegar I can afford in whatever proportions taste good to me. I often do this right in the bowl of greens I'm about to dress. Drizzle in the vinegar first, then the oil, then a bit of salt and toss lightly. The greens will be unevenly coated, which is fine when you use fresh greens and excellent vinegar and oil. Why should every bite of salad taste exactly the same?

To improvise a seasoned vinaigrette, first make a base. Chop ingredients such as shallots, capers, herbs, garlic, mustard, spices, and dried fruit—however fine or coarse is up to you—so they nestle comfortably in a spoon, then mix them into the vinegar. Add the oil in a stream as thin as spaghetti, using a food processor for a creamier, smoother dressing or a bowl and a whisk for a looser, chunkier one. Start with the same amount of oil as vinegar, adding more oil to mellow the flavors and a little salt to balance sharpness. Taste the vinaigrette with a piece of the leaf you are going to eat it with; it's easier to judge seasoning this way than if you sample it from a spoon. Take care not to oversalt the dressing; you can always salt the salad greens directly, once they're tossed.

In general, vinaigrettes should be pungent and bold. You'll want thicker dressings, such as those that use mustard or egg yolk, for sturdier leaves, and thinner ones without emulsifiers for herbs and baby greens. But these aren't strict rules. For example, you can whisk a few drops of warm water into creamy Mustard Vinaigrette (page 364) to make it light enough for tender greens.

Most vinaigrettes are best used at room temperature, but sometimes their texture improves when chilled. Especially for vinaigrettes that separate quickly, such as Cumin-Sherry Vinaigrette (page 364) and Parsley Vinaigrette made with lemon (page 69), chilling for about 15 minutes before using will give you a dressing with better body. Once the oil thickens and sets, you can even use these vinaigrettes as spreads for sandwiches. Whisk any vinaigrette well and frequently as it comes to room temperature, reinforcing its fragile emulsification.

Coriander Vinaigrette

I like the crunch of coriander seeds, but you can decide if you'd like to keep them in the vinaigrette or strain them out after they steep a while in the vinegar. Spoon this vinaigrette over Whole Roasted Fish (page 246) or use in a salad with ramp leaves (page 39).

→ **MAKES 1 GENEROUS CUP**

6 tablespoons coriander seeds, well crushed

½ cup apple cider vinegar

1 teaspoon coarse kosher salt

⅔ cup or more excellent olive oil

Combine the coriander seeds, vinegar, and salt in a small bowl. Let stand for 10 minutes. If you prefer no seeds, strain the vinegar into another bowl.

Whisk the vinegar as you slowly drizzle in the oil. Use immediately or store in the refrigerator for up to 1 month. Bring to almost room temperature before using, whisking to re-emulsify it as it warms up.

ABOUT VINEGAR

I often use vinegar when I want to wake up a dish. Both sharp and sweet vinegars offset the slight bitterness of greens in dishes like Collard Ribbons with Sharp Vinaigrette (page 48) and Roasted Radicchio (page 60). Vinegar gives a quick lift to vegetables like cucumber and cabbage. When you add vinegar to heated ingredients like mushrooms and sunchokes, the flavor announces itself loudly, then quiets as the ingredient absorbs it.

Green-Peppercorn Vinaigrette

This vinaigrette is pungent and unique; you need only a little bit for great effect. I toss it with Pickled Beets (page 162) or Boiled Potatoes (page 175), or spoon it liberally on top of warm Whole Roasted Fish (page 246).

Green peppercorns are the unripe berries of the black pepper plant. They can be as spicy as hot red pepper flakes but are made approachable when preserved in brine. You'll find them in Mediterranean markets.

→ **MAKES 1¾ CUPS**

¼ cup green peppercorns in brine, drained

2 teaspoons coriander seeds

2 tablespoons whole-grain mustard

2 tablespoons white wine vinegar

1½ cups or more excellent olive oil

Combine the green peppercorns, coriander, mustard, and vinegar in a food processor. Pulse several times to bring the dressing base together. With the processor running, pour in the oil in a very thin stream.

Use immediately or store in the refrigerator for up to 1 month. Bring to room temperature and whisk before using.

Cumin-Raisin Vinaigrette

Salty, sweet, sour—this vinaigrette has it all. You can use a food processor to make it, or chop and mix it by hand. The processor will emulsify it, making it creamier. You can double or triple the recipe with equal success.

→ **MAKES ABOUT 1½ CUPS**

1 cup golden raisins

¼ cup sherry vinegar

2 tablespoons cold water

1 tablespoon whole-grain mustard

2 teaspoons fresh lemon juice

1 small shallot, minced

1¼ teaspoons ground cumin

2 tablespoons capers, drained

1 teaspoon caper brine

½ cup excellent olive oil

⅓ to ½ cup warm water, if needed

Combine the raisins, vinegar, and cold water in a small saucepan. Bring to a quick boil over high heat. Immediately turn off the heat; cover the pan and let steep until cooled.

If mixing by hand. Combine the mustard, juice, shallot, and cumin in a bowl. Chop the capers and add them to the bowl, along with the brine. Chop the plumped raisins and add them and any remaining vinegar to the bowl. Whisk well as you drizzle in the oil, a little at a time.

If using a food processor: Combine the mustard, juice, shallot, cumin, capers and brine, and the raisins and vinegar in a food processor. With the machine running, pour in the oil and process until just creamy. Do not blend completely; a little texture is nice. Pulse in warm water as necessary to loosen if the dressing is too pasty.

Store in a jar in the refrigerator for up to 2 weeks. Bring almost to room temperature before using, whisking to re-emulsify it as it warms up.

Toss with

→ fresh spinach as a bed for Salted Roast Chicken (page 253)

→ Parsnips Braised in White Wine and Cumin (page 172)

Spread on

→ slices of baguette and top with cheddar cheese

Whisk into

→ Roast Chicken in Pan-Drippings Sauce (page 255)

Use in

→ Roasted Eggplant, Gruyère, and Cumin-Raisin Gratin (page 132)

DRESSING A SALAD

You'll need a bowl large enough to loosely fit all the lettuce. Spoon some dressing directly into the bottom of the bowl. With your fingers, loosely spread the dressing over the bottom and sides of the bowl. Add the lettuce, only as much as you think the dressing can coat nicely. With your fingers spread open, gently stir the greens in one direction around the bowl. This should dress them sufficiently without bruising. Unless you are trying to wilt or soften the greens, you should never aggressively stir or fold them. If you need more dressing, add it to the sides of the bowl, never directly on top of the greens. Season lightly with salt and pepper, then add any other ingredients.

Cumin-Sherry Vinaigrette

This vinaigrette is sharper than Cumin-Raisin Vinaigrette (page 363); it is also heavier on the spice. You can make it in a food processor or by hand. The processor will temporarily emulsify the vinaigrette, making it creamier; mixing this by hand will keep the consistency more like that of a traditional vinaigrette, and the flavors more defined. Prepare it in advance and refrigerate, which makes it easier to emulsify.

⟶ **MAKES A GENEROUS ¾ CUP**

2 tablespoons cumin seeds

¼ cup sherry vinegar

2 small garlic cloves, minced

2 teaspoons whole-grain mustard

2 teaspoons fresh lemon juice

2 tablespoons finely chopped golden raisins

2 pinches of coarse kosher salt

½ cup excellent olive oil

Toast the cumin seeds in a small dry skillet over medium heat until fragrant and lightly toasted, about 1 minute. Turn off the heat and add the vinegar and garlic. Let the garlic cook in the residual heat for about 30 seconds. Stir in the mustard, juice, raisins, and salt. Transfer to a small bowl or a food processor. Let cool.

If mixing by hand: Whisking, drizzle in the oil a little at a time.

If using a food processor: With the machine running, pour in the oil in a steady stream and process for about 30 seconds, until creamy.

Store in a jar in the refrigerator for up to 2 weeks. Bring almost to room temperature before using, whisking to re-emulsify it as it warms up.

Mustard Vinaigrette

Pair this pungent, creamy classic dressing with young spring vegetables such as radishes, asparagus, and baby turnips. Or pour it, gently warmed, over roasted potatoes, seared steak (page 280), or Salted Roast Chicken (page 253).

⟶ **MAKES ⅔ CUP**

¼ cup Dijon mustard

¼ cup red wine vinegar

½ cup excellent olive oil

½ teaspoon coarse kosher salt

Water, as needed

Mix the mustard and vinegar together in a small bowl. Add the oil, whisking it in a little at a time. Add the salt. If you want the dressing a bit thinner, whisk in water a single drop at a time.

Store in a jar in the refrigerator for up to 2 weeks. Bring to room temperature before using; if it separates, whisk to re-emulsify it as it warms up.

Spiced-Apple-Cider-Honey Vinaigrette

Toss with red leaf lettuce and croutons, or on Shaved Brussels Sprout and Swiss Chard Slaw (page 116). Or mix some into a bowl of slightly warm Freekeh in Garlic Tea (page 337) or Toasted Rye Berries (page 334).

⟶ **MAKES 1¼ CUPS**

¼ cup honey

½ cup apple cider vinegar

½ teaspoon ground cinnamon

½ teaspoon freshly ground black pepper

½ teaspoon coarse kosher salt

Pinch of hot red pepper flakes

Pinch of ground cumin

½ cup excellent olive oil

Mix the honey and vinegar together in a small bowl to dissolve the honey. Add the cinnamon, pepper, salt, red pepper flakes, and cumin. Slowly whisk in the oil.

Store in a jar in the refrigerator for up to 2 weeks. Bring almost to room temperature before using, whisking to re-emulsify it as it warms up.

SAVING BRINE: THE PICKLE BANK

The pickle bank is a reusable jar of pickle brine you like. Into the jar go both things you prepare to pickle and things for which you find no other use. These may include a few spare radishes; tender inner stalks of celery; a wedge of onion; even scrubbed, extra-thick carrot peels. The pickle bank doesn't just have its eye on the season's harvest, but on the loose things in your fridge.

Deposits into the pickle bank are like coins you find around the house, not worth much on their own, but valuable in aggregate. The bank keeps you rich with pickle options, a grab bag of eclectic brined bits and scraps, a sweet-and-sour miscellany, a safe haven for things that would otherwise end up as trash.

Anything can go into a pickle bank, but note the effects of one ingredient on others: A red beet will tinge carrot peels pink; asparagus may make them odoriferous.

Vegetables will pickle at different rates. You can avoid this somewhat by blanching raw vegetables before adding them to the cold brine. A thick green bean, for instance, will take forever to cold-pickle unless it is first blanched. You can also thinly slice the raw bean to speed up the pickling effect.

I use apple cider vinegar for pickled beets (page 162), apples (page 208), and squash (page 190); distilled white vinegar for garlic cloves (page 24); and white wine vinegar for eggplant (page 134), green tomatoes (page 145), and herbs (page 66).

Dried Fruit

Balsamic-Poached Figs

These figs are delicious served as a sweet compote, especially good over dark chocolate ice cream or alongside Savory Ricotta Custard (page 386).

Making the quick caramel is easy—and worth it. As long as you don't make it too dark, there is little you can do wrong. The inclusion of lemon juice reduces the risk of crystallization, a common problem when making caramel.

Prepare all of the ingredients ahead, so you are ready to mix in the spices, vinegar, and juices just as the syrup caramelizes.

makes **ABOUT 2 CUPS**

½ cup water

1 teaspoon fresh lemon juice

1½ cups sugar

½ cup balsamic vinegar

2 tablespoons fresh orange juice

½ cinnamon stick

1 star anise pod

1 allspice berry

2 whole black peppercorns

1 fresh thyme sprig

2 cups dried Black Mission figs, stems trimmed, cut in half or quartered

Bring the water to a boil in a medium saucepan. Turn off the heat; add the lemon juice and then the sugar, a little at a time, so no granules cling to the sides of the pan. Do not stir.

Turn the heat to medium-high and bring the sugar and water to a boil undisturbed. The bubbles will be rapid at first; as the syrup thickens, they will grow larger and slower, about 2 minutes. Meanwhile, combine the vinegar, orange juice, cinnamon, star anise, allspice, peppercorns, and thyme in a small bowl.

Watch the syrup closely: As soon as the entire surface becomes an even, light caramel color, carefully—but all at once—add the vinegar and spice mixture. The caramel will bubble up. Cook, stirring and scraping the bottom of the pan, for another 30 seconds. If the caramel seizes, it will quickly remelt. Once it is smooth, turn off the heat, stir in the figs, and let cool. Store in a covered container at room temperature indefinitely.

Use in

→ Dried Lemon, Balsamic Fig, and Cocoa Compote (page 220)

→ Polenta with Balsamic-Poached Figs and Bacon (page 317)

→ Braised Chicken Legs with Balsamic-Poached Figs (page 259)

→ Wild Rice with Swiss Chard and Balsamic-Poached Figs (page 328)

Fig, Olive, and Walnut Relish

I can eat this relish by the sweet and salty spoonful. But it also makes a terrific sandwich spread with prosciutto and Parmesan, a dressing for Raw and Ribboned Collard Greens (page 48), and with the help of roasted oranges, turns Popcorn Quinoa (page 329) into a fantastic fall side dish (page 330).

Although I prefer the jammy Black Mission figs for this relish, you can use larger Turkish ones too. Currants substitute in a pinch. Kalamatas are the choice utility olive, but oil-cured are especially delicious here. With either olive, be cautious about their salt content; use fewer olives to start if they are especially salty, then add more olives to taste. I call for Marsala wine, but a semisweet sherry works too. Finally, if you have saba (an Italian syrup also called *vincotto* or *mosto cotto*), use that instead of the vinegar.

makes **2 TO 2½ CUPS**

2 tablespoons excellent olive oil, plus more if needed

1 cup finely chopped red onion

Packed 1 cup dried figs (about 7 ounces), stemmed

2 tablespoons balsamic vinegar or saba

2 tablespoons water

½ cup pitted kalamata or oil-cured olives

Coarse kosher salt

Freshly ground black pepper

1½ to 3 teaspoons sweet Marsala wine

½ cup finely chopped toasted walnuts (page 368)

Place the oil in a small skillet over medium-low heat. Add the onions and cook slowly, stirring often, until translucent, about 20 minutes.

Meanwhile, combine the figs, vinegar, and water in a small saucepan. Bring to a quick boil, immediately turn off the heat, cover, and let steep for 10 minutes.

Drain the figs, gently squeezing any excess liquid back into the pan. Chop the figs very fine, then transfer to a bowl. Finely chop the olives and add them to the figs.

Reduce the steeping liquid until just syrupy, to about 1 tablespoon. Add to the figs and olives, and season with salt and pepper. When the onions are cooked through, add those as well. Stir and taste for salt, adding cautiously if the olives are salty. While the relish is still warm, add the Marsala and walnuts; let sit for 5 minutes. Taste again. You have the option to add more oil at this point if you think the relish can absorb it.

Store in the refrigerator for up to 1 month.

Maple Currants

Sweet and lightly spiced, this condiment belongs on oatmeal with buttermilk, next to thick slices of ham, and in Roasted Cauliflower and Maple Currants with Cumin Vinaigrette (page 105).

makes 1 CUP

1 cup dried currants

2 tablespoons maple syrup

1 tablespoon plus 1 teaspoon red wine vinegar

¼ teaspoon ground allspice

¼ teaspoon coarse kosher salt

Place all the ingredients in a small saucepan over low heat and cook just until steaming. Stir once, turn off the heat, cover, and let sit for the currants to plump and cool.

Store at room temperature for up to 3 months.

TOASTING AND BLANCHING NUTS

Blanched nuts are nuts without their skins. Typically—pecans and walnuts aside—blanched nuts are what we want to eat. Except for hazelnuts, blanched nuts are easy to find. If you can't find blanched hazelnuts, you can blanch and toast them at the same time (see below).

If you need to toast an assortment of nuts, keep the different kinds separate—they will toast at different rates. I set the oven low, so the nuts toast evenly with little risk of burning.

TO TOAST NUTS: Preheat the oven to 300°F. Spread the nuts on a baking sheet lined with parchment paper. (The parchment helps you collect them in one fell swoop at the end.) Bake until fragrant and lightly toasted, stirring once. Check after 12 minutes, but they may require up to 20.

TO BLANCH AND TOAST HAZELNUTS: Preheat the oven to 400°F. Spread the hazelnuts on a baking sheet lined with parchment paper. Bake until the skins begin to crack and turn black, 8 to 10 minutes—you'll see the brown nut peeking out underneath. Remove from the oven and pour the nuts into the center of a large, clean dish towel. Gather the towel into a bundle and repeatedly smash and roll it on the work surface, releasing the skins. Spread the towel out and let the nuts cool. Pour the nuts into a strainer and shake to settle the skins to the bottom. Don't worry if some stubborn skins stick. Lift out the blanched nuts and discard the skins.

It's best to toast nuts as you need them, but you can store extra toasted nuts in an airtight container at room temperature for up to a week. Taste before using.

Nut Cream

This infused cream can be used just like plain heavy cream. It is thicker, in part because it's reduced, and in part because the nuts release their own fat into it. If you like to make your own ice cream, this is a great way to flavor the cream (omit the sage leaves).

I call for hazelnuts, but you can substitute almonds or pistachios. To extract the most flavor from the nuts, warm them to "wake up" their oils, grind them while still warm, and heat the cream.

It's best if you can steep the nuts in the cream overnight.

makes 1 CUP

1 cup chopped blanched, toasted hazelnuts or other nuts (opposite)

2 cups heavy cream

6 sage leaves (see headnote)

A few gratings of nutmeg

Coarse kosher salt (optional)

Preheat the oven to 325°F. Line a baking sheet with parchment paper. Spread the nuts on the baking sheet and put them into the oven to warm thoroughly, 3 to 5 minutes. Monitor them so they don't toast further or burn.

Meanwhile, heat the cream and sage in a medium saucepan over medium heat.

Once the nuts are hot, lift the parchment like a chute to pour them into a food processor. Pulse the nuts fine, but don't turn them to paste. Immediately add the warm ground nuts to the cream. Bring to a quick boil—be

careful not to let the cream bubble up over the top—then turn the heat down and simmer slowly for 10 minutes, until reduced by almost half. Remove from the heat and let cool to room temperature. If possible, place in the refrigerator and let the nuts steep overnight.

If you have chilled the cream, bring it back to room temperature. Strain, allowing all the thickened cream to drain and pressing on the nuts to extract all their flavor. Season with nutmeg and a bit of salt, if you like. Discard the nuts.

Store in the refrigerator for up to 5 days or freeze for up to 1 month. Thaw in the refrigerator overnight to use.

Use in

→ Braised Celeriac Soup (page 171)

→ Mussels with Braised Fennel and Hazelnut Cream (page 234)

Nut Stock

Nut Stock is rich without being heavy; toasty but not bitter. To extract the most flavor from the nuts, warm them to wake up their oils, grind them fine while still warm, and add them immediately to the rest of the ingredients.

It's best if you can make this a day in advance and steep the nuts in the stock overnight before straining.

makes ABOUT 2 QUARTS

⅓ cup excellent olive oil

4 medium onions, thinly sliced

12 garlic cloves, thinly sliced

3½ cups blanched, toasted nuts (such as almonds and hazelnuts, see page 368; 1 pound)

4 teaspoons coriander seeds

12 cups water (preferably filtered)

1½ teaspoons coarse kosher salt

Preheat the oven to 325°F. Line a baking sheet with parchment paper. Heat the oil, onions, and half of the garlic in a large saucepan over low heat. Cover and cook until the onions are translucent, stirring occasionally, about 20 minutes.

When the onions and garlic are nearly completely soft, spread the nuts on the baking sheet and put them into the oven to warm thoroughly, 3 to 5 minutes. Monitor them so they don't toast further or burn.

Using the parchment as a funnel, carefully spill the warm nuts into a food processor. Grind fine, but don't turn them to a paste.

Immediately add the nuts and coriander seeds to the onions and garlic and stir well. Add the water, cover, and bring to a quick boil over high heat. Remove the lid, turn the heat down to low, and simmer for about 20 minutes. Add the salt and cook for 15 minutes more, until reduced by about a third. Turn off the heat and add the remaining garlic. Cover the pan and let cool to room temperature. If possible, let the stock steep overnight in the refrigerator.

Rewarm the stock and pass it through a fine-mesh strainer or a medium strainer lined with cheesecloth, pressing on the solids to extract all of their fat and flavor. Discard the contents of the strainer.

Store the stock in the refrigerator for up to 3 days or freeze for up to 6 months. Stir well before using.

Use in

→ Mushroom Risotto with Nut Stock and Roasted Garlic (page 325)

→ Triple-Braised Wild Mushrooms (page 194)

Tahini Sauce

Tahini takes you far with the help of pantry friends. Use as a dip for warm pita or for crudités of early spring vegetables. Or dress Whole Roasted Fish (page 246) with it; the unusual addition of anchovy makes this an especially delicious pairing.

This is best made in a food processor or blender. Its creaminess is the result of speedy whipping.

makes 1 CUP

5 or 6 anchovy fillets

1 large garlic clove

¼ cup fresh lemon juice

¼ cup excellent olive oil

⅓ cup tahini

⅓ cup cold water

With the machine running, drop the anchovies and garlic into a food processor for an initial quick chop. Scrape down the sides. Add the lemon juice, oil, tahini, and water all at once, and blend until smooth.

The dip will thicken as it sits. The garlic may be very strong at first, but will mellow. Store in the refrigerator for up to 2 weeks.

Spice Salts and Rubs

It can be difficult for even an experienced cook to taste how spices might work together, since each spice is hard to taste on its own. Straight from the jar, ground spices taste dusty, not distinctive. Whole seeds taste bitter, not of the aromas they'll lend. The key to tasting spices alone and in combination is to do so with a medium that carries flavor. One medium is salt.

Spice salts can be used more frequently, liberally, and creatively than single spices. Take bay leaves: Peppery and woodsy, pedestrian but full of gravitas, they lend maturity to bright flavors like lemon and tomato, and direction to legumes. Their elusive contribution is often mistakenly seen as optional, but they are the uncelebrated herb of a serious cook. However, they are structurally off-putting: a known choking hazard in soups and stews. So the first step in finding a broader use for these leaves must be to turn them to a friendlier form. Hence Bay Salt (page 374).

You can make spice salts with ground spices too, so you can discover new ways to taste and use even those spices most familiar to you. You can make spice salts on a cutting board by chopping or crushing whole seeds, or with a mortar and pestle, or in a spice grinder. For a rub, add olive oil.

Mix together the ingredients for each salt. In a tightly covered jar away from light, each will keep for about 3 months.

Fennel-Thyme Salt

Use with pork loin or leg of lamb.

makes ABOUT 3½ TABLESPOONS

2 tablespoons fennel seeds, crushed

1 tablespoon dried thyme

2 teaspoons coarse kosher salt

Cumin-Coriander Salt

This is particularly good on cauliflower, fregola, and garlic scapes.

makes ABOUT 4 TEASPOONS

2½ teaspoons coriander seeds, roughly crushed

¾ teaspoon ground cumin

¾ teaspoon coarse kosher salt

Za'atar Salt

Sprinkle on flatbread and roast asparagus. Use to season roast chicken.

makes 3½ TABLESPOONS

2 tablespoons za'atar

1½ tablespoons coarse kosher salt

Pork Spice Rub

I like to make a triple batch of this spice mix.

makes 4 TO 5 TABLESPOONS

1 tablespoon coriander seeds

1 tablespoon coarse kosher salt

1 tablespoon fennel seeds

1 tablespoon dried thyme

1½ teaspoons whole white peppercorns

3 small garlic cloves, peeled

2 tablespoons excellent olive oil

Place all the ingredients in a food processor. Process until the garlic is finely ground. The seeds will be mostly crushed; you can grind them to a fine paste if you prefer.

Keep in a covered container in the refrigerator for up to 3 months.

Add to

—→ melted butter

—→ A Cup of Broth for a Cold Day (page 268)

—→ Julienned Celeriac (page 168)

—→ A Single Deviled Egg (page 350)

Use in

—→ Orange-and-Fennel Pulled Pork (page 288)

Bay Salt

I grind bay leaves together with salt to a fine green-gray powder. It stays well blended and eliminates sharp pieces of leaf. Make sure your bay leaves are army green, not twig brown. Keep this salt on your counter and see how quickly you'll work through the jar.

makes **ABOUT 4 TEASPOONS**

15 large dried
bay leaves

1 tablespoon coarse
kosher salt

Break up the bay leaves with your fingers and place in a spice grinder. Add the salt and whirl to a fine powder. If necessary, pass through a fine-mesh strainer to remove any larger pieces of leaves.

In a tightly covered jar away from light, this will keep for about 3 months.

Sprinkle on

$\longrightarrow$ Roasted Beets (page 161)

$\longrightarrow$ Triple-Braised Wild Mushrooms (page 194)

$\longrightarrow$ sliced raw sea bass with lemon

$\longrightarrow$ Poached Shrimp (page 228)

$\longrightarrow$ A Single Deviled Egg (page 350)

$\longrightarrow$ roast chicken

$\longrightarrow$ Charred Corn (page 125)

Use in

$\longrightarrow$ Roasted Beets and Pickled Onions with Pistachios and Bay Salt (page 162)

$\longrightarrow$ Whole Roasted Fish with Wine-Pickled Garlic and Bay Salt (page 248)

$\longrightarrow$ Mushroom Risotto with Nut Stock and Roasted Garlic (page 325)

$\longrightarrow$ Olives with Lemon and Bay Salt (opposite)

Olives with Lemon and Bay Salt

Good olives don't need a marinade but are happy for a hint of spice or citrus. Here, I toss meaty Castelvetrano olives with Bay Salt and fresh lemon. I serve them as a small plate or snack or as "vegetables" in a meal.

→ **MAKES 2 CUPS**

2 cups Castelvetrano olives

Strips of zest from 1 lemon (white pith removed)

1½ tablespoons fresh lemon juice

1 teaspoon **Bay Salt** (opposite)

Place the olives in a bowl. Bend the lemon zest strips in half to release their oils and aroma, and toss in with the olives. Add the juice and bay salt. Stir once or twice to combine. These are best served at room temperature the day they are made.

Seasoned Butters

Cutting-Board Butter

Impromptu seasoned butters are simple to devise on your own, with whatever ingredients you like or want to use up, including the bits on your cutting board you might otherwise trash. If you are using briny ingredients like capers or anchovies, reduce the salt. For sweet ingredients like dried fruit, add a pinch more.

makes **5 TABLESPOONS**

2 tablespoons any herb, roughly chopped

½ teaspoon any crushed spice (such as fennel seeds or cumin seeds)

1 teaspoon flaky sea salt

1 teaspoon fresh lemon or orange juice

4 tablespoons (½ stick) unsalted butter, at room temperature

Pile the herb, spice, and salt on a cutting board. Sprinkle with the juice. Use a pastry scraper or the side of a knife to smear the butter over the other ingredients. Fold everything together until thoroughly mixed.

Store tightly wrapped in parchment and plastic in the refrigerator for up to 2 weeks, or freeze, rolled into a log for quick portioning and tightly wrapped, for up to 6 months.

Prune Butter

Use this as you would other savory butters—for example, to finish Roast Chicken in Pan-Drippings Sauce (page 255) or to reheat White Wine–Braised Duck Legs (page 273). It is perfect for a turkey sandwich too.

makes **A HEAPING ½ CUP**

2 whole cloves

1 star anise pod

1 cinnamon stick

2 tablespoons water

2 tablespoons fresh orange juice

½ cup pitted prunes, chopped

4 tablespoons (½ stick) unsalted butter, at room temperature

½ teaspoon coarse kosher salt

Tie the cloves, star anise, and cinnamon in a piece of cheesecloth.

Bring the water, juice, and prunes to a boil in a small saucepan. Turn off the heat and nestle in the spice bundle. Cover the pan and let sit for 10 minutes. Remove the lid and let cool to room temperature. Remove the cheesecloth and squeeze any liquid back into the pot; discard.

Put the prunes and liquid, butter, and salt in a food processor. Pulse to make a slightly chunky paste, scraping down the sides as it comes together.

Storetightly wrapped in parchment and plastic in the refrigerator for up to 3 weeks, or freeze, rolled into a log for quick portioning and tightly wrapped, up to 3 months.

Herb-Infused Butter

This recipe infuses and clarifies the butter, so its milk solids separate out and it will melt seamlessly into broths and sauces. (It will yield about 25 percent less butter than you started with.)

You can make infused butters in larger or smaller quantities, as you like, and with other ingredients you might not readily think of: saffron, dried mushrooms, even tea. Unlike typical clarified butter, you do not want to use this butter to cook at high heat; it will lose its fragrance and flavor. It is best slipped in at the end of a dish, as in Rustic Polenta (page 314) and Quick Spring-Stock Risotto (page 325).

makes ¾ POUND

1 pound (4 sticks) unsalted butter

2 cups assorted fresh whole or chopped herbs, including stems (such as thyme, parsley, oregano, and sage)

A handful of fennel fronds (optional)

4 bay leaves

8 whole cloves

2 teaspoons fennel seeds

½ teaspoon whole black peppercorns

Place the butter in a medium saucepan over very low heat. Pile the herbs and spices on top. Once the butter has melted, stir once to submerge the herbs. Continue cooking slowly until the herbs are wilted and the butter is tinged green, about 20 minutes.

Remove from the heat, cover, and let cool to room temperature.

Strain into a small container, pressing on the herbs to extract their full flavor. Chill well. The butter will separate into a glossy greenish-gold brick on top of milky white liquid.

To release the butter, invert the container under lukewarm water. The milky liquid will spill out too. Under *very cold* water, gently rinse off any milky residue from the brick of butter. Blot the butter with a dry, clean towel.

Store tightly wrapped in parchment and plastic in the refrigerator for up to 1 month, or freeze, rolled into a log for quick portioning and tightly wrapped, for up to several months.

Use in

→ Spring Vegetable and Herb Sauté (page 77)

→ The Only Pasta Recipe (page 309)

Green-Peppercorn Butter

I make this butter once a year for a local sale just before Thanksgiving, and sell out every time. What people don't use for turkey sandwiches, they eat with cured ham, or freeze and save for summer's Charred Corn (page 125). I've used this butter sparingly in the filling of fresh peach pies too.

makes ABOUT 1¼ CUPS

3 tablespoons plus ½ teaspoon green peppercorns in brine, drained

1 tablespoon plus 1 teaspoon Dijon mustard

½ pound (2 sticks) unsalted butter, at room temperature

Put the green peppercorns in a food processor and pulse until coarsely chopped. Add the butter and mustard and pulse to combine well.

Store tightly wrapped in parchment and plastic in the refrigerator for up to 2 months, or freeze, rolled into a log for quick portioning and tightly wrapped, for up to 6 months.

Anchovy Butter

Use this potent butter anytime you want the addition of something rich and salty, such as for seared steak (page 280) or to reinforce the flavor of a companion fish, like seared tuna (page 240) or for steamed mussels (page 232). Anchovies vary widely in quality and size; adjust the number of fillets to your taste.

If you can't find green peppercorns in brine, slightly increase the amount of capers and add coarsely ground black pepper to taste.

makes 1 CUP

About 12 anchovy fillets (see headnote)

10 green peppercorns in brine, drained

2 garlic cloves, roughly chopped

⅛ teaspoon freshly grated nutmeg

¼ cup excellent olive oil

¼ teaspoon Dijon mustard

2½ teaspoons fresh lemon juice

12 tablespoons (1½ sticks) unsalted butter, at room temperature

2½ teaspoons capers, drained

Combine the anchovies, garlic, oil, juice, capers, peppercorns, nutmeg, and mustard in a food processor. Process to a smooth paste. Add the butter and pulse until creamy. If you want the anchovy butter perfectly smooth, pass it through a fine-mesh strainer.

Store tightly wrapped in parchment and plastic in the refrigerator for up to 3 weeks, or freeze, rolled into a log for quick portioning and tightly wrapped, for up to 3 months.

Anchovy Dressing

If you like anchovies, you'll eat this by the spoonful. Toss with escarole or other bitter greens, fresh turnips, or radishes, or use as a dip for crudités. I add egg yolks for creaminess and to tame and distribute the strong anchovy.

makes 1¾ CUPS

2 (2-ounce) cans anchovies, drained

8 large garlic cloves, roughly chopped

¼ teaspoon hot red pepper flakes, or to taste

2 large egg yolks

1 cup excellent olive oil

Up to ½ cup water

Combine the anchovies, garlic, and red pepper flakes in a food processor and blend to combine. Add the egg yolks and blend until finely chopped. With the processor running, add the oil in a slow, thin stream. The dressing will be thick. With the processor still running, add the water, 1 tablespoon at a time, to thin to a smooth, creamy consistency. You may have water left over.

Store in a covered container in the refrigerator for up to 2 weeks.

Use in

→ Spring Turnips with Anchovy Dressing and Walnuts (page 186)

Toss with

→ Roasted Broccoli Rabe (page 103)

Buttermilk Dressing

If you're going to buy buttermilk to make pancakes, you might as well use the extra to make something else.

Here, enriched with sour cream, aromatic with tarragon, and brightened with lemon juice, the buttermilk mounts to a full, tangy dressing that clings beautifully to milder lettuces but also stands up to meat and poultry. I pair it with peaches, celery, asparagus, duck, and more.

makes ½ CUP

¼ cup sour cream

Up to ¼ cup buttermilk

Grated zest of 1 lemon

2 tablespoons fresh lemon juice

¾ teaspoon coarse kosher salt

¼ teaspoon freshly ground black pepper

1 tablespoon finely chopped fresh tarragon

Combine the sour cream, 2 tablespoons of the buttermilk, the lemon zest, lemon juice, salt, pepper, and tarragon in a bowl and whisk vigorously until smooth. Add more buttermilk to get the consistency you want. Store, covered, in the refrigerator for up to 1 week.

Garlic Yogurt Sauce

Garlic, lemon, and salt transform yogurt into a refreshing, creamy sauce that's good on sliced raw cucumbers; braised meats; blanched, slow-cooked, or roasted vegetables; grains; grilled breads; and flatbreads.

You can vary the recipe by substituting lime juice or pickle brine for the lemon juice; hot red pepper flakes or ground cumin for the black pepper; and oregano or mint for the parsley. Add crunch with scallion greens, minced shallots, pickled onions, grated zucchini, or chopped toasted nuts. Use a yogurt with at least 2% fat, or the sauce will taste chalky and uneven.

makes 1 HEAPING CUP

1 cup Greek yogurt (at least 2% fat)

1 small garlic clove, very finely minced

2 teaspoons fresh lemon juice

1¼ teaspoons coarse kosher salt

A few grinds of black pepper

¼ cup chopped fresh flat-leaf parsley

Mix all the ingredients together in a small bowl. Let sit for 10 minutes for the flavors to develop. If not using immediately, store in a covered container in the refrigerator for up to 5 days. Stir well before using.

Whole-Grain Mustard Aioli

I like store-bought mayonnaise, but I *love* this aioli. You can alter the sauce after it's made by adding, for example, capers and green peppercorns. Garlic is essential.

makes A SCANT **2** CUPS

2 large egg yolks

2 small garlic cloves, roughly chopped

1 tablespoon fresh lemon juice, plus more as needed

3½ teaspoons whole grain mustard

½ cup canola oil

¾ cup excellent olive oil

1 to 2 teaspoons coarse kosher salt

Up to 3 tablespoons warm water, as necessary

Spread on

→ bread with Best Roasted Green Peppers (page 136)

Use in

→ Poached Chicken and Braised Celeriac and with Whole-Grain Mustard Aioli (page 265)

→ Roasted-Pepper Breakfast Sandwich (page 137)

Put the yolks, garlic, lemon juice, and mustard in a food processor and process until well mixed. With the processor running, add the oils very, very slowly (see box). Season carefully with salt to taste. Thin the sauce with water, as you like, a tablespoon at a time.

Let the aioli sit for 10 minutes for the flavors to come together; taste again. It should taste bright, fresh, and creamy—not of oil. Tweak with lemon and salt until it becomes addictive enough to eat from a spoon.

Refrigerate for up to 5 days. Do not freeze.

Use as a dip for

→ spring vegetable crudités

→ Salt-Roasted Little Potatoes (page 178)

MAKING AIOLI

If you've never made aioli before, follow these tips:

→ Blend the base ingredients well before adding the oils.

→ Use only excellent oils with no acrid aftertaste.

→ When you add the oils, do so in the slowest possible way to avoid breaking the emulsion, pouring them in a stream as thin as spaghetti; if your hand is too unsteady for that, then drop by drop.

→ Use all the oil the recipe calls for.

→ Let it mellow for 10 minutes.

Refrigerator-Door Relish

This combination of preserved ingredients becomes the jumping-off point for a potent mustard, a coarse, piquant "salt," and a bold vinaigrette.

If you don't have green peppercorns in brine on hand, substitute hot red pepper flakes and double the amount of anchovy.

makes ABOUT 1 CUP

1 cup capers, drained

¼ cup green peppercorns in brine, drained and rinsed

4 anchovy fillets, drained

Coarsely chop all the ingredients by hand or in a food processor and combine well. Store in the refrigerator. The relish will keep for up to 1 month.

explorations

Refrigerator-Door "Salt"

Keep this bold seasoning on your kitchen counter or dining table and play with it a pinch at a time. It becomes crunchy and brittle, and makes a great finish for warm potatoes, Skillet Flatbread (page 357), or A Single Deviled Egg (page 350). I like to sprinkle it on roasted meats and into rich broths.

⟶ MAKES ABOUT ½ CUP

½ cup **Refrigerator-Door Relish** (at left)

Spread the relish evenly on a parchment paper–lined baking sheet or plate, in a thin layer. Leave out overnight or until completely dry. You should be able to crumble the mixture between your fingers.

Store in an airtight jar, out of direct light. It will keep for several weeks.

Refrigerator-Door Mustard

Serve alongside cheese or use as a rub for skirt steak.

→ **MAKES ABOUT ½ CUP**

½ cup **Refrigerator-Door Relish** (opposite)

1½ tablespoons whole-grain mustard

1½ teaspoons Dijon mustard

Chop the relish fine. Mix with both mustards. Store in the refrigerator for up to 1 month.

Refrigerator-Door Vinaigrette

Spoon this vinaigrette over Cumin-Roasted Eggplant (page 131), Roasted Radicchio (page 60), or Whole Roasted Fish (page 246).

→ **MAKES 2¾ CUPS**

½ cup white wine vinegar

½ cup **Refrigerator-Door Mustard** (at left)

1¾ cups excellent olive oil

Combine the vinegar and mustard in a bowl; whisk well. Add the oil in a thin stream, whisking continuously.

Refrigerate for up to 3 months. As it sits, the vinaigrette will separate; bring it to room temperature and whisk before each use.

Cheese

I keep four or five kinds of cheeses in my pantry at all times:

→ Creamy, single-note salty cheeses, like **chèvre** (soft goat cheese), which I like with raw and spicy ingredients such as radishes, or warmed with vegetables as part of a gratin (page 111).

→ Salty, stinky cheeses, like **Gorgonzola** or creamy **Bulgarian feta**, that range from crumbly to creamy. I serve these with other bold ingredients, like raw radishes and tart tomatillos, Apple-Core Mostarda (page 211), or Spicy Lemon-Onion Slaw (page 36).

→ Milder cheeses, like **mozzarella** and **ricotta**, which should taste of lightly salted, sweet fresh milk. The good ones are highly perishable. If your ricotta isn't delicious straight out of the container, or if your mozzarella slices well but tastes like filler, you aren't buying the right stuff. Cheese is never neutral. Don't invest in long shelf life at the expense of taste. Typically, you'll need to use these cheeses within 3 days of purchase.

→ **Pecorino** and **Parmesan**. They aren't interchangeable, though I often have only one or the other. Parmesan is such a good snacking cheese and has a funk that pecorino lacks. But there is almost no substitute for pecorino when you want the flavor of cheese accompanied by a bit more salt (Savory Ricotta Custard, page 386, and Rustic Polenta, page 314).

→ Raw-milk **Gruyère** or **aged Gouda**. I use these when I want to deviate from Parmesan and pecorino. Gruyère and Gouda together make very grown-up macaroni and cheese. Save the hard cheese rinds in a freezer bag for up to 6 months for Cheese Stock (opposite).

Cheese Stock

There is no better use for old cheese rinds than to reincarnate them as this rich stock. Use it as a base for soup, in a pasta sauce, in risotto—anywhere you want the sharpness of a hard-rind cheese. Sherry, at the end, adds needed structure to this stock and makes it more savory.

Don't use anything soft or semisoft, and nothing too stinky; I like Parmesan, Gruyère, and aged Gouda rinds, and old hard nubs of pecorino.

makes **6 TO 7 CUPS**

1 pound cheese rinds and/or old, hard cheese (see headnote)

¾ cup thinly sliced onion

2 large garlic cloves, thinly sliced

10 whole black peppercorns

7 fresh thyme sprigs

8 cups cold water

1 tablespoon or more dry sherry

Use a sharp knife or fine grater to shave any paper, mold, or wax from the cheese. Rinse under cold water. Using a heavy, sturdy knife, cut the rinds into ½ inch pieces.

Place the cheese in a large pot. Add the onion, garlic, peppercorns, thyme, and water. Bring to a quick boil over high heat, then turn the heat down to very low and partially cover the pot. Cook at a bare simmer, stirring from the bottom with some frequency to release any sticking rinds, for 1½ hours, until you taste a pronounced cheese flavor

Strain well through a fine-mesh strainer, or a colander lined with cheesecloth. Season with the sherry.

Refrigerate overnight to allow any cheese solids to separate from the stock. Skim them off and discard.

Store the stock in the refrigerator for up to 5 days. Or freeze for up to 6 months. Consider storing in 1-cup portions for single servings of soup.

Use in

→ Cheese Stock and Onion Jam Soup (page 35)

→ Cheese-Stock Risotto with Spring Vegetables (page 325)

→ Poached Cauliflower, Peanut, and Cheese Bisque (page 107)

Savory Ricotta Custard

The best ricotta cheese is highly perishable, and it will smell and taste funkier with each passing day. The following recipe not only doubles the cheese's shelf life, it makes it sturdy, which is especially welcome when you want to slice it for a sandwich, crumble it into pasta, or serve it on a cheese plate. It is especially good served as a not-too-sweet dessert with Dried Lemon, Balsamic Fig, and Cocoa Compote (page 220).

You can add other things to this custard, such as herbs or thick marmalade.

makes ABOUT 2¼ CUPS, ENOUGH FOR 10 TO 12 SERVINGS

Butter, for the pan

28 ounces (about 3 cups) excellent ricotta

2 large eggs, beaten

½ cup finely grated pecorino cheese

1 teaspoon coarse kosher salt

Scant ¼ teaspoon freshly grated nutmeg

Freshly ground black pepper, to taste

Preheat the oven to 300°F. Tightly wrap the outside of a 6-inch springform pan with a double layer of foil (to prevent leaks) and lightly butter the inside of the pan, or lightly butter a 2-quart silicone mold.

Combine all the ingredients in a bowl and mix well. Taste for salt, if necessary adding a couple pinches more to sharpen the flavor without masking the ricotta's fresh, milky taste. Transfer to the pan, smooth the top, and wipe the edges clean.

Cover the top tightly with foil and place in a larger baking dish. Pour hot water into the baking dish to rise halfway up the pan.

Bake the custard until a thin knife inserted in the center pulls out looking "beady" or barely clean, about 1 hour and 20 minutes. The finished custard may jiggle slightly when tapped and should still look moist. You do not want it to darken or seize up.

Remove from the water bath. Uncover, place on a rack, and cool to room temperature. Chill well before unmolding onto a plate.

Store in the refrigerator, tightly covered, for up to 7 days.

exploration

Ricotta Dumplings

These dumplings are easy to make. Keep dumpling wrappers around to make however many portions you need at a time. One recipe of custard will make 50 to 60 dumplings. While the ricotta custard itself doesn't freeze well, these dumplings do. To boil frozen dumplings, add about 2 minutes more to the cooking time. I choose the shape of the dumpling wrapper based on how I want to serve the dumplings: round ones to lie flat, as for ravioli, or square ones to stand up, as for soup.

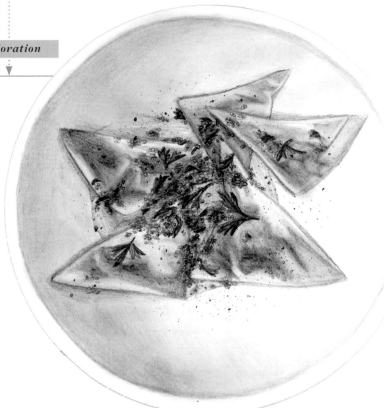

→ **FOR 10 TO 12 SERVINGS**

50 to 60 round or square dumpling wrappers

1 recipe (about 2 cups) **Savory Ricotta Custard** (opposite)

Fill each wrapper with a scant 2 teaspoons of the ricotta custard. For flat dumplings (to mimic ravioli), wet the edge of a round dumpling wrapper with water; fold over in half, pressing around the cheese to remove any air bubbles, and seal. For dumplings to serve with broth or in a sauce, place the custard in the center of a square wrapper. Wet the edges of the wrapper with water and lift up the four corners to meet above the filling. Make sure to press out any air around the custard before sealing the edges tight. (*You can freeze the dumplings at this point on a parchment paper–lined baking sheet in a single layer. Once frozen, carefully transfer to a freezer bag.*)

Bring a large pot of well-salted water to a boil. Add the dumplings and cook for 30 seconds to heat through to the center, or about 2½ minutes if frozen. Quickly test one by removing it from the water with a slotted spoon and sticking a thin knife through the wrapper into the center of the filling. Pull out the knife and test where it stabbed the ricotta; the knife should be hot. Once hot, carefully remove all of the dumplings from the water with a slotted spoon, blot them on a clean towel, and serve.

Use in

→ Ricotta Dumplings with Spring Stock and Seasonal Vegetables (page 78)

Serve with

→ Melted butter and bread crumbs (page 355)

→ Wine-Braised Leeks (page 28)

→ Confit Tomatoes (page 148)

Ricotta Dumplings with Butter, Herbs, and Bread Crumbs

A pretty, elegant dish, and with ricotta custard on hand, it's one of the easiest, quickest pasta plates to put together. It stands on its own alongside a salad, or as a first course in an extended meal.

Don't use store-bought bread crumbs; you'll need the toasty, salty flavor and coarse, uneven texture of ones you make yourself.

⟶ **FOR EACH SERVING**

Coarse kosher salt, for the cooking water

5 **Ricotta Dumplings** (page 387)

2 tablespoons unsalted butter

1 tablespoon chopped fresh herbs (such as oregano and/or parsley)

1 tablespoon **Toasted Bread Crumbs** (page 355)

Flaky sea salt and freshly ground black pepper

Bring a pot of water to a boil. Salt it well and add the dumplings. Cook for 30 seconds to heat through to the center; if the dumplings are frozen, boil for up to 2½ minutes. Use a slotted spoon to remove them from the water and place them on a clean paper towel.

Meanwhile, slowly melt the butter with the herbs in a small pan. Once it has melted, add the dumplings and bread crumbs and toss to coat. Arrange the dumplings on a plate and spoon any remaining butter and bread crumbs over them. Finish with a generous amount of flaky salt and pepper.

Index

greens, *continued*
    prewashed, note about, 56
    spring, wild rice, and
        sunchoke soup, 327
    see also specific greens

H

hazelnuts
    blanching and toasting, 368
    nut cream, 369
herb(s)
    any- , lemonade, 71
    any- , simple syrup, 71
    -infused butter, 377
    many- , salad, 64–65
    -scallion salad, 65
    and spring vegetable sauté, 77
    storing: the herb tank, 63
    see also specific herbs
honey
    -apple-cider vinaigrette,
        spiced, 365
    and cayenne, squash and
        rosemary compote with,
        189
    dried lemons in, 219
    and fish sauce, roasted
        glazed turnips with, 187

J

jam
    onion, 34
    Swiss chard stems, 54

K

kale
    cleaning and storing, 46
    hearty greens with bacon
        and fig, olive, and walnut
        relish, 49
    ribboned, preparing, 48
    sautéed, and walnuts, spiced
        lamb meatballs with, 301
    seared, and pork loin in
        broth, 287
    seared, with dates and
        cream, 51
    seared, with garlic and
        lemon, 50

seared, with roasted lemon
    and Parmesan, 51
stems, braised and pickled, 52
kimchi
    cucumber-peel, 130
    mussels, 235

L

lamb
    meatballs, spiced, with
        chickpeas, pickled parsley,
        and yogurt, 300
    meatballs, spiced, with pan
        sauce, 299
    meatballs, spiced, with
        sautéed kale and walnuts,
        301
    meatballs or patties, spiced,
        297–98
    shanks, pine nuts, and mint,
        flatbread with, 305
    shanks braised in two
        vinegars, 302–3
    shanks with apple-endive
        slaw, 304
    shanks with roasted lemon, 304
    spiced, with cherry tomatoes
        and rye berries, 299
leek greens
    -and-dill pesto, 32
    -and-dill pesto and wine-
        pickled garlic, smoked
        trout with, 244
    blanched, 31
    cream cheese, 33
    creamed, 32–33
leek(s)
    braised, and ricotta custard,
        linguine with, 312–13
    braised- , shaved cabbage
        salad, 113
    and pork meatballs, 291–92
    wine-braised, 28
    wine-braised, and bacon,
        squid with, 30
    wine-braised, and potato
        broth soup, 30
    wine-braised, skewered, with
        sunchokes, 30

lemon(s)
    any-herb lemonade, 71
    and bay salt, olives with, 375
    dried, balsamic fig, and
        cocoa compote, 220
    dried, in honey, 219
    juiced, 218
    lemonade for one or more, 218
    -onion slaw, spicy, 36
    parsley vinaigrette, 69
    rhubarb lemonade, 98
    roasted, and Parmesan,
        seared kale with, 51
    roasted, and raisins, braised
        duck leg with, 275
    roasted, dressing, 221
    roasted, lamb shanks with, 304
    roasted, shallots, and olives,
        braised chicken legs with,
        258
    roasted whole, 220–21
    watermelon lemonade, 154
lentil(s)
    green, and bread salad with
        olives, 345
    green, and cabbage with
        orange vinaigrette, 345
    green, with cardamom, 344
lettuce
    caper Caesar salad, 57
    cleaning and storing: the
        wedge, 56
    confit duck salad with
        buttermilk dressing, 277
    sautéed wedge salad with
        warm vinaigrette, 58
    wedge Caesar salad, 57
liver, chicken, seared, 269
livers, chicken, with triple-
    braised wild mushrooms,
    269

M

maple currants, 368
meal planning, note about, 14
meat
    cooking notes, 280
    raw, storing, 280
    see also beef; lamb; pork

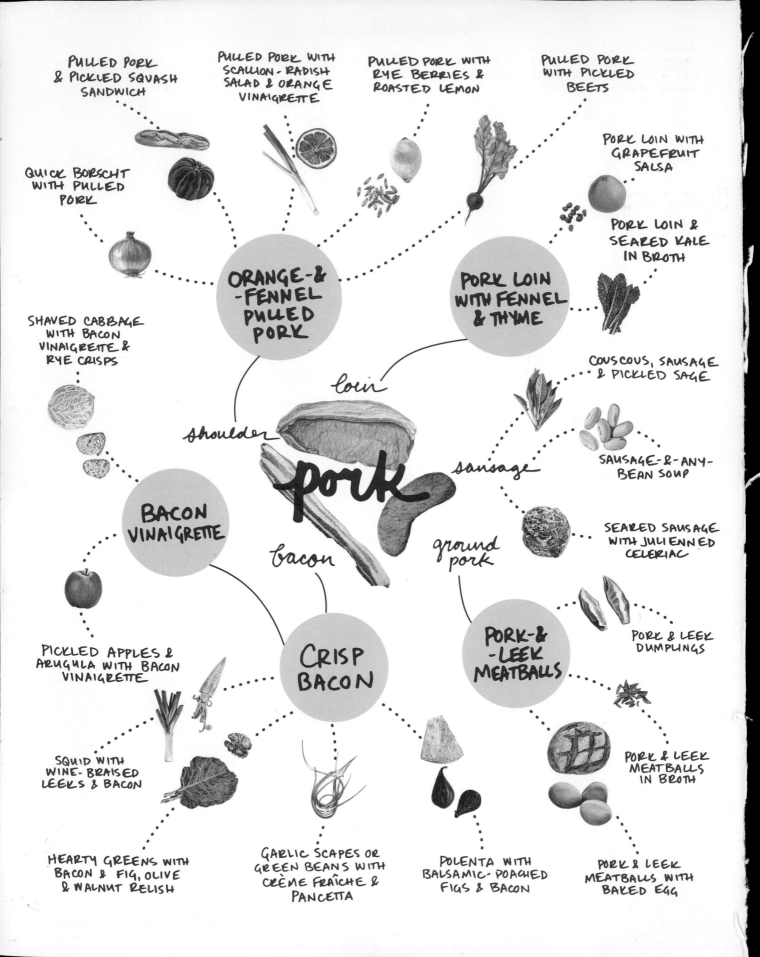

PULLED PORK
& PICKLED SQUASH
SANDWICH

PULLED PORK WITH
SCALLION-RADISH
SALAD & ORANGE
VINAIGRETTE

PULLED PORK WITH
RYE BERRIES &
ROASTED LEMON

PULLED PORK
WITH PICKLED
BEETS

PORK LOIN WITH
GRAPEFRUIT
SALSA

QUICK BORSCHT
WITH PULLED
PORK

PORK LOIN &
SEARED KALE
IN BROTH

ORANGE-&-
-FENNEL
PULLED
PORK

PORK LOIN
WITH FENNEL
& THYME

SHAVED CABBAGE
WITH BACON
VINAIGRETTE &
RYE CRISPS

COUSCOUS, SAUSAGE
& PICKLED SAGE

loin

SAUSAGE-&-ANY-
BEAN SOUP

shoulder

pork

sausage

SEARED SAUSAGE
WITH JULIENNED
CELERIAC

BACON
VINAIGRETTE

ground
pork

bacon

PICKLED APPLES &
ARUGULA WITH BACON
VINAIGRETTE

PORK-&-
-LEEK
MEATBALLS

PORK & LEEK
DUMPLINGS

CRISP
BACON

SQUID WITH
WINE-BRAISED
LEEKS & BACON

PORK & LEEK
MEATBALLS
IN BROTH

HEARTY GREENS WITH
BACON & FIG, OLIVE
& WALNUT RELISH

GARLIC SCAPES OR
GREEN BEANS WITH
CRÈME FRAÎCHE &
PANCETTA

POLENTA WITH
BALSAMIC-POACHED
FIGS & BACON

PORK & LEEK
MEATBALLS WITH
BAKED EGG